MW00425467

Praise for *Too Close to the Flame*

"IN *TOO CLOSE TO THE FLAME,* Joe Ingle references the ancient Christian call to be a Fool for Christ. In his pastoral and prophetic work against the 'killing machine' that is the death penalty over nearly 50 years, Joe reminds us that the call of Christ is a foolish one. To follow the Christ is to refuse to look away. May more of us who profess to be Christian in the Southern U.S. follow Joe Ingle into the foolish work of proclaiming the light of the Crucified Christ against the idolatry of state killing."

—The Right Rev. Brian L. Cole
Diocesan Bishop
Episcopal Diocese of East Tennessee

"THIS IS A POWERFUL TESTAMENT to Reverend Joe Ingle's decades of death row ministry, and the personal cost of that ministry. His stories expose the toxicity of the death penalty to everyone it touches, from those who carry out executions to the families of murder victims trapped for decades in a system that doesn't support their healing. The trauma felt by Rev. Ingle and those he counseled is palpable, the pain is visceral. This book should be a catalyst for us to reimagine justice in a way that is focused on safety, healing, and accountability—not on extracting punishment and inflicting harm."

—Reverend Stacy Rector
Tennesseans for Alternatives to the
Death Penalty Executive Director

"JOE'S BOOK IS A RARE GEM that straddles the necessity for proximity to pain and practicing self-care. His ministry to those on death row and advocacy against the 'ritual slaughter' that is the death penalty is both awe-inspiring and daunting. He weaves a series of traumatic vignettes into a work of hope, horror, and healing."

—Sam Heath
Equal Justice USA Evangelical Network

TOO CLOSE

TO THE

FLAME

TOO CLOSE
TO THE
FLAME

With the Condemned
Inside the Southern
Killing Machine

JOSEPH B. INGLE

Forefront
BOOKS

Published by Forefront Books, Nashville, Tennessee.
Distributed by Simon & Schuster.

Library of Congress Control Number: 9781637632918

Print ISBN: 978-1-63763-291-8
E-book ISBN: 978-1-63763-292-5

Cover Design by Jonathan Lewis, Jonlin Creative
Interior Design by Mary Susan Oleson, Blu Design Concepts

Printed in the United States of America

For Becca

"Je me révolte, donc nous sommes."
("I revolt, therefore we are.")
—Albert Camus

Contents

CODA

Preface

THE WEEK BEFORE my wedding in October 1979, I guided a tour of historical and active Southern landmarks. My tour group consisted of foundation executives from around the country who were interested in supporting the work of the Southern Coalition on Jails and Prisons, the group I directed. The tour began in Nashville, my hometown, at the Tennessee State Prison, which opened in 1898. After meeting with prisoners and visiting death row, we left the castle-like "Walls," which resembled the entrance to Disney's Magic Kingdom, and headed south.

Parchman is the site of the Mississippi State Penitentiary. Unlike the penitentiary style of the Walls in Nashville, Parchman is a plantation prison and exists on thousands of acres. The men work the fields, the land of the fertile Mississippi Delta. Cotton is the main crop. As David Oshinsky describes it in *Worse Than Slavery: Parchman Farm and the Ordeal of Jim Crow Justice*, Black lawbreakers were to learn "proper discipline, strong work habits, and respect for white authority." Governor James Vardaman founded it as a reform of the convict lease system. It was easy to see how Parchman helped birth the blues.

After Parchman, our tour concluded with a trip to the Louisiana State Penitentiary at Angola, Louisiana. The prison goes by the name Angola. Its reference to Africa indicates what race of people Angola was designed to exploit.

Preface

In 1896, Major Samuel James reported that there were 216 convict deaths that year through the convict lease system in Louisiana. This report and the many abuses of convicts in the lease system led to public outcry and the system's abolition in 1901. It is estimated that between 1870 and 1891, three thousand Black convicts died in Louisiana.

The Louisiana State Penitentiary, like its sister institution, Parchman in Mississippi, was the answer to the abuses of the convict lease system. By 1900, Blacks comprised 84 percent of the prison population. It was also a home of the blues.

Our tour drove the winding two-lane road through the backwoods toward Angola, the landscape clearly revealing how difficult it is to escape from the eighteen-thousand-acre prison farm. The Tunica Hills provide one barrier and the Mississippi River another. In addition, hound dogs could unerringly track a scent.

We arrived at the front gate into Angola. The guards at the gate checked the memo on us and called the warden's office. We were given directions on how to get to the administration building and were waved through the gate.

I had arranged this tour through the courtesy of Warden Frank Blackburn. We found his office, where he greeted us cordially. We would be able to spend the day touring Angola, he said, and then he would host us for dinner at his home. Everyone was taken with his friendliness and hospitality.

There are two schools of thought regarding prisoners: (1) They are locked up for punishment, and that is it. (2) They are capable of rehabilitation and should be provided the opportunity to change their ways. Warden Blackburn was an ordained Methodist deacon and a devotee of the rehabilitation school.

Angola, the largest maximum-security facility in the country with 6,300 prisoners, is a plantation. Its specialty is sugar cane, and if one thought working cotton at Parchman was difficult, the sugar cane experience at Angola is equally brutal.

Our first stop on the tour was a housing unit. It was large, dormitory style, with many double-bunked beds. No one was there because everyone was in the fields. As our group walked around, imagining how loud and crowded this place would be with the men in it, one person asked me, "Joe, what is that?"

High on the wall was a wooden plaque. Inside the frame were numbers and letters, much like you would see hymn listings in a rural church. But rather than hymn numbers, we read the following:

W-24

B-251

C-193

I interpreted for the guests: "The *W* stands for the number of whites. The *B* for the number of Blacks. The *C* for the number of Colored or Creole. It is the count of the number of prisoners housed here to sleep."

It was clear that South Africa, an apartheid society, was not the only place where individuals were kept under control and designated solely by the color of their skin.

We moved on from the housing unit to observe the men at work in the fields. Just as in the movie *Cool Hand Luke*, the men were doing stoop labor under the supervision of guards with rifles on horseback. There was little to say. It seemed we were in the nineteenth century rather than the twentieth.

The new Maximum-Security Unit (MSU), Camp F, had recently opened. Unlike the old MSU at Parchman, which was literally falling down, this was the Brave New World of penology, and we were about to enter it.

This MSU was new, but it was hardly an improvement. Metal doors shut on the cells. The electric light was controlled from the outside. There was no window. If a prisoner were enclosed by the metal door, he would essentially be in a tomb. It was true solitary confinement.

Preface

I asked the guard to open a door so I could talk to a prisoner. The door swung open, and an African American stood blinking in the light. He needed some minutes for his eyes to adjust. He asked, "What day is it?" I told him. I asked him if that metal door was frequently closed, and he indicated it was. I asked how long it had been shut. He told me he lost count of the days and nights after twenty days. I thought, "Sweet Jesus, have mercy."

By the time we completed our visit to the MSU, it was time to proceed to the warden's house for dinner. The guards drove us up into the Tunica Hills to Frank Blackburn's abode. The house was situated on top of one of the hills, with the thousands of acres of Angola fields stretched out below. We watched as the sun began to set and the men marched out of the fields, returning to their dormitories. Armed guards on horseback accompanied them. Although it was the autumn of 1979, the scene of the white guards and the Black convicts felt like it was a hundred years earlier.

Frank Blackburn arrived as we were absorbing the sunset scene. He greeted everyone jovially and invited us all into the dining area. My colleagues were being served iced tea and water, and Frank said, "Joe, come with me."

I followed Frank out of the dining area, through the house, to the adjacent garage. Frank opened the garage door. In the fading light lay a pile of wood. Frank asked, "Joe, do you know what that is?" I had no clue. "No, Frank, I don't know." Frank replied, "That is the electric chair. And the way the Supreme Court is going, we are going to have to put it back together."[1]

We stood there gazing at the heap of wood. Then Frank pulled the garage door down, and we went back to join the guests for dinner.

We were seated at tables covered with white tablecloths. The food was produce and meat grown at Angola. Our iced tea

---

1 The United States Supreme Court had struck down the death penalty in 1972 but reinstated it in 1976, allowing Gary Gilmore's execution in Utah in January 1977.

and water were immediately refilled, and coffee was available with dessert. We were treated with the utmost courtesy by Black prisoners in white coats and pants. As night settled over Angola, we reminisced about the day and asked Frank Blackburn questions about his job and the prison.

The evening complete, I left for the rehearsal dinner and wedding awaiting me in Huntsville, Alabama.

* * *

The electric chair in Frank Blackburn's garage was reassembled. I next saw it when my friend Tim Baldwin was strapped into it and electrocuted at Angola on September 10, 1984. I walked with Tim down to that electric chair.

What I provide through my experiences is a keyhole through which the reader can view the caging and killing machinery of the South. Mass incarceration and state-sanctioned killing are merely the latest manifestations of an old story in my region. The South is the most religious region of the country. It is also the largest killing field and imprisoning machine in the United States. Those two facts are intertwined.

Unfortunately, this is nothing new. From the enacting of the first slave laws in Virginia in the 1660s until today, the South has pioneered the oppression of the Black, the Indian, and the poor. The history breaks down into periods: the Slavery Regime (1662–1865), the Genocide Regime (1830–1890), Reconstruction (1866–1876), the Regime of Segregation (1883–1953), the Second Reconstruction (1954–1976), the Regime of Disfranchisement I (1980–1992), the Regime of Disfranchisement II (2000–2008). I detail this history in *Slouching Toward Tyranny: Mass Incarceration, Death Sentences and Racism.*

Dr. Martin Luther King Jr., quoting abolitionist Theodore

Parker from the 1850s, opined that "the arc of the moral universe is long, but it bends toward justice." Yes, it would be heartening to agree with that viewpoint. However, my experiences in Southern prisons, jails, legislatures, courtrooms, governors' offices, and mansions have led me to a different conclusion. Justice for the oppressed is rare and elusive. And that is no accident. It is the way the system has been designed from the beginning and continues to function today. The myth of American exceptionalism is belied by racial tyranny. Alexis de Tocqueville, who came to the United States to study the prison system, observed this phenomenon and termed it "the tyranny of the majority" in his book *Democracy in America*.

For those who speak of American exceptionalism—yes, this might be true if we are talking about per capita prison population. We lead the Western world in that category and also in executions. No country can belong to the European Union and have capital punishment. But if one would compare American history on that point, merely consider the founding documents and laws regarding the treatment of Blacks and Indians. Walter Benjamin understood what all such documents stand for: "There is no document of civilization that is not at the same time a document of barbarism."

My invitation to you is to experience a portion of our barbarity firsthand through this book and to join me in the work of restorative justice.

Foreword

SHANE CLAIBORNE

THERE WAS JOHN EVANS in Alabama. And Jimmy Lee Gray in Mississippi. And James Hutchins in North Carolina. There was James Adams in Florida, and David Washington also down in Florida. Tim Baldwin in Louisiana. And Robert Wayne Williams. Bob Sullivan. Willie Watson. Philip Workman. Velma Barfield in North Carolina. Billy Irick in Tennessee. Warren McCleskey. Alvin Ford. Willie Darden. Steve West. John Spenkelink. Don Johnson in Tennessee, and Nick Sutton also in Tennessee. And of course, Ed Zagorski.

Those are a few of the names of people condemned to death and executed who you will get to know in this book . . . and I'm pretty sure I forgot a few. There are too many, and that's the point. They will come to life as you flip these pages.

Some of them were innocent, some were guilty of the crimes for which they were convicted. Some were Black, some white . . . almost all of them were poor, because there aren't many rich folks on death row. Aside from being executed by the state, all these people had one thing in common—they had the privilege of calling Joe Ingle their friend.

And so do I.

Joe is more than a friend—he is a mentor, an inspiration, a national treasure, a legend in the movement for a better world.

Foreword

This is a book of stories, stories that you will never forget, some of which you will probably wish you could. They will disturb you, move you, make you sick at your stomach, and make you laugh in your gut. Some of these stories happened before I was even born, and some of them I got to be a part of as I walked, literally, alongside Joe Ingle.

When it comes to caring about the most vulnerable people in our society, I've become convinced that our biggest problem is not compassion but proximity. It's not that we don't care about people on the margins, it's often that we don't *know* them. It's hard to love people you don't know. And we are good at having opinions about issues that affect people we don't know. Love compels us to get proximate, to lean into the suffering and pain of the world. But that comes at a cost, as you will see on the pages of this book. In fact, that's where the title *Too Close to the Flame* comes from. Most of us are too far from the flame, but Joe Ingle got a little too close. His story is one that can help all of us find the right equilibrium.

The death penalty has survived because there are layers of anonymity that allow for a system that kills while protecting the people who are a part of the machinery of death. This book is a rebuke of that system.

It's easier to kill people if you don't know them. That's why the system creates carefully designed barriers between executioners and those they are being asked to kill. The burden of death is carefully divided among many different people in the hopes that no one carries its full weight.

You see it even when you look at the crucifixion of Jesus, the most famous execution in history; he was executed not just by some Roman soldiers but also by a host of other contributors, none of whom wanted to carry the shame and burden of the execution—Judas, and the Sanhedrin, and Caiaphas, and Herod, and the angry mob, and Pontius Pilate washing the blood from his hands.

And so it goes.

We have attorneys who open the door to death.

We have a jury that finds someone guilty.

A judge (or judges) who sentences the convicted prisoner to death.

A governor who nods in approval or signs a warrant.

A clemency board that removes all obstacles.

A warden who oversees the execution.

Prison guards who prepare the person to die.

A "death team" that performs the execution.

A technician who inserts the needle.

And a coroner who pronounces the defendant dead.

We have a system that kills, but no one wants to be a killer. So we have tried to sterilize and bureaucratize state killing. But at the end of the day, on the death certificate of a person executed by the state, the manner of death is listed as "Homicide." We have a system that has mastered the sterilization of state-sanctioned, legal homicide.

This book takes you inside the "system," into the bowels of the "machinery of death" so that all can see that there is no such thing as a system that kills without any killers. Joe Ingle brings you deep inside the convoluted apparatus of state killing. And it has come at a cost. It is hard to stare death in the face, to look into the eyes of the devil . . . and go on with life as usual.

Foreword

This book is a gift to us all, a gift to the church, and to a world that is plagued with violence. These pages are filled with stories that put a face on the "issue" of mass incarceration and state killing.

You'll hear about Terry King trying to donate a kidney as a prisoner on death row. Billy Irick and the guys on Unit 2 painting the Stations of the Cross on a twenty-foot scroll, literally reflecting on the execution of Jesus as they awaited their own fate and counted the hours they had to live. Bob intentionally getting caught with a handcuff key so that he would be separated from his cellmate so his execution would be less traumatic.

Imagine what it would be like to have a prison chaplain who supported your execution ask you to pray with them. These stories mess with you. A man who was too sick to get executed and had to be sent to the hospital to get healthy enough to be killed. Sweet Velma calling the corrections officers "the help" as she knitted on death row, as if they were there to bring her yarn and sweet tea, as if she were in a rocking chair on her front porch. You hear about Ed doing ten thousand push-ups before his execution as a way of coping with the machinery of death.

I could feel the hard concrete as Joe lay outside Willie's cell singing Sweet Honey in the Rock through the night before his execution. I could smell the cigar smoke as they smoked a Jamaican cigar to celebrate the birth of Joe's newborn baby girl, as the state prepared to take the life of another friend.

And you hear about the governors who are Christians, or are pretending to be Christians, who have the power to kill or not to kill as if they were God, as if they were "the one without sin" with the right to throw a stone.

I got to the chapter on Don Johnson, about two-thirds through the book. I knew Don; he's one of the guys Joe introduced me to on Unit 2, Tennessee's death row. I have a lighthouse he made me here in my office. I was with him days before his execution . . . it tore

22

my heart out to stand outside the prison as he sang "Soon and Very Soon" as he was being executed. It took every ounce of discipline I had *not* to get arrested for protesting that execution, because Don asked us not to. It was then that I realized Don Johnson was one of nearly forty people Joe has known intimately and witnessed the state kill . . . and whose execution he has witnessed a Christian governor sign off on. These stories, these people have shaped Joe Ingle, and they have shaped me. I know they will do the same for you.

In addition to his friends on death row, Joe also introduces you to the other friends who helped him keep his hope alive in hope-crushing moments—Will Campbell, Hector Black, Dan Berrigan, Søren Kierkegaard, Dorothy Day, Thomas Merton, John Egerton, Albert Camus, Billy Moore, and Harmon Wray . . . some of those names I recognized and some I know now, all a part of the cloud of witnesses that carried Joe through desperate times. And, of course, there are also the friends in the natural world that helped Joe make it through—the pileated woodpecker outside his window, the redbud trees, and wild ginger, bloodroot, trillium, phlox, and iris that showed a God who was still beautiful, life that is defiant in a world that can crush the human soul. It's an invitation to find ways to keep your hope and joy and faith alive as you get proximate to the pain and cruelty of this world.

Even though I've known Joe Ingle for about fifteen years, I discovered as I read this manuscript that Joe was nominated for the Nobel Peace Prize, that he went to Harvard, and all kinds of other stuff that would make him blush if he confessed it to you. That tells you something about this man, about his humility and integrity.

Joe has visited pretty much every maximum-security facility and death row in America. In fact, he was one of the first people to take me inside to visit Tennessee's death row, which I've been visiting now for about ten years.

There is not much redemptive within our criminal justice

system, but whenever you see a faint sign of dignity or beauty or hope inside the concrete walls, Joe Ingle probably had a role in creating or protecting that glimmer.

He has also been one of the steady, reliable, prophetic voices critiquing the worst of our system—prison conditions, violations of human dignity and rights, health care . . . Joe has even got into "good trouble," stirring up holy mischief of the best sort, even risking arrest at times to protest and expose the injustices of the criminal justice system, or as Joe prefers to call it "the criminal legal system" (since there is so little justice there).

When I first met Joe, I wasn't sure if he was a lawyer or a pastor. Eventually, I came to find that he is a little bit of both. There's that place in Scripture where the apostle Paul says, "I have become all things to all people so that by all possible means I might save some" (1 Corinthians 9:22, NIV). Joe Ingle puts a new spin on that one. He never compromises who he is, but as you will see in this book, he became all kinds of things to help save lives—a friend, a counselor, a comedian, a listener, a teacher, a student, a pastor, a mentor, a theologian, an activist, a legal aid, an accomplice, a witness, a liaison . . . but most of all he has been a friend to those on death row, and to their families—like no one else I know.

This book is a memoir, but it is more than a memoir. It is a case study on how to love. And by love, I mean the kind of love Dostoyevsky spoke of—not the anemic, sentimental love of fairy tales but the "harsh and dreadful love" as Dorothy Day called it—the love that won't let you sleep some nights. The love that leads you to sacrifice, the love that can land you on a cross asking for forgiveness for the people nailing you to it—the kind of scandalous, offensive love that wants the best even for one's enemies. But it does raise some eyebrows, especially these days when many people are more concerned about self-care than self-sacrifice and we have made a business out of social work that often cares more about "professional distance" than befriending people and walking alongside them.

It's hard to find the right equilibrium between caring for ourselves and caring for others. One of my mentors invited me to imagine a new spin on "love your neighbor as yourself" by asking me, "Are you loving yourself as you love your neighbor?" That's the question at the heart of this book: How do we love well?—love ourselves, love our spouses, love our families, love the marginalized, and love those in the forsaken places like death row, who are condemned to die . . .

How do we do it well, and for the long haul?

The best part about this book is that, in typical Joe Ingle style, it is not anecdotal. It is definitely not cliché. It is not preachy. It is a deep dive into the darkness. Just as Jesus is said to have descended into hell, this is a story of descending into hell and living to tell the story. It's a tale of learning the limits of one's own finite capacity to love, even as we aspire to love with the infinite love of God. But like Moses at the burning bush, we discover that we cannot stare into the face of God or we will go blind. How do we allow the fire of the Holy Spirit to consume us without it burning us up . . . or burning us out?

Honestly, I haven't read many books that are this honest, this raw, this unresolved . . . and that's why it is so spectacular. Too many people write books trying to answer all the questions. This book is more about questioning the answers. It is a book for folks who are tired, and it is a book for folks who have a fire inside their bones to change the world. It's a book for old people and young activists. It's a book for folks who want to abolish the prisons, and for the folks working within them. It's a book for those who have doubts and questions, and for those who think they've got it all figured out. It's a book for those who have great faith and those who wish they had more.

This book, like Joe Ingle, is a gift to the world.

A Letter about Joe
from Death Row

TERRY KING

I FIRST MET Joe Ingle in August 1983. After my arrest for two homicides in Knox County, Tennessee, the state publicly announced that they would seek the death penalty. I received a letter from Joe asking if I had an attorney and what he could do to help me.

When Joe wrote to me, he was the director of the Southern Coalition on Jails and Prisons. They had eight chapters in eight different states, all in the South.

I have known Joe almost forty years, and he has been there for me more times than I can count. He has been a champion for all the guys on the row. He always sided with us in our struggles with the state over any issue we had, including the struggles with getting proper medical care. Joe has helped all the guys on the row in one way or another. Every guy here has been offered by Joe to be paired with someone to visit them when their family cannot or won't.

In 1988, the state doctor messed up a medical procedure with my left knee and did not have the expertise to fix it. I needed ACL reconstruction. It was Joe who got some wonderful surgeon to agree to fix my knee at no cost to the state and likewise got the hospital to agree to allow me to come there at no cost to the state. This was in January 1989, and the doctor did an amazing job repairing my damaged knee.

I cannot think of a single time that I have needed Joe's help that he hasn't been there to help me.

In 1997, when my grandfather passed away, I wanted to attend his funeral. However, both Warden Ricky Bell and the commissioner of corrections denied me permission to attend his funeral. That denial didn't stop Joe from helping me. Joe knew someone who worked in the governor's office and reached out to them to explain that state policy allowed me to attend. All of a sudden, with a phone call from the governor's office to the commissioner, I was allowed to attend the funeral. Because the prison waited so long to take me, when I did arrive there were at least seventy-five family members at the funeral home. Some of the family I had not seen in years. Being there allowed me a level of closure that I wouldn't have been given had it not been for my friend Joe Ingle. I will forever feel a debt that I can never repay to my friend.

Over these many years, Joe has been a loyal and caring friend to me and to the guys on the row. A couple of years ago, he asked me whether I knew anyone who didn't have a family member to get them a Christmas food package. I asked around the unit and found about a dozen guys who didn't have the means to get a food package. I gave Joe the list, and when the packages were passed out, the guys on the list all got one. They all had smiles on their faces.

Of all the good folks I have known over the years who God has blessed me with, no one has been involved in my life longer than Joe Ingle. I will forever be grateful to Joe for the many blessings he has been instrumental in providing for me.

A Letter about Joe from Death Row

TERRY KING has been on death row over thirty-nine years at the "gated community" known as Riverbend Maximum Security Institution. In some ways, his story is not unique, but he certainly is. As he likes to say, despite these walls and bars of steel, "I am the freest man you will ever meet! God has forgiven me and set me free."

CHAPTER ONE

Maundy Thursday

I DROVE MY SILVER 2009 Toyota Tacoma pickup truck up the incline into the parking lot around two in the afternoon, when the lot was mostly filled with vehicles. I pulled into a parking space facing the buildings spread out before me—structures I was very familiar with because I had been entering them since October of 1989, when they were opened. It was Maundy Thursday, March 29, 2018, and I was at the Riverbend Maximum Security Institution (RMSI).

I stepped out of the truck onto the asphalt. I removed my driver's license from my wallet, put the license in my shirt pocket, and slid the wallet under the seat. I shut the door and clicked the remote lock. The bed of the pickup still contained the leftover debris of coffee grounds and compost from preparing my blueberries, some two hundred plants, for the summer. Two college buddies had come to town to help me, and my muscles were still sore from the stoop labor. *I really need to get this truck washed*, I thought.

I strode across the parking lot to the sidewalk leading to the administration building—a single-story building among the concrete structures. An aerial view would show the building I was entering as the stem of a sprig of clover, with two four-leaf arrays composed of concrete structures, one on either side of the stem. It

31

looked something like a college campus. But this was no college.

When I entered the administration building that day, I was following a life path I had traveled almost weekly since the prison opened twenty-nine years ago.

In the late 1970s, a group of us—lawyers, ministers, prisoners, and concerned citizens—filed suit against the state of Tennessee and the Department of Correction for the deplorable conditions at the Tennessee State Prison (TSP, built in 1898) and other prisons. That suit brought to the attention of the courts the violence, lack of health care, and overcrowding that characterized the facilities, and as a result, a federal court judge ordered relief (*Grubbs v. Bradley*). That order included closing down TSP and building a new prison, RMSI.[1]

My involvement in that suit began a life working with the condemned that has lasted now for over forty years. They have been Black, brown, and white, women and men, straight and gay, old and young, some mentally impaired or insane, all poor, in settings from trial to death row to execution chamber.

I entered the prison through the glass doors and walked fifty feet to a checkpoint. As I signed in, I teased the two African American guards, one female and one male, whom I knew well: "Well, here we are again. One of you is kind and professional every week when I come out here. The other's just a mean man." We laughed, at ease with each other. I took off my shoes and belt and placed them with my truck key and ID in an opaque plastic container on the conveyor belt. Everything moved through the X-ray machine, just like at an airport, and I went through a separate metal detector.

Cleared by the metal detector and patted down, I gathered my things and headed through the door that led outside along a concrete sidewalk toward Unit 2—death row at RMSI. Unit 2 was on the

---

1 For a detailed account of the prisoner rebellion that led to the lawsuit, see my book *Last Rights: Thirteen Fatal Encounters with the State's Justice* (New York: Union Square Press, 2008).

high-security side of the prison, known as the "high side," to my left. The "low side" was to my right.

I proceeded through Building 8, the control area of the prison, from which many doors can be opened and shut remotely. Building 8 also contains the large visiting area for the prison. Low-side prisoners visit here. Behind the visiting area are the four holding cells and the death chamber, complete with lethal injection equipment and the electric chair. That was the deathwatch area. I turned in my volunteer badge at the control room, showed a guard my stamped hand, which illuminated under the fluorescent light, and told the guards behind the glass that I was going to Unit 2.

I left Building 8 and walked down the sidewalk toward Unit 2. The chain-link-enclosed recreation area, which featured a handball wall, weights, and basketball goal, was on my left. It was "the yard" for Unit 2, although there was no grass in view—it was all concrete. The guys using the yard shouted, "Hey, Joe, what's up?"

I yelled back, "Good to see you! Let me know if you need to talk to me."

At Unit 2, I pressed the button on the intercom. There were cameras, of course, that had no doubt alerted the guards that I had arrived. Awaiting the buzz that would permit me to enter, I gazed at the sky and then down at the red-and-white impatiens planted on either side of the door. I placed my hand on the dark metal door handle, a change from the gray-painted buildings that surrounded me. I was standing now within the four-leaf clover of the high side. The buzz, when it came, was loud and tingled my hand. I jerked the heavy metal door open before the buzzer stopped. Entering "the trap"—the area between the two locked doors—I pulled the first door shut with a slam. Only after the first door closed did the second buzzer sound. I pushed the second door open and entered Unit 2. The door closed behind me.

A desk sat to the right. During designated visiting hours, a guard sits behind the desk. My visits were generally not during visitation hours but rather during designated volunteer periods. I moved through the visiting gallery to my left. The chairs there were linked underneath by a bar that connected and held them in place. There was also a microwave where snacks could be warmed and children's books in a small bookcase. It was quiet and deserted now, but I could easily imagine the hubbub during visiting hours.

I walked down a passageway to the next locked door—metal, but with a glass window taking up the top half, through which I could see into the unit. This door has no button to sound a buzzer, so I knocked on the window. A prisoner walking past saw me and shouted to the guards in the room to the right, "Volunteer on the door!" Then I heard the familiar buzz and pushed the door open. Now I was in the heart of Unit 2. My volunteer status enabled me to visit the guys in their cells, go over to the program building, 2-A, or out into the rec area. I nodded at the two guards to my right.

"Think I'll start with Terry King."

Their reply: "He's in 2-A."

Then one guard spoke into a walkie-talkie: "Inner/outer doors 2-A."

From where I stood at the center of Unit 2, the doors to the pods of each unit were easily accessible. The doors to 2-A buzzed to my right, and I walked briskly to reach the door before the buzzer stopped. Grabbing the brass handle and swinging the heavy door open, I stepped into the trap and closed the door behind me. Then the next door buzzed and slid open. Stepping through that door, I was now outside in a walkway bordered on either side by chain-link fence and topped by a solid metal roof. But I wasn't outside for long; I walked up the slight incline to the metal door leading into the program building of 2-A. I was buzzed into the unit and proceeded down the corridor to another gray metal door on the right, where I was buzzed into another trap. Once the door behind me closed, the solid door ahead of me buzzed and I pushed it open.

The big room I entered was divided in half by bookcases full of books of general interest. The law library was to my right, and the smaller art room was next to it. In the middle of the area to my left was the Table of Reconciliation, a large white table with, in its center, an African design symbolizing reconciliation. Several guys sat at the table, talking. One was Terry King. When he saw me, he jumped up and we embraced. I greeted the other men at the table, and then Terry and I sat down for a visit. Terry and I have been friends for over thirty years.

* * *

Inadvertently, I had helped build this prison. After we filed suit against the state of Tennessee for unconstitutional prison conditions in the late 1970s, the judge issued court orders to bring the deplorable conditions in our state prisons under control. Those orders had resulted in a special session of the legislature in 1985. Millions of dollars had been appropriated to bring the prison system into the twentieth century. My particular interest had been death row, and in fact, my fellow plaintiffs and I had also filed a separate death row–conditions lawsuit, *Groseclose v. Dutton*. Along with the Department of Correction, we had worked with Pat McManus, the court-appointed special master, to build a unique death row at RMSI, configured using behavior modification as a management tool.[2]

In this new death row, when the prisoner entered from the trial court, he was placed at level C, the lowest level. He was locked down except for an hour a day to exercise. If his behavior was good for a year, he would move up to level B. This allowed for more out-of-cell

2 Pat McManus had been appointed by the court to be the special master to ensure that the orders of the court were carried out. Pat was a former corrections commissioner of Kansas. He worked with those of us who initiated the litigation and the Department of Correction to upgrade the entire prison system in Tennessee, which had been declared unconstitutional.

time, for contact visits while handcuffed but without shackles on the ankles. After another year of good behavior, the prisoner was made an A-level prisoner. A-level convicts could be out of their cell all day, take GED and college courses, go to the law library, do arts and crafts, and have contact visits unencumbered by handcuffs. Death row prisoners never left Unit 2, which meant they did not touch grass, but they could go to 2-A, the adjacent program building, to participate in programs.

In the 1970s and 1980s, my work took me to every death row in the South. I made friendships with prisoners throughout the region. My colleagues in the Southern Coalition on Jails and Prisons (SCJP) and I labored for criminal justice reform and the abolition of the death penalty. I visited men and women on all the death rows in the South. I developed a very clear idea of what I wanted the new Tennessee death row to be. And it was not the almost total lockdown of every other Southern death row.

When we began the SCJP with a meeting at Will Campbell's farm in the spring of 1974, we authored a statement we called "Where We Stand." We thought there were too many people locked up in the country—some 250,000 at that point, though in the decades since it has grown to 2.2 million. We opposed the death penalty, and at the time we wrote "Where We Stand," there were no executions taking place in the United States because of *Furman v. Georgia*, a Supreme Court decision that struck down capital punishment in 1972. In 1976, a different Supreme Court, with four justices appointed by President Nixon, reinstated the death penalty. Since then, there have been 1,576 executions.

We were in favor of a range of alternatives to incarceration, and some of them have been implemented at the state level. But the age-old practice of state killing, combined more recently with the growing industry of mass incarceration, continued the process begun with slavery and lynching.

Some of those racially discriminatory practices had been recognized and either overturned or condoned by the courts—especially the US Supreme Court, in such cases as *Batson v. Kentucky*, a 1986 Supreme Court decision in which the conviction of James Batson, an African American man, for burglary, was overturned on the basis that peremptory challenges cannot be used to eliminate all jurors of the same race as the defendant, as they were in Batson's trial. Another prominent case was *McCleskey v. Kemp*, a 1987 decision in which the Supreme Court supported the sentencing to death of Warren McCleskey, an African American man and a friend from visits to Georgia's death row, for armed robbery and murder. *McCleskey* became a landmark legal case that established uncontroverted statistical evidence that the death penalty was racially discriminatory on the basis of the race of the victim. That case has been described as the *Dred Scott* decision of our time.[3] Despite or because of cases such as those, the racially discriminatory practices observed in Southern states included trials of African Americans conducted with all-white juries, sentencing laws written with disproportionate impacts on Blacks (such as reserving the death penalty almost exclusively for those who kill white people), and the fact that 98 percent of all prosecutors in the South are white.

As a result, the South, the most avowedly religious section of the country, also led in racially discriminatory practices and state-sanctioned or state-tolerated killing (both official and unofficial—Jim Crow and the New Jim Crow—including lynching, mass incarceration, and executions). It was possible to envision the South as a giant crucifix; its "Christian" religiosity brought about the erection of the two beams of the cross. The vertical beam, which was race, has crucified millions of people since the inception of the

---

3 *Dred Scott v. Sandford* was a landmark US Supreme Court decision stating that enslaved people were not citizens of the Unites States; therefore, they did not have the same rights, privileges, and protections offered by the US Constitution.

country. The horizontal beam of the cross represented class. It was almost always the poor who were killed. These malevolent factors continued to claim victims daily.

*   *   *

"Terry," I said, as we sat down at the table, "I saw Governor Haslam recently, and he was okay with your kidney donation as long as the commissioner [meaning the commissioner of corrections] is. The commissioner signed off on it as well. Now we're back to getting a hospital and transplant surgeon lined up. Dr. Johnson and Kathy are working on that. So we just have to wait and hope."

Terry shook his bald head. "Man, I hope this is finally it. We've been this close before, only to have it fall through. I just want to donate this kidney to make somebody's life better. I was in my cell thinking about this the other day. You know how long it's been since we started trying to get this approved? Eighteen years."

I smiled. "Sounds about right. We get half the equation, the state, lined up. Then the other half, the hospital or the surgeon, falls through. It seems never-ending."

After we'd chatted awhile, I said goodbye and stood. Terry was my main lifeline to death row, and we were in constant communication as to what was going on there.

Across the room, I passed three men painting on a twenty-two-foot-long white canvas background. They had been working on this project for over a month. The three of them were depicting Jesus as he labored through the stations of the cross. The various images had been sketched out, and the guys were hard at work. Derrick Quintero, known as Taco, enthusiastically said, "Joe, see how far we've come since last week? We can get this done before Lent is over." He pointed out each completed panel in the two-foot-high scroll.

Maundy Thursday

"Derrick, man, this looks so real. It's as if you guys were there watching the entire crucifixion in real time." I marveled at the spirit that emanated from their portrayal of the final journey of Jesus. These condemned men, it seemed, knew all too well what Jesus felt under sentence of death, making his way to execution.

Harold Nichols, known as Red even though his hair was now graying, concentrated on the figures he was painting on one panel. His presence in the room illustrated the arbitrariness of the death penalty. Recently, he had stood before a state post-conviction judge, and it appeared that Red would be granted relief, perhaps a reduction to a life sentence. But the attorney general's office appealed, and Red lost. Out of luck and out of options, he was now hurtling toward an execution date.

Billy Irick was the third artist. He had been given an August 9 execution date—remember, today was March 29. Through his artwork while on death row, Billy had found a medium to communicate and overcome the horrific abuse suffered during his childhood. That abuse had come not only from his parents but from the state of Tennessee as well. When Billy was a child, the state had no facilities for mentally disturbed children. To deal with ten-year-old Billy's acting out, he was placed in an adult mental institution. When that didn't control him, he was exiled to solitary confinement. Some months later, a social worker found the naked child languishing there.

Today, Billy was hard at work on the sky and rocks in one of the panels. I teased him that if he wasn't careful, this work would make a Christian out of him. He shook his head, all long gray beard and hair.

Taco said, "He says God abandoned him. At least that's what Red says."

Billy just kept silently painting.

I thought of Jesus on the cross: "My God, my God, why hast

39

thou forsaken me?" Billy and Jesus shared the feeling of being, in the midst of their execution, abandoned by God.

As I surveyed the panels of the stations of the cross, I suggested that we try to get the finished banner displayed in churches in Nashville. "Guys, I know we can get it displayed in Christ Church Cathedral. Probably at St. Paul's in Murfreesboro and St. Ann's in East Nashville." James Booth, a Catholic volunteer, had already offered to lead the effort of placing it in Catholic churches around town.

Taco said, "What about Edgehill Methodist?"

"Probably," I said. "They have a new minister I don't know."

Red and Billy just kept painting, and when I said I'd see them later and turned to walk away, Billy was so intent on his painting he never looked up.

I left 2-A and went back down the chain-link corridor to Unit 2. There, in the middle of Unit 2, the crossroads where the hallways to all the pods converge, David Duncan—"Slim," a tall African American—greeted me. He gestured to an empty room, where he began updating me on his case.

"Judge Nixon granted me a hearing. The state is willing to settle the case. They want me to serve thirty-six years before parole. Joe, I've already done thirty. Can't I get something less than thirty-six?"

"I can see Ray Whitley, the DA. We had a cordial talk last time, but, David, I have to be honest—I don't see him moving from his position. He did agree to talk to the victim's son, so I'll follow up with him on that."

"Joe, you know I feel terrible about what I did. I'm willing to meet with the victim's son if he would like. I've changed my life. I know most people on death row say that, but with me, it was God who changed me—this really is a God thing. Maybe he would agree to just hear from me."

"I promise I'll check it out. I think Whitley said the guy may even be a minister. I'll call him." We hugged, and I moved on into B pod.

Maundy Thursday

The pods are on two levels, containing single cells on each level. I climbed the stairs to the second level. I looked through the small window in Mike Rimmer's door. He was in a familiar posture—seated, leaning forward over his electric typewriter, no doubt working on his case. I tapped on the hard plastic window. He looked up and smiled. "Joe, how you doing?" He stood, and as he approached the door, I flashed back to the vigil we'd held outside the Memphis Criminal Court building last fall. The hearing was to review Mike's frame-up by the police and prosecutors in Shelby County. Mike's cousin; his visitors through our Visitation on Death Row program, Ann and Jerry Calhoun; several local death penalty abolitionists; and I had congregated on the sidewalk in front of the Shelby County Criminal Court building and held up signs demanding justice for Mike. After the hearing, we'd had lunch with Mike's parents at a local eatery.

Mike stuck his hand through the pie hole in the metal door and we shook hands. Then he updated me on his case. Of all the cases on Tennessee's death row, Mike's was a doozy. The police and prosecutors in Memphis (who have sent about half of the state's death row population to Riverbend) conspired to convict Mike and sentence him to death not once, not twice, but three times in separate trials. Forget the facts that eyewitnesses identified other people at the crime scene and that there was no physical evidence that connected Mike to the crime. The prosecutors suborned perjury from law enforcement officers to overcome those deficiencies in their case. The sentencing was overturned once by a Memphis judge who found egregious error, and the lead prosecutor was sanctioned.

The prosecutors and officers did not like Mike or his attitude— he does not back down. He had previously assaulted his girlfriend, so when she was murdered, they assumed Mike must have killed her. So Mike was sentenced to death a second time, despite prosecutorial malfeasance during the trial. Those of us who are activists against the death penalty have many times heard or sensed an old notion, the same notion that led to the prosecution and death sentence of Philip Workman, another innocent man out of Memphis: *This is a bad guy. If he didn't do this murder, he will do something else. Let's take care of him.*

I liked Mike a lot, but he could be his own worst enemy. On a trip to Washington, DC, I recruited a law firm to represent him in appealing his second conviction. But Mike decided, based on what little research he could do, that he would not accept them because they did not meet his standards. I respected his choice, but now he was stuck with Tennessee-based counsel that he also found inadequate, and on this day he wanted to talk about nothing but his latest frustration with his lawyer. I could barely find a hole in his string of grievances into which to insert a comment, and there was nothing I could do about his case in any event.

Finally, trying to change the subject, I said, "Mike, how is your dad doing?" His father suffered from serious heart trouble. A year before, I had arranged for a cardiologist friend at Vanderbilt Medical Center to see Mr. Rimmer.

"He's still doing great, Joe. The medicine he's on has really helped. He'll probably live another five years, maybe longer. I appreciate your helping to get him squared away."

"He just needed the right doc. You know, I'm very fond of your folks. How are the visits with Darlene going?" I asked. Darlene Kimbrough was Mike's volunteer visitor in our Visitation on Death Row (VODR) program, which we started in 1975 at the Tennessee State Prison. VODR matches "free world" people with prisoners for one-on-one visitation. The goal is to provide every prisoner who desires one with a visitor from outside. Currently, all of the forty-nine men on death row in Tennessee are matched with a visitor. This has created a real experience of community, especially among those who visit on Monday evening. I had matched Mike with Darlene because she was a spirited soul I was confident could deal with Mike's intensity.[4]

"Going great!" he said enthusiastically. "We're reading and discussing Bible passages. She's a real pistol. Doesn't know much law, but that's okay. She's become a good friend. Helps keep me honest."

When I was finished talking with Mike and a few other guys on the walk who wanted to talk, I headed back down the stairs and went to find Ed Zagorski. Ed's was a name that, over the many years of our relationship, had etched itself into my thoughts and prayers and emotions. These relationships, and the one I had with Ed in particular, were so much more than friendships—they were life-altering experiences.

When I entered A pod, Ed waved me over to a table in a small room. We pulled up chairs and began to talk.

"Ed, did your lawyer come out to discuss the execution date with you?" The Tennessee Supreme Court had recently set an execution date of October 11 for Ed.

"Yeah, we had a good talk. I don't have a lot of options. But he's optimistic about clemency. I heard you've been working in your blueberry field."

I laughed. "Yeah, blueberries wait on no man. My college buddies helped me get them ready for summer."

He was quiet for a while, looking pensive, and then said, "You know, Joe, I see it like a mercy killing. It's hard growing old in prison." He was sixty-three. "It's hard enough growing old on the outside, but in here it's even harder. There's no health care, your body is breaking down . . .

"When you're out there speaking against the death penalty, you should tell them that the thing that's hardest, that makes us suffer the most, is getting old in here. That's even worse than the death penalty.

---

4 For an in-depth look at the VODR program, see *He Called Me Sister* by Suzanne Craig Robertson.

Man, when they kill me, it'll be like a mercy killing."

An animal lover, Ed asked about Molly, my brindle mutt, as he always does. I told him I would send him a picture of her. "She's not much to look at," I said, "but I can always count on her."

"Like me," Ed said, then grew quiet again. For a long time. What he said next surprised me: "Joe, I'd like you to be with me when the time comes—assuming this execution ever actually happens. Not as a religious person but as my friend. I'd like to have my last conversation with you."

The seriousness and intimacy of his request took me aback. It was my turn to be quiet for a moment. "Ed," I said finally, "you know I'll be there for you if it comes to that. But let's concentrate on keeping that from happening."

He nodded.

Next up was Don Johnson. Don was out of appeals and expecting an execution date to be set by the Tennessee Supreme Court. He had recently helped me understand the prison's regulations regarding telephone use because we wanted some of the guys on death row to participate in *Lifelines,* a podcast created and developed by the Lifelines Project, based in Philadelphia. The program shared the religious perspectives of death row prisoners with the public. Don had his own religious broadcast on the radio and understood the rules of the prison regarding religious transmissions. Under Don's tutelage, Abu-Ali Abdur'Rahman had sung three beautiful hymns over the phone for a *Lifelines* episode.

Don said, "Joe, I know you're aware that John Dysinger is my religious adviser. But I'm worried about that. He and his family are wonderful people. I'm afraid that my execution will mess him and his family up. If it comes down to it, I want you to be with me at the end as my religious adviser."

For the second time that afternoon, I was sitting and looking into the eyes of a friend as he asked me to be with him when the state kills him. Once again, I responded, "Don, you know I'll do anything to help you."

During the fifteen-minute drive home, all I could think about was Ed and Don, what they had asked of me, and what I had agreed to do. I knew all too well what the "deathwatch" role entailed—I had done it before.

There had been only six executions in Tennessee since 1977, when the death penalty law passed the legislature. I had been involved with death row prisoners across the South since 1975 and lost too many of them to the executioner. But Tennessee, with the exception of Philip Workman's killing in 2007, had always been my safe harbor. It now appeared that my safe harbor was about to vanish.

CHAPTER TWO

A Judicial Lynching

AS SPRING GAVE WAY to summer and my weekly visits to death row continued, I grew increasingly concerned about Billy Irick's fate. He was convicted of the 1985 rape and murder of seven-year-old Paula Dyer in Knoxville, Tennessee. In the weeks before that crime, he had chased an invisible demon down a Knoxville street with a machete. He was profoundly mentally ill and had been since he suffered abuse and abandonment by his parents as a child. He heard voices and demonstrated a variety of psychotic behaviors. On the night of the attack, he'd been speaking off the back porch into the air. Nonetheless, the child's parents, who were friends of Billy's, left Paula in Billy's care as her babysitter and went out.

In the bizarre world of death penalty litigation, the only obstacle between Billy and the death house was litigation concerning the state's chosen method of execution: lethal injection. There was a trial in state court on the efficacy of Tennessee's killing protocol. This was the fourth iteration of such litigation because the state kept changing the drug protocol. Indeed, the latest change had taken place just four days before the July trial on lethal injection began.

On February 20, 2018, lawyers for death row prisoners filed a complaint in chancery court claiming that the latest lethal injection protocol would result in the "[needless] experience of terror, pain and suffocation during execution." The lawyers made that claim because of the inclusion by the state of midazolam as the initial drug in the injection process. This drug renders the prisoner asleep—but not insensate. When the acidity from the injection of the next drug, vecuronium bromide (a paralytic), acts to fill the lungs with water, creating pulmonary edema, the prisoner feels as if they are drowning. An NPR study of autopsies found that 84 percent of prisoners executed by lethal injection suffered this feeling of drowning during an execution.[1] It is like being waterboarded. The second drug renders the prisoner paralyzed so that he cannot move, not even an eyelash. He cannot reveal the pain he is experiencing. A chemical veil is created so that the witnesses will see a peaceful death when the prisoner may in fact be suffering excruciating pain but cannot show it due to paralysis. The third drug, potassium chloride, painfully stops the heart. The lethal injection protocol is a recipe for torture.

This drug renders the prisoner asleep—but not insensate.

Arizona, one of the states that pioneered the use of midazolam, stopped using it for the reasons stated above. Those problems were of no concern to the state of Tennessee in its rush to crank up the machinery of state killing.

The chancery court hearing went on for almost two weeks as the plaintiffs provided detailed scientific proof of the torturous

---

1 Noah Caldwell, Ailsa Chang, and Jolie Myers, "Gasping for Air: Autopsies Reveal Troubling Effects of Lethal Injection," NPR, September 21, 2020, https://www.npr.org/2020/09/21/793177589/gasping-for-air-autopsies-reveal-troubling-effects-of-lethal-injection.

nature of the latest lethal injection protocol. The leading scientists in the research on midazolam testified; witnesses to executions in other states shared their observations of how the drug had gone wrong before their eyes. The state was unmoved, seemingly taking the position that it was interested only in what it had the power to do, not in what was right to do.

It all climaxed with closing arguments on July 24. The presentation of Kelley Henry of the Middle Tennessee Federal Public Defender's office was a tour de force on behalf of the prisoners. Her closing argument recounted the details of the scientific testimony and the witness observations. It was clear that this protocol had no analgesic component. The question was: Would Chancellor Ellen Hobbs Lyle see it that way? The answer came swiftly. Her decision denied the scientific and anecdotal evidence, concluding there was "some analgesic effect" when in fact there was none. The decision was rendered on July 26 at 6:32 p.m.

* * *

As American citizens, we have certain rights. One of those rights is the "due process of law" guaranteed by the US Constitution. This enables us to go to court to pursue legal remedies for wrongs committed against us. If that court rejects our petition, we can appeal it to a higher court where we are entitled to a careful, reasonable, objective review of the findings of the first court. That right was a given until the Tennessee Supreme Court (TSC) denied that option to Billy Irick on August 6, 2018.

The hearing Chancellor Lyle presided over featured twenty-three witnesses and 139 exhibits and provided an in-depth examination of the cruelty of the new lethal injection protocol that leads with the drug midazolam. The prisoners' experts were the premier experts in the field on what this drug can and cannot do. The state's experts were inadequate. Chancellor Lyle acknowledged the superiority of the plaintiffs' experts, but she dismissed the prisoners' claims, primarily because she took the word of the Tennessee Department of Correction (TDOC) that they could not find the drug alternative for execution that the plaintiffs had been required to suggest under law. That Chancellor Lyle accepted the state's word for this when prisoners in Texas and Georgia had recently been executed with alternative drugs made for a curious conclusion.

The case moved to the Tennessee Court of Appeals on July 30 with Billy Irick facing an August 9 execution date. The Court of Appeals looked at the record and the evidence and decided that it did not have time to fairly review the information contained in the trial record before Irick's execution date. The Tennessee Supreme Court (TSC) reached down and assumed the case on July 30.

Common sense suggests that with a record as deep and extensive as the lethal injection case, the Court of Appeals made a wise and just decision. It is one that the TSC should have followed. Instead, on August 6, that court, rather than issuing a stay of execution to consider the record, decided by a 4–1 vote that there was not a "likelihood of success" in Billy Irick's claims. They declined to conduct the proper review that the Court of Appeals had thought necessary to render a fair decision. Instead, a majority of justices simply opined that it did not look like Billy Irick's case would prevail—so why bother? The TSC denied Irick's right to a full and proper review, clearing the way to proceed with the execution.

As dissenting Justice Sharon Lee pointed out:

> The question is not whether the state will execute Billy Ray Irick, but whether the state will execute Mr. Irick before an appellate court can review the chancery court's dismissal of the claims that Tennessee's newly adopted method of lethal injection is unconstitutional. In his

motion to vacate the August 9, 2018, execution date, Mr. Irick has shown a likelihood of success on appeal by asserting error in the chancery court's factual findings, its legal conclusions and its denial of his motion to amend. Unless the execution date is vacated, Mr. Irick—unlike the other thirty-two death row inmates who have challenged the state's method of execution—will not live to see whether the chancery court's decision is correct.[2]

Why the haste by the TSC? The majority opinion reveals a thinly veiled hostility to the parties bringing this claim and a frustration caused by the repeated changing of the drug protocol by the TDOC, which resulted in continued challenges via litigation. By adding to their opinion a footnote that death penalty abolitionists precipitated this litigation by convincing drug companies not to make these drugs available for execution, the highest court in the state was going out of its way to deflect the focus from the constantly changing execution protocols offered by the TDOC. At the time of the trial, the most recent protocol alteration had occurred just four days before the trial began. This failure to acknowledge the continued incompetence of the state directs attention away from the testimony of the leading experts in the field during the trial—experts who offered uncontroverted proof that the use of midazolam would result in "the feeling of drowning while being consumed by a chemical fire."

The TSC wanted to get on with executions, and to accomplish that, didn't mind denying a fair appellate hearing to Billy Irick. If it's torture, who cares? It was a shameful day in the legal history of Tennessee that saw basic constitutional rights denied so that the state could proceed with executions. It literally was a judicial lynching.

2 *State of Tennessee v. Billy Ray Irick,* filed August 6, 2018, https://www.tncourts.gov/sites/default/files/docs/irick_dissent_order_8-6-18.pdf.

As all of this was going on, I continued my weekly visits to death row. I had encouraged Billy Irick, Harold Nichols, and Derrick Quintero to keep painting after they finished their rendition of the Stations of the Cross. Billy was totally absorbed in their new work—three paintings: *The Crucifixion, The Laying of Jesus in the Tomb,* and *The Ascension.* Billy brought a real sense of color to the backgrounds. When my wife, Becca, and I were in Arles, France, in May of that year I saw seven Van Goghs in one museum. I sent Billy a postcard of a work by Vincent van Gogh from that exhibit, struck by their mutual love of bright color in their art.

I visited death row on Tuesday, August 7. The guys there told me Billy had continued painting through Monday afternoon. He had his visit Monday night in the visiting room with other guys and their visitors. Then guards took him to deathwatch in Unit 8.

It had been almost eight years since an execution. One day when Billy had first come to death row some thirty years before, he was playing the card game pinochle with several others. When he lost the game, he was so upset he struck himself in the cheek with his fist. In his many years on death row, Billy had grown from that emotionally damaged individual into a convict who helped others, whose word was his bond—a man who loved to paint. Now he was about to be executed, and that prospect was unnerving and depressing for his death row brothers.

As I left the prison that day, I noted all the fresh painting taking place in the hall of the administrative building. I had seen this often in Southern prisons on the eve of executions: a desire to spruce things up for the general public and press before an execution.

Many of the volunteers who participate in our Visitation on Death Row program were there on the Monday night when Billy had his last visit. Those volunteers wanted to be together again on the eve of the execution. We gathered outside the prison in a field at 6:00 p.m. on August 9.

A Judicial Lynching

There were about fifty people gathered in the field to protest the execution. There was also a service at the Fisk University chapel for others in Nashville who wished to protest. In an area adjacent to the field, there were five people gathered in support of the death penalty. They blasted out "Hell's Bells" by AC/DC on a boom box into the summer evening. Unbeknownst to the celebrators of the execution, AC/DC was Billy Irick's favorite rock group. They yelled out their gleeful approval of Billy's approaching killing.

Those in the group who visited death row gathered in a circle and shared Billy stories. Almost everyone had a story to tell about Billy. It felt good to renew those bonds. As the execution, scheduled for 7:00 p.m., drew nigh, we joined in a larger circle with everyone in the field to protest. We shared what brought us to the gathering; we prayed.

The five death penalty celebrators next to us, beyond the roped-off area, grew loud: "He's a monster! Why don't you pray for Paula! He's a monster!" Of course, we *were* praying for Paula. Our point was that we are all children of God and deserve to be treated as such. No one should be killing anyone. The response to killing should not be more killing.

We began singing. Everyone in the circle sang "Amazing Grace." Then "Precious Lord, Take My Hand." We lifted one song after another into the night air. The yelling from the celebrators died down. We kept singing past the designated execution time, holding hands in the circle.

I left the circle to check with a journalist to see if she knew what was going on. I feared that, based on the evidence presented in the hearing concerning lethal injection, Billy would suffer a prolonged and gruesome death. The reporter I spoke to had also attended the hearing, so she was also aware of that danger. She kept checking the newsfeed for any word about the execution. Finally, the Department of Correction announced that Billy had been executed. The time given was 7:48 p.m.

After being strapped to the gurney, Billy had said, "I just wanna say I'm really sorry, and that—that's it."

Steven Hale, a witness and writer for *Nashville Scene*, gave the following account:

> He jolted and produced what sounded like a cough or a choking noise. He moved his head slightly and appeared to briefly strain his forearms against the restraints. In a statement following the execution, federal Public Defender Kelley Henry said those were signs of the kind of trouble warned about in [the lethal injection] lawsuit . . .
>
> This means that the second and third drugs were administered even though Mr. Irick was not unconscious. The descriptions also raise troubling questions about the State's attempt to mask the signs of consciousness, including by taping down his hands which would have prevented the witnesses from observing the failure of the midazolam.
>
> At about 7:37 p.m., the color in Irick's face changed to almost purple. After that, we watched for nearly 10 minutes as he lay there. He did not appear to be breathing any longer.[3]

* * *

The morning after Billy's execution, I received a call from Gene Shiles, Billy's lawyer, who had represented Billy for some twenty years. He always thought someone would recognize Billy's mental illness and have mercy. He had witnessed the execution.

"Gene, how are you?" I asked.

---

3 Steven Hale, "The Execution of Billy Ray Irick," *Nashville Scene*, August 10, 2018.

"Okay, Joe," came the reply. He had called because he wanted help with an affidavit. Billy had told him that he didn't want an autopsy because it violated his Native American religious beliefs. Gene was filing an emergency petition in court to prevent the autopsy, and he needed someone who could vouch for the authenticity of Billy's beliefs. I had known for twenty years that Billy felt this way and was happy to put that in an affidavit.

Just before we hung up, Gene said, "Joe, in my last five minutes of conversation with Billy, he mentioned you. He said, 'Tell Joe Ingle I really appreciate the time he spent with me.'"

"Gene, thank you for letting me know that. I feel I failed Billy in so many ways. We just couldn't do enough. It was heartbreaking."

Gene reassured me that I had done a great deal. We discussed the utter desolation and hopelessness of everything having to do with the death penalty in Tennessee and Billy's case in particular.

A hearing was held in chancery court on the petition Gene had filed on Billy's behalf. Chancellor Perkins granted Billy's request. The state could draw fluids but would not perform an autopsy. We had pioneered this litigation after Cecil Johnson's execution nearly eight years before. Gene spoke to Brad MacLean, who handled that litigation, and drew on that work in crafting the petition and argument in Billy's case.

There is no doubt in my mind that Billy died a horrific death. Steven Hale had reported in the *Nashville Scene* that Billy's face had turned purple—an indication of pulmonary edema, which gives one the feeling of drowning. Since the midazolam did not render him insensate, he would have experienced what the scientists described as "chemical burning"—at the same time, he was experiencing the sensation of drowning.

It's no wonder that in my conversations with guys on death row after Billy's death, they considered the electric chair the lesser of two evils. They thought the electric chair would be less torturous.

Among those who told me that was Ed Zagorski, whose execution was scheduled for October 11.

After Billy Irick's execution, as I discussed it with my colleagues fighting the death penalty, we thought it appropriate to raise our concerns about this method of extermination. I contacted a prominent Nashville lawyer to arrange a meeting with the governor's legal counsel, Dwight Tarwater. The meeting took place at the state capitol from 3:00 to 5:00 p.m. on August 20.

The group that came to express our concerns consisted of two lawyers (Brad MacLean and Brant Phillips), Dr. Jane Easdown (an anesthesiologist at Vanderbilt Hospital), and me. We met with Dwight Tarwater and two of his colleagues. Brad had prepared a detailed analysis of how the brain functioned on midazolam, complete with graphs, which he distributed. A lengthy discussion ensued, and the point was made that despite Chancellor Lyle writing in her decision that there was "some analgesic effect" of midazolam, in reality there was none. When Dr. Easdown spoke, she was very clear on the total inability of the drug to render someone insensate. Rather, it was used to ease people into sleep but provided no analgesic effect, leaving the prisoner subjected to lethal injection unprotected against excruciating pain.

As the discussion progressed, I flashed back to my trip to Huntsville, Texas, in December of 1982 for the execution of Charlie Brooks. It was the first lethal injection performed in the country. And it was bungled. Here we were, thirty-six years later, and we still had an inhumane, barbaric ritual disguised as a medical procedure. Rather than improving over time, this method had actually become worse.

After a lengthy discussion of the medical implications of the drugs in the lethal injection protocol, Dwight Tarwater asked me what I thought clemency meant. I responded, "Grace." After a discussion of the religious implications of executive power, Mr. Tarwater asked me about Paul's letter to the Romans, chapter thirteen. "Dwight," I said, "I'm a Jesus man first. He is clear about the death penalty in the eighth chapter of the Gospel of John, which describes his encounter with a woman convicted of what was a capital crime in those days—adultery. When the crowd clearly wanted to execute her by stoning, Jesus replied: 'Let he who is without sin cast the first stone.' After her accusers left, Jesus told her, 'Go and sin no more.'"

He nodded and responded, "Yes, I doubt that the men had to worry about the same punishment." He was right—the laws of the day did not carry the same punishment for men as women.

Then I turned to Paul and Romans 13. This passage—"the state does not carry the sword in vain"—has been abused for centuries by those in power to justify not only the death penalty but whatever horrific act they wish to perform.

"Paul was writing to a small Christian community in Rome," I said. "It was literally under the boot of the empire. The Romans regarded Caesar as divine, and if someone denied that and asserted that Jesus was Lord, it meant death. Paul knew the realities of Rome and wanted his little flock to survive. He did not want them challenging the state, because he knew that would mean extermination. So in this passage, he was providing not a proscription of what should be but rather a description of the political situation as it was. Unfortunately, governments ever since have used this passage to justify their own ends."

It was chilling to contemplate Dwight Tarwater, Governor Bill Haslam, and Attorney General Herbert Slatery, all from Knoxville and members of the same Bible study group, using Romans 13 as a justification for what they were doing.

Our pitch to Governor Haslam, through Dwight Tarwater, was to establish a commission to review this new lethal injection protocol because of the strong evidence that it was actually torturous. Governor Bredesen, the previous governor, had taken similar action when issues emerged concerning a prior protocol. We requested that Haslam stop further executions until the protocol issues were thoroughly addressed, just as Governor Bredesen had.

* * *

Before Billy's execution, I had arranged for several bishops to see Governor Haslam about clemency for Billy. He would not see them. I asked evangelicals to see him. He refused to meet. I had met with him previously and attempted to see him again. He denied my request for a meeting. The signals were clear about what was going to happen to Billy Irick, but I refused to accept them and continued to work on his behalf. In the end, my efforts accomplished nothing. Billy died a wounded, broken man. He'd been abandoned by the state of Tennessee at an early age because of his mental illness, and Tennessee abandoned him again at the end when it killed him.

CHAPTER THREE

Dated Up

THE WEEK AFTER Billy Irick's execution, I went back to death row. The guys were sober. After almost eight years with no executions, Tennessee—and death row—had entered a new legal world. Two more execution dates had been set, and a cluster of men had exhausted their appeals. Nick Sutton was in that group.

> ## After almost eight years with no executions, Tennessee—and death row— had entered a new legal world.

On this visit, I sat down with Nick to talk about his situation. I was preparing an affidavit for Nick's lawyer about the growth and maturation I had observed in Nick in his many years on death row. He had recently completed a conflict resolution class and was a certified mediator. But on this day, Nick wanted to talk about Billy Irick: "Billy was as good as his word. He didn't get in anyone's business. He helped out others when he could. He was a real convict. I hate to see him go. Joe, I'm in the next group. I'm going to get dated up. When should I file for clemency? After what happened to Billy, I just don't know."

Nick wasn't the only one reeling from Billy's execution. I was finding it hard to talk about.

"Nick, I don't put a lot of faith in Governor Haslam after what he did to Billy," I said.

Nick nodded. "Yeah. It *was* a horrible crime Billy committed, and it happened in Haslam's hometown. But I hear you. Right now, I just need to decide when to file for clemency. I'm thinking of filing before I'm dated up."

Ed Zagorski, my last guy to visit that day, already had an October 11 execution date. After Billy's killing, we all knew that date was firm—and time was running out. "I'll be here every week to talk to you," I told Ed. Because I had agreed to stand deathwatch with him, I needed to know him better.

The next week, Ed and I began meeting weekly so that he could reveal to me the journey of his life from Michigan, where he grew up, to Louisiana to Tennessee. Why was that important? It has been my experience that, in working with someone on deathwatch, it's best to get to know them as well as you can. I have experienced that at both extremes. For instance, I met Morris Mason the night of his electrocution in Virginia on June 25, 1985. On the other hand, my friendship with Philip Workman in Tennessee led to several deathwatches as he went through six death warrants over the years. I visited him weekly for seven years before his execution on May 9, 2007. The role is to be there for the prisoner and best meet his needs. The more you know him, the better you can serve him.

Clemency papers on Ed's behalf had been filed with Governor Haslam, and Ed's entire legal team was hopeful Ed would receive clemency. The facts were compelling: First, he had not received one write-up in almost thirty-five years on death row. (I have known no other prisoner incarcerated for that long of whom that was true.)

Second, when Ed was tried, there was no Life without Parole (LWOP) sentence. Six of the jurors in that trial, when recently contacted, said that they would have voted for LWOP if it had been available. And third, testimonial statements on Ed's behalf had been given by guards, prison employees, and even a former warden.

The role is to be there for the prisoner and best meet his needs.

As Becca and I discussed Ed's clemency prospects, she was encouraged by the optimism of the legal team. But when she asked me what I thought, I had to say, "Honey, I've heard so many predictions of clemency by defense lawyers over the years. And I end up arranging the funerals. I have a bad feeling about Ed's chances."

Ed's conviction decades before had been for killing two people over marijuana dealing. Although Ed didn't kill those two, it's true that he was a marijuana dealer working with folks who had a network across the South. He wasn't a kingpin—just a trusted soldier in delivering the drugs and collecting money. He had come to Hickman County, Tennessee, from Louisiana; he had been a marijuana dealer there too. An avid hunter, Ed had originally been attracted to Hickman County to hunt deer. But once he was living in Tennessee, he realized that it would be a good place to expand the marijuana business. He contacted his associates back in Louisiana, who sent a team of men to investigate the viability of making Hickman County a drug distribution point. A major interstate, I-40, bisected the remote, forested county. There were rural roads that could accommodate large trucks. The advance team decided it would be an ideal place to run drugs. They agreed to expand into Tennessee, and Ed began moving large quantities of marijuana through Hickman County.

Ed and his friend Jim Blackwell would shoot deer at night with a spotlight. Ed would be positioned in the back of the pickup truck with a high-powered rifle. Jim would drive since he was a local and knew the woods well. Jim would find the deer, transfix them with the beam of the spotlight, and Ed would shoot one or two. Sometimes the two of them would be seen and chased by police. Jim would always escape. He could drive the truck through the narrowest of passageways between trees to safety.

After Ed and Jim had been friends for several years, Ed cut Jim into the marijuana trade on a modest basis. But he didn't tell Jim who his associates were. Jim dealt only with Ed.

When Ed's associates moved into an area, they wanted any competition—as well as anyone who wanted to work for them—to know they meant business. They had a system. They would bring prospective dealers to a van and put them, their heads covered with a hood, in the back. When the van arrived at the rendezvous and the hoods were removed, the prospective new employees faced several armed men in camouflage gear, their weapons drawn and their faces covered. The new people were told in no uncertain terms what was expected: If anyone betrayed them, not only would they face the consequences but so too would their families. At that point, they would be handed a photo of their family members to show that they could make good on their threat.

In the early 1980s, the marijuana business in Tennessee was booming, and the music folks in Nashville were among the best customers. In 1984, Ed was told that there would be a major rendezvous to deliver a large shipment of marijuana. He was concerned, though, about Jim. Jim had been wanting a bigger piece of the action, but Ed had been keeping him at bay; and he sensed that Jim, frustrated, might create problems at the rendezvous—perhaps by attempting to steal the shipment. So Ed took precautions. He told Jim to be at a particular place—far from the rendezvous point—to pick up ten pounds of marijuana Jim had already paid for.

The evening of the shipment arrived; the rendezvous point was on a road in the woods near a trout farm in Hickman County. Some small-time local prospective dealers (Dale Dotson and Jimmy Porter) arrived with $35,000, their good-faith pledge that they hoped would allow them to move up a level in the drug trade. As Dotson and Porter walked up the road toward the rendezvous, as they had been instructed, Ed, armed and dressed in camouflage, stepped out of the woods, his face exposed so they would recognize him. Then a host of armed men in camouflage gear appeared from the woods. Ed explained to Dotson and Porter that everything was cool. They were going to be interviewed.

As some of the other armed men led Dotson and Porter to the boss for their interview, Ed walked some distance away into the woods. He was one of the sentinels posted to prevent anyone approaching the marijuana shipment from any direction. The boss conducted the drug interview, complete with pictures of the families of Dotson and Porter so that they would grasp the gravity of entering into this arrangement.

Hidden in the woods, keeping vigil over the shipment, Ed heard a rustling sound. He spied two men sleuthing toward the marijuana bales. He shot twice into the darkness. Responding to the gunshots, the armed men on the road immediately killed Dotson and Porter, fearing that a trap had been sprung on them.

When the shooting was over, everyone still standing came together to confer. The boss decided that the bodies would be dropped in nearby Robertson County to serve notice to a drug dealer who lived there that he was facing serious competition and should be careful with whom he interfered.

When Jimmy Porter and Dale Dotson's bodies were found,

Sheriff Frank Atkinson of Hickman County went looking for one of his favorite informants—none other than Ed's friend Jim Blackwell. At first, Blackwell denied knowledge of the killings but later changed his story. Even though Blackwell was a suspect in the murders, Sheriff Atkinson allowed him to actively assist in the investigation. Indeed, years later, Blackwell said that he "worked for" Frank Atkinson on "the Ed Zagorski case." All of this information was withheld from defense counsel at trial and on appeal.

Jim Blackwell was the only person who could incriminate Ed Zagorski. He was a confidential informant and a drug dealer. In fact, Sheriff Atkinson was aware that Blackwell could be a murderer. A witness came forward who saw Blackwell emerging from the woods near the time of the slaying of Hugh McKinney. Others alleged Blackwell paid the sheriff $5,000 not to link him to the McKinney murder. Yet now Blackwell was assisting in the investigation of the Porter/Dotson murders—killings that he had at first said he had no knowledge of. It was this "reliable source" who disclosed to authorities that Ed Zagorski had killed the two people whose bodies they found. The only problem was it wasn't true.

After the murders, Ed fled to Ohio. One night, he decided to host a party. Cleaning up in preparation, he took some trash to the dump and then went to the liquor store to purchase booze. While Ed was in the liquor store, a plainclothes policeman entered to purchase some alcohol. "He recognized me from the police sketch," Ed said. "But he was smart. He didn't let on he recognized me. And I had become arrogant. I hadn't altered my appearance. I had left most of my weapons back at the farm. I did have on my Kevlar vest and cap."

The policeman left the store and radioed for backup. When Ed drove away from the store, the policeman followed. Realizing that he was being followed, Ed estimated that if he could make it to an access road ahead that led to some difficult terrain, then he might get away with his four-wheel-drive truck. He sped up.

Unfortunately for Ed, the police had acted quickly; they had already set up a roadblock. Ed would have to run that roadblock to reach the access road. As Ed approached, a policeman jumped out of the lead car and pointed a shotgun at him. His partner knelt behind the opposite door, gun drawn. Ed lifted his automatic and fired first, shooting through his windshield; then the officer with the shotgun fired. Ed was hit. His truck plowed into the police car. The impact sent the second policeman to the ground, and his legs were run over. The shotgun blast had hit Ed in the head with buckshot, and blood was running down his forehead into his eyes. He couldn't get his truck through the other police cars. He was trapped.

While being treated in a West Virginia hospital, he gave a statement to police after being denied legal counsel. He did not acknowledge killing anyone.

Ed was brought back to Tennessee. Although the murders had occurred in Hickman County, the bodies of the slain drug dealers were found in Robertson County. The counties dueled for jurisdiction, and Robertson County prevailed.

While the police were searching for Ed, they had thoroughly investigated his background. They found little accurate information, because Ed always used an alias and hid his true background and identity from everyone, even his associates. They found a little information about a former drug charge, but for the most part, Ed was a mystery man. They did know from Jimmy Blackwell that Ed was hooked up with a major drug cartel, and they believed that Ed knew who ran it and how it was organized. It was that knowledge the authorities were determined to extract from Ed.

After being treated for his wounds, Ed was discharged from the hospital and transported to the Robertson County jail. Law enforcement officers sought to interrogate him, but he repeatedly stated, "I want a lawyer." They placed him in the drunk tank that first night.

The next day the sheriff moved him into an unventilated metal box about six feet high inside a cell. The cells were not air conditioned. It was June, with heat building in Middle Tennessee. The heat would reach one hundred and twenty degrees that summer, while Ed sat in the box. Their intention was to torture him into talking.

In my visits to Angola prison in Louisiana, I learned that a similar device—called the Red Hat Box, because the prisoner was placed into the metal box wearing a red hat—had been used for difficult prisoners. Their punishment was to broil in the Louisiana sun until authorities decided to remove them. This was precisely what the district attorney, sheriff, and jail officials sought to do to Ed Zagorski in Robertson County. Except that Tennessee's Red Hat Box was inside an un-air-conditioned jail cell in the Tennessee summer heat. Ed was in there for 120 days, twenty-four hours a day.

Ed's interrogation by the sheriff and associate district attorney was the classic good cop–bad cop routine. One would promise to get him out of the box if he would just give up one name of someone in the organization. The other would threaten him with the electric chair, accompanied by gruesome descriptions of eyeballs popping out and blood boiling through various orifices of the body.

Ed wasn't about to tell these guys anything. For one thing, he wasn't someone who would betray confidences. He had sworn not to identify his colleagues in the marijuana trade, and his word was good. Secondly, he knew the guys he worked with. If he did what Jim Blackwell had done and informed to the police, he and his family would be killed, just as he knew that Jim Blackwell would eventually be slain for informing on Ed. The torturous conditions did result in two rambling statements—"confessions"—but again, Ed didn't admit to killing anyone. Other than that, all Ed would tell his interrogators was, "I want a lawyer."

Ed's lack of cooperation left the prosecution in a bind. All they had was Jim Blackwell's word about what happened. There was no physical evidence linking Ed to the crime. Gradually, they pieced together stories about Ed's activities, but it was all hearsay. They really needed a statement from Ed.

One day they brought Ed in for the usual interrogation—from the hot box into a room frigid from air conditioning turned low. Standard practice for Ed's interrogations. Since Ed would say only, "I want a lawyer," or discuss things not on point for the murders, his interrogators needed to trick him into making a statement that would convince a jury. And that meant using Jim Blackwell.

Blackwell provided authorities with so-called evidence that became critical in the case. He turned over shell casings he said were from Ed's gun from a time he and Ed had gone target-shooting in Hickman County. Authorities found a shell near where the bodies were found in Robertson County that matched those shell casings. But that's odd for at least two reasons. First, the shell casing was found at that crime scene the day after it had been thoroughly processed by sheriff's department personnel. Why hadn't they found the casing then, if it was there? And second, recall that the murders, and therefore all the shooting, had actually occurred in Hickman County, and then the bodies were moved to Robertson County. Why would a shell casing related to the murders have been in Robertson County at all?

The case against Ed Zagorski relied on an informer who "found" shell casings, who allegedly paid the sheriff of Hickman County $5,000 not to link him to a murder he very likely committed, and who had been a drug dealer in Hickman County for years. None of this information was provided to defense counsel, who repeatedly requested any and all information pertaining to the *Zagorski* case.

Who knew about Jim Blackwell's unprosecuted crimes? Hickman County law enforcement knew of Blackwell's drug activity. Prosecutor Joe Baugh suspected it. In fact, even as the murders of Porter and Dotson were being investigated, the prosecutors had evidence that Jim Blackwell was a drug dealer. Indeed, county and state authorities made no attempt to stop Blackwell from selling drugs while he was helping to get Ed Zagorski convicted. Again, none of this information was relayed to defense counsel. The refusal to turn over such information upon request is a clear *Brady* issue—meaning that by law any items in possession of the prosecution, including possible exculpatory evidence, must be provided to the defense—and should have resulted in a new trial.

This was the foundation of the case against Ed Zagorski, who was convicted on March 2, 1984, and sentenced to death on March 27, 1984.

CHAPTER FOUR

What a Tangled Web We Weave

ED ZAGORSKI WAS moved to deathwatch the night of October 8 around 11:30 p.m. This meant that he was placed in a holding cell in Building 8 near the execution devices (electric chair, lethal injection paraphernalia) and put under twenty-four-hour observation by a guard outside his cell. He would remain there until his killing on October 11, unless he received a stay of execution from the courts or governor. Neither prospect seemed likely.

As Ed's spiritual adviser, I could see him from 3:00 to 5:00 p.m. On October 9, I made the fifteen-minute drive from my house to Riverbend Prison, timing it to arrive at 3:00 p.m. I would return on the 10th and 11th.

Although I have been into prisons many times since my initial visit to the Bronx House of Detention in New York City in 1971, it has never felt normal. I am always highly aware that I am entering the caging and killing machinery, especially when entering a maximum-security prison like Riverbend, and even more so when entering deathwatch. It reminded me of my visits to Auschwitz, Majdanek, and Mauthausen. In those places, I imagined the horror of all the exterminated bodies. Here I would actually be seeing one after the state killed him. And it would be someone I knew and cared for.

Prisoners were applying fresh paint to the walls of the administration building as I entered—the same thing that was done two days before Billy Irick's execution in August. It's the "let's pretty everything up for the execution" routine. There's nothing like the prospect of an execution to make a prison shine.

*Prisoners were applying
fresh paint to the walls
of the administration building
as I entered—the same thing
that was done two days before
Billy Irick's execution in August.
It's the "let's pretty everything
up for the execution" routine.
There's nothing like the
prospect of an execution
to make a prison shine.*

The guards on duty when I arrived, female and male African Americans, were cordial. During my weekly visits, we often teased one another. This time we were polite, but tension permeated the building.

Usually, I get through security with just a volunteer badge. This is different. This is deathwatch. Getting in requires a memo from the warden.

I took off my shoes, emptied my pockets, and placed my truck key along with the other items in a plastic container on the conveyor belt, which then carried my items through a metal detector. I walked through another metal detector, emerging on the other side beside a metal pole. I turned around 360 degrees, then lifted each socked foot up to the pole. The light on the pole flashed green—I passed. I still had to be patted down by the male guard, who then summoned an escort to walk me to Building 8, in the rear of the general population visiting room.

The guard took me to the door, and I was buzzed into the trap. After a brief wait, the second door buzzed and I opened it.

This door opened into a waiting area. An enclosed, darkened glass observation booth was to my right. A guard greeted me and patted me down again. I signed into the logbook, giving my name, occupation (minister), and purpose (pastoral). After a few minutes' waiting, I was led through another door into a foyer. Ahead was the visiting booth I would occupy. A glass partition divided the space; Ed would be on one side and I on the other. There was a small bathroom in the foyer behind me.

I waited for Ed to come into the booth.

The holding cells were out of sight but only a few feet away. I could hear Ed being shackled, locked to the black box that attached his handcuffs to a waist chain, and he soon shuffled his way to the entrance door on his side of the visiting booth. Then came the ritual of undoing the black box and the cuffs, and Ed turned fully toward me. We smiled at each other and fell into an easy discussion.

"I've been thinking about my childhood," he said. "I had a good one. Growing up, I fell in love with bikes. Dirt bikes, then motorcycles. Man, when I was a teenager, we had fun baiting the cops on our bikes. We usually got away from them." He smiled at the recollection.

"My mom, I guess she was mentally ill. She did some strange things. My dad was always protecting me. He sent me to be with my Aunt Lorraine every summer. I really loved being with Aunt Lorraine."

His execution was now less than seventy hours away, but Ed maintained his equanimity. He felt he had lived a good life. He'd had his adventures, his loves, his motorcycles—it had been a good ride. Now, he believed his body was beginning to break down. His eyes had been giving him problems. He'd been experiencing a vague pain in his belly. Ed didn't want to end up like our friend Charles Wright, a death row prisoner who died not by lethal injection but in the infirmary due to lack of prompt treatment for his prostate cancer.

"Man," Ed said, "Bill Stevens, they just didn't do anything for him. By the time they did his cancer was too far gone and they left him to die alone in the infirmary."

"Don't forget Gary Cone," I said. "His sentence was set aside by the courts and then he fell in his cell and pierced his back on the metal corner of his bunk. Rather than properly cleaning it out and treating it, the medical staff left it to putrefy. When I visited Gary in Vanderbilt Hospital, he was paralyzed with an infection throughout his spinal cord."

Ed nodded. "Yeah. He eventually made it out of the hospital, but he was still paralyzed, never truly recovered, and he died from it."

Those men, and the twenty-one others I knew of who had died from lack of medical care while on death row over the years, were examples Ed had no desire to emulate. He would take the electric chair.

Ed was pleased that his lawyers had tracked down a woman he had been quite fond of back in the day. After Ed had moved on, he'd had some regret and asked his lawyers to find her if they could. What they'd found, instead, is that she had died. They brought him a picture of her gravestone. "I really appreciated them doing that. I had always wondered about what could have been. Now I know there's nothing more to say or do about it."

I think of Ed Zagorski as an outlaw. To me, that's distinct from being a criminal in that an outlaw like Ed operates within the boundaries of an unwritten code. Ed was part of an organization that delivered massive amounts of marijuana. He focused totally on that task and on maintaining silence about those with whom he was involved. Although he held a steady job, he literally lived outside the law in a world that had its own rules, preeminent among them being that one did not snitch. Ed's word was his bond.

> *Those men, and the twenty-one others I knew of who had died from lack of medical care while on death row over the years, were examples Ed had no desire to emulate. He would take the electric chair.*

In over forty years of working with prisoners, I had known a lot of men like Ed—especially in the 1970s and 1980s. As mass incarceration inundated the prison system, the world of the code became less prevalent. Even so, I knew I could trust my life with such hardcore convicts as Ed Zagorski. Race didn't matter to them, but honor did. Indeed, there had been several occasions in my visits to prison when my life had been protected by men like Ed. Outlaws? Yes. But I counted them as true friends.

Ed had begun doing push-ups on deathwatch. As we talked on the afternoon of October 9, he had done three thousand. A guard had challenged him to do nine thousand before his execution on the evening of the eleventh. The guards posted outside his cell twenty-four hours a day during deathwatch chronicled his every move. They even had a record of his push-up count. Ed was already up to nine thousand push-ups and thought he could be over ten thousand before the following evening. He got along well with the guards, some of whom had done push-ups themselves along with him. Ed chuckled. "They can barely do a hundred. And most of them are ex-military."

"You remember the first time we met?" Ed asked me. I did. It was in 1990. "You remember that pain in my wrist?" I remembered that too. The prison medical care system had simply refused to treat it, so I brought a doctor into the prison. He diagnosed Ed's problem as severe tendinitis—painful, but treatable. The doctor wrote the prescription, and the prison provided the pills. "After months of hurting," Ed reminded me, "I took those pills for thirty days. And the pain really subsided. After thirty more days, I felt I was well. But the doc had told me to take them for ninety days, and I did. After that, no more problems with the wrist." Ed smiled and rotated his hand to show his pain-free flexibility.

Our two hours sped by, and it was time for me to go. "I'll see you at three, tomorrow afternoon," I said. We smiled, put our hands to the glass in a farewell gesture, and I exited deathwatch.

Back home in my study, I emailed Kelley Henry: "I can't believe I'm saying this, but Ed reiterated his desire to be electrocuted—which means we have to advocate for his electrocution." State statute gave Ed a choice of methods of execution, and he was unalterably opposed to lethal injection. Kelley wrote back that, yes, it was bizarre to be arguing for electrocution for her client, and she couldn't believe she would have to file such an appeal. But she was doing it.

There was a legal whirlwind around Ed. The Tennessee Supreme Court had denied his appeal of the chancery court's decision on lethal injection. It was now under appeal to the US Supreme Court. The appeal of Ed's 60-b petition, denied by the US district court, was granted on October 10 by a 2–1 vote of a panel of the Sixth Circuit Court of Appeals. The Sixth Circuit also entered a stay of execution. The state appealed it to the US Supreme Court. And now there was the litigation requesting electrocution.

I met with Ed on Wednesday, October 10, once again in the noncontact booth. Judge Aleta Trauger had granted his request to be electrocuted. Barring a reversal in the appellate court, Ed would be strapped into the electric chair the next day.

His mordant humor was on full display during our visit that day.

"Joe, I'm planning on sitting in that chair," he plopped down in the blue plastic chair with his arms on the armrest, imitating being strapped in the electric chair, "and looking at you and Kelley. I'll say, 'Hey, Kelley, come sit in my lap. It could be quite a ride.'" He shook and jerked as if electricity were running through his body, laughing at his own humor. "Before they hit the juice, I'll ask you to take care of Molly." Molly was my stray, abused brindle puppy who had appeared at the side door of our house some ten years before. Ed was fond of her and kept her picture in his cell.

"Ed, just to remind you—I'm not going to watch them kill you. One of my cardinal rules is to not watch the state kill my friends. I made an exception with Willie Darden in Florida in 1988—that's something I'll never do again."

Ed nodded. "I know. It's cool."

*   *   *

October 11, the day of the execution, arrived bright and beautiful. All the painting inside the prison had been completed. The place was spruced up for company—as it always was for an electrocution. Billy Irick had been executed by lethal injection in August 2018, but before that, it had been almost eight years since an execution.

As I entered the prison parking lot that day, black tape placed on my truck window to indicate I had permission to park in a designated space in the lot, I had a feeling of dissonance. The Sixth Circuit Court of Appeals had issued a stay of execution, but everyone in the prison was tense, expecting the stay to dissolve and the electrocution to proceed. Not me. I felt, for reasons I could not have explained, that the stay would hold. It certainly wasn't because of prior experience; I had been there too often, throughout the South, when stays of execution were dissolved by higher courts and the killing went ahead. Still, I had a weird feeling of being split in two. My outside was taking note of the planning and preparation for an electrocution that my inside felt would not happen. This was not an example of good mental health.

When I finally made my way through the hallways and security checks back to Ed, complete with a plastic water bottle that the warden had kindly provided me, Ed was his regular self. "Joe, I'm *walking* to that electric chair. I am strong, and I'll be that way to the end. If it's my time, it's my time."

As I had expected, he was determined to be strong—to show no fear and welcome death. The prison personnel stationed near him matched their attitudes to Ed's. Despite the stay, he truly believed that in less than four hours he would be dead.

"I told them I didn't want a last meal, Joe. Some of the guys scraped together some ingredients and made pizzas in the microwave before I came over here. That was my last meal."

We talked at length about how he had evolved as a person on death row, how he had made some good friends, and how he would miss them. And he made clear his feeling that it was his time to go.

He described being a boat captain in Louisiana: "I was piloting a 121-foot boat filled with supplies and sometimes men, out to the oil rigs in the Gulf of Mexico. I did that at night and during the winter. Not many people wanted to pilot out there in the winter at night."

One of Ed's lawyers, Paul Bottei, had created a ship captain's license for Ed and given it to him, along with a fictitious letter from President Reagan, thanking Ed for his hard work and commending him for getting his pilot's license. (Ed had once said, "The one thing I really regret in life is voting for Ronald Reagan.") The captain's license and letter were a big hit with Ed.

Ed's experiences piloting boats were real and dramatic. One night, when loading his boat with supplies to transport to an oil rig with his two crewmen, a drilling rig exploded out in the Gulf, sending a fireball up into the night sky. No one wanted to shut the rig down for repairs because it would be too expensive to get going again. Now it was ablaze.

Ed looked at his crew. One was a veteran sailor from Maine. The other was a young kid. Ed said, "Guys, I'm for going out there to the rig. There could be survivors in the water. But let's put it to a vote. We have to decide as a crew."

The Mainer didn't hesitate: "Let's go." They both looked at the kid, who turned his gaze to the inferno, clearly visible from the shore. "You're going out *there?*"

Off they went, accompanied by several other boats.

Near the burning platform, they began picking survivors out of the water. Sparks rained down on them, and long tongues of flame arced over them. Finally, when the heat became too intense and the flames too close, they motored away. Ed's boat and the others saved twenty-four men that night.

Perhaps that memory is why it was Ed's desire that his remains be scattered in the Gulf of Mexico, a place he loved. Earlier in the day, I had discussed this with Gaye Niece, an investigator on his case for many years. She had lived on the Gulf Coast and shared Ed's love of the area. She agreed to take his ashes and spread them there.

The one thing we could do for our friends after the state killed them was make sure they had a dignified burial, whether at sea or on land. We would honor them for who they were, not for the way the state viewed them because of one frozen moment in their past. We had been doing this since John Spenkelink was electrocuted in 1979. No pauper's grave for the people who had become our friends.

As the time approached, Ed proudly informed me that he had done twelve thousand push-ups—an accomplishment that, given the short time allowed him, boggles the mind. It was part of his tough-guy routine, and he also enjoyed the physical challenge.

As we talked, I could see the crease on his head from the shotgun blast by the police in the Ohio shootout. At that showdown, it was shoot or be shot. Ed the outlaw gave as good as he got.

At about 4:15, there was a sudden knock on the door behind me. When I opened it, the guard told me the visit was terminated. Puzzled, I asked, "Why?"

The guard said, "The warden said to end the visit." Then he looked at Ed. "Your lawyer's on the phone. He needs to speak to you."

Ed thrust his hands through the pie hole in the door so the handcuffs could be put on. He looked at me, confused.

"Ed, let's have a prayer," I said. We bowed our heads: "Lord, give Ed strength, mercy, and compassion. Amen." Then his door was opened, they put the black box back on his wrists, and I turned and exited my side of the booth.

As I left deathwatch and was escorted back to the administration building, no one would tell me what was going on. It felt bizarre and strange and unfinished leaving the prison before the conclusion of my final visit with Ed. My only guess was that something had stopped the electrocution train.

Emerging into the sunlight from the administration building, I noticed the press packing up and leaving the media tent. I hopped in my truck, drove over to a reporter, and asked what was going on.

"The governor gave a temporary stay of execution," he said.

The stay of execution was to last through October 21, my birthday. Later, discussing it with colleagues, I learned that the Department of Correction wasn't sure that the electric chair would work properly. The state was deeply concerned with the optics of killing people. The sight of Ed Zagorski's head bursting into flame, as had happened with a man on Florida's death row with whom I worked, was to be avoided at all costs. Hence, the governor gave the prison ten days to be sure the electric chair was ready to go.

Ed had revealed himself, in our conversations during his death-watch, as a man who approached his own killing calmly. He was pleased that his attorney's requests for clemency had been turned down because, in truth, Ed preferred to either remain on death row, where he had been for thirty-four years, or be executed. He had no desire to be moved into the general prison population. And he was, I knew, disappointed with the stay of execution—he had prepared himself for his own demise and saw no point in any delay.

*   *   *

On October 26, a Thursday afternoon, Ed and I were having a leisurely discussion in a room off his pod. He was the same mentally prepared, story-telling guy I had last seen on deathwatch. The Tennessee Supreme Court had set his new execution date: November 1, 2018—All Saints' Day on the Christian calendar.

When our discussion that day wound down, we closed by noting the obvious. I would see him on deathwatch next Tuesday at 3:00 p.m. We knew there would be no stay of execution this time.

CHAPTER FIVE

Déjà Vu

AFTER NAVIGATING the usual security checkpoints, pat downs, and door openings and closings, my escort and I arrived at door 116. I walked through, endured a final pat down, and signed into the log. Then a sliding metal door opened into the foyer. It was October 30, 2018, at 3:00 p.m. I opened the door and walked into the cubicle. Ed was on the other side of the glass. "Déjà vu," he said. I nodded.

Of course, this wouldn't truly be déjà vu, because we both knew this time there would be no stay of execution. On the evening of October 11, the US Supreme Court had reversed the stay of execution of the Sixth Circuit Court of Appeals and dismissed Ed's appellate issues. (New justice Brett Kavanaugh weighed in on the wrong side of this appeal. This would be one of the first of many actions he would take against the poor, the condemned—"the least of these," as Jesus put it). Now Ed's lawyers were asking the Court to review electrocution and ineffective assistance of counsel. Neither of those issues had a real chance of success.

Ed was his usual upbeat self. He was determined that his execution be by electrocution and relieved that he would not suffer the torturous death Billy Irick had endured by lethal injection in August. Not that electrocution was humane; it just seemed like the less horrific method of being killed between the two. (Other death row prisoners had filed suit in federal court seeking death by shooting as an option, but that had not been fully litigated.) As Ed put it, "I may have to drag them to the chair with me if they aren't moving fast enough." Then he smiled.

Other death row prisoners had filed suit in federal court seeking death by shooting as an option, but that had not been fully litigated.

Ed was still doing hundreds of push-ups. He was proud of his ability to do so many. After he told me how many push-ups he was up to, he said, "Did I tell you about my trips out West, and the times I met with the Lakota?" He knew he had, but he just enjoyed talking about it. He had gotten to know the Indians through his trips to the annual motorcycle rally in Sturgis, South Dakota. "Back in those days, Joe, it was just the real bikers who showed up in Sturgis. Not the lawyer and doctor types who buy Harleys now. Back then, Sturgis was for hard-core bikers." Each year, Ed would spend three weeks of his two-month vacation in Sturgis, just hanging out with fellow bikers.

Several of those who attended the rally were Lakota Sioux, sometimes called the Yellowhairs because their ancestors had scalped George Armstrong Custer at the Battle of Little Big Horn. On one occasion, Ed told me, they took him home, and he met their shaman, who was also their brother. This shaman didn't do drugs or alcohol; he was a practitioner of the traditional ways and medicines.

"That was an impressive man," Ed said. "He's the one who introduced me to traditional Lakota life."

Déjà Vu

Through his repeated visits to the Lakota over the years, Ed grew to appreciate and value their ways. Like Billy Irick, he incorporated some of their spiritual outlook into his own.

A little after four we paused the visit so the nurses could take his vital signs, check his blood sugar, and do a basic physical. The state of Tennessee was ensuring that Ed would be in good health to be killed in two days. The dissonance of this health check amid the machinery of killing was stunning. Ed passed with flying colors. The nurse then gave him a handful of pills, and he chose the ones he would take and told them why he chose those and declined the others. I noticed when Ed received his pills from the nurse that his hand had a slight tremor—the only indication of stress I could see. His relationship with the nursing staff and the guards was friendly and often jocular. Many of them had known Ed for years. I knew it was hard on them to be involved in killing someone they had befriended and respected.

One of the ironies of the death penalty is that the guards in the prison are the flip side of the same coin as the prisoners. None of them are people of means. The prisoners are poor. The guards work underpaid jobs with atrocious hours. Many of the guards and a surprising number of prisoners have military experience. Only those who direct the machinery of killing from a distance, many of them wealthy, somehow see capital punishment as a necessity. Most of the people I encountered within the killing machinery itself showed little enthusiasm for it. They were just doing their job.

As we had frequently before, Ed and I discussed the facts of the crime for which he would be executed. The irony of his being condemned for killing two people he hadn't actually killed struck me once again. How often had I seen this? Again and again, the flawed, corrupted process of the criminal legal system manifested itself.

* * *

83

One of the ironies of the death penalty is that the guards in the prison are the flip side of the same coin as the prisoners. None of them are people of means. The prisoners are poor. The guards work underpaid jobs with atrocious hours. Many of the guards and a surprising number of prisoners have military experience. Only those who direct the machinery of killing from a distance, many of them wealthy, somehow see capital punishment as a necessity. Most of the people I encountered within the killing machinery itself showed little enthusiasm for it. They were just doing their job.

* * *

Déjà Vu

The next day, Ed shared more stories of his life as a marijuana smuggler. He told me again about turning down the deal for a life sentence the prosecutors had offered. He hadn't been about to plead guilty to killing someone he hadn't killed.

Even at this late date, he wouldn't reveal which smugglers and dealers he had worked with or for. He shook his head at the thought: "They actually thought by putting me in that hot box I would talk." I was struck again by how thoroughly the cops and prosecutors had misjudged this man. He was no common criminal—if he gave his word, you could count on it. He would not snitch anyone to law enforcement. The prison population mostly consisted of two groups: prisoners who were code-bound and those who would sell their mother for a song. Ed was the polar opposite of Jim Blackwell and his ilk, who were all about transactional relationships.

The authorities could put him in a metal box in the summer heat of Tennessee, they could try the good cop, bad cop routine—but if they had taken the time to learn to understand him, they'd have realized how futile those efforts were. It's not surprising that they didn't take that time, though. This was just another chapter in the death penalty game, where prosecutors and police notch convictions on their belts without regard to truth.

As they had the day before, the nurses came to do a physical. They recorded Ed's blood pressure, listened to his heartbeat with a stethoscope, and took his pulse. They pricked his finger to check his blood sugar level. They administered his pills. They asked a few perfunctory questions and were done. In less than twenty-seven hours, Ed would be strapped into the electric chair, but the state of Tennessee wanted to make sure he was healthy first.

When the nurses left, Ed expressed gratitude, one by one, for all who had worked with him over the years. "Joe, Kristen [one of his lawyers] brought a shrink out here to see me. I was reluctant, but I talked to her. She really helped me get in touch with some feelings and memories I had forgotten about. Believe it or not, I learned a lot about myself. I'm deeply grateful for that." Then he smiled and said, "Tell Kristen she's turned me into a wuss!"

We chuckled together, and I said, "I'll tell her."

It was one of those memories recovered through his sessions with the psychologist that Ed wanted to discuss next. "You remember I told you about Laurie, the woman I cared for back in the day?" I nodded. "I think that could've worked out. I just walked away. She was the one I could really have stayed with." I suppose it would be more accurate to say that he rode away on his Harley. He had chosen a lifestyle—that of the hard-core biker, living free—over a matter of the heart. A choice that now—at the end of his life—he regretted.

"Joe," he said, changing the subject, "it's interesting that it's all 'the Christians' who are executing me. That prosecutor—you told me that he taught Sunday school. The governor, he lets you know what a Christian he is. The attorney general. They all claim to be followers of Jesus." This was amusing and ironic to Ed. It opened the door for a discussion of the simple life of the Jewish peasant from Galilee and his teaching of forgiveness, love, and reconciliation. These marks of discipleship were remarkably absent in the state killing machinery.

I told Ed about my two visits with Elie Wiesel in Boston. "Ed, he was kind enough to meet with me even though I wasn't one of his students. His book *Night* describes his experience at Auschwitz and the Nazis marching him and a column of Jews in the bitter winter cold to flee the Russians who were on the verge of taking the camp. We discussed the Holocaust and the death penalty. A statement Wiesel made still sticks with me: 'The Christians ran the death camps.' Now they run executions. Some things have not changed."

Soon it was time to go. We bid each other goodbye, and I was on my way home, leaving the insanity of what US Supreme Court Justice Harry Blackmun termed "the machinery of death."

CHAPTER SIX

All Saints' Day, November 1

THE CELEBRATION OF All Saints' Day is one of my favorites on the church calendar. The hymn "For All the Saints" is magnificent. The occasion to recall the saints provides an opportunity to remember my own saints, many of them executed: John Spenkelink, Bob Sullivan, James Adams, David Washington, Robert Wayne Williams, Warren McCleskey, Velma Barfield, Tim Baldwin, Willie Watson, Willie Darden, and Philip Workman, for starters. And then some "free world" folks who died natural deaths: Daniel Berrigan, Thomas Merton, Søren Kierkegaard, Dorothy Day, Will Campbell, John Egerton, Albert Camus, Harmon Wray.

There are some who will surely say, "But those people you list as saints, at least the prisoners, did bad things. Besides, they aren't officially recognized by the church as saints." All of which is true. It is reminiscent of King David, who arranged for Uriah's death because he lusted after Uriah's wife and impregnated her. David was literally a murderer, but he repented and was a man after God's heart.

As the pressure grew with each passing day of Ed Zagorski's deathwatch, Daniel Berrigan, Catholic priest and poet, dissident extraordinaire, kept popping into my mind. That might have been because it was now November, the month that Dan came down to Tallahassee, Florida, in 1983 to join in civil disobedience before Governor Bob Graham to protest Bob Sullivan's execution.

In particular, I recalled fragments of the statement Dan had written on behalf of the Catonsville Nine—the name given to him and eight other Catholic activists who burned draft board files in 1968 so that the information identifying young men due to be drafted was turned to ashes. That undoubtedly kept some young men from being summoned into the military and perhaps Vietnam. It also sent Dan and his colleagues to prison.

On the afternoon of All Saints' Day, before I left for the final deathwatch with Ed Zagorski, I sat on my back porch and rewrote Dan's statement on behalf of the Catonsville Nine to use at our vigil that night protesting Ed's execution:

> Our apologies good friends, for the fracture of the good order, the burning of candles instead of people, the angering of the orderlies in the front parlor of the charnel house. We could not, so help us God, do otherwise.
>
> For we are sick at heart, our hearts give us no rest for thinking of the Land of Burning People in Electric Chairs. And for thinking of that other man, of whom the poet Luke speaks. As an infant that man was taken in the arms of an old man, whose tongue grew resonant and vatic at the touch of that beauty.
>
> And the old man spoke: "This child is set for the fall and rise of many in Israel, a sign that is spoken against." Small consolation; a child born to make trouble and to die for it, the first Jew (not the last) to be subject of a "definitive solution," as we saw in the synagogue in Pittsburgh

this past weekend. He sets up the cross and dies on it; in the executive mansion of Tennessee, on the Legislative Plaza downtown, in the middle of the Dept. of Corrections.

We see the sign, we read the direction: you must bear with us, for his sake. Or if you will not, the consequences are our own. For it will be easy, after all, to discredit us. Our record is bad; troublemakers in church and state, assembled here to say no to state killing.

We have records, we have been turbulent, unchari-table, we have failed in love for the brethren, have yielded to fear and despair and pride, often in our lives. We are no more, when the truth is told, than ignorant beset people, jockeying against all chance, at the hour of death, for a place at the right hand of the dying one.

We act against the law at a time of poor people marching through Mexico to our border, at a time more-over when the government is announcing ever more massive paramilitary means to confront disorder in the cities. At a time when a computer center has been built in the Pentagon for millions of dollars to offer instant response to outbreaks anywhere in the land; and moreover, the government takes so seriously a view of civil disorder that federal troops are dispatched to the border and our streets with responsibility to quell disorder. The impli-cations of all this must strike horror in the mind of any thinking person.

The ways of killing are more and more literally brought home to us. Their inmost meaning strikes the American ghettos, in the servitude to the affluent. We must resist and protest this crime.

Finally, we stretch out our hands to our brothers and sisters in our prisons and jails. We who are religious and our fellow religious. All of us who act against the law, turn to the poor of the world, to the immigrant, the victims, to the condemned, for the wrong reasons, for no reason at all, because they were so categorized by the authorities of the public order which is in effect a massive institutionalized disorder.

We say: killing is disorder, life and gentleness and community and unselfishness is the only order we recognize. For the sake of that order, we risk our good name.

The time is past when good people can remain silent, when obedience can segregate people from public risk, when the poor can die without defense. We ask our fellow citizens to consider in their hearts a question which has tortured us, night and day, since the death penalty began. How many must die before our voices are heard, how many must be tortured, dislocated, abused, maddened? How long must the world's resources be raped in the service of legalized murder? When, at what point, will you say no to this barbarity? We have chosen to say, with the gift of our presence tonight, and if necessary, our lives: the violence stops here, the death stops here, the suppression of the truth stops here, this state killing stops here.

We wish to place in question by this act all suppositions about normal times, about longings for an untroubled life in a somnolent congregation, about a neat timetable of ecclesiastical renewal which in respect to the needs of people, amounts to another form of time serving.

Redeem the times! The times are inexpressibly evil. Our religious bodies pay conscious tribute to Caesar and Mars; by the approval of overkill tactics, by brinkmanship, by nuclear liturgies, by racism, by support of genocide, by allowing state killing to proceed. They embrace their society with all their heart, and abandon the cross and the prophets. They pay lip service to Christ and Yahweh and provide military service to the powers of death. And yet, and yet, the times are inexhaustibly good, solaced by the courage and hope of many. The truth rules. God is not forsaken.

In a time of death, some people—the resisters, those who work hardily for social change, those who preach and embrace the unpalatable truth—such people overcome death, their lives are bathed in the light of the resurrection, the truth has set them free. In the jaws of death, of contumely, of good and ill report, they proclaim their love for the brethren. We think of such people, in the world, in our nation, in the congregations; and the stone in our breast is dissolved; we take heart once more.

When I'd finished my rewrite of Dan Berrigan's work, it was time to get dressed—for one final deathwatch with Ed Zagorski on All Saints' Day, November 1, 2018.

* * *

During the short drive to the prison, I steeled myself for the inevitable, my adrenaline on overdrive. Approaching the left turn leading up the incline to the parking lot, I noticed that the heightened security typical just before an execution was in effect. I pulled to a stop and rolled down my window.

During the short drive to the prison, I steeled myself for the inevitable, my adrenaline on overdrive. Approaching the left turn leading up the incline to the parking lot, I noticed that the heightened security typical just before an execution was in effect.

"Can I see some ID?" the prison guard asked.

I handed it to him, along with my volunteer badge. "I'm Ed Zagorski's spiritual adviser."

He went to check my name against the memo the other guards had on a table to the right of my truck. Then he returned and handed me back my ID and badge and placed a piece of black tape in the upper left corner of my windshield. "You're in parking slot 8. Just go up to the next checkpoint and they'll tell you how to proceed."

I thanked him and drove up into the parking lot to the next checkpoint. The media tent was to my left. Once again, I had to show them my ID and volunteer badge, then they pointed the way to my designated parking slot. I thanked them and drove forward, then did a U-turn to reach number 8, on the front row of the parking lot facing the administration building.

Once out of the truck, I did the same inventory that I've done for over forty years: I removed my driver's license from my wallet and placed it in my pocket along with my volunteer badge, left the wallet and cell phone in the truck, patted all my pockets to be sure I'd removed everything, and finally left all keys but my truck key in the vehicle. Then I locked the truck and walked toward the administration building.

After I'd cleared security, my escort took me to deathwatch. I entered through the two doors, signed into the logbook, received a final pat down, and then went through the door to the foyer. I entered the noncontact visitation booth and Ed was already waiting on the other side of the glass. He smiled—he was excited. His enthusiasm surprised me.

"Joe, I have to tell you about the dream I had last night. I can't believe it. You know about my fantasy of the afterlife—women in bikinis no older than twenty-one, a Harley, and no cops." He chuckled.

I smiled and nodded.

"Well, last night I slept soundly, and I had a dream about what I think the afterlife is *really* like. And I saw Laurie, the woman I cared so much for years ago. She was waiting for me after this. She reached out and took my hand, and we walked across a grassy area. She told me everything was going to be all right. It was an incredible feeling. Peaceful.

"Then she told me to hold tight. She squeezed my hand, and I held hers tightly. Then we took off. We were flying! I couldn't believe it! I wasn't afraid, but it felt strange. Then I saw trees ahead. We were headed right for them. I pointed them out to Laurie. I thought we would smash into them, but she didn't seem concerned. And we flew right *through* them! We came out on the other side and landed. We were back on the green grass again."

Ed was bubbling with excitement as he shared the dream.

"Ed," I said, "that seems more like a vision than a dream." Whatever it was, it made a powerful impact on Ed. He discussed his relationship with Laurie again, how much he cared for her and how he believed that she would be waiting for him, extending her hand, after he was killed in the electric chair. It was hard to believe we were less than four hours from his execution. He was as excited as a kid with a new toy.

Ed's dream obviated the discussion I thought we would have

about death and the afterlife. His dream, along with the mishmash
of beliefs he had accumulated over his life from various religious
traditions, told me that Ed was spiritually prepared for whatever the
state of Tennessee brought to him.

Once again, the nurses showed up for his physical. For the
three days he was on deathwatch, they monitored his health daily
in a way they never did while he was on death row. It was a bizarre
health care ritual in the bowels of the killing machinery. God
forbid Ed Zagorski should die before the state could kill him!

After the nurses left, Ed turned to a topic we had often discussed
previously. In Ed's outlaw world, you did not "rat" someone out to
the cops. Jim Blackwell had done that to Ed. And for that, Ed knew
that Jim would be marked for death.

When Ed arrived on death row years before, his former associates
communicated with him in code. They would frame Jim Blackwell—
nicknamed "Diamond" Jim Blackwell—for murder. Unfortunately, it
was a cruel and bloody process. They began to abduct and kill women
they found walking along the roadside, planting evidence with the
bodies that would incriminate Diamond Jim. Their theory was that
the police would find the bodies and follow the trail of evidence to
Blackwell, convict him, and sentence him to death. But the police
never found the women's bodies. So eventually Ed's former associates
killed Jim Blackwell. He had paid for ratting out Ed. But that still left
the matter of the innocent women who were abducted and murdered
in the failed attempt to incriminate Blackwell.

*It was a bizarre health care ritual in
the bowels of the killing machinery.
God forbid Ed Zagorski should die
before the state could kill him!*

"Joe," Ed said, "there could be ten or so bodies. I know about where they are, and I want the cops to find them. Those families need to know what happened to them. They'll want to give them a proper burial. I want you to bring the Tennessee Bureau of Investigation [TBI] or Ray Whitley in here so I can tell them what I know."

I took a deep breath. Ray Whitley had prosecuted Ed. I knew Ray and had discussed the death penalty with him. He would surely attend Ed's execution. Maybe I could somehow get word to him. "Ed," I said, "I'll give it a shot. But if we approach the police with this, you know they're going to want more. They'll want to know who killed those women."

Ed shook his head. "We're not in the crime-solving business. We're in the helping victims business. The guys who did that are my age now. I don't want to think of them in prison growing old like I am. Just do the best you can."

I stepped out of the booth and found a guard. "Listen," I said. "Ed has something to say. Something important, related to his crime. We need to reach Ray Whitley, the prosecutor."

The guard held up a hand to stop me. "This is above my pay grade. I'll send you to the shift commander." He spoke into his walkie-talkie, and soon I was on my way out of deathwatch, back up to the administration building, and waiting outside the training room. When the shift commander came out, I explained what Ed had told me. He asked a few questions and said he would follow through. I went back to deathwatch and reported back to Ed.

As we were talking, I noticed Associate Warden Lewis in the foyer behind me. I stepped outside the booth and let him know that Ed really wanted to see Ray Whitley or the TBI. "Warden Lewis, Ed's desire is simply to share this information, which he will do as soon as the TBI gets here. He isn't trying to slow down the execution. Would you be sure this information gets to the commissioner?"

Warden Lewis nodded. "I'll be sure he gets it."

This chaotic activity consumed most of my visitation time with Ed. We discussed a few final matters, and I heard the door open. Kelley Henry, his lawyer, was entering the foyer for a final visit before his electrocution. My time was up.

I placed my fist on the glass. "Ed, I love you."

He placed his fist on the glass opposite mine. "I love you too, Joe." Then the guards led him out so he could change his clothes.

As I came out of the booth, Kelley and I embraced. I told her, "Keep hugging me. I need to tell you what is going on." I whispered of my efforts to locate Ray Whitley or the TBI and why. I explained how important it was to Ed that we get this accomplished if we could. I stepped back and she nodded that she understood.

We talked a minute more, and I noticed that Ed was back in the booth. Kelley opened the door to enter, then said to me back over her shoulder, "Maybe the Supreme Court will do something."

"What are the issues?" I asked.

Entering the visitation booth, she said, "Ineffective assistance of counsel and electrocution."

There was no doubt Ed had lousy trial counsel and that the electric chair was barbaric. There was also no doubt that the majority of the justices on the Supreme Court didn't care.

I walked across the foyer and signed out of deathwatch. Walking toward me was Warden Tony Mays, with a retinue of people. I stopped him. "Did you get my messages?"

"Yes, and I answered them all," he said. Thinking that he might be referring to several previous emails I sent him about other issues, I said, "No, I mean the messages of the last hour or so about Ed."

Warden Mays said, "I took care of it."

As I stood there, my hyper-vigilance, my total focus, crashed into the realization that there was nothing more I could do for Ed Zagorski. I shook Warden Mays's hand and thanked him. I said, to no one in particular, "Well, I've done all I could." And I walked out of the room.

I met Becca and my old friend Doug Magee at Wendell Smith's Restaurant near the prison for a down-home supper. I shared with them some of the chaos and beauty of the last two hours with Ed. As I sat there numb and emotionally exhausted, I found myself saying, again and again, "I got too close to the flame."

Exhausted or not, I still needed to join the vigil and attend to the cremation of Ed's body. Becca and I gathered with others at 6:30 p.m. on a windy heath outside the prison. The electronic candles that the Reverend Matthew Lewis, who was leading the service, brought from Christ Church Cathedral encouraged us in the face of a twenty-mile-an-hour wind.

Holding our candles, we joined in a large circle. By the time we finished the liturgy, several people had spoken, and I had read my reworking of Daniel Berrigan's poem, the media informed us the electrocution had taken place.

Ed's last words: "Let's rock."

Those who didn't know Ed might mistake his last statement as bravado. Much like the pig's knuckles he had for his last meal. But I knew that as he sat in that electric chair, awaiting the current, he was focused on Laurie and her extended hand of welcome and love. The sooner he reached her, the better.

*   *   *

The events of the week necessitated that I organize Ed's cremation. I was in touch with the people handling that job, and an understanding had been reached with the medical examiner's office that there was no need to do an autopsy, just draw fluids. The body was taken from the prison to the medical examiner's office. The crematory staff picked it up Friday. I arranged to view the body on Saturday morning.

Kelley Henry and I arrived separately at the crematory Saturday morning. We entered a small, dark room. Ed's body was laid out. I removed the white covering from his head, and we gazed at his face. I was struck by the redness of his complexion. He had been pale when alive; this redness accentuated what two cycles of 1,750 volts of electrical current can do to the skin. There was a small dark hole above his left eye and another burned into his shaved head. I placed the palm of my hand on his cheek. With heart breaking, I thought, *Ed, look what they have done to you.* Kelley left. I remained for a few more minutes of prayer and thought.

Becca and I picked the ashes up Saturday afternoon. While she drove our green Prius, I placed Ed's cremains on the floor of the car between my feet. They were in a plastic bag inside a gray cardboard box, along with a cremation certificate. Back home, I placed them on the mantle in the living room above the fireplace. I had promised to deliver them to Gaye Niece, the investigator on Ed's case. I found myself unable to look at the box. I felt totally detached from myself. Stunned. Traumatized. I felt as if I were just going through the motions.

When I finally felt up to the task and tried to reach Gaye, I discovered that she wasn't easy to reach. She was out of the office working other cases. Desperate, I emailed her boss, Henry Martin, and asked if I could bring Ed's ashes to him. "I have to get them out of my house," I said. "I can't bear to look at the box holding the ashes."

Henry kindly told me to bring the ashes to him and he would deliver them to Gaye.

Two deathwatches in eighteen days—it had all been too much for me. One of them had unexpectedly stopped shortly before the execution; the other had ended with Ed's electrocution and the sudden severing of the intense emotional bond Ed and I shared. I was an emotional wreck.

At some basic level, I was functional. I was completing tasks—but as I did, I felt dislocated from my body. I had two trips scheduled for that week, one to Huntsville, Alabama, and one to Savannah, Georgia. I hoped that leaving the state would give me the break I needed.

Alas, not even a change of scenery and time with relatives and close friends could provide the relief I needed. Flying from Huntsville to Savannah, I caught a taxi from the airport to the hotel. But the hotel's front desk had no record of me. That's when I realized what truly bad shape I was in: I didn't even know what hotel I was staying in. A call to Becca provided that information, and soon I was settling into my room on the eighth floor of my hotel, looking out the windows at the Savannah River.

Savannah is a lovely town. It was my first visit, and I'd been looking forward to it all autumn. Now the events of the previous week had left me stunned—numb and with a feeling of being dislocated from my body. Later I would learn the term for this: *disassociation*. Could I function? Yes, although not at full capacity, as the hotel fiasco revealed. I could put one foot in front of the other. I could carry on a conversation. But I couldn't feel anything. Here I was in a lovely new city, and I couldn't experience it. I had intellectually taken in the words on the historical markers in the park as I'd walked to the hotel, but I did not feel the beauty of the park, and I wasn't moved by the poignancy of the history.

I had been too close to the flame with Ed. I was burned emotionally, to the extent that I had damaged myself.

The flight home, despite feeling utterly exhausted, gave me time to reflect. The idea of taking a trip out of state after Ed's execution still seemed a good one. The things I did there, and the time spent with loved ones, distracted my conscious mind. However, I realized it wasn't just my conscious mind I needed to be concerned about. There was also the unconscious and what two deathwatches in eighteen days had done to me.

As I flew, my mind was full of Ed Zagorski. On October 9, 10, and 11, Ed and I were together in a small booth as time wound down on his killing. We were preparing for his extinction. But that execution, to our surprise and completely against all our expectations, was halted some two hours before the electrocution. Then on October 30, 31, and November 1, it was deathwatch redux. Only this time, there was no stopping the electrocution.

Although I had been working with the legally condemned since 1975, I had never been through the ordeal of two deathwatches over the space of eighteen days. I learned early in my time working with those on death row not to witness the execution. That was my protective hedge. Yet any thought of protection or borders had, in this case, been overwhelmed by the compressed experience of twice being with someone who is being coldly, calculatedly, systematically prepared to be murdered.

Sitting in the visiting booth, Ed and I, our time together framed by the reality that he was to be killed in less than seventy-two hours, mentally counting down (whether we wanted to or not) was hammering to the soul. When I emerged into the sunlight of the parking lot on October 11, I tried to find out why the execution had been stopped. On November 1, I came out into that same parking lot after an exhausting and chaotic last visit with Ed. The darkening of the evening matched my mood, although my adrenaline was still running high. I knew, this time, Ed would be electrocuted. But rather than gearing down, my body retained its hyper-alert state through the entire weekend and did not begin to ease up until I passed Ed's ashes on to Henry Martin on Monday. My motor was still on high when I'd traveled to Huntsville and Savannah. But the macabre trifecta, of visiting Ed on Thursday evening, viewing his body Saturday morning, and cradling his ashes in a cardboard box between my feet on the floor of the car as Becca drove us away from the crematory late that afternoon, had imploded internally.

The emotional ripples of repercussion were repressed—but building.

CHAPTER SEVEN

The Aftermath

THE NEXT WEEK, when I went back out to death row to see the guys, I realized how truly messed up I was. Although it was good to see them, I had little to offer. I couldn't feel a thing. My conversations felt perfunctory.

I needed help. I sought out a trauma therapist.

I had been working with the condemned since 1975—more than forty years. I had been through executions previously, but never before had one affected me with this much power and confusion. Perhaps it was the surprise and daunting reality of doing two death-watches with Ed within eighteen days. I needed to find out.

Two weeks after Ed's electrocution, I went to my initial trauma therapy session with Dr. Lee Norton, whom I had known for thirty years. She had assisted me with a difficult death penalty case with a prisoner who appeared almost normal but dwelled in fantasyland. We had interviewed him, then traveled together to visit his family. Having observed her work, I knew I was in excellent hands. Her office was in her home, and I sat across from her as we talked. I relayed my entire experience with Ed to her, then sat back and waited, hoping that she could make sense out of something that made no sense to me.

"When you experience trauma," she said after a short,

thoughtful pause, "the left side of the brain shuts down. That means that the executive functions, along with the language function and your ability to think creatively, are all impaired. Your right hemisphere takes over, and that hemisphere has a different purpose: to enable you to survive. The impulse to flee or fight is primary. But you were in a booth on deathwatch, where you could neither fight nor flee. You were locked in, attempting to navigate survival in a situation in which the options you most needed weren't available to you. You froze."

I had been working with the condemned since 1975— more than forty years. I had been through executions previously, but never before had one affected me with this much power and confusion. Perhaps it was the surprise and daunting reality of doing two deathwatches with Ed within eighteen days. I needed to find out.

No wonder I felt numb. My mind shut me off from the outside world to protect me from the trauma I was experiencing. In a sense, the state's process of killing Ed Zagorski, to a certain degree, killed me.

The Aftermath

I went back to my therapist a week later. This time, she placed laminated cards on the couch across from me, along with legal pads. We did EMDR—a rapid-eye-movement exercise that accesses trauma. She introduced it by saying, "I want to begin with the one image of Ed that comes to mind today. Right now. Don't think, just go with the image. Then go to the next one." And while I concentrated on the images, she moved her index finger slowly back and forth before my face and instructed me to follow it with my eyes.

I began with the image of Ed that was most deeply imprinted in my mind: his pretending to be electrocuted during one of our visits. He was joking about it, writhing as he pretended the powerful shock was blasting through him. I held this image in my mind as my eyes followed her index finger. Then I segued into the next most traumatic image—his body laid out in the morgue, his face red, burn marks above his left eye and on his head.

In a sense, the state's process of killing Ed Zagorski, to a certain degree, killed me.

We continued, back and forth, image after image.

She diagnosed me with post-traumatic stress disorder (PTSD). As she succinctly put it, "If this were a medical wound, you would be in the ICU. You need to think of this as you would a sucking chest wound." As I digested those sobering images, she added, "You will get better. It will take time—but we will get you through this."

* * *

Meanwhile, I, along with others, were trying to obtain clemency for a prisoner named E. J. Harbison, and those efforts were reaching a climax. Almost eight years before, I had recruited Keith Simmons, the managing partner at Bass, Berry, and Sims, to prepare a clemency presentation on behalf of E. J., who was on death row and faced imminent execution. With the help of Brant Phillips and a team of colleagues, Simmons had done a superb clemency petition and met with Governor Bredesen. The governor commuted E. J.'s sentence from death to life without parole. This spared E. J. and also allowed incoming governor Bill Haslam to avoid a decision of life or death in February, when E. J.'s execution had been scheduled.

Now we were appealing for clemency again, seeking a life sentence so he could make parole. I agreed to set up a visit between E. J. and Keith Simmons so that E. J. could sign the letter authorizing Keith to represent him in clemency. Naturally, there were complications. When I arrived at the RMSI checkpoint in the administration building, the necessary memo should have been awaiting us there, but it wasn't. I requested that the guards call their superiors to obtain clearance for the visit. In the midst of the flurry of phone calls, Keith Simmons arrived, and we sat down to wait. I was examining my hand, trying to keep my focus on it because it was all I could do to hold myself together. As I sat and waited, I realized that I was too traumatized from Ed's killing to be back at the prison. I thought it would be all right since I was going to the low-security side of the prison. It wasn't all right. Just being there was triggering my trauma.

"Mr. Ingle," said a voice nearby. I looked up and there was Mr. Lewis, the associate warden for security, a large, burly African American. Our last encounter had been during Ed Zagorski's death-watch. I jumped up, shook his hand, and explained the situation. I introduced Mr. Lewis to Keith.

Associate Warden Lewis said, "I just talked to E. J., and he confirmed that he wants to see you today. Let's see what we can do."

The Aftermath

The associate warden cleared us through security, and I walked with Keith out of the administration building down the sidewalk into Building 8, where E. J. awaited us. I had come down this passageway on my visits to Ed Zagorski on deathwatch, which was just a couple hundred feet beyond the room where E. J. waited.

We opened the door and E. J. stood up. I embraced him. I was so occupied with events on death row I had not seen him in seven years. We sat and talked for over an hour, discussing his case and explaining the steps that would happen next. The time passed quickly. As we prepared to leave, E. J. said, "I understand there are no guarantees. But I want to thank you for what you're doing. I really appreciate it. It means a lot to me." We shook hands and left.

When I recounted this visit to my therapist on my next visit, she looked me in the eye and asked, "How do you feel?"

"I still feel numb. I'm just going through the motions."

"How did you feel at the prison?"

I paused and thought. "Warden Lewis helped us out in a difficult situation. He made it possible for us to do what we came to do. And yet it felt so strange—this man helped kill my friend, and now I was asking him to help me with E. J. This whole process leaves me feeling contaminated. Dirty. I know it isn't just me. Everyone who comes into contact with the official killing machinery is affected, including those who do the killing."

She considered this, then said, "The prison is a trigger. I don't want you going back out there for a while."

Then we began to delve into my layers of sadness.

CHAPTER EIGHT

Insights

DAVID MILLER WAS on death row for almost thirty-seven years, longer than anyone else. He was a wounded, broken man who suffered horrific abuse as a child. His cousin sexually assaulted him at age four or five, and later one of his grandfather's friends did the same. His mother raped him and would whip him with a belt, an extension cord, a wire coat hanger, or an umbrella. But perhaps the worst was his stepfather, who once "knocked David out of a chair, hit him with a board, threw him into a refrigerator with such force it dented the refrigerator and bloodied David's head, dragged him through the house by his hair, and twice ran David's head through the wall."[1] It was no wonder that David had a recurring nightmare about his stepfather: "I'm at my execution, strapped to the gurney so I can't move at all, and my stepfather is present. I see him sitting in the viewing gallery. I don't see any expression on his face, but I hear him say this to me: 'I hope you have nightmares about this you sorry bastard!'"

Dr. David Lisak, the clinical psychologist who evaluated David Miller, said that David's attempts to be a responsible adult "were ultimately undone by his meager reservoir of coping resources, by the tragic death of his grandfather, and the deep wellspring of rage that

---

1 Quotations in the first two paragraphs provided by Dr. David Lisak, clinical psychologist.

he harbored. This rage that was periodically directed at women, and that ultimately was directed at Lee Standifer, stemmed directly from the incestuous abuse he suffered at the hands of his mother and from the brutal physical abuse he suffered at the hands of his stepfather."

This rage took over on a date David had with Lee Standifer on May 20, 1981. David was drinking and taking LSD. He struck Ms. Standifer multiple times with a fireplace poker, killing her. At the time he was living with a fifty-year-old Baptist preacher who established a coercive relationship with David. The preacher made David swap sex for room and board.

So it was that the subsequent death penalty conviction brought another broken soul to death row. Billy Irick, Ed Zagorski, and David Miller all lined up for killing by a governor and state that had no room for mercy, only vengeance.

Helen Standifer, Lee Standifer's eighty-four-year-old mother, provided the best evaluation of the killing process when interviewed by the *Nashville Scene*: "I don't see that it accomplishes anything at all. It's immaterial. It doesn't bring my daughter back. It doesn't accomplish anything. Frankly, I don't see any reason to be there."[2]

I didn't know David well. We talked over the years but not in depth. His execution was scheduled for 7:00 p.m. on December 6, 2018. His final words while seated in the electric chair were concise: "Beats being on death row." I was with my trauma therapist; we had planned to meet that day from 4:30 until 7:30, when the execution was announced.

The Dream

I was deep into my PTSD after David's execution. I had a dream. In the dream, I was in New York City. (In the 1970s and 1980s, I was in New York at least twice a year raising money for the Southern

---

2 Steven Hale, "The Execution of David Earl Miller," *Nashville Scene*, December 7, 2018.

Coalition on Jails and Prisons for our fight against the death penalty and mass incarceration.) I was near Columbus Circle, at the offices of the NAACP Legal Defense Fund (LDF). I had friends who worked there, and LDF had been the litigation leader in the fight against the death penalty.

In the dream, I was taking a shower in the LDF offices. When I was through, an LDF friend gave me towels so I could dry off. I felt clean, restored, no longer dirty or contaminated.

When I awoke, I discussed the dream with Becca. It was significant, I thought, that in my dream I was in New York, a state that did not have the death penalty. Significant, also, that I was among friends who were fighting the death penalty with me but had the protection of the LDF. And they had reached out to me—handed me towels so I could wipe off the water that purified me. I felt renewed and restored. The dream pointed the way to hope.

And by now I was grateful for any indication of hope. I was still feeling stunned, numb—feeling what I imagined a zombie might feel like.

On the night of December 17, 2018, Becca raised the possibility of my taking antidepressants. At other times in my life, I might have strongly resisted, but this time I said, "I'm willing." I was, after all, actually feeling depressed. It might seem odd to view feelings of depression as a positive sign, but actually, I did. I thought depression was an improvement from feeling emotionally numb. We agreed that I would see my doctor as soon as possible.

Two days later, I saw my doctor and explained my experience with Ed Zagorski's execution. He said, "But you've been through this before, right?"

"Yes," I said, "but not two deathwatches so close together. It was too much."

His diagnosis was "situational depression." He prescribed a course of antidepressants but cautioned that it might take a month to take full effect. And that concerned me, because I knew I would struggle just to make it through the next twenty-four hours.

"Do you mean you're harboring thoughts of suicide?" he asked.

"No," I said, and I meant it. But I was totally miserable, and I wondered how much of this interior blackness I could take before suicide began to sound like a good idea.

I felt as if I needed all of the emotional support I could get, and one way I set out to get it was by emailing all of the approximately thirty volunteer visitors in the Visitors on Death Row (VODR) program. VODR had been operating since 1975 at the old Tennessee State Prison and had transferred to Riverbend. In my email, I informed them of my condition and asked that they each share that with the prisoner they visited. I wanted everyone who was involved in the death row community, inside and out, to be aware of what was going on with me.

Letters from death row and from VODR volunteers containing expressions of love and support began arriving at my house. I should have felt uplifted and supported, and would have if I could only have felt the emotion behind the words. But I was too far gone inside, too down, too numb and dark inside. I saved the letters for a better day.

Despite my emotional fragility, the work had to go on. E. J. Harbison's clemency petition had been prepared, and it was time for a meeting with the governor's legal counsel, Dwight Tarwater. On December 19 at 2:30, Keith Simmons, Brant Phillips, and I met with Mr. Tarwater in a conference room at the state capitol—the same room in which I had read the transcripts of Philip Workman's two clemency hearings while researching the story of his twenty-five-year journey from Memphis frame-up to execution for *The Inferno: A Southern Morality Tale*.

Since my initial meeting with Dwight Tarwater back in August, I had learned that he and I had a distant connection. His late wife was the daughter of Richmond Flowers, the attorney general of Alabama in the 1960s. Flowers had opposed segregation despite Governor George Wallace's adamant insistence on it. My late father-in-law, Emile Joffrion, was an Episcopal priest in Huntsville, Alabama, during that time. He integrated the Church of the Nativity over the objections of his senior warden and about a third of his parish, who subsequently left. He had been an admirer of Richmond Flowers.

I shared that story to begin our meeting about E. J. Harbison, and Mr. Tarwater responded by sharing stories about Richmond Flowers. The meeting was off to a convivial start.

Brant served as our main spokesman in the meeting. Keith explained the granting of the previous clemency. I described the personal dynamics of E. J.'s life. Our presentation went well, and we answered all of the questions Mr. Tarwater and his colleagues raised. We could only hope Governor Haslam saw a way to commute E. J.'s sentence from life without parole to a life sentence, which would make him eligible for parole. I had been concerned that my depression would inhibit my ability to make E. J.'s case, but Brant and Keith assured me I had done well.

While I may have passed muster at the meeting with Dwight Tarwater, two details helped me realize how far I had fallen. The first was my empty bird feeders. I love watching birds. Yet for over a month, I had not had the energy to fill the feeders. They were swinging empty in the wind in the backyard. The second was the next morning when I came into the kitchen to make coffee. I stood at the counter looking at the plastic filter on the coffee maker that held the grounds. I realized suddenly that if there were old coffee grounds in that filter and I had to summon the energy to empty them, I would be utterly defeated. With trepidation, I gently slid the filter out of the coffee maker. It was empty. No coffee grounds. Thank you, Jesus!

* * *

December 28 found me reclining in a lounge chair at the outpatient infusion center at Ascension St. Thomas Hospital Midtown in Nashville for my intravenous injection of monoclonal antibodies. This was a relatively new treatment for multiple sclerosis (MS), with which I had been diagnosed in 1989. I still remembered the words of the neurologist who delivered the diagnosis: "We don't know how to cure this. However, it is best if you avoid stress and becoming too tired. It could worsen your condition." Clearly, my work did not comport with the doctor's advice.

My previous IV treatment had been six months before. It was a five-hour process that my doctor and I hoped would reduce the onset of left-side numbness and tingling, which I experienced from the MS. With nothing to do but wait, I leaned back in the comfortable chair and eyed the clear liquids flowing down the IV tube into my vein. For someone with MS, I realized I was fortunate. The left-side numbness and tingling were fairly mild symptoms and susceptible to treatment. MS is a progressive disease, but over three decades of living with it, I've found that my symptoms respond to that treatment. On those occasions when the symptoms just will not go away, I've taken massive amounts of IV steroids. Although this left me bedridden in a "steroid psychosis," it did clear the numbing and tingling. Hopefully, the monoclonal antibodies would eliminate the need for the IV steroids.

Executions at a Teaspoon Dosage

The Tennessee Supreme Court (TSC), the body that sets execution dates in Tennessee, had authorized three executions over three months: Billy Irick on August 8, Ed Zagorski on November 1, and David Miller on December 6. For a state that had historically executed fewer prisoners than any other Southern state, this rate of killing was unprecedented in modern times. It established Tennessee as the leader in the country in executions for this three-month span.

The Tennessee Supreme Court (TSC), the body that sets execution dates in Tennessee, had authorized three executions over three months: Billy Irick on August 8, Ed Zagorski on November 1, and David Miller on December 6. For a state that had historically executed fewer prisoners than any other Southern state, this rate of killing was unprecedented in modern times. It established Tennessee as the leader in the country in executions for this three-month span.

Perhaps this newfound notoriety of Tennessee as a leader in state killings proved to be too much for the TSC. Although about ten men remained on Tennessee's death row who had exhausted their appeals, the TSC parceled out the next group of execution dates.

The next one was scheduled for May 16, 2019—Don Johnson. Then Steve West for August 15, 2019, and Charles Wright for October 10, 2019. The final one for the year was Lee Hall, on December 5. In 2020, two more were scheduled. One was Nick Sutton, whose fear of being "dated up" was realized when his execution date was set for February 20, 2020. The other was Abu-Ali Abdur'Rahman, set for April 9, 2020. The TSC was now offering up execution dates by the teaspoon rather than by the bucketful. Perhaps the rapid execution rate in the autumn of 2018 had brought unwelcome attention.

Frankly, when the dates in 2019 and 2020 were announced, I was emotionally unable to connect them with living, breathing souls—nor did I try. It was all I could do to get through the day. It was hard to see forward into 2019, much less celebrate it, but 2018 had come to an end.

However, I was resolute on one matter for 2019. I would not let it end with the emotional carnage that concluded 2018.

A Reservoir of Sadness

New Year's resolutions can be fine things. For mine to come true, I needed help. Sessions with my trauma therapist and medication were steps in that direction. Yet, as the numbness of the experience with Ed began to wear off, sadness permeated my soul. I can't find the words to describe the complete saturation of sadness I experienced. I felt physical heaviness in my chest, I leaked tears intermittently from my right eye all day long, and I had little energy and no inclination to tackle any task. I continued to visit with friends, watched a lot of detective series on television (the complete series of *Endeavour*, *Inspector Lewis*, *The Closer*, and *Bosch*), and attended Vanderbilt basketball games. I also read mystery books. And I talked to Becca. All of this was intentional distraction, forcing me to focus on something other than myself. If I spent time thinking about how bad I felt, how long it had been since I felt good, how long it would be before I might feel good again, it would be like walking to the edge of a cliff and looking below. I would plummet into the abyss.

In church one morning, Ann Walker King—a friend and retired investigator for the Office of the Federal Public Defender, who had investigated Ed Zagorski's case—asked if I would like to meet with her after the worship service. We rendezvoused downstairs in a large room that served as a dining area and kitchen, not far removed from the rooms in which Sunday school for the younger children was conducted. Ann and I sat at one of the round tables in the ubiquitous gray metal folding chairs.

"How are you doing?" Ann asked.

I answered honestly, describing my feelings in reaction to the two deathwatches and Ed's electrocution. The conversation turned out to be a turning point—an eye-opener. As we talked, I began to get a perspective on the events surrounding Ed's death for the first time.

The people involved in death penalty cases try for a team approach. There are lawyers, investigators, religious people, friends and family—all working to provide support for the condemned, who have often experienced abuse and receive little, if any, help from the machinery of state killing. At the Office of the Federal Public Defender, Ann had been a part of such a team for many years. Even after Ann retired, Gaye Niece carried on as an investigator working Ed's case. The supports were in place—there was a team to help Ed through the deathwatch nightmare. But most of that had been like background music. I was focused on his personal and spiritual needs, trying to navigate a path through the deathwatches. By the second deathwatch, the rest of the team was gone, either because of job changes or because their role had been completed. Everyone but me. The team approach had collapsed. I was alone. I was isolated. And I was crushed by the experience. When Ed was killed, a chunk of me went with him.

By the second deathwatch,
the rest of the team was gone,
either because of job changes
or because their role had been
completed. Everyone but me.
The team approach had collapsed.
I was alone. I was isolated.
And I was crushed by the experience.
When Ed was killed, a chunk
of me went with him.

The conversation with Ann enabled me to see clearly what had happened for the first time. During the events, I was too enmeshed with Ed to have perspective. After the electrocution and cremation, I was too stunned to see things rationally.

That conversation was so refreshing. Ann and I shared stories about Ed—somebody we had both loved—about his goodness, the ways he had helped others, his love for his Aunt Lorraine, his adventures on motorcycles, his enjoyment of his job on the Gulf of Mexico. We laughed. And I cried.

I emerged from that conversation with a viewpoint beyond my own misery. I was able to take a step back and glimpse why it had been such a blow to me. My sadness had reasons.

CHAPTER NINE

How It All Began: John Spenkelink

SITUATED ON HIGHWAY 301 in north-central Florida, Starke is an aptly named town. Pine trees line the pastures where Brahman-bred cattle graze, their white outlines accentuated by the cattle egrets perched on their backs pecking parasites. The land is unremittingly flat, and the highway, once an artery for traffic in this part of the state, has been depleted of traffic by interstates.

The major industry in Starke is incarceration. The Florida State Prison is the county's largest employer. Located just outside town, the prison houses death row and maximum-security prisoners. Three shifts of prison personnel a day maintain the imprisoning and killing machinery in Bradford County.

During the Christmas season, there's a sentinel over the town of Starke: a red neon cross, affixed on the top of the water tower, shines through the winter night, the highest mark on the horizon. But given the setting, it serves more as a reminder of the blood spilled by the state of Florida, supposedly in the name of public safety, than the birth and teachings of Jesus.

On my visits, I would drive into Starke from Jacksonville. The flight from Nashville, through the aerial merry-go-round of the Atlanta airport, would usually land in Jacksonville in the early

117

afternoon. Then I would rent a car and drive the hour and a half to Starke.

Highway 301, the main drag of Starke, is a tertiary tourist road now, lined with motels, fast food, and the flotsam of the old tourist trail. The choices for lodging, all of which I sampled over time, occupied a rather narrow spectrum: at one end, the Dixie Motel, which gave the appearance of having barely survived the Civil War, and at the other, the Best Western and Holiday Inn, which provided nicer lodging. After several trips, I settled on the Best Western. The manager, Wanda, was a nice thirtyish woman working hard to support her child. I figured that, considering the lack of tourist traffic on 301, my few shekels could help her out a bit.

My trips to Starke began in 1977. I was the director of the Southern Coalition on Jails and Prisons. We had offices in eight Southern states; our charter was to oppose the death penalty and mass incarceration. My goal on my first trip was to visit John Spenkelink, a resident of death row at the Florida State Prison. I had been corresponding with John for several months, and now I wanted to meet the man with the small, neatly scribed handwriting whose signature was the smiley face he also sealed his envelopes with. Given the evolving calculus of capital litigation, I feared that John might become the first person executed against his will in the United States since the US Supreme Court reinstated capital punishment in 1976. In January of 1977, I had gone to Salt Lake City, Utah, to join a religious witness against the execution of Gary Gilmore, who had dropped his appeals and sought the firing squad. That experience renewed my determination to try to prevent the madness of state killing that might blossom in the South.

The Florida State Prison (FSP) appeared to occupy the middle of a large cow pasture. Cattle grazed on either side of the road from Starke that, on its way to the prison, wanders near a small airstrip that services the prison administration building. The pastures are framed by Florida's ubiquitous pines. The prison itself squats behind chain-link fences like a malevolent beast caged by barbed and razor wire and guarded by emaciated German shepherds trotting down a run behind the fence. The administration building sits at the end of the parking lot, an air-conditioned haven beyond the reach of the prisoners and guards inside FSP.

> *I feared that John might become the first person executed against his will in the United States since the US Supreme Court reinstated capital punishment in 1976.*

An aerial view of the prison might appear something like a prehistoric creature splayed out on the plain. The ribs of the beast extending from the backbone are the housing wings where prisoners are locked up: R wing, S wing, P wing, and so on. The building itself is three stories high and has a flat roof, which guarantees some flooding with every serious rain. The tail of the beast extends straight out behind the backbone: Q wing, the killing wing, where the holding cells and electric chair await any prisoner whose death warrant has been signed by the governor.

My visits with John Spenkelink occurred in the colonel's room, a large area with small rooms for professional visits. The colonel had his office there, hence the name, and it served as the prison's interior command post. It was air conditioned, and we could close the door and have a private visit in a small interview room, although we were visible at all times through glass windows.

John Spenkelink was striking—angular, prison thin, but in

good shape with a lean and muscled body, his orange death row T-shirt and blue pants fitting loosely. But it was his head that captured attention. His hair was prematurely gray and combed straight back. A white shock of hair ran down the middle of his head, from his forehead over the crown. He looked as if he'd walked in off a London street rather than the R wing at FSP. Despite the white hair, John was barely thirty years old.

On our first visit, John and I shook hands and fell into an easy conversation. His accent was clearly not Southern. John had been born in Iowa, but his family moved to California when he was a child. But the Southern California life he had left behind was no Beach Boys idyll of sun and surf. As a twelve-year-old, John had discovered his father dead in the family garage, asphyxiated by the exhaust he had rigged to enter the family car from its running motor. After his father's suicide, John was in and out of trouble—never hurting anyone but not coping well with life. At age eighteen, strung out on speed, he robbed six stores in one night. He was caught, given an indeterminate sentence, and sent to the adult penal system.

Entering the adult prison system in California, no place for an eighteen-year-old, was a turning point for John. Racial gangs ruled the prisons; violence was endemic. The guards, rather than running the institution, were more than happy to let the violence explode and play the gangs off each other. John wanted out. He escaped a medium-custody facility and fled to Canada with his girlfriend.

He could have remained in Canada during the Vietnam War era and had a productive life, but he missed the United States. He came back. Driving through a Nebraska snowstorm, John stopped to pick up a hitchhiker. That act of compassion would cost John his dignity, his self-respect, and eventually his life. The hitchhiker, Joseph Szymankiewicz, was older, a hardened convict and a violent man. Armed, he commandeered the car and John along with it. John was sodomized, terrorized, and forced to play Russian roulette as the two careened about the country.

John looked for an opportunity to escape, which finally came in Tallahassee, Florida. When Szymankiewicz fell asleep in their hotel room, John quietly packed a few things and prepared to leave. But Szymankiewicz awoke and challenged him. John grabbed the gun. In the fight that followed, Szymankiewicz was shot and killed.

John Spenkelink's case should not have been a death penalty case. If the case had been prosecuted in the Miami area, it would have been a second-degree murder charge at worst. But John was in the northern part of the state. A death penalty law had just been enacted by the Florida legislature in Tallahassee in an effort to overcome the United States Supreme Court's 1972 decision in *Furman v. Georgia*, which struck down the death penalty nationwide. John wasn't from the area, he had a funny-sounding last name, and he looked weird with his prematurely gray hair with the white shock down the middle. Naively, John thought that if he just told the truth during his trial, the jury would understand that he'd killed in self-defense. But his court-appointed lawyers didn't prepare him to testify during his trial, and he stumbled through his testimony, was caught by the prosecutor in contradictions, and was convicted and sentenced to death.

Most of us who knew John felt that it had been a case of self-defense. But my visits to death row across the South had taught me that John's case was all too typical. Again and again, I met people on death row who were there not because of a particularly brutal murder but because of poor legal representation at trial. Ninety percent of those on death row could not afford a lawyer, and this ensured their doom. Court-appointed lawyers were notorious for their lack of effort in capital cases.

Then there was the prosecutorial discretion as to who received

121

the full power of the state. Prosecutors frequently decided which cases to pursue, and with what degree of resolve and effort, on the basis of what would best enhance their reelection chances rather than out of concern for justice. And the political calculus to make that decision, and to decide whether to pursue the death penalty, almost always included these two questions: What color was the victim? And what color was the accused? Black life was still not valued as highly as white life in American society, nor is it now. Indeed, from 1608 to 1976, there were approximately 18,500 executions in the United States, and of those, thirty-one were instances of whites executed for killing a Black person. Of those thirty-one, ten were executed for destroying their own property—that is, killing their own slaves—under the laws of the day. Now factor in the shameful record of extra-judicial executions—lynching—in America: over 6,500 documented. Overwhelmingly, those were Blacks lynched for supposed attacks on whites. The death penalty and its sister institution of lynching were inherently *political* processes in the South, rather than judicial, with little regard for justice or truth. The fear of Black people permeated white America.

Into that web of misery John Spenkelink fell because he killed a white man. Had his "victim" been Black, his trial might have ended with a very different result. And once John came to death row, he became the poster boy Florida could use to show that the system was not prejudiced, because a white man was the leading candidate for execution.

John introduced me to other death row prisoners, and soon, as director of the Southern Coalition on Jails and Prisons, I was also visiting the other Southern death rows. The South, the Bible Belt, was also the Death Belt. The South housed more people on death row than any other region in the country, even though its murder rate was not the nation's highest.

Prosecutors frequently decided which cases to pursue, and with what degree of resolve and effort, on the basis of what would best enhance their reelection chances rather than out of concern for justice. And the political calculus to make that decision, and to decide whether to pursue the death penalty, almost always included these two questions: What color was the victim? And what color was the accused?

The South also led the nation in the politics of death. Politicians were building careers posturing as "tough on crime" and supporters of the death penalty, even though it had not proven to have deterrent value. In short, politicians were killing their citizens without reducing crime in any meaningful way. The hard truths about the death penalty were carefully hidden—no mention that it was reserved almost exclusively for the poor, that it discriminated on the basis of race, or that, since murder was the least repeated crime in the country, the likelihood of the death penalty deterring killers was nil. The old saying was apropos: Those without capital get capital punishment. Or as my friend Steve Bright, a veteran death penalty lawyer, put it, "It's not those who commit the worst murder who receive the death penalty. It's those who have the worst lawyer." And it was the machinery of state killing and incarceration, created in response to the success of the civil rights movement,[1] that propelled New South governors like Jimmy Carter (Georgia), Bill Clinton (Arkansas), Bob Graham (Florida), and Jim Hunt (North Carolina) on their political course.

All of this was abundantly clear to me simply from the preponderance of Black and brown faces among the death row prisoners I visited. John Spenkelink put it best: "Joe, I'm at the front of the bus here. But once they get me, they'll be moving the Blacks up front. That's what this is really about. I'm just the poster boy they can use to show they don't discriminate. Walk back through death row, and it becomes clear who the death penalty really targets."

*　*　*

As a philosophy major in college, I sometimes felt the need to step back and ponder the bizarre nature of the institution of state killing. As a phenomenology student, I liked to separate the layers of the onion, as Edmund Husserl described the process of considering the phenomena of life.

For instance, consider a typical trip to visit John and other prisoners at FSP. The men would be brought down in groups and placed in a cage outside the colonel's room. I divided the visits up so I could see three or four men before lunch and three or four after lunch. The entire cohort for the morning would remain in the cage, with no chair or other means of making themselves comfortable, very much like animals in a zoo. As I called them, one by one, each would come in escorted by a guard. The guard would remove the shackles. The prisoner and I would shake hands and visit in the small

1 See Joseph B. Ingle, *Slouching Toward Tyranny: Mass Incarceration, Death Sentences and Racism* (New York: Algora Publishing, 2015).

room. After lunch, the same scenario unfolded. By the end of the day, I was exhausted and I'm sure the men were too.

These men were confined almost twenty-four hours a day in a six-by-eight-foot cell. They could exercise on the yard once a week. They could have a weekly visit if fortunate enough to get a visitor. Otherwise, they were in their cell following a tightly proscribed routine that repeated itself week after week, month after month, and year after year. The ennui of death row, despite the noise and the compactness of human existence, could be overwhelming.

Jerry Wayne Jacobs, a death row prisoner in Alabama, once performed a bit of phenomenology for me. He asked if I had ever been in a slaughterhouse. Although I'd been to the family farm many times, the only animal I had seen killed was the chicken my Uncle Ben beheaded for Sunday dinner. I shook my head, and Jerry continued. "Well, you keep the cattle all herded up in one place. Then, one by one, you run them down a chute. When they get to the end, you kill them quickly with a blow to the head. But it's one by one, so none of the cattle can look ahead and see what is in store for them. That's what it's like on death row. They keep us penned up, then one by one they take us down the chute to kill us. Just like a slaughterhouse."

John and Jerry Wayne were right. The institution of state killing was formally elaborated in the marble halls of the US Supreme Court, where it was upheld in 1976 in *Proffitt v. Florida*, *Gregg v. Georgia*, and *Jurek v. Texas*. These decisions were a macabre marker of the two-hundredth anniversary of the American Revolution, delivered on the weekend of July 4, 1976. However, those decisions were implemented through trial, conviction, and sentence not in the elegant atmosphere of the US Supreme Court but in mostly Southern courthouses that operated on the legacy of racism and randomness recognized in the 1972 decision, *Furman v. Georgia*, that struck down the death penalty. This process culminated in the death house

Jerry Wayne described, where condemned prisoners were separated like cattle in a slaughterhouse and led one by one into a room to be exterminated.

On one of my visits with John at FSP, he mentioned that the chaplain had come to see him. Chaplain Savage was on the payroll of the state, as are almost all institutional chaplains, and he'd had no real contact with John over the four years he had been on death row. Still, he came to John's cell door one day and asked if John wanted to pray. John said, "Chaplain, I understand you are for the death penalty. Is that true?"

The chaplain nodded. "Yes, I am."

"That means you're in favor of me being executed. How can I pray with a man who wants to see me killed?"

John told me that Chaplain Savage looked down at his shoes, shuffled his feet, and then moved off down the walk.

Once again, John had demonstrated a knack for getting to the heart of the matter. He had illustrated the duality inherent in the work of institutional chaplains. On the one hand, they are employed by the state and beholden to the warden. How does a prisoner trust an employee of the state with confidences, especially when those confidences may be relayed to the warden? Chaplain Savage wasn't the only chaplain in favor of the death penalty—many of them were, which compromised them in the eyes of death row prisoners. Over 90 percent of chaplains in the United States were Christian, yet they were employed by the state, which was killing their would-be parishioners. They were hopelessly compromised. As John put it, how could someone pray with him who sought his killing?

In his work *Christ and Culture*, H. Richard Niebuhr, a theologian at Yale University, delineated different archetypes of Christianity: Christ against Culture, Christ with Culture, and Christ above Culture. *Christ against culture* represented the prophetic tradition and Jesus of Nazareth, *Christ with culture* signified the meld of religion and state, and *Christ above culture* was an interaction of the previous two types that could become a transformative force.

Niebuhr pointed out the dangers of the Christian faith lining up with the culture, as many prison chaplains certainly were doing with the death penalty. I thought that, as Christians, the appropriate category we should pursue had to be *Christ against culture*. Jesus of Nazareth would in no way condone or cooperate in the modern machinery of state killing, nor should his disciples. Niebuhr held out hope that the paradigm of *Christ transforming culture* would win out, but from the bowels of the Florida State Prison, I think the best we could do was make a faithful witness, as John had done, and say no to state killing. It was *Christ versus culture*.

John and I shared many conversations about the Christian faith. I had given him a medallion of the Committee of Southern Churchmen, an ad hoc group of folks scattered about the South who shared with Will Campbell—the director of the committee, an Anabaptist—a sort of bootleg Christianity that led to confrontations with the state over integration, civil rights, prison ministry, and opposition to the death penalty. John appreciated the gift and felt it spoke for his own view of the Christian faith.

Thanksgiving of 1978 was delightful. My girlfriend, Becca Joffrion, and I drove the two hours from Nashville to Huntsville, Alabama, to be with her family for the holiday. Becca and I had been dating since 1976, and I had come to love our time with her family. Becca's father, Emile Joffrion, was an Episcopal priest at the Church of the Nativity; her mother, Martha, was a high school guidance counselor. Their children—Becca, Tina, Paul, Peter, and David—made for the large family I had always longed for but never had due to Dad's early death and Mom's decision not to remarry.

On Thanksgiving Day, the table was laden with turkey, dressing, cranberry sauce, and all of the treats of a Southern Thanksgiving feast. We laughed, caught up with each other's doings, talked sports, and savored the joy of a close-knit family. We had brought Scarlet, my black Labrador retriever, and after dinner we played fetch with Scarlet and tossed a football around in the backyard. It was an easy, relaxed time in Huntsville.

The contrast with Thanksgiving at FSP couldn't have been more harsh. There, the day before Thanksgiving had been filled with anticipation of family visits. Since Starke was so remote, the holidays offered families an opportunity to take a long bus ride and see their incarcerated loved ones.

But in 1978, that was not to be. Bobby Lewis, a death row prisoner, donned a guard's uniform and walked out of the prison. The embarrassment was acute for the officials, who had no clue how Bobby had managed the feat. Their response, on the day before Thanksgiving, was to cancel Thanksgiving visits for the other prisoners—a classic case of closing the barn door after the horse was out, and all too typical of the prison mindset.

Because the prison canceled the family visits at such a late date, many of the families could not be reached in time (remember, this was 1978) and thus they would travel many hours only to be turned away at the gates. John Spenkelink requested a legal phone call to his lawyer. That request was denied. Nor was he allowed to call his mother. Likewise, the other prisoners were not allowed to notify their loved ones that the visits were canceled.

John decided to protest nonviolently. Death row prisoners were fed on a tray shoved through a "pie hole" between the bars of their cells. When they were through eating, the prisoner trusty who delivered the food would pick up the tray in the pie hole. Initiating passive resistance, John withheld his lunch tray when the trusty came to pick it up. Word spread quickly. John informed a guard he would return the tray when he was allowed to make a phone call to either his lawyer or his mother, who was coming to visit him. Other prisoners withheld their trays also.

128

How It All Began: John Spenkelink

The other prisoners followed his lead because, in the five years John had been on death row at FSP, he had emerged as a leader. He was no longer a troubled kid but a mature and thoughtful adult. In our visits, I had been struck by his compassion, his thoughtfulness, and his authentic Christian commitment. He was trying to live the life of a faithful follower of Jesus while on death row. It was not an easy task, but it earned him respect from the other prisoners.

A counselor came to see why John had not returned his food tray. John quietly informed the counselor that he would return the tray when he had access to a telephone. After promising that either John would get access to a phone or else the counselor would make the call himself, the counselor left. John hung on to his tray, but the other prisoners, on the basis of that promise, gave theirs up. The first counselor didn't return, but a second counselor appeared and reassured John. John gave up his tray. The day wore on, but they heard nothing more. They were not given access to a telephone.

By suppertime, tension was high on R wing. There had been no contact from anyone, and Thanksgiving was hours away. When it came time for the trusty to pick up the supper tray, John once again refused to give his up, as did the rest of the men in R wing, in solidarity with John. The lack of basic decency on the part of the prison administration had created a potential flashpoint.

John was clear, articulate, and nonthreatening in his dealing with the guards. He just wanted use of the telephone to inform his mother not to come, and then he would surrender his tray. The guards, however, saw this as a refusal to obey a direct order. A goon squad composed of six armed guards approached John's cell.

"You're going to kill me?" John said. "Why not just let my mother visit me?"

The words bounced off the visored helmets, batons, and fiberglass shield with which the tactical squad was equipped. John didn't want anyone else to get hurt. He urged the other prisoners to give up their trays. They did.

John kept his.

The guards opened John's cell door and sprang through behind the five-foot vertical shield. The force of their attack knocked John back; his head struck his sink as he went down. He was pummeled with batons until he was unconscious. Then the guards dragged his limp body down the walk to Q wing—the punishment wing.

I heard about the attack on John the Monday after Thanksgiving, November 26. I was stunned by the brutality of the response to what had been a peaceful protest. The state had acted on the basis of its *perception* of John as a hardened convict, a killer, rather than on the basis of the reality that John was a soft-spoken, compassionate Christian. I determined to go to Florida as soon as possible to see him.

Later that week, I was sitting in the colonel's room waiting for John to be brought in. He was fully shackled this time, feet and hands. When the guard unlocked him from his chains, we shook hands—but when I reached to embrace him, he said, "Easy." I gently hugged him and took a good look. His neck had a knot on it from a billy club, and there were lacerations and bruises on his face and shoulders. He lifted his orange T-shirt, revealing bruises and more lacerations. He also had a broken rib. But what really hurt to see was the look in his eyes. For the first time in my two years of visiting him, John looked completely vulnerable.

John was a kind, compassionate man who had a basic faith in our system of justice in the United States. Despite his prior incarceration and his daily exposure to the rank injustice of death row, he felt that the system would eventually work for him, through clemency. It was an attitude I found only in white prisoners. Black prisoners knew how the system worked; they had no expectation of justice. Now, though, John's faith in the system had been shaken to its roots. The beating he'd been given after his nonviolent protest had removed any veil of privilege his white skin had bestowed on him. He knew now that these people would kill him without a moment's hesitation.

* * *

As winter gave way to spring, I was filled with foreboding. John's case was nearing the end of the legal process. He had an appeal pending before the US Supreme Court, but no one held out much hope for its success. This meant that John's fate depended on the decision of newly elected governor Bob Graham to grant clemency or not.

David Kendall, John's excellent appellate lawyer, presented a persuasive clemency case to Governor Graham. He detailed John's troubled background, his father's suicide, the maturity John had demonstrated on death row, and the positive force he had become there. John was always helping prisoners who had no stamps for food or commissary. He even had one of the mentally ill prisoners, a man who constantly babbled and got on everyone's nerves, placed in the cell next to him because John could tolerate the man and communicate with him.

Governor Graham, a Democrat, had come into office with a significant political problem. As governor of Florida, he presided over the largest death row in the nation. How would he respond to this challenge? The decision of whether to grant John Spenkelink clemency would probably answer the question of what the other 134 condemned prisoners might expect from him.

Governor Graham was a member of the United Church of Christ (UCC) in the Miami area. As a United Church of Christ minister, I believed it would be helpful to have a dialogue about the death penalty with Governor Graham and religious leaders. We could discuss how to address the dilemma of Florida's death row, the largest in the country, as well as John Spenkelink's case.

A meeting to broach these topics with Governor Graham in

Tallahassee was arranged for March of 1979. I contacted a professor of Christian ethics at Union Theological Seminary, Roger Shinn, who was also a UCC minister. Mary Charlotte McCall of the Southern Presbyterian Church and C. K. Steele, a prominent civil rights activist and Baptist minister, agreed to attend as well.

The meeting with Governor Graham would be one of many with Southern governors over the years. In 1979, I was thirty-three years old, a five-year veteran of death row ministry, and swimming against the political tide. But I held dear matters of truth and justice—and although those things were not virtues for politicians concerned about getting elected, perhaps an ecumenical appeal to Governor Graham would not fall on deaf ears.

Governor Graham welcomed us into his office. We sat in a semicircle with his two aides behind us. He began by telling us that he believed the death penalty was a deterrent. I considered this tactic an opening gambit. Bob Graham was an intelligent man, and he surely knew that the death penalty was not a deterrent.

"You may be aware," I said calmly, "that in 1976, when it reinstated the death penalty, the US Supreme Court stated that the deterrence argument had not been proven."

But Governor Graham dug in his heels on the deterrence argument.

Dr. Shinn asked, "Governor, do you find retribution an adequate moral justification for implementing the death penalty?"

The governor's response was swift: "I do not. I certainly wouldn't sign a death warrant for somebody for no other reason than vengeance."

My group had done their homework. Mary McCall explained the various denominational positions on the death penalty. Almost every major denomination that *had* a position on the death penalty was opposed to it. C. K. Steele raised concerns about the discriminatory effect of the death penalty.

How It All Began: John Spenkelink

"I think the decisions of the US Supreme Court cleaned up the discrimination problem," the governor said.

Did it? I cocked my head. "Governor Graham," I said, "it's a long way from the marble halls of the US Supreme Court to the county courthouses in Florida. Decisions authored in Washington, DC, seem to be woefully out of touch with the reality of the administration of the death penalty in the South."

As a matter of fact, the first studies on the administration of the death penalty in the South since the enactment of the 1973 death penalty laws were emerging at about that time. The results revealed significant racial discrimination in the application of the law, including Florida. The Gross-Mauro study indicated a much greater likelihood of receiving the death penalty if you killed a white person than if you killed a Black person. Obviously, the Supreme Court did not have this evidence when it ruled in *Proffitt v. Florida* in 1976.

The governor seemed engaged by this line of discussion and asked a few questions. Finally, I suggested he appoint a commission of prominent social scientists to examine the evidence of these studies to ascertain whether the law was discriminatory and perhaps even undertake such a study itself. Governor Graham nodded and asked me to call his secretary the next day with my suggestions for the commission members. My hope was that he would forgo signing any more death warrants until the commission had reported its results. We left the capitol feeling better than when we'd walked in.

In May of 1979, the Southern Coalition on Jails and Prisons sponsored the March Against Death in Atlanta. After the march, Becca and I visited at Sunset Beach, North Carolina, seeking rest after the hectic spring of my work against the death penalty and her work as an oncology clinical specialist. Walking the sandy North Carolina shore, we decided to become husband and wife. The wedding, we decided, would be in Huntsville at the Church of the Nativity in October.

Heading out to the beach on Friday, the last day of our vacation, I was surprised to be summoned to the telephone by the motel manager. Puzzled, I picked up the manager's phone. My colleagues back in the Nashville office of the Southern Coalition on Jails and Prisons apologized for disturbing my vacation but said, "We knew you'd want to hear this. Governor Graham just signed John Spenkelink's death warrant. The execution is set for next Wednesday at 7:00 a.m."

The irony was striking: Governor Graham had responded to our proposal that he establish a commission to study the application of the death penalty in Florida by signing John's death warrant. This was my initiation into the peculiar institution that had resumed once again in the last quarter of the twentieth century: state-sanctioned killing.

Becca and I rearranged our plans, and I arrived in Starke on Sunday evening. I called Superintendent David Brierton at home and arranged a meeting with John for the next morning, May 21. The execution was scheduled for Wednesday, May 23.

David Brierton sat behind a desk whose glass top was mounted on a hunk of farm machinery. He was a big man who obviously worked out with weights. Our previous dealings had been cordial. However, I knew he was under an enormous strain. John's would be the first execution of a man who did not want to be killed since the death penalty was reinstated. The last thing Brierton wanted to see was the Circus Maximus atmosphere Gary Gilmore's execution had created in Utah in January of 1977. He said that he would limit visits due to "security concerns." I had worked with enough wardens to understand that "security concerns," real or not, was the protective mantle wardens threw over their operations to maintain control.

I assured Brierton that no one visiting John would smuggle anything to him so that he could kill himself. We were all desperately fighting to keep him alive. Indeed, at that very moment his lawyer, David Kendall, was arguing before the Florida Supreme Court on several vital legal issues related to John's case. However that decision went—and it would probably go badly since the judges were political creatures subject to election—it would be appealed. The fight would be carried into the federal courts.

Superintendent Brierton and I negotiated a visitation schedule for John that included clergy, legal, and personal visits. We also negotiated the details of a final visit—such as who could hug him, who could kiss him and how many times, and whether the visits would be contact or noncontact before the final visit, which would be contact. For reasons that were unclear, Brierton would not allow John's sister Carol, who had traveled from California with her husband, Tim, to visit her brother. We agreed to meet again the next morning as well to review the day's schedule.

I left the prison administration building, walked across the parking lot, buzzed the speaker, and told them I was there to see John Spenkelink. The chain-link gate slid back, and I stepped into no-man's-land between the two high fences topped with razor wire. German shepherds, desultory in the heat, moved slowly toward me in the run between the fences.

Once the gate behind me slid shut, the one in front of me opened. This is the cardinal rule regarding the movement of visitors or other personnel in a prison: the gate or door behind has to close before the one in front of the visitor opens. I moved through the opened gate, up the steps, and into the Florida State Prison.

At the control booth, I identified myself to the guard behind the tinted glass and signed into the logbook. Then the barred gate across the hall in front of me opened, and I walked into the noncontact visiting area. A guard locked the door behind me. The room was about thirty feet long with booths attached to the glass that bifurcated the room. I found a booth and sat down. Since John was under death warrant, we would visit here. Our conversation would be through a metal opening in the middle of the glass.

This would be my first time visiting noncontact at FSP. My previous visits had always been up a level in the colonel's room. As I waited, I considered John's situation. He should have been charged with second-degree murder at worst, and yet now here he was on deathwatch. The inadequate representation of his court-appointed lawyers during his trial limited his possible grounds for appeal—despite the lack of a willful murder.

A door opened on the other side of the glass. John and two guards came in. The guards unlocked the shackles on his hands and his feet. We waved at each other. He pulled up a chair and sat. We greeted each other by placing our hands on the glass, palms facing each other through the partition.

A short time into our conversation, John said, "I'm concerned about my mother. And my sister Carol. Will I get to see them? How are they holding up?"

"I talked to them by phone," I said. "Your mother will be coming by for a visit. Here's the bad news, though—Superintendent Brierton isn't going to allow Carol to visit."

John was dismayed. "But why?" he asked, incredulous that his family should be denied this final contact.

I couldn't serve as Brierton's apologist—it wasn't my job to justify his decisions. But I could at least explain. "It isn't really clear why he's denying it," I said, "but in his eyes it falls under the rubric of security." John and I agreed that I should discuss it with David Kendall. When I shared with John the superintendent's concern about his committing suicide, he shook his head. "If he knew me, he would know I wouldn't do anything to take myself out. If I have to die, I'm going to show these people for what they really are: killers."

John and I talked for about an hour, then ended our

conversation hurriedly because we were both anxious that I be with John's mother, Lois, and his sister.

"I'll be back later," I assured him.

When I drove into the residential neighborhood where Lois Spenkelink was staying, I shook my head at the sign in the yard of the next-door neighbor: "Fry Spenkelink." Lois was staying with Junior and Lila Boruff, originally from East Tennessee; they had retired to Florida due to Junior's health. They had generously opened their home to Lois some months before. In my previous visits to Starke, I too had enjoyed their warm hospitality and Lila's fine cooking.

Lila opened the door and welcomed me. Crossing the living room was Lois—white-haired, overweight, ponderous in her movements, and full of warmth. We embraced and held each other for a while. In my previous visits, I had come to love Lois, and I hated to see her in such distress.

We sat and talked about the day's events. Carol and Tim came by and joined the conversation. When Carol heard that she would not be permitted to visit her brother, she was justifiably angry and left the room in tears. Lois and Tim filled me in on the events in Tallahassee over the weekend, where protests of John's execution were being held. Lois had tried to visit Governor Graham, but he'd refused to see her—and his denial had become a focal point for the protesters and the press. Lois was somewhat bewildered by the amount of attention the press was giving her.

Lila served us up one of her sumptuous meals. It was home cooking at its best, and we relaxed around the kitchen table in the fellowship of those who cared deeply for one another. After lunch, Lois went to take a nap before her visit with John.

* * *

That evening, I met with Lois after her noncontact visit. Of course, it had been distressing to her, but she was holding herself together. We went back to the Boruffs' for supper and spent the evening talking about the case. Lois turned in early. Tim and Carol told me who they and Lois had been calling on John's behalf: Senator Ted Kennedy of Massachusetts, Governor Jerry Brown of California, and President Jimmy Carter. President Carter had been of particular interest to them because he was an avowed Christian. Lois didn't understand how someone could claim to be a follower of Jesus and be *for* the death penalty. I had a hard time understanding that as well. I cautioned Tim and Carol about letting Lois get her hopes up about President Carter, despite his public professions of Christian faith. He was a practitioner of the politics of state killing. As governor of Georgia, Jimmy Carter had signed the death penalty bill into law.

I drove to the motel where the lawyers were staying. David Kendall and his colleague Debbie Fins were due to arrive at about midnight. We had a meeting with Mr. Brierton scheduled for Tuesday morning, and I wanted to brief them on the first meeting. I also wanted their analysis of where things stood legally.

David and Debbie had been involved in court, in meetings, and in appeals all day long and into the night. Then they'd made the three-hour drive from Tallahassee to Starke. When we rendezvoused at 2:00 a.m., they were exhausted. I prepped them for the meeting with Brierton the next morning and reviewed how John and his family were doing. They updated me on the legal struggle. When we turned in after a long day, we knew the next promised to be even longer.

The Reverend Tom Feamster, an Episcopal priest who had been a professional football player and had become a priest later in life, had been visiting John over the last two years. Tom had a small parish near Starke, and the tension in his congregation about his ministry with John had grown as the execution neared. On the morning of the twenty-fourth, Tom, David, and I met for a pre-meeting before heading over to meet with David Brierton at the prison.

Mr. Brierton asked David what he thought our chances were in the courts. The denial in the Florida Supreme Court was a foregone conclusion, but perhaps we would fare better at the federal level.

When we brought up visitation, Superintendent Brierton surprised me: he agreed that Carol could visit John. He recognized that a brother and sister should be able to say goodbye to each other.

"By the way," he said, "I've visited John today. I'd have to say he's in the angry stage."

How else could he feel? I thought, biting my tongue. *You, whose job it is to see that he's killed, show up outside his cell. Should he rejoice in your presence?*

My own anger, as well as exhaustion, was getting the best of me, so I kept quiet. Tom and David were very articulate and fair with David Brierton. It was, all in all, a good meeting. My only contribution was to volunteer to handle the funeral arrangements if the need arose.

When I visited John later in the day, once again through the hated glass partition, he asked, "What are my chances, Joe? No bullshit. What are my chances?"

All I could say was what I took to be the truth. "It's going down to the wire, John."

Realizing that this might be the last time we'd see each other, John said, "I appreciate all everyone has done for me. Please tell them all that. I love you for who you are and for what you have done for me and my family. Stay strong and don't give up the struggle, no matter what happens to me."

I took a moment just to study my friend through the glass. His grave countenance, the mostly white hair combed back from his angular featured face, combined with his stillness made me want to touch and comfort him. But all I could do was say, "I love you, John."

Too Close to the Flame

As I placed my palm on the glass, John raised his hand and covered mine on his side. "I love you too, Joe."

* * *

The network television remotes, the national major dailies, and the Florida press and international reporters all converged in the field across the road from the prison. The prison administration had erected a tin-roof lean-to shelter in the middle of a cow pasture for any press conference.

Lois decided to give a statement to the press. From the tin-roofed shelter, she made an eleventh-hour plea to Governor Graham to stop the execution. She shared what a good son John had been and described his difficulties after he discovered the body of his father. Then we released a statement from John about his crime; it expressed his regret that the victim had been killed but insisted that it had been an act of self-defense. We also explained the rules for John's final visit with family:

- One embrace and one kiss would be allowed at the beginning of the visit.

- John could hold hands with a visitor as long as the hands were on the table in full view of the guards. John's wrists would remain handcuffed throughout the visit.

- One kiss and one embrace would be allowed at the end of the visit.

After the press conference, I drove an exhausted Lois back to the Boruffs'. She needed rest before going into the prison for the final visit that night.

Tom Feamster told me that the prison had refused to allow us—the ministers closest to him—to share a final Communion with John. Their reason: security, of course. A prison chaplain would provide Communion. Not only did the prison system want to kill John; they also wanted to control him, strip him of his dignity, and reduce to a minimum any spiritual contact beyond their own controlled clergy. Jerry Wayne Jacobs had described the state killing of a human being as a slaughterhouse—to my mind, it was worse. John was fully aware of what was going on, and the process was designed to not only exterminate him but to humiliate and demean him.

That evening, with the execution less than twelve hours away, I met with David Kendall in his motel room and told him of the denial of Communion with John's ministers. David was livid. He immediately called the governor's legal counsel and in no uncertain terms informed him that if John could not have Communion with the clergy of his choice, David would issue a scathing statement to the press blasting the governor.

When David had originally taken this case, he'd been with the NAACP Legal Defense Fund. But by the time of John's deathwatch, he was with a prominent Washington, DC, law firm—Williams and Connolly. Edward Bennett Williams, a founding partner in the firm, represented the *Washington Post*. The *Post* belonged to Katharine Graham. I knew Governor Graham would not want to tangle with the *Washington Post* on the issue of clergy for a condemned man.

As the night wore on, we waited anxiously for news from the courts. The Fifth Circuit Court of Appeals and the US Supreme Court were our final hope.

A demonstration of several hundred protestors had taken shape in the cow pasture across from the prison. Chants of "Death row must go!" rolled across the cow pasture, reaching the prisoners at FSP. It was a clear night, with the sky full of stars and the prison clearly visible under the moon. Suddenly, those of us in the cow pasture heard a loud metal clang ringing through the night, apparently from within the prison. Then lights went off and on rhythmically within the prison. Flaming towels and sheets were tossed out the prison's windows. The flames illuminated the prison as they fell harmlessly to the ground. Then we began to hear the answering chant from the prisoners—a stunning, loud demonstration of their affection for John: "Save John Spenkelink! Save John Spenkelink!"

Standing and witnessing it all, I could think only of John in Q wing. He could hear it all. This was an affirmation beyond anyone's expectations. The prisoners at FSP were doing all in their power to stand against the barbarity that the state of Florida had scheduled. John and I had discussed the power of resistance and witness. Now it was unfolding on his behalf in the most unlikely of places.

When I had described to John my meeting with Governor Bob Graham and we had plumbed the political depths into which the governor had descended to sign John's death warrant, John had said, "I don't hate Governor Graham. I don't understand why he wants to kill me or why he won't see me personally. But I don't hate him. In a way, I feel sorry for him because he is committing murder by killing me. It's kind of sad, isn't it?"

I felt caught in the maw of the giant machinery of destruction. We were on a conveyor belt with John designated for extermination. He couldn't get off. The rest of us would be dropped off the belt at the end. We had at least accomplished something powerful and good: the protest within and outside the prison. As powerful as the killing machinery might be, we could still oppose it, maybe even toss some sawdust into the gears to slow it down or stop it. We had to make our witness, to be steadfast in our faithfulness.

I went back to the motel to see if David had heard from the governor's office about Tom and I having final Communion with John. When I walked into David's room, he was on the telephone. Debbie Fins, his colleague, ran to me. The smile on her face surprised me, but the words from her mouth stunned me: "We have a stay! We have a stay!"

As Debbie and I embraced, I still couldn't quite grasp the news.

How It All Began: John Spenkelink

"How did this happen? What does it mean? How long will the stay of execution last?" I asked, and as my words tumbled out, Debbie sought to answer them. We actually had two stays of execution. One was from Judge Elbert Tuttle of the Fifth Circuit Court of Appeals and the other from Justice Thurgood Marshall of the US Supreme Court. It looked as if we would have months to sort through the legal issues.

David motioned me to the phone. He was talking to John. As soon as David handed me the phone, John said, "Joe, go right now to where my mom and sister are staying. Explain all of this to them so they'll understand." He was relieved, of course, and elated, but his thoughts were as much for his family as for himself. I told him I would leave right away.

I gave the phone back to David and in my joy swooped Deborah Fins off her feet. I carried her down the stairs on my way to the car, filled with sheer delight. Placing Debbie carefully down in the parking lot, I gave her another hug, jumped in the car, and drove off to the Boruffs' to visit with John's family.

A few minutes later, happy pandemonium reigned at the Boruffs'. Lila went into the kitchen to make some homemade biscuits to celebrate. Lois, Carol, Tim, and I hugged. Friends joined us, and we had a wonderful evening of thanksgiving and celebration.

Then I was spent. I turned in for a much-needed night's sleep.

* * *

The next morning, eating breakfast in the restaurant at the Holiday Inn, I spotted Superintendent Brierton and spoke to him. It happens surprisingly often, in small Southern prison towns, that the executioners and the opponents of killing end up eating at the same place. The coziness of state killing, Southern style!

Now that there was a stay of execution, I felt the freedom to return to Nashville—after a stop in Tallahassee. I had one last visit with Lois, Carol, and Tim. Lois's eyes were puffy and, not surprisingly, she seemed careworn. I urged her to catch up on her rest. They planned to visit John that afternoon; I told them to give him my love.

In Tallahassee, I went to the offices of the Florida Clearinghouse on Criminal Justice, the Florida office of SCJP. Scharlette Holdman, whom I had hired to direct that office, had helped organize the Tallahassee protests on John's behalf. About fifteen of us visited over fried chicken in the office. As we chatted, the local evening news came on and the attorney general, Jim Smith, was interviewed. He was clearly upset about the stays of execution and promised to have them dissolved so John's execution could happen on May 25, the last day of the death warrant. I was alarmed but everyone reassured me.

I stayed in Tallahassee the next day, wanting to confirm that the stays of execution would remain in place. At noon, as expected, the US Supreme Court dissolved Justice Marshall's stay of execution. The day wound down with no news from the Fifth Circuit Court of Appeals. I sat on the steps of the office, enjoying a pleasant evening, watching the Spanish moss that draped some nearby live oaks swaying in the breeze.

Relaxed by the sound of the cicadas, I went back inside the office to check on flights to Nashville. As I passed Scharlette's office, I could see that she was on the telephone and that her expression was anxious. She hung up. "Joe, the entire Fifth Circuit Court is going to review John's appeal over the telephone. And John's lawyers weren't given a chance to brief the issues raised on appeal." This meant that the judges would reach their decision without the benefit of the legal briefs detailing the significance of the issues brought up on appeal. This sounded ominous.

"I'm driving back to Starke," I told Scharlette.

During the monotonous nighttime drive back to Starke down

I-10, I struggled to maintain a clear radio signal. I figured that if the Fifth Circuit dissolved the stay of execution, I would hear it over the radio. Sure enough, in the middle of the drive, a crackling voice came over the airwaves: "The Fifth Circuit Court of Appeals has dissolved John Spenkelink's stay of execution. He is scheduled to die in the electric chair at ten o'clock tomorrow morning."

I leaned out the window and screamed into the Florida night: "God, is there no justice? Is there no justice?"

* * *

I arrived at Starke heartsick, in the middle of the night. The beauty of creation seemed to be mocking me. The entire week had been gorgeous weather and this last night was no different with its cloudless sky complete with stars and moon. Amid this beauty, the madness of state killing would commence in a few hours.

A final visit for John's family, I learned, had been set up. It would end at 6:00 a.m. Communion would be given by Tom Feamster, who would stay with John until 8:00 a.m. David Kendall had agreed to witness the execution.

I was exhausted from the emotional roller-coaster ride of the past few days. I felt as if I were coming unglued. I had no emotional reserve to say goodbye to John one more time. I would focus my time on Lois and hope we both held together.

I spoke with Tim and Carol. We were all concerned that the press knew Lois was staying at the Boruffs'. We didn't want her to be besieged by them as the execution neared. I arranged to pick Lois up at 9:00 a.m. and sequester her in a motel until the execution was over.

When I arrived to pick her up, Lois was moving as if in a daze. The exhaustion and the stunning change of events had taken a dramatic toll on her countenance. I urged her along as gently as possible, but it wasn't until 9:30 that we left the Boruffs' home. I glanced at the "Fry Spenkelink" sign in the neighbors' yard, but Lois, holding my arm and stumbling along, seemed to have tuned it out.

We drove to a rundown motel in Starke, a place so dilapidated that I couldn't imagine any reporters staying there. I asked the manager not to inform anyone of our presence. I told her that there would be phone calls and that I would screen them.

Lois had been amazingly indomitable up to this point. But when we entered the room, she was mumbling almost incoherently. The immense weight of the occasion was crushing her spirit. She sat on the bed, her face puffy and stained with tears.

"Have we heard from Senator Kennedy, Governor Brown, or President Carter?" she managed to ask.

"No, Lois, we haven't."

"How could they not call me back? They're killing my son!"

I had no answer.

The telephone rang, and Lois grabbed it before I could reach it. After a minute or two, she thrust the phone toward me and said, "I don't understand."

I identified myself as a minister with the family and asked who I was talking to. The reply: "This is Richard Carzini calling for President Carter. Please tell Mrs. Spenkelink the president sympathizes with her deeply. But as you probably know, this is a matter of state law, and he doesn't think it would be proper for him to intervene and call Governor Graham."

This bit of legal doublespeak was the last straw for me. My anger, although controlled, was surely evident as I responded, "Don't you understand why we called? Carter claims to be a Christian. We are pleading with our Christian brother in the name of Jesus Christ to call Governor Graham and stop this execution. Would you please deliver that message?"

There was a pause that seemed to stretch into eternity. "I'll be sure the president gets the message."

How It All Began: John Spenkelink

I hung up. Lois had stretched out on the bed, her head on the pillow. She was mumbling something about Senator Kennedy. Within what seemed like seconds, she had fallen asleep.

Surprised, I watched as she slept. Exhaustion had taken her to a much-needed rest, and I was not about to interrupt it. The tension of waiting for word of John's electrocution would not be a conscious problem for Lois. Sleeping, she would be sheltered from the principalities and powers storming the gates of her life.

Neither Lois nor I wore a watch, nor did the motel room have a clock radio. David Kendall had promised to call after the execution to inform us, but I feared that might take too long. Lois would need to know as soon as the deed was confirmed so that she could begin taking phone calls from family and friends. I decided to turn on the television with no sound and wait for some bulletin on the screen.

As I watched, I glanced out the window and saw the same blue pellucid sky I had seen all week. It was a bright light on a dark business. Despite my anxiety, I took a moment to soak up the beauty of creation in the midst of the madness that surrounded me.

But I couldn't sit long. Nervous energy coursed through me. I paced, wondering why David had not called. Maybe another stay of execution had come through. I glanced back at the television—now a rerun of the sitcom *All in the Family* was broadcasting. As I alternated between watching Archie Bunker yell at his wife and glancing out the window to see if anyone was approaching, a bulletin scrolled across the bottom of the screen: "At 10:12 a.m. John Spenkelink was executed at the Florida State Prison . . . The US Supreme Court denied his final appeal." I turned the television off.

Lois remained peacefully slumbering. Unbeknownst to her, her only son had just been electrocuted a few miles down the road at the Florida State Prison. Sorrowfully, I approached the bed to wake her—and noticed through the window that the motel manager was

147

walking toward our room. I slipped out the door and intercepted her midway across the parking lot.

"That's Mrs. Spenkelink in there, isn't it?" she asked.

I nodded.

"Please tell her that I'm sorry. If there is anything I can do to help just let me know."

I asked her to screen all our calls. I didn't think a crank caller could find us, but I wanted to be sure.

"I'll be glad to," she said.

I eased back into the room as quietly as possible. Lois was still asleep, breathing deeply. I sat on the edge of the bed and gently shook her shoulder. There was no response. I shook again, harder. She slept on, oblivious. The third time I shook even harder. Her blue eyes fluttered open and sought out mine.

"Lois, I'm afraid I have bad news."

Her response was instantaneous: "They've killed my Johnny." She spoke it as a fact, not a question.

"Yes, Lois. They've killed John."

Lois sat up, her gaze still locked on mine. Then tears welled up in the corners of her eyes and spilled onto her cheeks. She began to weep.

Through the sobs, I heard her words of self-accusation: "What else could I have done? Who else should I have called? Did Senator Kennedy call back?"

I pulled her hands away from her face. "Lois! Listen to me. You did all you could. All of us did what we could for John. We all loved him. There is simply nothing else we could have done. Don't second-guess yourself. Please don't punish yourself."

We sat holding hands. Eventually her weeping subsided, but the tears continued to roll down her cheeks. "Would you like to pray?" I asked.

She nodded. We prayed, then continued to talk softly to each other, holding hands.

How It All Began: John Spenkelink

The telephone rang and I reached for it. It was Lois's brother from California, John's uncle. While he and Lois talked, I walked into the cramped bathroom. I turned the water in the sink on full blast and flushed the toilet. Then I leaned on the wall, banging on it with my fists. As softly as I could, I screamed to God: "God, why? Why? Why is there no justice?" Leaning against my arms, braced against the wall, I broke down and sobbed.

But not for long. I had to pull myself together for Lois's sake. I washed my face, then I stepped back into the motel room, where Lois was still talking with her brother. When she had hung up, Lois wanted to talk about John. We quietly shared stories and memories about him, invoking his presence.

The door opened, and in came Carol and Tim. They embraced Lois and joined us in talking about John. After a while, David Kendall, looking wan and spent, joined the conversation—though, after watching his client die, a man he deeply cared for, David couldn't muster much energy for conversation.

Other friends and supporters came over the next hour or so, forming a circle of love that held us all up. It had been a long day and night for most of us, and sleep and food had been scarce. We decided to go to a local steakhouse for lunch.

The intimacy of dining together united us in both grief and healing. We were broken, sad, but not in despair. Somehow, God had pulled us through the experience of John's killing.

Suddenly, Carol rose from the table and went to the restroom. I didn't think anything of it until Tim, Carol's husband, nodded toward the parking lot. Through the window, I could see Tom Feamster crossing the lot, fresh from the inventory of John's final belongings. Tom's presence there was no surprise, since he'd been planning on joining us there when he was free. What surprised me was that he was talking to Superintendent David Brierton, who had just presided at John's electrocution. Evidently, Brierton had just arrived and was about to enter the same steakhouse in which the Spenkelink family was dining. After a brief discussion between the two men, Brierton returned to his car and drove away. Tom entered the restaurant.

Carol remained in the restroom for a while—we found out later she'd been vomiting there from the shock and renewed grief brought on by that glimpse of Brierton in the parking lot. The whole experience was so intense and personal, this Southern-style politics of killing. It was too much to comprehend. It could only be endured.

The week culminated with a memorial service for John at First Presbyterian Church in Tallahassee, where the Reverend Bruce Robertson was pastor. It was a beautiful and consoling service created by those who loved John, and every pew was filled.

* * *

Back in Nashville, I didn't realize how profoundly the ordeal of John's ritual slaughter had affected me until the following weekend. The first Saturday of June, I was driving my blue pickup down Broadway, the main street of downtown Nashville, headed to Acme Farm Supply, a stone's throw from the Cumberland River. Early Saturday morning in summer was a slow traffic time in downtown Nashville. Fan Fair, the annual country music extravaganza held in early June, had not yet begun. I approached an intersection, glanced at the traffic light, and drove straight through. A car honked to the right, and I realized that despite looking at the light I had not cognitively registered it as red. Fortunately, an alert driver had not proceeded on his green light before scanning the traffic. I was saved a collision I justly deserved.

Five blocks further, at Acme Farm Supply, I parked my truck and sat in the cab gripping the steering wheel with white knuckles. I was shaking and struggling to think clearly. I was, I realized, in shock—and not from my close call at the traffic light.

How It All Began: John Spenkelink

I spent the rest of June regaining my equilibrium. Meanwhile, reports from the prisoners on death row at FSP, along with a few guards, revealed that John had kept his promise to me and made the prison personnel show who they really were. When the death squad came to John's cell to escort him to the electric chair, he refused to cooperate. Their response was a replay of the brutality that had taken place the previous Thanksgiving holiday. He was beaten and dragged to the death chamber, strapped into the electric chair, and gagged, with a mask placed over his face so no one could see the gag in his mouth. He was like a penned animal awaiting slaughter when the blinds opened in the execution chamber for the witnesses to observe the execution. Tom Feamster told me his eyes reflected sheer terror. Although prison rules mandated a last statement, John was not given the opportunity to make one. Instead, 2,100 volts of electricity charged through his body three times.

The prisoners had seen and heard how John had been abused. The publicity surrounding the allegations of brutality prompted Governor Graham to appoint a commission to investigate. I went to FSP to observe the investigation hearings and was not surprised to discover a well-orchestrated charade designed to prevent the truth of John's beating coming to light.

The irony was striking. Governor Graham had declined to appoint a commission to examine the evidence that the death penalty in Florida was being administered in a racially discriminatory manner. He did not care to inquire into the merits of the death penalty in Florida. Allegations of brutality during the killing of a prisoner, however, garnered an investigative commission. As Jerry Wayne Jacobs might have put it, Governor Graham was concerned about the appearance of the slaughter, not the actual slaughter itself. For Governor Graham, it was all about optics. How embarrassing it would be if Florida officials roughed up prisoners on the way to the electric chair! However, strapping the prisoners into the chair and electrocuting them was of no concern. Nor was denying them a final statement.

As a result of the investigation, future executions would have an "independent observer" who would be stationed on deathwatch to ensure proper procedures were followed and prisoners were not abused—just killed.

* * *

On June 22–26, 1979, the United Church of Christ held its Twelfth General Synod in Indianapolis, Indiana. I was at the general synod to shepherd a resolution against the death penalty (which I had drafted) through the voting process. The denomination was already on record against the death penalty, but this resolution would be different. It would speak to the current events of a reinstated death penalty as well as the ongoing issues of race, class, and morality. The resolution specifically mentioned the state of Florida, with the largest death row population in the country, and the governor of Florida, Bob Graham, our "Christian brother."

While in Indianapolis for the general synod, I roomed with my mentor and friend, Bill Webber, from East Harlem. He was immensely helpful in pushing the resolution through the two conferences to the floor of the general synod. We dealt with the usual objections and with parliamentary procedure, and in due course the resolution was ready to come to the floor of the general synod for a vote.

When the day for voting on the resolution came, I was on the floor explaining the resolution and answering questions. The prospects for passage looked good, but one can never tell until a vote is completed. As I stood at the back of the room full of UCC delegates from around the country, I was approached by a representative of the Florida Conference of the UCC. He came with a request from the conference minister, Chuck Burns, that we drop Bob Graham's name

from the resolution. The representative provided some weak explanation, but as I listened, I realized that the Florida Conference probably received a significant amount of financial support from Bob
Graham, who was from South Florida. Plus, he was the governor,
and having a UCC member as governor provided a definite cool
factor that likely gave him some clout.

But I had a potent memory: As a United Church of Christ
minister, I had visited Governor Graham, a UCC layman, in March
to discuss the death penalty and our Christian position regarding
it. His response was to sign John Spenkelink's death warrant, which
led ultimately to his electrocution on May 25. All I could see as
this representative made his pitch were the faces of John and Lois
Spenkelink. A son killed by Bob Graham's death warrant and a
mother Graham refused to meet.

When the request was complete, I said, "No, we can't take his
name out. If Governor Graham is going to kill people, then he needs
to get accustomed to having his name associated with those he kills.
We all know the denomination's position on this issue."

He continued to try to argue his point until he realized I was
resolute and left. I immediately alerted the resolution's supporters on
the floor to expect an amendment to the resolution and to spread the
word to defeat it.

The resolution passed as drafted.

CHAPTER TEN

January 2019

BOOM!

On Tuesday, January 22, I awoke with a heaviness in my chest and the old familiar feeling of doom. The whole day was one of misery. I felt like I had reverted to where I was in November. Before that morning, I had begun to think that the meds were positively affecting me. The days hadn't seemed bottomless anymore. I still had no energy, no real will, but at least I wasn't enervated. Maybe I was making progress.

And then, *boom*.

I kept reminding myself that the therapist and psychiatrist had both warned me it could be like this, that I could feel better and then bottom out again, that it was not a straightforward process. There would be many ups and downs before I navigated my way out of the melancholia. I understood their message intellectually, but it did not make me feel better.

In fact, back in mid-January, I had visited a psychiatrist who prescribed an additional antidepressant. As we talked, he told me he thought I had a "moderate depression."

"If this is moderate," I said, "I would hate to see severe."

"Yes, you would."

I wondered if now I was in fact experiencing "severe depression."

I immediately thought of my friend who had undergone ECT and other friends who had been in psychiatric wards. In truth, I had been wondering whether I should check myself into the Vanderbilt psychiatric unit. But, as bad as I felt, I had at least—so far—been able to put one foot in front of the other, to imitate the motions of living. So maybe *moderate* was an accurate term. It just didn't feel moderate.

Now, on the twenty-second, I wondered whether there was a reason for my attack of more extreme despondence or if it might be random, which it often is. And then it hit me: the etching of Ed Zagorski.

Just three days before, I had received the etching from Ann Walker King. It had been done by our friend Susie Ries some years before. Ann thought it captured Ed. Without thinking of what effect the picture might have on me, I had asked Ann to send it. It did indeed capture his liveliness. But I hadn't been able to look at it very long. It was too traumatic. Seeing him so clearly brought back all the trauma: his pretend writhing in the electric chair, his reddened, burned face and head, the ashes. *Jesus, let it stop.* But now it was once again front and center. The picture became a trigger for the trauma I was now experiencing on the morning of January 22.

* * *

Don Johnson had an execution date of May 16, 2019. He was the next man up and the first opportunity for the new governor, Bill Lee, to deliberate a condemned man's fate. As I had learned in Florida with John Spenkelink decades before, first in line is a position no prisoner wishes to occupy.

My last conversation with Don in the fall had been hopeful. He thought he had a chance at clemency, but Governor Haslam had denied him. His lawyers would reapply with Governor Lee.

January 2019

Regardless of what happened with Don Johnson's case, my trauma therapist had been very clear: "No more deathwatches." And I knew she was right. But even before he had an execution date, I had already agreed to Don's request to be with him on deathwatch. Since agreeing to that, I had experienced the emotional devastation of two deathwatches with Ed Zagorski over only eighteen days. Now Don had a date—and I knew I could not be with him due to my own trauma.

I pulled out my personal stationery and wrote Don a letter in my scrawl. I explained my situation. I knew he would understand. I was very fond of Don; I had known him for thirty years. He was a serious Christian who did a radio show every weekend with faith communities in Tennessee. I very much wanted to keep my commitment to him. But I simply couldn't.

For me to be away from death row this long was a major departure from the norm. My weekly visits had become a mainstay for both the condemned and me. The men were my peeps.

* * *

My standing appointment with my therapist is at 9:30 a.m. every Friday. I arrived a few minutes early on January 25. Her office, in her home, was a relaxed environment. Rosie, the big black dog, licked me in greeting. I sat across from the therapist. Rosie occasionally wandered through. Throw pillows were scattered around. It felt homey and safe.

I began that session by telling my therapist about something that had happened that week. About midweek, when I woke in the morning, Becca asked me, "Do you remember anything from last night?"

"No—should I?" I said.

"I woke you twice. Each time, you were beginning to scream.

157

Do you recall what it was about?"

"No," I said. "But, as often happens, when I was going to sleep I couldn't get Ed's image out of my mind. So when I fell asleep my mind was dwelling on Ed."

The therapist listened, then said, "What is the image you have of Ed that causes so much trauma? Let's start with that."

Through the process of EMDR, my therapist guided me through one traumatic image after another, back and forth, as my eyes followed her finger. The current trauma had indeed been triggered by seeing the etching of Ed Zagorski. It had relaunched the experiences of the two deathwatches, and from there back through a lifetime of trauma: John Spenkelink, Bob Sullivan, Robert Wayne Williams, Velma Barfield—and that was only a partial list of state killings starting in 1979 and continuing into 2018. Those four names—Spenkelink, Sullivan, Williams, Barfield—are the ones I focused on for this session. I talked rapidly, clearly needing to unpack the trauma of the killing of those friends. Even though some of it had happened thirty-five years before, the pain was layered deep.

John Spenkelink, Bob Sullivan, Robert Wayne Williams, Velma Barfield—and that was only a partial list of state killings starting in 1979 and continuing into 2018.

* * *

January 2019

As I struggled to comprehend my feelings, to understand my experiences, I turned to the poetry of W. H. Auden. When living in East Harlem while attending Union Theological Seminary in New York, my tenement mate and I telephoned Auden and invited him to dinner. The kind man we spoke with wrote the poem "Death's Echo," which includes these four lines near the end:

> The desires of the heart are as crooked as corkscrews,
> Not to be born is the best for man;
> The second-best is a formal order,
> The dance's pattern; dance while you can.[1]

Then there was his description (from his famous poem "In Memory of W. B. Yeats") of intellectuals besotted with history and illusion before the Soviet Union aligned with the Third Reich:

> In the nightmare of the dark
> All the dogs of Europe bark . . .
> Intellectual disgrace
> Stares from every human face[2]

Hannah Arendt described the era: "The time when it looked for quite a while as if the worst could happen and sheer evil would become a success."[3]

This description by Auden and Arendt applies to my feelings. My experience with state killing looks as if sheer evil has become a success. It grinds people down. It is unrelenting. And yet Auden could write, in his poem "Precious Five:"

> I could (which you cannot)

---

1 W. H. Auden, "Death's Echo" (1937).
2 W. H. Auden, "In Memory of W. B. Yeats" (1940).
3 Hannah Arendt, "Remembering W. H. Auden," *New Yorker*, January 20, 1975.

Find reasons fast enough
To face the sky and roar
In anger and despair
At what is going on,
Demanding that it name
Whoever is to blame:
The sky would only wait
Till all my breath was gone
And then reiterate
As if I wasn't there
That singular command
I do not understand,
Bless what there is for being,
Which has to be obeyed, for
What else am I made for,
Agreeing or disagreeing.[4]

Auden also caught me with the following verse, again from "In Memory of W. B. Yeats":

Follow, poet, follow right
To the bottom of the night,
With your unconstraining voice
Still persuade us to rejoice;
With the farming of a verse
Make a vineyard of the curse,
Sing of human unsuccess
In a rapture of distress;
In the deserts of the heart
Let the healing fountain start,
In the prison of his days

---

4 W. H. Auden, "Precious Five" (1950).

January 2019

Teach the free man how to praise.

This "human unsuccess," I believe, is at the heart of the death penalty struggle and also of my melancholia. Some of us have been gifted to know those who are an "unsuccess" in the eyes of the world. Our calling is to translate to the free world the reality we encounter with those deemed an "unsuccess," people we know as caring and generous despite their status. We do so "in the deserts of the heart" so that we may let "the healing fountain start." Then we may all know that "in the prison of our days" we will "teach the free man how to praise." The freedom and the love come from unsuccess. We will never understand the condemned if we view them from the eyes of success. It is only when we recognize "human unsuccess," especially our own, that we can see one another mutually as children of God.

CHAPTER ELEVEN

Bob

THERE JUST SEEMED to be something about Florida, the condemned, and Thanksgiving.

In 1978, the guards known as "the goon squad" had attacked John Spenkelink at the Florida State Prison for withholding his dinner tray as a passive protest against the prison administration for canceling Thanksgiving visits for the prisoners. Five years later, I was headed back to the Florida State Prison to be with Bob Sullivan on deathwatch.

Although Bob was the second man on the verge of execution in Florida, the intervening years since John's killing had taught us a lot. Governor Bob Graham was in the process of signing more death warrants than any governor in Florida's history. The warrants hurried the cases along, and now Bob's case had risen to the top. It mattered not if you were a Democrat like Graham or a Republican, the politics of state killing won votes in the South. Later, George Bush, the Republican governor of Texas, would become the next great expediter of death warrants to rival Bob Graham.

By the time I arrived in Florida in late November 1983 to join the protest against Bob's execution and to be with him, I had worked closely with a few men exterminated by the state: John Spenkelink in Florida, Frank Coppola in Virginia, John Evans in Alabama, and in

September of 1983, Jimmy Lee Gray in Mississippi. Now it was Bob Sullivan, and on the near horizon, in mid-December, Robert Wayne Williams in Louisiana.

During the almost five years since John's electrocution, I had visited the Florida State Prison quarterly and come to know Bob well. He wasn't a typical death row prisoner. He hailed from New Hampshire, and his adopted father was a surgeon. He had spent four years at the University of Miami. He was a fervent Boston Red Sox fan—and since I was a Los Angeles Dodgers fan, we frequently teased each other about our baseball teams.

Bob was a chunky man with blue eyes and a sparkling wit. Despite a severe stutter, he was articulate, and his intelligence shone through his observations. As a devout Catholic, he fervently hoped the Catholic Church would become involved in his case. Priests from Boston visited him. He was deeply involved in his legal appeals and knew as much about the law as many lawyers. His letters were full of legal points and suggested courtroom strategies. A friend back home had set up the Robert Austin Sullivan Legal Defense Fund to raise money for his legal battles. This money enabled Bob to hire a private investigator to find evidence to support his claim of innocence.

Bob was on death row because he'd been convicted of murdering the assistant manager of a Howard Johnson's restaurant in Homestead, Florida, about forty miles away from FSP. Bob was himself a former manager of the restaurant. When he was convicted in November 1973, the jury recommended a life sentence—but the judge imposed the death penalty.

As part of Bob's appeal of his conviction, a private investigator obtained two sworn affidavits from witnesses who said Bob was in a Miami bar at the time the robbery-murder took place. Other evidence suggesting that Bob might be innocent of robbing and murdering the assistant manager of the restaurant included the allegation that the restaurant manager, a different person, had disappeared after stealing $5,000 from the establishment. The victim's widow filed a federal suit charging that restaurant employees had carried out the crime—and Bob, of course, was no longer an employee. Further complicating his case was the fact that two of Bob's potential defense witnesses were murdered under circumstances similar to the murder of which Bob was accused.

When he was convicted in November 1973, the jury recommended a life sentence— but the judge imposed the death penalty.

After Bob's murder trial, his lawyer and the lawyer's investigator contradicted each other on an important aspect of the case. The lawyer stated before the trial that he had given the investigator a list of potential witnesses—witnesses whom Bob had said would provide an alibi. Five years after the trial, the investigator provided an affidavit in which he swore that the lawyer hadn't approached him until a year after the trial and that the lawyer hadn't given him specific names of potential witnesses but had just asked him to try and find somebody who could corroborate Bob's story. The investigator's statement raised fundamental questions about the competency of Bob's defense during the trial and the initial appeal of the conviction. This was no surprise to me—I had learned by this time that inadequate trial counsel and insufficient investigation plagued virtually all death penalty cases in the South.

As a minister, I sought to involve religious leaders in speaking against the death penalty. I asked René Gracida, the Catholic bishop of the Diocese of Pensacola-Tallahassee, to raise Bob Sullivan's case with Governor Graham. Bishop Gracida and some other Florida Catholic bishops met with Governor Graham for breakfast in March of 1983. They pled for mercy on Bob's behalf, asking the governor to commute his sentence to life. Several months passed with no reply, so they followed up with a petition to Graham asking that he intervene in the case. In a cold, formal reply, Governor Graham stated that the case was still in the courts and that he had no intention of intervening.

Technically, Governor Graham was correct—the case was under appeal. But death penalty cases are *always* under appeal, often to the eve of execution. What we needed for Bob was time for his legal team to investigate the claims and issues that had come to light in the ten years since his trial. We hoped Governor Graham would wait until 1984 before signing Bob's death warrant.

But on November 8, 1983, Governor Graham signed Bob Sullivan's death warrant. The execution was set for 7:00 a.m. on November 29.

When I learned of the execution date, I contacted Bishop Gracida again, now bishop of the diocese of Corpus Christi, and also Bishop Snyder of St. Augustine, requesting of each of them that they contact the Vatican's representative to the United States, the Apostolic Delegate, in the hope that they would contact Pope John Paul II and request that he intervene with Governor Graham on Bob Sullivan's behalf.

My colleagues and I set up a meeting of PAX, People Against Executions, in Tallahassee on November 27, with the goal of organizing acts of civil disobedience—coordinated nonviolent direct actions in Tallahassee—to protest Bob Sullivan's execution. Father Daniel Berrigan, the veteran peace and social justice activist, had corresponded with Bob and agreed to join us.

On November 27, the PAX planning meeting lasted until

after midnight. We decided on a protest: the group would don black executioner's hoods and stand outside the governor's office door from 2:00 p.m. Monday until the governor left for the day. On Tuesday, another group would stage a mock execution in front of Governor Graham and his cabinet (with whom he conferred on death penalty cases) at their regular meeting. Then the governor would sign a death warrant. Determined not to allow protestors to disrupt the daily work of government, including the routine of killing, he had informed police and security guards not to arrest protesters unless they attempted to stop the government from carrying out its business.

Monday morning, I received word that I could visit Bob Sullivan that evening at 7:00 p.m. Starke is a three-hour drive east from Tallahassee. I would need to leave by 4:00 p.m.

But before I left, there was a serious issue troubling me that I was anxious to resolve. I telephoned my friend the Reverend Bruce Robertson, minister at First Presbyterian Church in Tallahassee. He agreed to have lunch and listen to my concern, which was that Bob Sullivan had asked me to witness his execution if his lawyer could not do so.

Over lunch, I explained my dilemma to Bruce. My cardinal rule was not to witness the killing of my friends. If I did, I felt it would do me such harm that I could no longer continue my work visiting those on death row. Bruce listened and we discussed the issue from all sides. By the discussion's end, I decided that I would witness the execution if the lawyer did not show up.

When lunch was over, Bruce offered to drive me to the prison. I was relieved because I was tired and didn't want to make that long drive alone.

I rented a car for the drive. Just before leaving, I called the Tallahassee office of the Southern Coalition on Jails and Prisons to check on the legal status of Bob's case. Sounding tired, Jimmy Lohman gave me the bad news: "We lost in the Eleventh Circuit [referring to the Eleventh Circuit Court of Appeals] 2–1." With that setback, it appeared that Bob's appeal would be headed to the US Supreme Court—"the Supremes," as we called them. Given the conservative makeup of the court, that could only be bad news. My stomach tightened as I realized Bob would be killed despite all the evidence and arguments discovered post-trial. If there were only more time!

When Bruce and I drove into Starke on US Highway 301, we passed the town water tower, topped by the blood-red neon cross glowing garishly in the Florida night. The nearby prison held more than two hundred condemned men. This blood-red replica of an ancient device for execution spoke eloquently of the business of Starke and the state of Florida.

As we checked into the Best Western motel, the clerk gave me a message to call Scharlette Holdman at the Florida Clearinghouse of Criminal Justice, the SCJP Florida office, ASAP. (This was 1983, before cell phones.)

I called her from my room. Scharlette picked up and answered: "Clearinghouse."

"Scharlette, it's Joe. We just checked in and I'm—"

"Joe! Joe! We got the pope. We got the fucking pope! The pope asked Graham to stop Bob's execution."

"What?"

"Archbishop McCarthy conveyed the message directly from Pope John Paul II to Governor Graham, asking him to stop Bob's execution. Of course, Graham turned him down."

Through the hard work of a number of Catholic bishops and priests from Boston, Pope John Paul II had heard our request. And for the first time in US history, a pope had intervened in a death penalty case. Despite the historical nature of that intervention, Governor Bob Graham had been indifferent to what Pope John Paul II had requested.

Shortly after 7:00 p.m. I met with Bob's lawyer inside FSP. The legal prognosis looked bad, he told me. But I was greatly relieved when he told me that he had decided to witness the execution the next morning. I would not have to.

I was cleared by security and entered the visiting room, where I found Margaret Vandiver, a paralegal who was close to Bob, and three Catholic priests from Massachusetts. I hugged Margaret and was introduced to the priests. Then I turned to greet Bob.

Behind the glass partition of the visiting room—this was a noncontact visit—Bob looked out somberly, his eyes red and puffy. Clearly, he was suffering greatly. The calm, intelligent, witty Bob Sullivan I knew and loved was weeping at the prospect of death the next morning.

Bob splayed his manacled hand flat against the glass partition in a sign of greeting. I pressed my hand against the partition, covering his hand. The cold, hard glass kept us from touching.

> *Bob splayed his manacled hand flat against the glass partition in a sign of greeting. I pressed my hand against the partition, covering his hand. The cold, hard glass kept us from touching.*

The six of us spent the next two hours talking. Bob's voice came through a tinny speaker in the partition. We all, including Bob, shared soda pop and snacks. We cried together. I briefed Bob on his current legal situation, which was grim. I told him that Governor Graham had reached a new low. "When you turn down the pope, that is cold!" I said.

Five heads snapped toward me.

"What did you say?" Bob asked, his surprised voice thin and tinny through the speaker.

I had assumed they all knew about Pope John Paul II's intervention on Bob's behalf. Clearly not. I told them all I knew about it.

"Joe," said Bob, now smiling, "that is an answer to my prayers. I had prayed that the Holy Father would intervene. To me, it matters less that the governor turned him down than that my church has done all it could for me. That's what matters. I'm grateful."

Toward the end of our three-hour visit, we sang hymns and prayed together. But Bob stopped us in the midst of our informal service. "I don't want this to be a downer," he said. "It's getting too sad. As serious as this is, I want us to end in a way that's uplifting for us all. There's a lot to be grateful for. Let's think of that and celebrate it."

Over the course of the three-hour visit, Bob had come full circle emotionally. Whether it was the news of the pope's action or the grace of the Holy Spirit, Bob was transformed. He was composed. Now he was leading us, shifting the tenor of our prayer and conversation.

When the time came for me to say goodbye, I pressed both my hands against the glass partition in farewell.

I waited while Margaret and one of the priests joined Bob for a contact visit. As their visit neared completion at 11:55 and they began to say their goodbyes, the door opened. A prison guard said, "The warden wanted me to inform you that there was a stay."

We were all stunned. We bombarded the guard with questions to which he had no answers. Bob was escorted back to his cell. I went directly to the prison administration building to call Scharlette in Tallahassee and find out how the stay of execution had happened. I refused to get my hopes up. I remembered how hard the governor and attorney general had worked to override the stays of execution for John Spenkelink. I was sure they would work just as hard to kill Bob.

Bob

When I reached Scharlette, she laughed and said, "We got a stay from Judge Godbold."

"Why? And for how long? Will they still try and kill him tomorrow?"

"For some reason, Anderson [the dissenting judge on the panel] wanted a poll of all the judges on the circuit, but apparently this had not been communicated. That's a request that must be honored, so the judges must be polled about the panel's decision. Our lawyers don't think this can be done overnight."

"Scharlette, I thought this was already before the Supremes."

"So did we all," she said. "But it's still in the jurisdiction of the Eleventh Circuit."

As we spoke, I could see through the window that the extra shift of guards brought in for the execution was leaving the prison. Clearly, the prison authorities had called it off—there would be no execution at 7:00 a.m.

I hurried back to the prison to tell Margaret and the priests what I had learned. Then I met with reporters outside the prison. When, emotionally drained and physically exhausted by the day's events, I returned to my motel room, there was a message to call the office in Tallahassee. Doug Magee, my friend from seminary and a member of PAX, asked, "Joe, can you be here for the civil disobedience we've planned for the cabinet meeting tomorrow?"

My spirits sank. "Doug, you know it's a three-hour drive back to Tallahassee. I wouldn't get in until almost four in the morning. After the day I've had, do you really need me?"

"Over two hundred people turned out at First Presbyterian Church to hear Dan Berrigan read the pope's message to Governor Graham. Berrigan called for protests of the execution. He also called upon Governor Graham to reconsider Bob Sullivan's situation. The plan is to build on the momentum of today's events and make a strong statement of protest on Tuesday."

171

I asked Doug to hold the line and turned to Bruce Robertson, who had been my chauffeur from Tallahassee. Would he drive me back now, in the middle of the night, while I slept in the car?

He would.

"Doug, I'll be there. What time?"

"We're meeting at the office at 8:30 in the morning."

The middle-of-the-night drive from Starke to Tallahassee reminded me of the late-night journeys while we were trying to save John Spenkelink. Those memories haunted me as the miles rolled by, but finally adrenaline and emotional turmoil gave way to exhaustion, and I dozed off.

After another two hours of sleep at Bruce's house, I joined fellow protestors at the Florida Clearinghouse office. We formed a plan: Dan Berrigan and other PAX members would stage the mock execution in the cabinet meeting room during their meeting. Bob Gross, Jimmy Lohman, and I would don black executioner's hoods and point fingers of responsibility at the governor as the mock execution unfolded. The "dead" body would be laid at the feet of the governor and the cabinet members.

We entered the cabinet room under the watchful eye of security guards. We each found a seat in the area where we had arranged for the action to occur. We waited for Governor Graham and his cabinet to enter.

Reporters and photographers swarmed the entrance leading to the dais as members of the cabinet entered and sat behind a long, curved table. Governor Graham walked in at about 9:10 and stopped to answer questions from reporters about the postponed execution. He said, in effect, "I'm concerned about the continuing delay and the effect it must be having on the men on death row, especially Bob Sullivan."

"Can you believe that?" I whispered to Dan Berrigan, sitting beside me. Dan just shook his head.

172

Then the governor walked to his chair in the middle of the table and asked everyone to stand for the invocation. With all heads bowed in prayer, a small-town Baptist minister indulged us in a display of civic religion, asking the Lord to "strengthen those in leadership, especially in these times of grave decisions."

"Bullshit!" Father Berrigan whispered loudly.

Each time the minister called on God to bless these officials, one of whose acts we considered to be ritual murder, Berrigan stage-whispered "Bullshit!" I admired his courage and agreed with his sentiment, but I hoped he wouldn't be removed before we could complete our civil disobedience.

Mercifully, the prayer ended and everyone sat. As the governor read the first item on the agenda, the protestors sprang into action. There would be no "business as usual" for the governor and his cabinet this day.

One of the PAX members covered her head with a black hood. Dan and the other PAX member grabbed her by the arms and dragged her down the aisle toward Governor Graham and his cabinet. She screamed, "No! Please no. No! *No!*"

Dan yelled, "We're going to execute you. It's the law! It's the law! It's the law!"

When they had dragged the hooded woman to the front row, Bob Gross jumped out of his first-row-center seat. Dan shoved her into the seat and tied her down with imaginary straps. The other PAX member threw an imaginary switch, and she convulsed in her chair. Three times he hit the switch. Three times she quivered and arched her body as the imaginary killing charge of electricity coursed through her. She collapsed in the chair. Dan untied the straps and threw the limp body at the feet of Governor Graham.

Then Bob Gross stepped forward, his head now covered by an executioner's hood. He read the official decree of death and threw the paper at the governor's feet, near where the apparently lifeless body still lay crumpled on the floor. A profound silence hung in the room.

Governor Graham sat straight, rigid in his chair, his face betraying no emotion. He seemed determined not to let this action move him. Apparently, the security guards had been ordered not to respond to acts of peaceful resistance. No one interfered with the mock execution.

Dan picked up the limp body and carried her out of the cabinet room. The remaining four protesters remained in our seats, black hoods over our heads, and extended our arms to point our index fingers directly at Governor Graham, emphasizing his responsibility. We sat there silently as the cabinet meeting began, and the governor tried to carry on as though nothing had happened. After about fifteen minutes, we protesters all rose and left the room together.

We met back at the office, jubilant that we had carried out our guerrilla theater—and relieved that we weren't in the Leon County jail!

Gradually we came down from our emotional peak and focused once again on Bob Sullivan's legal situation. We hoped the stay of execution would take us past the week during which the death warrant was in effect. Twenty-eight hours was all we needed.

Tired as I was, I decided to return to Starke and the Florida State Prison. Chuck McVoy, an elder in Bruce Robertson's church, offered to drive Bruce and me to Starke. I was grateful and relieved. Bruce and I were both too weary to get behind the wheel of a car. As we were getting ready to leave at about 4:30 p.m., I made one last call to the Florida office. Jimmy Lohman answered the phone and gave me the bad news: The entire Eleventh Circuit Court of Appeals had declined to hear Bob's case. The stay of execution was dissolved.

Bob's lawyers had been ready for this. They had already filed legal papers with the US Supreme Court, but none of us held out much hope for that appeal. We anticipated the worst. It reminded me of John Spenkelink's situation.

We were on the road on the way to Starke when the radio gave us the news: "The United States Supreme Court has denied Bob Sullivan's appeal. He will be executed in the Florida State Prison at 10:00 a.m. tomorrow." I knew with painful certainty that this time they would kill Bob.

At the prison, I was cleared by security and headed straight for the visiting room. I felt calm and desolate as I went in to visit Bob Sullivan for the last time.

Margaret Vandiver and the three priests were already in the visiting room. I greeted them and turned to Bob, placing my open hand against the glass opposite his. It was a cold and sterile substitute for a handshake or an embrace, but it was all we were allowed in a noncontact visit with a man who had only hours to live.

Bob was composed. He told us he had seen the mock execution on the national evening news (NBC) and was pleased and grateful for that demonstration. He had also read news accounts of the service Dan Berrigan had led at First Presbyterian Church in Tallahassee. He was thankful for the people who had rallied around him in his hour of crisis.

As the six of us talked, our conversation transcended talk of legal battles and executions. It rose to a spiritual plane where, as Bob said so well, "My death is a victory." Bob had been transformed in his final twenty-four hours. He had integrated the reality of his upcoming execution with his genuine Christian faith so that he now saw his execution in that light. Bob kept us buoyed through the evening, joking, sharing stories, expressing his deep appreciation for what had been done for him and for the friendships that had endured through the years.

One of the priests suggested that we read Psalm 62. I looked it up, and we listened as the priest read it:

For God alone my soul waits in silence;
from him comes my salvation.
He alone is my rock and my salvation,
my fortress; I shall never be shaken.
How long will you assail a person,
will you batter your victim, all of you,
as you would a leaning wall, a tottering fence? . . .
Once God has spoken;
twice have I heard this:
that power belongs to God,
and steadfast love belongs to you, O Lord.
For you repay to all
according to their work.
(Psalm 62:1–3, 11–12 NRSV)

The psalmist was writing as if he had our situation in mind! The only succor we had was from God, just as the psalm recounted. The politicians had decided to sacrifice Bob at the altar of the god of political expediency. Governor Graham was the man of "delusion," from verse 9 of that psalm, who believed that it was his right to play god and decide who would live or die, to feign omnipotence in the name of civic duty and political power. As the psalmist put it, God would "repay to all according to their work."

After the reading of the psalm, Bob and I talked through the glass partition. I realized how much I would miss him. My eyes brimmed with tears as I fought to keep the upbeat mood he so clearly wanted to maintain.

"What do you think my epitaph should be?" he asked me.

It was a question I wasn't ready for. "Bob, that is a personal decision. I wouldn't begin to advise you about it."

He nodded, and our conversation moved on to other things.

But a few minutes later, he said, "I've got it. How does this sound—'The cause is just.'"

"I think that is an excellent epitaph," I said.

The six of us huddled together as best we could, divided by the glass partition. We prayed for strength, for the grace of our Lord. Bob prayed for those who sought his death, especially Governor Graham and Attorney General Jim Smith.

When we'd finished our prayer, we sent for some food. In an informal Communion, we broke bread and drank soda pop and orange juice. Bob Sullivan ate with the relish of a man who enjoyed food and knew he would have no need of it the next day.

It was time for two of the priests and me to leave. Margaret and the other priest would remain for a contact visit with Bob. The priest would stay the night outside Bob's cell.

The others moved away so I could have a moment of private conversation with Bob before leaving. "Bob, I haven't told anyone else on death row this, but I regard it to be true of you. I think you are dying the death of a Christian martyr. You have triumphed through the strength of the Spirit in circumstances designed to conquer you. You have provided a witness to all of us of the power of reconciliation. You have been able to pray for Bob Graham and Jim Smith. I know I should pray for them too, but right now I am too full of anger. I pray that my anger will subside, and that the reconciling presence of the Spirit will reside in me as it does in you.

"Your witness has been powerful, not only to those of us here but to many. The letters you have written to folks all over the world, the interviews you have given to newspapers and television, the presence you have shared with the other men on death row—those things have been, and will continue to be, a powerful beacon shining in this darkness surrounding us. I want to thank you for being my friend."

His eyes moist with tears, Bob responded—and as I heard his words through the staticky speaker, I wondered who was ministering to whom. "Joe, I'm worried James might be lost without me. I knew this was coming, and I tried to wean him to greater independence, but I don't know if he can make it." His gratitude, his thanksgiving, his encouragement overwhelmed me. His final concern was that I make sure that a fellow death row prisoner with mental retardation was taken care of and nurtured after Bob was killed.

I agreed to see to it. We pressed our hands on the glass in a parting gesture.

A guard was at the door waiting to usher us out. His grim face indicated that, on this night, he bore no message of reprieve.

* * *

I called Scharlette Holdman, who told me that the US Supreme Court Chief Justice Warren Burger, like Governor Graham, had chastised Bob Sullivan's lawyers for dragging out his stay on death row. We saw our efforts as trying to save Bob's life, but according to Burger, these delays caused emotional suffering for the prisoner. I was appalled. The people involved in moving the gears to kill Bob were actually criticizing those who fought to save him. In a total inversion of reality, we were the ones causing him unnecessary suffering. Really? What irony! This was an example of the most malevolent action coming from those who believed they were doing no harm. That certainly described Chief Justice Burger and Governor Graham, who expressed their "concern" for the feelings of the condemned while killing them.

I had discussed Governor Graham's similar comment with Bob. Bob had been actively involved in his own legal appeals, and he continually thanked his lawyers for their work and support. As he put it, "It's *my* ten years on death row, and if anyone should be upset with the lawyers it should be me, not Graham." Or, a few days later, Burger.

Bob

At Scharlette's request, Bruce and I drove to Jacksonville to deliver some legal papers for a last-minute appeal to be filed. By the time we made it to Jacksonville and dropped the appeal in the lawyer's mailbox, it was 4:00 a.m. We looked for a restaurant to have breakfast, and then lingered over it, watching dawn light the sky. Our conversation meandered, exhaustion reducing us to talk that required little thought but kept us awake.

Breakfast over, we drove back to Starke, arriving at about 7:00 a.m. After a shower and a short rest in the motel room, we drove to the prison around nine o'clock. I made a statement to the press and then joined the protesters for a worship service in the cow pasture across from the prison. When the service ended, we all turned to face the prison and waited. It was 9:45 a.m. Bob Sullivan had fifteen minutes to live.

A white hearse drove into the prison grounds.

Memories of Bob swept over me. I thought of his friendship with James Hill, the death row prisoner Bob had asked me to look after. Hill was a twenty-five-year-old whose psychiatric evaluation revealed him to have the emotional age of eleven. His severe retardation made it difficult for him to understand his environment. Sometimes forgetting to take his medication, he suffered epileptic seizures. During one seizure he had broken several ribs. Bob had taken James under his wing, arranged to have James placed in the cell next to him, taught him to read and write, and helped him adjust to prison life. James looked to Bob daily for advice and help. He could not grasp the reality that the state was about to kill Bob.

In our visit on that last night, Bob had told me, "I got a handcuff key and made sure they caught me with it. That sent me to the punishment wing, Q wing, away from James. My not being there with him forced James to deal with death row on his own. He has to learn how—he'll have to cope with it himself after I am gone."

This was a typical action for this man the state of Florida was about to kill in mere minutes. Whatever had happened ten years ago, whether Bob Sullivan committed the crime or not, was no longer the central issue. Bob was a caring, giving, deeply spiritual human being with a lot to offer the world. It was cruel and insane to kill him.

Minutes later, the reporters passed the word that Bob Sullivan had been electrocuted. A short while later the hearse, gleaming white in the Florida sun, emerged from the prison gate. I was tired, spent, and numb.

We drove back to Tallahassee. By the time we reached the office, it was deserted. Everybody had gone home to collapse. I left a note on the door telling Scharlette of a memorial service organized for Bob in Gainesville. Then I went to Bruce's home.

I called my office in Nashville and retrieved messages. Several reporters had called. I returned those calls and went to bed. November 30, 1983, had come and gone. The state of Florida had killed Bob Sullivan.

I flew home to rest and relax with Becca. Then I focused on Robert Wayne Williams, whose execution was scheduled for December 14 in Louisiana. I dearly loved Robert Wayne and his family. I prepared to journey to Baton Rouge and Angola prison.

CHAPTER TWELVE

Ongoing Trauma

ON JANUARY 25, I returned to my trauma therapist. We did EMDR and discussed the traumatic experiences I'd encountered working with the condemned. After we'd relived several stories of friends I'd lost to state killing, she said, "You have a gift. You help people die well."

"I would rather that they live," I said.

> ## "You have a gift.
> ## You help people die well."
> ## "I would rather that they live,"
> ## I said.

She nodded. "I know. But that is beyond your power, and even beyond the power of the lawyers. Instead, you are the one there at the end, either with the condemned or their families.

"Look at Ed Zagorski. You agreed to be with him on death-watch. And ended up doing two deathwatches with him. You talked to Kelley at Ed's request, and she filed the legal papers that resulted in his choice of dying: electrocution. Your constancy with him, meeting with him week after week during the summer, hearing his story, brought you so close together. You midwifed his dream about Laurie. When he shared that with you, you told him it seemed more like a vision. By saying that, you validated his experience. He took it with him to the electric chair. You actually got the TBI in there at the end so Ed could tell them about the bodies.

"You were the one person he could rely on through the entire ordeal. Everyone else fell away for one reason or another. You were his brother."

Yes, I could see all of this. But those things had an emotional cost, and that was what brought me to her. "It was like my two hands were clasped together," I said. "We had become that close. Then someone amputated one of those hands, and suddenly I had only one hand. I felt alone, angry, hurt, abandoned, devastated, bleeding—and there was no one to talk to about this. The defense team had evaporated, and it was just me. No one who hasn't lived this reality can understand, no matter how hard I try to explain it to them, because it is too surreal. Only those who have gone through this horror can hear me. They're the only ones who won't flee from the trauma."

It was as if I had put all my emotions in a container, locked it down tight, and then hidden it high up on a shelf in a closet so I could be present for Ed and meet his needs—just as I had done with every one of my friends who were executed. I was focused on the other, not myself. To some extent, this hyper-alert state served me well in terms of navigating my survival during the deathwatches. In Ed Zagorski's case, it allowed me to function despite the horror of what we were experiencing, and even to accomplish things Ed needed and desired. The unavoidable cost came later, after I had passed his ashes on to others.

That cost is what brought me back to my psychiatrist on January 28. I described how the meds seemed to be working. I had been able to take a two-mile walk with Becca in a local park the day before. I still had bad days—but not bad weeks. He told me, "If you have three bad days in a row, email me and we'll increase the medication." It seemed like a good plan.

> ## *It was as if I had put all my emotions in a container, locked it down tight, and then hidden it high up on a shelf in a closet so I could be present for Ed and meet his needs—just as I had done with every one of my friends who were executed.*

Until the bottom fell out that afternoon. Suddenly I was as low as I had ever been, as low as I felt I could go. But I decided to hold to the three-day plan. Fortunately, I arose on the twenty-ninth feeling better. But then the sadness returned on the thirty-first. It seemed to be random. I could see no trigger. Where did the sadness come from? It would just suddenly appear.

My trauma therapist and I met on February 1. She asked me where I felt my sadness. I didn't have to think: "In my head, behind my eyes. And in my chest." She nodded.

We spent that session in a long discussion of the cost of my working with the condemned. She reminded me that, twenty years before, I had been involved in the case of a death row prisoner living in a delusional world that was quite real to him and helped him navigate death row. I spent several hundred hours with him over the years. In order to understand how he had arrived at this mental state, I interviewed his family. In doing so, I had found the "meaning maker" or "truth teller" who provided the necessary insight into the family dynamic so that I could grasp how my prisoner friend had reached cloud cuckoo land.

"You were able to get that family to talk," my therapist said.

"It felt natural," I said. "I really liked them."

"And that is the point," she said. "They *felt* that you cared for them, so one of them felt safe enough to step up as the meaning maker, to tell you what you needed to know to understand the fantasy in which their family member lived."

Fortunately, on federal appeal, the state psychiatrist who had testified against that prisoner at trial acknowledged that he was truly delusional. That testimony effectively stopped the express train to the death house for him.

"Becca says I can talk to anyone," I said. "I suppose that's because I really like people. I'm interested in them." I paused and thought. "Of course, that's true only when I'm feeling okay."

Our two-hour session ended with EMDR.

Three and a half days went by in which I felt total sadness. On the night of February 2, I emailed my psychiatrist, telling him I needed to increase the medication. He tripled the amount of antidepressant I was taking.

In the waiting room for a routine doctor's appointment two days later, images of Ed Zagorski flooded my mind. The body in the crematory, the ashes at my feet in the car as Becca drove away from the crematory, the deathwatches—it all rolled through. *God*, I prayed, *I hope this medication kicks in soon.*

*   *   *

One of my friends on death row called me. His mother had died after a prolonged hospitalization. Over twenty years before, I had helped him obtain a pass to attend his grandfather's funeral. Of course, it was a different set of actors working for the state now, but I told him I would try to get him to his mother's funeral. He had a visitor forward all the information about the visitation and the burial. Nothing involving death row is quick or easy, and all of this took several emails and phone calls. Finally, I had what I needed and submitted the request. I was not hopeful.

Compared to much of what I've done for prisoners, these tasks were simple. Even so, the effort of performing them exhausted me. All I had done was gather information and forward it to the Tennessee Department of Correction. But afterward, I crawled into bed, spent.

"What does that exhaustion tell you?" my trauma therapist asked.

"It tells me how far I have to go in my recovery if responding to a solitary request like that wore me out. You told me to avoid situations of controversy, such as arguments or disputes. You were right. I just no longer have the mental strength to survive in situations like that." It seemed I couldn't do the smallest task related to death row.

The TDOC denied the prisoner's request, by the way.

At this session, we began the EMDR with me imaging the most traumatic scene about Ed as if it were happening today. The scene I envisioned was Ed pretending to writhe in the electric chair as he sat in his blue plastic chair across from me. He was making a joke, but it had burned itself into my mind. (Of course, no one writhes in an electric chair—they are too tightly bound with brown leather straps.)

My mind started with that image, and after that I let it go where it would as I did the rapid eye movement. Every now and then, the therapist would stop and ask me to return to that image. "What do you see?" she would ask. This went on for quite a while—I lost all track of time. When I returned to Ed's image one final time at the end of the exercise, he was no longer in the blue chair. He was sitting with me and smiling. I explained that to the therapist and said, "I was honored that Ed invited me to share his last hours, not once, but twice. An absolute honor. And as difficult as the last few months have been, I am glad I did it."

In our next session, my therapist asked about my childhood. I summarized for her my growing-up years, moving around North Carolina. My parents were educators. My father became a high school principal in Jonesville, North Carolina. My mother taught high school English. But when I was seven years old, that "normal" family life was shattered by my father's fatal heart attack. Kay, my sister, was almost four. George Z. Ingle was forty-two years old when he died in the winter of 1954. My therapist requested I share the experience of my father's death. She thought it "might provide a template for how I spent my adult life working with the condemned."

CHAPTER THIRTEEN

Robert Wayne

IN THE SPRING of 1982, I drove through a Black neighborhood in Baton Rouge, Louisiana, searching for the home of Rose Williams. When I found the house and knocked on the door, Rose opened it. I introduced myself. Rose's clear eyes and unlined ebony face gave the appearance of a woman considerably younger than her fifty-three years. She smiled, extended her hand in greeting, and invited me inside.

"My mother made some tea cakes in honor of your visit," Rose said. "Won't you have some?" I readily agreed, and she disappeared into the kitchen. In her absence, I surveyed the room. Above the couch hung a beautiful photograph of a man with a serious expression and searching brown eyes. His face was clean shaven and tranquil. I recognized the son of the woman I was visiting: Robert Wayne Williams, who lived on death row at the Louisiana State Penitentiary at Angola.

Directly across from me was a smaller picture of Robert Wayne. He was smiling in this one, and he wore a mustache and goatee, the look I knew well. The picture was inserted into a burnt-tip wooden-match frame, which I assumed Robert Wayne had handcrafted and given to his mother. Adjoining the picture was a small mirror framed by the matchstick foldout. The carefully constructed folder was a common sight since many prisoners used the wooden matches for various hobby crafts—or at least they had at one time. This picture folder must have been several years old, since the warden of the Louisiana State Prison no longer allowed matches to the men on death row.

In my ten years of work throughout the South for reform of the criminal legal system, I had met numerous families of prisoners, both Black and white. My initial education about race had come first through my mother and subsequent schooling in the public schools of North Carolina, then living in East Harlem while in seminary and visiting the Bronx House of Detention. Those experiences had shaped me to begin my work with prisoners regardless of race. Almost every family I visited was hardworking and not well off. Rose Williams fit that description. She worked the night shift as a nurse's aide in a local hospital and often went a week or more without a day off. Yet as she came back into the living room carrying a tray with the tea cakes and coffee, serenity emanated from her. My colleagues in the Louisiana office of the Southern Coalition on Jails and Prisons had spoken of her admiringly, in almost reverential tones.

As Rose and I conversed about her son over cakes and coffee, I was immediately impressed by her concern for not just Robert Wayne but all of his fellow prisoners on death row at Angola. She was a caring and humble person with a deep sense of God's call on her life. She was a lay minister in the Church of God. I had the distinct notion that this woman was going to do all in her power for her son and everyone else on death row at the Louisiana State Penitentiary at Angola.

We talked until midmorning. I knew Rose must be exhausted from the previous night's work at the hospital. I prepared to leave to visit her son and others. She asked if we could close with a prayer. I nodded.

The prayer Rose spoke was not for herself or her son. Rather, it was for me and my work with death row prisoners at Angola and across the South. I felt a sense of genuine grace, and my soul was lifted. As we held hands during the prayer, I knew that I was in the presence of a woman who had been touched by God. After Rose prayed, I offered a prayer for Rose, for Robert Wayne, and for others on death row at Angola. We said "Amen," and I left to drive the back roads to the Louisiana State Penitentiary.

In my ten years of work throughout the South for reform of the criminal legal system, I had met numerous families of prisoners, both Black and white.

* * *

I had come to know Robert Wayne Williams through his friend Tim Baldwin, whom I'd befriended during his near-execution in the spring of 1982. Tim spoke warmly of Robert Wayne, and I began to include him on my visiting list at Angola. Robert Wayne was in many ways a counterpoint to Tim. Tim was white and Robert Wayne was Black. Tim was an older convict, almost forty-two when he arrived on "the Row." Williams was only twenty-seven when he came to Angola. Yet they shared a fierce independence and a concern for everyone on death row.

A joint project Tim, Robert Wayne, and I shared was putting together a lawsuit over the barbaric conditions on Louisiana's death row. Such basic amenities as electric lights in the cells were being denied the death row prisoners. We chose this course after my overtures to the warden had been flatly rejected and conditions remained intolerable.

Robert Wayne Williams, along with Ralph Holmes, had robbed a drugstore in Baton Rouge. Robert Wayne was carrying a shotgun and shot and killed the security guard, Willie Kelly. Robert had had no intention of shooting anyone. This is one of the common crimes that results in someone receiving the death penalty: a robbery-murder while under the influence of drugs.

Slim, as Robert Wayne was nicknamed by prisoners on the Row, delighted in the visits of his family on the weekends. His face creased into a big smile whenever he discussed his three daughters and son, who visited him often. The children scampered about the visiting room while Robert Wayne visited with other members of his family through the wire mesh screen separating them.

Robert Wayne Williams was an example of the difference a good lawyer could make in a death row case. In the summer of 1983, he was being defended by the director of the Southern Prisoner's Defense Committee (a law project SCJP had created in an effort to address the lack of lawyers for prisoners in the South). Although Robert Wayne's petition was denied by the US Supreme Court in July of 1983, quick work by his lawyer prevented a new execution date from being set by filing a rehearing petition. This meant the petition would not be decided until the fall. Even with able representation, I feared for Robert Wayne. The Supreme Court decisions regarding the death penalty that summer could hasten his execution. I had no illusions concerning his chances through clemency because the Republican governor, David Treen, was running for reelection. Robert would be used as a pawn in a political game, and weighed against political ambition, his life would be forfeited. It would be the "Vote for me, I'm tough on crime" gambit.

After the US Supreme Court denied a rehearing, the trial court judge set Robert Wayne's execution date for October 26—three days after the gubernatorial election but before the inauguration, so no matter who won, Governor Treen would make any clemency decision. Although Robert Wayne had lost by a 4–3 vote in the Louisiana Supreme Court and 6–5 in the Fifth Circuit Court of Appeals, the substantial dissents indicated the strength of the case. Yet I was worried that after the Supreme Court's *Barefoot* decision over the summer, successor habeas corpus petitions such as Robert Wayne needed might not be well received.

I stayed in touch with Robert Wayne and his mother, Rose, throughout the month, then journeyed to Louisiana on Saturday, October 22, to be with them. After settling into a friend's house in Baton Rouge, I scheduled a visit with Rose the next day. The execution date of October 26 was uncomfortably close.

On Sunday, Rose had an extended visit at the prison, so it was evening by the time she made the forty-five-minute trek back to Baton Rouge. I arranged to see her after supper.

Rose and I talked about the impending execution and decided that she needed to go see Governor Treen. We would simply drive to the governor's mansion and ring his doorbell. As we bundled up against the chilly night, I gazed around the small house and the family that had come together at this time of peril. Before we left, Sister Mary, an ordained minister in the Church of God, as Rose was, asked if she could pray. Soon a small circle gathered about Sister Mary as we bowed heads.

As a native of North Carolina and a resident of Tennessee, I had heard some prayers in my time. Yet the fervent, eloquent focus of Sister Mary overpowered me. All my worries disappeared as her words caressed my soul. When she finished, I was calm and prepared for any eventuality. As I glanced at each face in our prayer circle, I saw that everyone had been moved by the prayer. I thanked God for the blessing of being with such people.

Rose, two of her children and their spouses, and I set off to meet Reverend Pitcher of New Prospect Missionary Baptist Church, who had volunteered to accompany us to the governor's mansion. We arrived at the church at what we thought was the conclusion of their Sunday evening service. Rose went in to get him but returned quickly. "They're still going on. They're getting ready to have Communion, and I think I'll join them."

I decided to go with her. We walked into the church together and sat in a pew.

As the only white person in the building, I must have seemed out of place to the members of the congregation. Even so, I was welcomed as a brother in the faith. We sang a hymn, witnessed a baptism, and partook of Communion. As I listened to the joyful singing, observed the warmhearted fellowship, and shook hands with members of the church at the conclusion of the service, I was grateful that I had joined Rose rather than waiting in the car with the others. The Spirit was moving on this night in Baton Rouge, and I felt greatly comforted despite the impending reality of Robert Wayne's killing.

Reverend Pitcher joined us, and we drove to the governor's mansion. It was a beautiful, white-columned building. Governor Huey Long had built it with the intent that it would look as good as Mount Vernon, President George Washington's home. A camera peeked down at us from the porch roof as we rang the bell.

A young man with a holstered .38-caliber handgun opened the door. "I'm the Reverend Joe Ingle, and this is Robert Wayne Williams's family along with Reverend Pitcher. We would like to see Governor Treen to talk about Robert Wayne Williams's situation."

The young man replied, "You have a stay of execution. It came at 7:23 tonight."

I was too surprised to be anything but matter-of-fact: "Do you have any details?" I asked.

"Only that the Fifth Circuit Court of Appeals gave the stay."

I thanked him and we walked back to the car. As soon as we slid into our seats, I cautioned the family about becoming too excited before we'd had a chance to talk to the lawyers. I had seen stays of execution dissolve quickly. We drove back to the house amid building excitement.

Robert Wayne's grandmother met us at the door. "It's hallelujah time! It's hallelujah time!" she said, clapping her hands and rocking back and forth. A big smile lit her face. As the children, teenagers, and adults mingled, hugged, smiled, and gave thanks, it truly was hallelujah time.

Robert Wayne received the news of the stay of execution about an hour after he had been moved to the death house. He called us, and for the next forty-five minutes, we took turns speaking to him on the phone.

The next morning, I caught a bus to New Orleans, where John Vodicka, a colleague who worked in the SCJP New Orleans office, met me at the bus station. We drove to the Fifth Circuit Court of Appeals to pick up a copy of the *Williams* decision. Reading it, my heart sank. Clearly, the stay of execution was temporary. The Fifth Circuit had denied all the legal issues but concluded in a final paragraph that since the appeals did have a substantial basis, and the US Supreme Court had not clearly delineated the parameters of some of the issues, a stay of execution should be granted. Robert Wayne's counsel could appeal the decision to the entire Fifth Circuit, which could carry the case well into next year. When I returned to Nashville, I wrote Robert Wayne a note expressing my relief, although the long-range picture did not look promising.

On November 7, the US Supreme Court vacated the stay of execution and took the highly unusual step of reaching into the Fifth Circuit, where the *Williams* case was under consideration, and denying all the issues. This meant the trial court could move immediately to set a new execution date for Robert Wayne. The message from the court was loud and clear: a majority of the justices wanted to get on with executions, and Robert Wayne Williams was the first person they could use to alert the lower court judges in the country of their new temperament. Clearly, this was no longer the same US Supreme Court that had abolished the death penalty in 1972.

I discussed the situation with Robert Wayne's lawyer over the phone. Our only hope was in mounting another clemency bid with Governor Treen. I decided to call a friend in Prison Fellowship who was an acquaintance of Governor Treen. I also talked to a prominent New Orleans lawyer about Robert Wayne. Both of these actions were long shots, but we could leave no stone unturned. I was not optimistic.

The morning of November 9 brought the announcement that Governor Graham of Florida had signed Bob Sullivan's death warrant. The execution date was set for November 29. Governor Graham had read the signals from the Supreme Court in the *Williams* case and pushed harder for executions in his state.

A week later, I learned that Robert Wayne was scheduled to be killed on December 14. Events were picking up speed. If Bob and Robert Wayne were both killed, it would bring the total number of executions to four for the year—the highest number of people executed since 1976—and presage what was to come. Each of the four would become mere statistics in news stories on the return of the death penalty in America. But they were my friends. The words of the forty-fourth psalm welled within me: "We are being massacred all day long, treated as sheep to be slaughtered."

This time, more people were organized in the effort to stop Robert Wayne's execution. Unlike Bob Sullivan, Robert Wayne had a supportive family who would be with him through the ordeal. My role was simply to support the family. I arrived in New Orleans on

Robert Wayne

Monday, December 12. The execution was set for the early morning hours of December 14. Although still reeling from Bob Sullivan's killing in Florida on November 30, I wanted to be with Rose and the family. I disembarked from the plane and hitched a ride with reporters going to Baton Rouge to cover the story.

The clemency board had voted against Robert Wayne, 3–2. That decision, the latest and last one-vote-margin loss for Robert Wayne, would seal his fate. A young Black man tried before an all-white jury in Baton Rouge (not exactly a city free of racism), who had no prior felony convictions, a man with a court-appointed lawyer, a man with a serious drug dependency at the time of the robbery, was going to be the first person killed by the state of Louisiana in the electric chair since 1961. In Louisiana, which billed itself as the "Dream State," the dream was now a nightmare for the Williams family.

A young Black man tried before an all-white jury in Baton Rouge (not exactly a city free of racism), who had no prior felony convictions, a man with a court-appointed lawyer, a man with a serious drug dependency at the time of the robbery, was going to be the first person killed by the state of Louisiana in the electric chair since 1961.

I visited with Rose on the evening of the twelfth. She and other family members had visited with her son most of the day. He was in good spirits despite the gravity of the situation. All the family members were leaning on Rose for support. Her quiet strength transmitted to everyone.

Rose and I went to the home of the leader of the local chapter of Amnesty International, who had spent an hour with Governor Treen earlier in the day. As I listened to him recount the meeting, I had to check my cynicism, born of painful experience. He actually felt that the governor was truly wrestling with Robert Wayne's case and was especially troubled by Robert Wayne's inadequate defense counsel at trial. I had been down this road too many times before. I had met with Governor Graham in Florida, worked to get Bishop Gray to visit Governor Winter in Mississippi, tried to move Governor Clement in Texas, and had in some of those cases heard of the same "concern" now supposedly expressed by Governor Treen. In each situation, the decision in the end was a political one, despite "much concern." I had no doubt it was about to happen again. Morality and religion don't get people elected. Being tough on crime does. Robert Wayne was doomed.

I telephoned Rose early Tuesday morning, as we had agreed. She really wanted to try to find a member of the victim's family who would make a public statement on Robert Wayne's behalf. Since the victim's son had asked for the death penalty at the clemency hearing, I had little hope of changing his mind. But I promised Rose that I would try to find a member of the victim's family willing to speak out. It sounded virtually impossible at this late date, but if Rose wished it done, I would give it my best effort.

I spent the entire day searching for a member of the victim's family to speak out. I was unsuccessful. Frustrated, I headed back to the home of the Amnesty International leader, anxious to find out whether Governor Treen had issued a statement regarding

Robert Wayne

Robert Wayne's case.

He had. Governor Treen had said that he would not intervene. He made the usual statements: the review in the courts was fair and complete, and it was not his prerogative to overturn the court's decision (blatant deceit, since he was empowered with clemency). In what was becoming a routine and nauseating exercise of Southern governors, he tied Robert Wayne's execution to the will of God.

The governor's statement infuriated me. He *could* intervene; he had the authority to do so. And his closing remarks about the "Invisible One" who would judge us all sent my anger above the boiling point. In no way, shape, or form could I discern the hand of God in this unmitigated evil of state-sanctioned murder. Robert Wayne was on death row because he had a poor trial lawyer, suffered from drug addiction, and was Black.[1] Invoking God's blessing for this action was the epitome of hypocrisy and duplicity; it denied the real factors of race and class. Of course, Governor Treen hadn't been willing to meet with Robert Wayne's family and tell them this to their face. For him, it was just politics as usual.

I was already at the Williams house when the family returned from their last visit with Robert Wayne. When Rose Williams, along with her children and mother, returned, she looked worn and weary but still determined. She had just seen her son for the final time.

We talked briefly about Robert Wayne. He had spent his last hours ministering to his family, encouraging them not to be burdened by his death. He had special words for each one, trying to speak to their pain and sorrow. His words were a precious gift to them, a gift no one would be able to take away.

The family had decided to participate in the protest organized against the execution. Although we would be late, they were

---

1 The latest study on racial discrimination in the administration of the death penalty, the Baldus study, was included in *McCleskey v. Kemp*. It was conclusive and uncontroverted. As a Black man tried before an all-white jury in Baton Rouge, Robert Wayne was a classic example of racial discrimination.

determined to join the vigil outside the governor's mansion. The worship service was over by the time we arrived, but the picket line was long, strung out down the sidewalk. Rose shook the hand of everyone there, thanking them for coming out on this cold night to bear witness against her son's killing. After half an hour of silent protest, a number of us journeyed to Angola for another protest there.

The family decided to make a statement to the press. I was glad—I wanted the citizens of America to glimpse the strength and suffering that this family displayed in the midst of the ordeal they were enduring. The media assembled just outside the main entrance to Angola. The prison was illuminated by floodlights as well as television camera lights. When Rose made her statement, one sentence lodged in my mind: "If God can forgive, why can't man?" When she was done speaking, Rose and other family members joined the protesters in a circle of more than fifty people. We held hands and proceeded with our planned religious service. Under the very nose of the god of death, we gave testimony to the Lord of life.

At about 11:45 p.m., the service ended in a moving and appropriate manner, with each of us remembering Robert Wayne and sharing a story about him, expressing thanksgiving for him.

As we huddled in the cold, the wind whipping our scarves and coats, we received unexpected news: a temporary stay of execution. The governor had extended Robert Wayne's life for one hour so that his defense counsel could rush its papers to the US Supreme Court.

We adjourned to the automobiles for warmth, and watched and waited. I sat in the car with Rose, thinking, *Oh God, be with Robert Wayne. Let him know that this delay is a result of our desperate fight to keep him alive. Give him courage for an extra hour.* I had no hope that the Supreme Court would actually do anything about this case. They would certainly not be concerned about what hurt this prolonging of the inevitable inflicted on Rose, the family, and Robert

Wayne. I told Rose not to be hopeful about the stay because it was simply a last-ditch effort.

At 1:15 a.m., a minister emerged from the prison gates. He looked shaken. He had been with Robert Wayne until he was killed. The minister's presence outside meant the state had accomplished what it had set out to do—Robert Wayne was dead.

Rose quietly cried in the car, and I peered into the Louisiana darkness. We prayed. There was little to say. Robert Wayne was gone.

We arrived back at the Williams house around 3:30 a.m. I was exhausted, emotionally drained, numb from the experience. The love and closeness of the Williams family burst forth in grief. Weeping echoed throughout the house; I watched helplessly as one relative after another broke down in tears. Rose moved from person to person, beginning with her mother and then on to other family members, comforting each of them. She refused to be overpowered by her own grief. Rather, she ministered to the pain of others. I was astounded at her strength and her gentleness. She had a word or a special comfort for each person. Simply watching her renewed my own strength.

The next day, I came back to the Williams house. Although it had been only a few hours since I left, I was struck by the transformation in the mood of the family as I greeted them. They had united, through Rose, to endure the loss and persevere in the work against the death penalty. The abiding Christian faith at the core of this family held them together like glue.

I could sense Robert Wayne's presence in the room as his children and their cousins scampered about our feet. Although there was grief, there was some gentle teasing and an occasional burst of laughter. The children reminded us of the simplicity and endurance of God, even in the face of the power of the state. They stood as visible examples of a determination to continue no matter what havoc was visited on their family.

Time passed swiftly amid the love of this family, and soon it was time to bid Rose and her clan farewell. One of the friends of the family volunteered to take me to the bus terminal, so I hugged my friends and promised to stay in touch and to continue together in our fight against executions. I gave Rose a long hug and spoke in her ear: "I love you, Rose."

As my bus rolled through the Louisiana countryside and onto the causeway across Lake Pontchartrain, I could still hear the piercing wail of Robert Wayne's aunt shortly after he was killed: "No more Robert Wayne! No more Robert Wayne! No more Robert Wayne!"

* * *

After I finished sharing my story of Robert Wayne with my therapist, she looked at me long and hard. John Evans in Alabama and Jimmy Lee Gray in Mississippi, whom I had also mentioned to her, had preceded Bob Sullivan and Robert Wayne Williams as friends I lost to the executioner in 1983. Of course, for me it felt as if Bob and Robert Wayne were part of a series of executions stretching into 1984, when James Hutchins in North Carolina, James Adams and David Washington in Florida, Tim Baldwin in Louisiana, and Velma Barfield in North Carolina were killed by the state. I loved and lost them all.

After a significant pause, my therapist spoke: "You are held together by this framework of faith. I don't understand it. I am not religious myself. Yet this knits you together amid all of the trauma. I don't know how it works, but clearly it does for you. When you speak of them, it is as if you resurrect them. They are a part of you."

CHAPTER FOURTEEN

The Victims

ELSEWHERE, SUCH AS in the next chapter, I describe how I coped with trauma by watching crime and detective television series. They required little serious thought and proved a much-needed distraction from myself and my emotional struggles. However, I was fully aware as I watched those stories that they are not an accurate portrayal of the criminal legal system. They serve merely to entertain, not to educate viewers about the facts of criminal prosecution.

The real criminal legal system is often trauma inducing. The retributive punishment model pays little heed to the needs of either the victim or the offender. It has sent 2.2 million people into prison and kept 6.8 million under state control through such vehicles as parole and probation. It has left millions of victims with unmet needs in its wake.

The retributive justice model we currently use is poorly equipped to deal with the human experience of suffering. Rather, it wishes to place blame. The system is designed to mete out punishment, not actually understand or work with the real issues behind being a victim of crime. This has resulted in 2.2 million people being incarcerated, 3,000 on death row, and very little assistance to victims.

The criminal legal system is an abject failure at addressing human suffering. Indeed, it creates more suffering as it seeks to inflict punishment on one category in the system (offenders) and neglects those in the adverse category (victims). This adversarial process that supposedly arrives at deserved punishment is helpful to no one except those who find careers in it or build prisons.

The real criminal legal system is often trauma inducing. The retributive punishment model pays little heed to the needs of either the victim or the offender. It has sent 2.2 million people into prison and kept 6.8 million under state control through such vehicles as parole and probation. It has left millions of victims with unmet needs in its wake.

Is there any way out of this destructive system? Fortunately, there is a tried-and-true model that has been developed in this country since the 1970s: restorative justice. As the name indicates, the object is not to cast blame or punish. Rather, it's a victim-driven process wherein the victim is able to express the harm done to her, after which a restorative solution is worked out between the parties. This requires that the victim and offender meet with a trained facilitator—first separately, then together. As much time as necessary is spent with the victim to be sure she is heard and her feelings are honored to enable her to express how she would like the offender to repair the harm done to her. The facilitator then meets with the offender. He is encouraged to explain why he did what he did. He is also assisted in seeing the victim as fully human and to understand how she feels about his harming her. The offender often details what was going on in his life that led to the crime. Then the offender is asked what he would consider to be restorative.

The parties are introduced by the facilitator. The victim shares her feelings about what happened—the sense of loss and fear, the wondering if it will happen again. The offender responds not by excusing his behavior but by explaining it. He also expresses remorse for what he did. The victim then responds, and a dialogue ensues. The facilitator's role is to ensure that the victim will not be revictimized verbally in the process. After each party has communicated fully and believes she or he has been heard, the parties discuss what is appropriate to repair the harm that has been done. At the conclusion of the meeting, a document is written that describes the understanding reached and the next steps to be taken in restoring the victim.

Howard Zehr pioneered restorative justice (RJ) in America. He began with juveniles in Elkhart, Indiana, in the 1970s. As a result of Howard's work, RJ has spread throughout the country and internationally. His book, *Changing Lenses*, provides a detailed description of the history and development of RJ and is considered the bible of the RJ movement. The title literally describes the need we face as a society. It is imperative to change the way we view crime. Our lens should be restorative, not retributive. Howard taught at Eastern Mennonite University for years, and has advocated RJ across this country and abroad. Eastern Mennonite is home to the Howard Zehr Institute, which continues to develop restorative justice throughout the world.

Restorative justice accounts for the needs of people as it deals with crime. None of us reach adulthood as a blank slate. We all experience some degree of suffering that is etched on our souls. RJ provides a means of addressing this reality.

Restorative justice accounts for the needs of people as it deals with crime.

* * *

The story of Hector and Susie Black and their adult children provides an example of a modified restorative justice effort in what was originally a death penalty case in Atlanta, Georgia. In June of 2001, I met Hector and Susie at a national Murder Victims' Families for Reconciliation Conference in Boston, a conference for families who had lost a loved one to murder. There were families from one end of the spectrum to the other: some had forgiven the murderer and visited him in prison, others had no desire to see the person who had killed their loved one. But all participants were united in the view that the response to murder was not more murder in the form of execution. This remarkable gathering of souls was trying to release the desire for vengeance in their hearts.

Even though the organic nursery farmed by the Blacks outside Cookeville, Tennessee, is a mere ninety miles away from my home in Nashville, it took a conference in Boston for the Blacks and I to discover each other. They were attending the conference in the wake of their daughter's murder in Atlanta the previous November.

We found a place to sit, and there we discussed Patricia's murder. The timing of the meeting was serendipitous. I had recently completed a weeklong training at the University of Minnesota led by Mark Umbreit: "Victim/Offender Dialogue in Serious Crimes."

I explained to Hector and Susie that if they chose to pursue initiating dialogue with Patricia's murderer, I would work with them through it.

The Black family was willing. But there were several obstacles we would need to address before fully exploring their feelings about Trisha's murder. We agreed that, upon our return to Tennessee, I would come to their farm and begin the process.

The Blacks had already met with the district attorney, Paul Howard, who wished to pursue the death penalty. The Black family had mixed emotions about that. Trisha's murder had occurred in Atlanta, where the Blacks had lived previously, and District Attorney Howard told the Blacks that, if they didn't seek the death penalty, the man who raped and murdered Trish would be eligible for parole in seven years. This was one of several misconceptions conveyed to the Blacks about the legal process in which they were enmeshed.

Our meeting took place around the kitchen table in the Blacks' farmhouse. Hector and Susie were there, along with their adult children (all daughters), including one patched in by phone from the West Coast. The purpose of the meeting was for them to share their emotions about Trisha's murder.

It was a painful session—not only because the family's feelings were raw from the murder but also because family members had different ideas about the appropriate response. Hector and Susie did not want the death penalty, based on their understanding of the Christian faith. That didn't mean they didn't want Ivan Simpson— the murderer—punished. They just didn't want him executed. The Blacks' children had a variety of feelings, and once everyone stated them, we began an honest, heartfelt exchange. In the end, all of the family decided to adopt Hector and Susie's position regarding the death penalty.

"You've been given misleading information by the district attorney's office," I said next. "If we were able to get the district attorney to agree to prosecute without seeking the death penalty,

Ivan Simpson would receive a life sentence and probably never live outside a prison again."

After I'd explained how the system works and answered their questions, the Black family was clear that they didn't want a trial. A trial, with the accompanying media, would reopen the wound of Trisha's loss. Their preference was to proceed to a hearing with no trial.

It was my job to facilitate the wishes of the family, and I began by contacting the defense attorney, Susan Wardell, by phone. "Are you familiar with restorative justice?" I asked. When she replied that she was, I explained that this was a modified restorative justice approach. It would require her client to plead guilty.

"Joe," Susan said, "Let me explain some things about Ivan Simpson. He was born in a mental hospital. His mother had repeatedly tried to drown him and his three siblings—in fact, he witnessed the successful drowning of one of them. Another sibling had been comatose after a drowning attempt. Ivan had been raped and nearly strangled to death by a brother. He was diagnosed with psychosis and a dissociative identity disorder and treated for it, but at the time of Patricia's killing, he was off his medication."

As Susan continued, it became clear there would be no personal discussion between the Blacks and Ivan Simpson. "Susan," I said, "the district attorney is insisting on the death penalty, and yet the Blacks don't want it. How can we best deal with his opposition?"

She thought a moment, then said, "We could go directly to the judge."

We agreed on a strategy: I would have Hector write a statement for the judge and forward it to him through Susan.

I telephoned Hector and explained. He liked our proposed path forward. I asked him to draft a statement to be read in court and send it to me.

Hector's first draft was heartfelt but short. I encouraged and coached him over the phone, and after several drafts, Hector came up with an eloquent expression of the feelings of the family. We forwarded it to the defense lawyer to convey to the judge.

After receiving the letter, Judge John Goger summoned the district attorney and defense lawyer for a discussion of how to proceed with the case. Reluctantly, with the urging of the judge, District Attorney Howard agreed to a hearing and accepted the guilty plea.

The hearing was held in Atlanta on January 14, 2002. After convening the hearing, the charges concerning the murder-rape of Trisha were read aloud. Hector and Susie had been informed that they did not need to listen to the eight-count indictment, but they elected to stay for it anyway. This was hard for them, because there were details of the crime they hadn't known about until they heard the indictment read. Simpson had broken into the house. When Trish came home, he was hiding in the closet. When she opened the closet, he burst out and tied her hands behind her back.

"You need to put burglar bars on your windows," Simpson said.

His mental illness came up. Trish: "You need to take your meds."

Simpson: "Do you want to have sex?"

Trish: "I'd rather die first."

So Ivan Simpson killed and raped her.

When the indictment had been read, Judge Goger made clear to Simpson he would receive a sentence of life without parole if he pled guilty. The judge asked him if he had agreed to plead guilty to the charges. Simpson then pled guilty to each count. The sentence was imposed for each charge: life without parole.

Then Judge Goger invited the reading of victims' statements. Michelle, Trish's cousin, read one. Then it was Hector's turn. He approached the judge. The following is taken from his notes written shortly after the hearing and printed in an article by Amanda Hoffman.[1]

1 Amanda Hoffman, "What Can Love Do?," *Friends Journal*, June 1, 2002.

"I have a couple of photographs with me. I would like to show them to you so that you would have an idea of who we are talking about here." One was of Trish the summer before she was killed . . . the other picture was Trish when she was a child maybe 10 years old. The judge thanked me, and he looked at them. I could tell that I was dealing with a real human being who knew how much this pained me. That was a comfort.

Then I read my statement:
My name is Hector Black. This is my wife, Susie. We first met Patricia Ann Knuckles when she was a thin and neglected child of eight, living with her mother and younger sister, in Vine City. We moved to Vine City in 1965, working in a tutoring program established by the Atlanta Friends Meeting. Although Patricia was not our child by any claim of birth, she was our child by every claim of love. She lived with us and became a much-loved part of our family. She was one year older than the oldest of our three girls. Because my wife is hand-icapped and mostly confined to a wheelchair, our children all learned to help with basic chores. Trish also took her turn—it somehow put her on an equal footing with our other children. I can still hear her scolding her sisters when they tried to avoid helping. Trish always took her responsibilities seriously. She became our daughter, our children's sister. We watched for 35 years as she grew into a beautiful woman, beautiful in every way. We thought we were helping her, but as can happen when we give, we received far more from her than we gave. She was God's gift to our family.

She was not ashamed of her background. Rather,

she used this experience to help others—especially children in the Emmaus House program on Hank Aaron
Drive, and in the Public Library in Kirkwood where she
worked with children such as she had been. She wanted
to make the world a better place. And she did. [Trish
parlayed her degree from Fisk University to a job at the
library in Kirkwood.]

November 21, 2000, was the darkest day our family
has ever experienced. Our lives, mine and the lives of
my wife and three daughters, were changed forever as we
learned, piece by piece, what had happened to Patricia,
our daughter, our children's beloved sister. Every day we
struggle to try and remember the beautiful and loving
person she was and drive out the horrible thoughts
and visions of how she died. Many times, it seemed as
though the darkness was stronger than we were, that this
terrible deed was so burned into our lives that we would
never be able to celebrate who Patricia was, how much
we loved her, and how much she loved us. I thought God
had abandoned me.

About three months after Trish was killed, I
remember looking at the table we had set out with
photographs of her from different periods of her life. The
one that caught my eye was a picture of her at about 9
years of age looking back over her shoulder with such a
sweet expression on her face, and I smiled for the first
time remembering her as a child. It was the first time I
had looked at those photos without a stab of pain.

We were not abandoned. The love of family and
friends surrounded us . . . a friend had given us a book
for people who have suffered loss. [In] it was a saying:
"All the dark news in the world cannot extinguish the

light of a single candle." Those words helped us. They are written on her headstone in the little graveyard on our farm where Trish is buried, where my wife and I hope to be buried.

I know that love does not seek revenge. We do not want a life for a life. Love seeks healing, peace and wholeness. Hatred can never overcome hatred. Only love can overcome hatred and violence. Love is that light. It is that candle that cannot be extinguished by all the darkness in the world. Judge Goger, that is the reason we are not asking for the death penalty. I know that 'Forgive our trespasses, as we forgive those who trespass against us' were not to be empty words. I don't know if I have forgiven you, Ivan Christopher Simpson, for what you did. All I do know is that I don't hate you, but I hate with all my soul what you did to Patricia.

My wish from my heart for all of us who were so terribly wounded by this murder, including you Ivan Christopher Simpson, is that God would grant us peace."

When I was reading that last line, I was looking directly at Ivan Simpson and he lifted his head. Our eyes met. Tears were streaming down his cheeks. Both of us were in great pain. It was one of those rare moments when raw wounds and pain will strip away all pretense, all falseness. It was somehow a moment of terrible beauty that I will never forget.

There was such torment in his look. How could I hate this man? Certainly, I could hate what he had done, but hate someone who had suffered so much as a child, someone tormented by what he had done and filled with remorse?

The Victims

After Ivan Simpson was given a life sentence without parole and was being led away, he said he wanted to say something. He turned and faced us and said twice, with tears running down his face "I am sorry for the pain I have caused. I am so sorry for the pain I have caused."

I could not sleep that night. I kept thinking about what had happened. It was as though a weight had been lifted from me. I knew that I have forgiven Ivan Simpson, that I must write him and tell him this, and encourage him that his life is not over. That he can help others in prison, perhaps especially in prison, where there is so much darkness. This forgiveness, like everything before, does not seem to be something I have "won" or "earned." It is a gift of grace.

In a letter postmarked January 23, 2002, Ivan Simpson responded to Hector Black's letter:

Dear Mr. Hector Black/family

I first want to say God bless you all in all things. Second, I have to go straight to the point. I know God has forgiven me, you have forgiven me, but I can't forgive myself, not yet anyway. I have so much anger at myself right now it's unbelievable.

This hardness I have against myself is a sort of strength to help others, that I draw from when I'm witnessing to others about God's love for them. From the moment I came to realize the hurt, pain, grief I've caused others from the evil act I did, I do things for others now. I used to pray for myself but I realize it's not about me, it's about giving God all the glory. I only pray for others now. I like writing. I should be asking is it alright to write you all?

I don't know the level of love Ms. Patricia had, but if it's anything like your example of it, it's great. God comfort you all, in everything. Feel free to ask me anything you like. . . .

Even if I forgive myself one day, I will always be remorseful. Maybe that's my thorn in my side, like the Apostle Paul had, that always reminded him about God's Love. I read Psalms 88 every day for the rest of my life. I used to hear God speak to me all the time. I used to see his Spirit in my dreams and visions, but I guess after I did what I did he took away his touch from me, for right now I miss his voice. I heard it in you that day in court in the way of compassion. I'll talk later.

Take care.

Sincerely,
Ivan Simpson

After months of negotiation, Hector Black was able to arrange a visit with Ivan Simpson in prison. As of this writing, Hector is ninety-five years old and unable to travel the distance to continue his visits with Ivan. They still correspond.

CHAPTER FIFTEEN

February 2019

MY PSYCHIATRIST'S TRIPLING the amount of antidepressant I was taking pulled me out of what I feared could have been a fatal slump. Alas, that improved mood was not a permanent state. I would have good days, then bad ones—the proverbial emotional roller coaster. Then one of our leading volunteer death row visitors died unexpectedly. Ronny had led the effort in Murfreesboro, Tennessee, recruiting a number of volunteers. He had helped me lead the orientation training for VODR the previous October. And now he was dead. I attended his funeral at St. Paul's Episcopal Church in Murfreesboro. Too much death. I seemed to be drenched in it.

Too much death. I seemed to be drenched in it.

Sometimes I think of the sadness as a sack of cement in my chest. It just weighs me down. In order to distract myself, I continued, and continue still, my viewing of mystery series via streaming. This, along with the intellectual stimulation of courses at Vanderbilt and elsewhere, prevents me from sinking into melancholia for too long.

When I awake, I don't know whether I'll be up or down.

Nor do I know how long whichever state I am in will last. It's random. I have no control over it. After a couple of good days in mid-February, I felt myself sinking in the late afternoon of the seventeenth. Fortunately, my old friend from college days, Bob Pryor, drove down from Kentucky to pay me a visit. As we talked that evening, he said, "If you don't want to talk about your condition, that's fine. But if you would like to talk, I'm here." I took him up on his offer. We talked through the whole history from Billy Irick to Ed Zagorski. I also shared the impact of PTSD on my life. It was a needed time of sharing.

Bob fed the birds for me the next two days, and they flocked to the too-long-empty feeders. My favorite, the red-bellied woodpecker, was one of the first arrivals.

After Bob left, I went to buy more birdseed. It was raining, as it did most of February—a local record of 13.5 inches for the month. The guy who waited on me offered to carry the bag of seed to the truck. When we reached the truck, I said, "Put it in the front seat." He did. I thanked him.

Suddenly, I felt overwhelming gratitude for this act of service. Someone, a stranger, had offered to do something for me, and had done it. Routine? Sure. Part of his job? Yes. But for me, that simple act of kindness from a stranger produced a sense of power I had not experienced since Ed's killing in November.

$$* \quad * \quad *$$

To combat my ennui, Becca and I, along with our friends Ed and Ran Ying Porter, planned a trip to northwest Tennessee. Our destination was Reelfoot Lake, where we planned to observe the bald eagles. We had planned to stay for two nights, but flooding from the record rainfall forced us to leave a day early. Fortunately, we were traveling in the Porters' car. The flooded creek, two feet deep, that we had to ford to get to and from our cabin would have been too much for our Prius.

There are approximately forty nesting pairs of eagles at Reelfoot Lake throughout the year. Plus, migratory eagles come through in January and February, so in those months there are literally hundreds of eagles around the lake. Two park rangers guided us and a few others through Reelfoot's extensive waterways. We rode in a white van. We saw bald eagles nesting and flying, and took pictures whenever we could.

At one point, as we drove across a levee, we saw just below us at the bottom of the levee's slope a magnificent bald eagle feasting on a kill. He was surrounded by eight turkey vultures, which kept a distance of ten to twelve feet from the eagle. The vultures were respectfully waiting for the eagle to finish the kill before they dined on the remains. We probably observed the eagle for fifteen minutes, noticing the blood on his beak as he ripped the kill apart. Finally, he pulled off a large section of red meat from the carcass and soared into the sky. He flew straight up at first, then circled behind us to a stand of trees across the levee road. He lit in the large eagle nest where his mate awaited, and he transferred the hunk of meat from his beak to hers. He then turned outward to keep watch while his mate dined as she warmed the eggs underneath her.

We had a good Southern meal for lunch and drove back to Nashville. Only a week later, we heard that a mudslide had rolled across I-24, the road we drove that day, and left so much loosened earth and rock on the road that one lane was closed for a month.

* * *

As February progressed, I developed a new state of consciousness. Rather than up or down, I was in-between. I nicknamed it being in a Tweener state of mind. It feels as if I'm on the cusp, capable of going either way and with no control over which way I go. As the Tweeners increase, the down days diminish. Perhaps this is progress, but if so, it is still completely random.

Reading Camus's *Myth of Sisyphus* prompted me to think about my situation. Camus gives new meaning to the Greek myth of Sisyphus pushing the boulder to the top of the mountain, only to have it come down again. Sisyphus is condemned to repeat that process infinitely. For Camus, the story of Sisyphus is the story of modern humanity, which must repeatedly make the effort even if it is hopeless.

In my case, I feel as if the boulder is rolling me. As I roll up the mountain and down the mountain, I am hanging on for dear life, not wanting to lose the boulder. In the Tweener state, which I occupy as I write this, the boulder has come to rest on a ledge, halfway up the mountain. I can do nothing but wait to see which direction I am taken.

In his novel *The Plague*, Camus provides insight into the human condition. The fictional doctor, Rieux, trying to treat patients suffering from the plague, understands the situation. The priest is lost in his piety and orthodoxy, unable to see what is taking place. A third party, Tarrou, initiates a conversation with the tired doctor:

"After all—?" Tarrou prompted softly.

"After all," the doctor repeated, then hesitated again, fixing his eyes on Tarrou, "it's something that a man of your sort can understand most likely, but, since the order of the world is shaped by death, mightn't it be better for God if we refuse to believe in Him, and struggle with all our might against death, without raising our eyes towards the heaven where He sits in silence?"

Tarrou nodded.

"Yes. But your victories will never be lasting; that's all."

Rieux's face darkened.

"Yes, I know that. But it's no reason for giving up the struggle."

"No reason, I agree. Only, I now can picture what this plague must mean for you."

"Yes. A never-ending defeat."

Tarrou stared at the doctor for a moment, then turned and tramped heavily toward the door. Rieux followed him and was almost at his side when Tarrou, who was staring at the floor, suddenly said:

"Who taught you all this, doctor?"

The reply came promptly.

"Suffering."[1]

I really can't imagine how anyone could more aptly describe my situation. My plague, state killing, seemed to be "a never-ending defeat." True, I have witnessed victories—some innocent people freed, some condemned friends now paroled—but for the most part it has been a never-ending defeat. Or what Nietzsche termed the "eternal recurrence of the same." And like Rieux, I have not learned this in the abstract world of theology, as did the priest, but through "suffering." It is only by being in relationship with those who suffer that suffering becomes the teacher.

Fyodor Dostoyevsky, a man condemned and almost executed, described the condition of the people I have worked with in prisons and jails: "The prisoner himself knows he is a prisoner; but no brands, no fetters will make him forget he is a human being."[2] Yet society in its madness inflicts cruelty on the condemned and

---

1 Albert Camus, *The Plague* (Everyman's Library, 2004), 115.
2 Fyodor Dostoyevsky, *Notes from a Dead House* (New York: Vintage Classics, 2015), 111.

imprisoned as if to justify its own existence through their suffering. It is literally insane that the US keeps a total of 2.2 million people locked up and has executed well over a thousand of them since 1976. And most US citizens don't seem to care. And if they don't care, then they won't act, and they certainly don't suffer because of their lack of action. Indeed, it is fools like me who suffer because of our experiences with the condemned. As the Christian ethicist Reinhold Niebuhr once put it, if you are a Christian, "you can be a fool for Christ or a goddamned fool."[3] Camus understands this madness and articulates it clearly. It does not matter that Camus is an agnostic and I am Christian—the heart of the matter is suffering and how we respond to it. That sense of connection is one reason Becca and I visited Camus's grave in Lourmarin in the South of France in May of 2018.

My plague, state killing, seemed to be "a never-ending defeat." True, I have witnessed victories— some innocent people freed, some condemned friends now paroled—but for the most part it has been a never-ending defeat. Or what Nietzsche termed the "eternal recurrence of the same."

---

3 A story told by the Reverend Bruce Robertson, a student of Reinhold Niebuhr at Union Theological Seminary, to Joe Ingle on a drive from Tallahassee to Starke, Florida.

February 2019

Albert Camus was a "Blackfoot" (a disparaging term for those French who grew up in Algeria rather than France). He knew first-hand of the dispossessed, the poor, and the power of the state. He experienced suffering as a child before attaining his adult literary heights (he won the Nobel Prize for Literature). This gave him a perspective that Jean-Paul Sartre, author of *Being and Nothingness* and other works, could not attain. Sartre, the Parisian sophisticate, could not bring himself to critique the Soviet Union's Gulag. The following exchange illustrates the chasm between a leftist who could not condemn the horror of the Gulag and a man who understood what Jesus meant when he talked of "the least of these, my brothers and sisters," no matter the political system.

Sartre: "Like you, I find these camps intolerable [the Gulag], but I find it equally intolerable the use made of them every day by the bourgeois press." On another occasion, Sartre said, "As we are not members of the Party, it was not our duty to write about Soviet labor camps; we were free to remain aloof from the quarrels over the nature of the system, provid[ing] no events of sociological significance occurred."[4]

*   *   *

At a John McCutcheon concert, I bumped into my trauma therapist during the intermission. As we chatted, she mentioned she would be leaving the country on vacation for a month.

"Whoa," I said. "I'm losing my therapist for a month?"

She said, "I thought I told you. We're leaving for the month of March."

I shook my head. This was news to me.

"Joe, you'll be fine. You can make it."

And as I thought about it, I realized she was probably right.

---

4 Anne Applebaum, *Gulag: A History* (New York: Doubleday, 2003), 19.

A month ago, I would not have made it without her. Now, with the support of my psychiatrist and our plan for increased meds if I experienced three consecutive days of melancholia, I believed I could make it through March. Thank God we had come this far.

On February 26, I had lunch with an old friend. Billy Moore and his wife drove up from Georgia to speak at the local anti–death penalty meeting. Back in 1975, my initial visits with Billy had been at the Georgia State Prison at Reidsville, where he'd been on death row. We'd continued our visits when death row moved to the Georgia Diagnostic and Classification Center in Jackson.

Billy and I usually visited with our dear friend Warren McCleskey. We shared our lives, talked about their cases, and discussed what it meant to be a Christian. It was a precious friendship, which lasted until Warren was electrocuted in 1991. (For a detailed discussion of Warren's case, *McCleskey v. Kemp*, see *Slouching Toward Tyranny: Mass Incarceration, Death Sentences and Racism.*)[5]

As Billy; his wife, Donna; and I ate lunch, I was thankful this man was free and sitting across from me. I tried to block out that Warren could just as easily have been with us, since he was one of the finest people I had ever known, in or out of prison. But the state of Georgia had other plans for Warren McCleskey.

Although I didn't discuss with Billy and Donna the trauma I was suffering, simply visiting with Billy brought back images from Reidsville and Jackson. Reidsville, where they'd imprisoned MLK for protesting, and where the condemned, on their way to execution, crossed a landing that was open to the sky. The prisoner could absorb a final vista of the stars and moon before walking back inside to be strapped into the electric chair. Jackson, a brave new world of penology, was in its modernity in many ways worse. The prisoners I'd visited in those places, Billy and Warren and others, careened

5 Joseph B. Ingle, *Slouching Toward Tyranny: Mass Incarceration, Death Sentences and Racism* (New York: Algora Publishing, 2015).

through my mind. Those flashbacks knocked me off the ledge on which I was teetering. The boulder was carrying me back down the mountain.

* * *

Our dogs, Ink and Molly, both adopted as strays, are a real comfort and excellent companions. Ink, the German short-haired pointer, is a hunting dog. Her white coat is dotted with small brown spots and several large liver-colored spots. Her brown head and white muzzle highlight an inquisitive face.

Molly, although spoiled by us for ten years, had been terribly abused before she wandered up to our door as a puppy. Her tail had been broken in three places and had to be amputated. She had vasculitis and took three to four pills twice a day to combat that skin disease. Now, in early 2019, she became quite sick. She ate nothing and developed diarrhea. The pounds dropped off her. She would not leave her bed; we had to bring a bowl of water to her so she could drink.

After a four-hour examination, the veterinarian determined several things. Molly had a mass adjacent to her liver. A biopsy would be required to determine whether it was malignant. Her joints were full of arthritis. The vet gave us four medications, including one for pain and one for diarrhea. Molly was now up to eight pills twice a day.

Becca spoke the obvious: Molly was probably dying. But when she began to discuss the possibility of having her cremated afterward, I interrupted. "Honey, I can't handle this conversation. It brings back what happened to Ed. Let's take it one day at a time."

* * *

For Albert Camus and William Blake, the meaning of life was not found in theology or philosophy. Rather, it was found in the doing, the action. It is all about ethics. Camus had written his master's thesis on Saint Augustine but left that behind and explored the importance of action even if it has no ultimate meaning. Blake became a fierce critic of church and state, which were much the same in eighteenth-century England.

I could understand both Camus and Blake from my own experience. I had written my master's thesis, titled "The Path of Thinking," on Martin Heidegger while at Union Theological Seminary. At the same time, I was visiting the men in the Bronx House of Detention. It was that experience that drove me back to the Bible and inspired me to read it from the perspective of those on the bottom of society looking up.

When I left New York to come back South, I was a changed man. I had left philosophy behind. Instead, I was focused on the ethical life and how the Bible informed that life. The institutional church seemed not to understand this perspective, and I became critical of the church just as Blake and Camus had been. I realized I would never be at home in the church. I went into the prisons and jails to find Jesus and meaning.

My trauma therapist had once said, "The only way you could have done what you have over the years is to operate out of this religious framework. I don't understand that, but for you it has held you together and impelled you forward. I suspect that it holds you together still, even amid your current trauma." And she was right. I was experiencing PTSD as a result of my work with the condemned. Yet unlike Camus, my suffering had meaning. I read it in the letters and heard it in the phone calls from death row. Even when I was unable to feel it, I knew that my life had had an impact for my brothers and sisters behind bars. For over forty years I had been in relation with those our society deemed unredeemable and whom Jesus termed, "the least of these, my brothers and sisters."

* * *

February came to an end. The rains stopped, and a cold snap settled in to kick off March. My thoughts turned to Velma Barfield. Dear Velma. It was time to consider her life and death in depth with my therapist. She had been, for me, the final chapter of 1983–84. She was executed at Central Prison in Raleigh, North Carolina, the city in which I attended high school.

CHAPTER SIXTEEN

Velma

AS THE AIRPLANE circled on its approach to the Raleigh-Durham airport, I gazed at the familiar scene below. Eastern North Carolina was flat and green from pine trees and newly green hardwoods. Farmland stretched toward the horizon away from Raleigh, but there appeared to be considerably less farming and considerably more urban sprawl than when I graduated from high school in 1964, twenty years before. I'm sure the Chamber of Commerce would see this as progress, but I wasn't so sure.

Mom met me at the airport, and after hugs I drove us to her east Raleigh home where I took up residence in my old bedroom. Mom seemed to be doing well. Although she had resumed drinking after a ten-year hiatus, she was in good spirits. She and I talked about Velma Barfield, my reason for coming to Raleigh.

Velma, an absolutely delightful fifty-three-year-old grandmother, was a good friend. We had known each other since 1979. I enjoyed our visits. Thoughtful and concerned about those around her, Velma always left me feeling as if she had entertained me at home, showering me with the warmest of hospitality. Her home, however, was near downtown Raleigh on death row at the Women's Prison.

There was no doubt that Velma had poisoned her husband. At the time of his death, however, no one thought much about it.

Velma was a hardworking member of the Parkton, North Carolina, community. She shopped in the A&P grocery store, worked in the hosiery mill, and was a proud mother. She was just plain folk.

When her husband's family insisted on an autopsy, the truth came out. He had died of arsenic poisoning. Velma had fed it to him for months until he died. For the prosecutor, Joe Freeman Britt, who had sent more people to death row than any other prosecutor in the country, Velma was a witch who had to pay with her life. Although Velma certainly was not the witch that Prosecutor Britt portrayed, there were other murders in which she was implicated but for which she was not tried, including her mother.

I had been working with prisoners full-time since 1974, plus a year in seminary, with a focus on death row since 1975. Although I was continuing to learn more about human behavior, there was little that surprised me. Nor was I being manipulated by inmates such as Velma, as prosecutors would suggest when I testified on behalf of prisoners at their trial or sentencing hearing. Rather, visiting death row, I found myself dealing with broken people who, out of their brokenness, had shattered other lives. Velma Barfield was another example of this suffering.

In 1978, when this trial occurred, North Carolina's death penalty law was in its infancy. The US Supreme Court had upheld the death penalty in its 1976 decisions but had struck down North Carolina's statute because of its mandatory nature. The state legislature rewrote the law in 1977. It was under this new law that Velma Barfield came to trial.

Velma's trial lawyer was ill equipped to manage the case. He had neither the training nor the resources to do it properly. He hired no experts to examine his client's mental health and made no real investigation of her family. Velma was basically at the mercy of Joe Freeman Britt, and mercy was not one of Mr. Britt's better qualities. Rather, he possessed a ruthless political ambition to ride the death penalty issue to a judicial position. Velma Barfield was soon on death row at the Women's Prison in Raleigh.

I began visiting Velma in 1979. She needed a lawyer, and I found a good one for her, Dick Burr. Unfortunately, she was shackled by the woeful trial court record. Her lawyer would have an uphill battle to understand why Velma had done what she did, and then to present it to a court in such a way that intervention could perhaps save her life.

*   *   *

As I drove to the Women's Prison to see Velma, I lamented that, in all likelihood, she would be denied by the US Supreme Court that summer. If so, a last desperate round of appeals would be launched highlighting new evidence about her mental health. Dr. Dorothy Lewis from NYU had worked with Velma and uncovered abuse at the hands of her father. One chilling episode that stood out was when her father found her dog in the house against his instructions. Screaming at Velma, he stomped the dog's head with his boot, crushing it. There was sexual abuse as well.

I stopped first at the office of the warden, Jenny Lancaster. Jenny was very fond of Velma. Indeed, the entire prison staff seemed taken with her. In turn, Velma was very kind to them, knitting them various things. In our conversations, she referred to the guards as "the help." I had a good talk with Jenny about Velma's legal situation. Clearly, Jenny did not want to see Velma Barfield killed on her watch.

I was as fond of Jenny as I was of Sam Garrison, the recently retired warden at the men's prison in Raleigh, Central Prison. Both wardens represented the best of North Carolina in corrections. Jenny was obviously schooled in modern penology, but Sam was a good ol' boy who knew how to work with death row prisoners. Sam once stopped me as I was leaving Central Prison after a long day visiting death row and invited me into his office. He had his boots up on his desk and gestured for me to sit down. I sat and gazed at the large man from Morrisville who wore his hair in a crew cut.

"Joe, what do you think about the death penalty?" he asked.

Obviously, Sam already knew what I thought about the death penalty, so instead of answering I asked him, "How does executing someone make you feel, Sam?"

"How does executing someone make you feel, Sam?"

He gazed at me over the desk silently for a moment, then said, "You know, no one has ever asked me that before. They send these guys here and I make sure they're taken care of. They get food, clothing, medical care, and I get to know them and their families. Then one day they tell me to take them out and kill them. Put 'em in that gas chamber." Sam, a bear of a man, shook his head. "Doesn't make much sense. And you know, I've talked to these men. None of them gave a thought to the death penalty when they committed their crime. Not a one. It ain't no deterrent, that's for sure."

If there was such thing as a modern good ol' gal, it was Jenny. She ran her prison fairly, and her relationship with Velma was almost mother-daughter. I told her I would keep her posted on legal developments and went back to see Velma.

Velma was brought in without shackles in a long, matronly dress. We caught up on our families; she had some new pictures to show me of her children and grandchildren. The time seemed to speed by, and before I knew it several hours had passed. We always closed our visit with a prayer.

Velma was interested in her legal situation, but dispassionately.

She believed that her lawyer was doing a good job, and she liked Dr. Lewis—but what she really wanted to talk about was her family and her faith.

One of the ironies of Velma's situation was that she was being visited by Billy Graham's daughter. Velma's strong Christian faith developed in prison and brought her into correspondence with many people and a few visitors. Billy Graham might have actually talked to the governor on Velma's behalf, if his daughter requested it. The problem with Billy Graham, however, was that he was a man who'd spent his entire career as a court prophet to the powerful. He was a modern version of 1 Kings 22:1–37. He never spoke truth to power, as did Micaiah the son of Imlah in 1 Kings. Instead, he cozied up to power, currying its favor, as did the court prophets who spoke against Micaiah. There was not a war he did not bless, and while some sat in during the civil rights movement, he sat it out. I doubted he would lift a finger to help Velma, even if his daughter asked him to. Jesus of Nazareth summed these folks up: "By their fruit you shall know them."

I gave Velma a goodbye hug and left. Driving back to my mother's house in east Raleigh, I felt a cold dread well up inside me. My experience with the politics of killing told me that Velma was in a world of trouble. Barring a miracle, I feared she would be killed in the gas chamber by the state of North Carolina.

As 1984 wore on, I lurched from one killing place to another. In Florida, James Adams was killed on May 10. Alvin Ford came within hours of death before getting a stay of execution in late May due to his madness. David Washington was electrocuted in July. And through it all, Velma's case wandered to completion. As I'd suspected, she was denied by the US Supreme Court in the summer. A November execution date was set.

In the fall of 1984, the incumbent governor, Jim Hunt, was seeking to unseat the incumbent senator, Jesse Helms. The Democratic and Republican parties were spending a fortune battling for this seat; it became the most expensive race for the US Senate in the history of North Carolina. As Senator Helms played to the worst passions of the electorate through a withering television campaign, Governor Hunt's early lead evaporated. As a native of North Carolina, I knew all too well that our liberal veneer hid a racism that ran deep in the state. Jesse Helms had spent a political career tapping into it, and he exploited it to keep his seat in the Senate.

In the midst of this political bloodletting, Velma Barfield's plea came to Governor Jim Hunt, trying desperately to salvage his senatorial bid. Velma's execution was scheduled for two days before the election—a classic example of the politics of killing.

The Reverend Randy Taylor, head of the Presbyterian denomination to which Governor Hunt belonged, talked to him. I too was raised in the Presbyterian church, and I knew that the stance of the denomination was that it opposed the death penalty. Velma's lawyer made a clemency presentation to Governor Hunt, and Jenny Lancaster spoke eloquently for Velma's life. Indeed, she wept and begged Hunt not to kill Velma, enumerating the many positive contributions Velma had made at the Women's Prison. Although the governor gave no immediate answer, the answer was clearly blowing in the political winds.

The mantra of almost every Southern politician was *I support the death penalty*. It was symbolic, a sine qua non, a no-expense way of being tough on crime. It didn't actually do anything about the crime problem. During the years of the nationwide moratorium on executions, espousing support for the death penalty had no real-world consequence. But by 1984, it actually meant killing people. Clearly, it was a long shot that Jim Hunt would grant clemency in the midst of the political race of his life. As expected, Billy Graham did not request clemency, and Governor Hunt did not grant it. Rather, he made some gratuitous comments about Velma's victim, which was pandering at its worst. All that stood between Velma and the gas chamber was a last legal effort.

> *The mantra of almost every Southern politician was* **I support the death penalty.** *It was symbolic, a sine qua non, a no-expense way of being tough on crime. It didn't actually do anything about the crime problem.*

And concerning that final legal push, there was reason for cautious optimism. Lao Rubert, on Velma's legal team, had unearthed the fact that when Velma had suffered from depression, she was prescribed antidepressants by her doctor. Research had recently shown that certain antidepressants could precipitate a psychotic state in people who suffered the abuse Velma had endured. She could appear perfectly normal but in reality, could be profoundly altered by her medication. She might, for instance, poison those near her because her drug-induced psychosis made her terrified of them. This had in fact become a pattern in her adult life and was why she poisoned her husband, Stewart Taylor, along with two other family members. This issue was brought before Federal District Judge Dupree in Raleigh as we sought to gain a stay of execution to put on our proof.

Judge Dupree was quite conservative, but he issued a certificate of probable cause, indicating that the issue had merit. Next stop: the Fourth Circuit Court of Appeals in Richmond, Virginia. Dick

Burr, civil rights attorney Adam Stein, and I left Raleigh shortly after
Judge Dupree's decision was issued at 7:30 p.m. on October 30. The
hearing in the Fourth Circuit Court of Appeals in Richmond was set
for 8:30 a.m. the next day.

I was no stranger to this drive from Raleigh to Richmond. When I
was growing up, we had occasionally made the drive to visit Aunt Pearl,
Ma-Ma's sister, who lived there. And during the summers of 1966–
1970, I'd been a counselor at Camp Hanover, outside of Richmond
near the Cold Harbor battlefield. I had also lived in Richmond after
college graduation. So I knew this road like the back of my hand—
and a good thing, too, because I was exhausted, and Dick Burr was
napping from utter physical collapse. Reliving those early memories
of the road helped keep me alert through the autumn night drive.

The South is still a small place. One of the three judges on the
panel hearing Velma's appeal was Dickson Phillips, a former dean
of the University of North Carolina law school. Tom John was a
neighbor of mine and good friend in Nashville and had grown up
in Laurinburg, where I had gone to college. The Phillips and John
families were lifelong friends from the Laurinburg area. I was more
than an interested observer in the argument for Velma Barfield's life.
I knew Judge Phillips would recognize me in the courtroom.

The physical layout of the Fourth Circuit Court of Appeals
was a graphic display of power. The judges were placed high above
counsel. Counsel was in a pit, looking up at the judges. It was a
bizarre setting—but then this was Richmond, Virginia, the capital
of the Confederacy.[1]

Judging by their rulings, the Fourth and Fifth Circuit Courts
of Appeal were in a race to see who could be the most regressive
appellate court in the country on the death penalty. Given that
reality and the continuing restriction on raising issues such as the

---

1 Unbeknownst to me at the time, the judges would sing "Dixie" at their judicial conferences. When Chief Justice Rehnquist of the US Supreme Court addressed the conference, he
sang "Dixie" as well.

one discovered in Velma's case, the certificate of probable cause and possibly Dickson Phillips were all Velma had going for her.

The oral argument did not go well. Dick, representing Velma, was fatigued from the work and pressure of the last few months and had developed a tic below his eye from exhaustion. The judges were not receptive to his argument. Judge Phillips raised some questions that gave Dick an opportunity to expound, but it was clear that at least two of the judges were against us.

After the argument concluded, the clerk informed us that the decision would be rendered shortly, since the panel knew we were up against an execution deadline in about twelve hours. I found my college buddy Bob Brewbaker, and he allowed us the use of his law office conference room to wait. Dick, Adam, and I began drafting a possible certiorari petition to the US Supreme Court.

About four o'clock we received a call from Velma through Mary Ann Talley, a lawyer helping back in Raleigh. Velma made it clear that if there was no relief in the Fourth Circuit, she did not want to appeal any further. It was less than twelve hours to the execution and she didn't want another futile appeal hanging over her head. She needed to prepare herself and her family for death. With the utmost gratitude for everything that had been done, she gently made it clear that enough was enough.

The clerk of court told us the decision would be forthcoming, so we went back to the Fourth Circuit. The decision came at 5:00 p.m.: a 3–0 vote against us. As Velma had requested, there would be no appeal to the US Supreme Court. The state of North Carolina would kill Velma Barfield in nine hours.

Adam and I drove back to Raleigh. Dick, the lead lawyer, flew back with the attorney general's staff in the state plane so he could have a last visit with Velma.

Back in Raleigh, I joined the crowd of several hundred people gathered to protest Velma's killing. It was a quiet, contemplative community in the field outside Central Prison. I arrived about 10:00 p.m. and had an opportunity to visit with many of the people who had done so much for Velma. She had attracted quite a fine crew of people through her kindness and ministry over the past five years. We hugged each other, wept, burned our candles, and the night slipped away.

Shortly before 2:00 a.m. on November 2, 1984, a smaller crowd across the street, celebrators of Velma's killing, erupted in shouts and curses. They were separated from us by Western Boulevard, but they made their presence known as the hour of killing approached. Screams of "Kill the bitch!" and other hateful, spiteful epithets were spat into the night. They cheered mightily when the clock passed 2:00 a.m. I saw Velma's brother peel off from our group and go watch the celebrators. I doubt that any of them knew Velma. They just reveled in the killing. Her brother watched them for a while, then shook his head and walked back to us. A Department of Correction spokeswoman came out and made the official announcement of Velma's killing by the state of North Carolina.

Esse quam videri is the motto of the state of North Carolina. The Latin translates, "It is better to be than to seem." On this night and over the course of Velma Barfield's trial, imprisonment, and deathwatch, she had been caught in political factors that gave lie to the state motto. The politicians were interested in promoting their careers, *seeming* to do justice rather than doing it. The more admirable part of North Carolina stood in that field in silent protest, maintaining a vigil. Our vigil was in the tradition of Paul Green, the great North Carolina playwright. Green maintained a vigil by himself, a lone vigil, outside Central Prison on the night of an execution. Green, from the previous generation of witnesses against state killing, passed the lighted candle to our generation. Our collective vigil that night was offered in a spirit that united us to Velma and to the state's motto of being, not seeming.

Esse quam videri.

CHAPTER SEVENTEEN

Alvin

AS IF THE REST of the death row stories from 1984 weren't enough, there was one other that figured prominently in my trauma work with the therapist, a story that was etched on my soul. It involved a man who survived the state of Florida's attempt to kill him. My friend, the dear, demented Alvin Ford.

Governor Bob Graham preferred to sign two death warrants at a time. In 1979, it had been John Spenkelink and Willie Darden. In May of 1984, it was James Adams and Alvin Ford. The death warrant signings placed the two men in adjacent holding cells near the electric chair in Q wing of the Florida State Prison. James had a May 10 execution date and Alvin a May 31 date. I was close to each man.

During my last visit with James Adams, on the evening of May 9, he was concerned about Alvin. James told me that this death warrant, Alvin's second, had driven him stark raving mad, and James was worried about him. I told James I would help with Alvin, but first we needed to focus on James for what little time we had left. I prodded him to mentally revisit his childhood, and he recalled a time as a child when he'd almost died. He described the experience of leaving his body and looking down at everyone in the shack. Suddenly, it was as if someone had grabbed his ankles, and he was drawn back into his body. At the time of that conversation,

James ("Tennessee" as his death row brothers called him, since he hailed from Covington, Tennessee) was hours from electrocution, even though he had not committed the crime for which he'd been convicted. His memory of that childhood near-death experience would sustain him to the end. James was electrocuted at 7:00 a.m. on May 10. I went back home exhausted and numb, needing to rest and recover so that I could return to Florida to be with Alvin at the end of the month.

Governor Bob Graham preferred to sign two death warrants at a time. In 1979, it had been John Spenkelink and Willie Darden. In May of 1984, it was James Adams and Alvin Ford. The death warrant signings placed the two men in adjacent holding cells near the electric chair in Q wing of the Florida State Prison. James had a May 10 execution date and Alvin a May 31 date. I was close to each man.

* * *

Alvin

It felt strange to return to the killing ground of Florida in late May. I was reminded of my first trip back to the Florida State Prison after John Spenkelink was electrocuted in 1979. After John was killed, I had thought I was driving the rental car to Starke when suddenly I saw a sign proclaiming "St. Augustine, 30 Miles." I had driven away from the prison! My subconscious had refused to let me make the correct turn, probably trying to protect me from more pain. But in May of 1984, I was determined to drive directly to Starke from Jacksonville, with no side trip to St. Augustine—even though my feelings were very similar to those of June 1979. I was, in fact, experiencing the same powerful mental undertow I'd felt five years previously. I did not want to go on this final visit with Alvin Ford. But he was helpless, and those of us who cared about him had to be there to do what we could for him and his family.

Although I had witnessed Alvin's mental deterioration over the months, I was not prepared for the man I encountered on May 30 at the Florida State Prison. Alvin hadn't eaten since being moved to Q wing after the signing of his death warrant almost thirty days before. He was emaciated. Watching him as he sat in "the cage" awaiting our visit, I recalled the smiling young man I'd first met in 1979. The starving man before me, mumbling incoherently, eyes closed and then fluttering involuntarily, did not seem to be the same person.

Alvin's vocabulary hadn't changed since our last visit. "RS, pipe alley, destiny, Pope II"—a cascading whisper of indecipherable code that enabled Alvin to navigate the trauma of death row. All I could do was express my support, let him know he was loved, and listen to an unintelligible language from a man whose appearance suggested a starving apparition more than a dear friend.

A community of people had gathered around Alvin as he descended into madness. Larry Wallen, a professor at Florida State University; Gail Rowland, a paralegal; Margaret Vandiver; his lawyers; and me. His mother, Connie Ford, visited when she could.

And the guys on the Row were looking out for him, trying to help him as best they could. Two of them, Jacob Dugan and Elwood Barclay, sat on either side of him in the holding cage when Margaret, Gail, and I came to visit. They spoke to him gently, telling him everything would be all right.

All I could do was express my support, let him know he was loved, and listen to an unintelligible language from a man whose appearance suggested a starving apparition more than a dear friend.

"Here comes Gail, Margaret, and Joe," they said, "to see you." He sat in the corner of the cage, eyes fluttering, gaunt, being ministered to by his death row brothers.

We entered the colonel's room and asked the guards to bring Alvin in to join us. Alvin came in, handcuffed, and sat down opposite us. Once again, we began the painful process of trying to connect with him through the madness as he babbled incoherently.

Clearly, the news we had received late the night before had not penetrated Alvin's mind. After a roller-coaster ride in the appellate courts, the US Supreme Court had just given Alvin a stay of execution. That court had decided to take the case to determine whether it was constitutional to execute the insane in the United States. *Ford v. Wainwright* would become landmark constitutional law. The stay had come just hours before his scheduled electrocution.

As we sought to reach Alvin, to let him know the good news, the words of the psychiatric report done by the state's panel of mental health experts kept rising in my mind. That evaluation, which determined that Alvin was competent to be executed, contrasted starkly to the man mumbling before me. The psychiatrists, sworn to uphold the Hippocratic oath to do no harm, apparently thought the ethics of the oath did not penetrate the Florida border.

Yet as I gazed at Alvin, I believed that somewhere, deep inside, beneath the rambling nonsense, behind the vacant stare and fluttering eyelids, the Alvin I loved was there. I tried to focus on that person as I spoke: "Alvin, they are not going to kill you. They aren't going to kill you. You have a stay. Do you hear me? Do you understand?"

Gail would try to communicate. Then Margaret. We sat close to Alvin, held his shackled hands, and peered into those shuttered, fluttering eyes. But nothing we said or did appeared to penetrate the gibberish.

Finally, as the morning wore on, I stood. I looked through the glass windows to the larger colonel's room. The runners, prisoners themselves, were bringing the luncheon trays to the prisoners with visitors and were busy unloading their cart. I stepped outside the interview room, stretched, and looked at the trays. Acting on intuition, I asked the runner: "How about giving one of those trays to Alvin?"

He looked at me as if I were nuts: "Man, are you crazy? He hasn't eaten in a month."

I opened the door to the interview room, and the runner placed the food tray at Alvin's feet. "Alvin," I said, "this food is for you. First, we're going to pray." Gail held one of Alvin's hands and I the other, and Margaret linked Gail and me together. "Lord, we are grateful for Alvin's life. For the Supreme Court giving a stay of execution. Please help Alvin to feel your love, to know he won't be killed. Amen."

Alvin, without responding beyond his usual unintelligible rambling, leaned over and picked up the tray. He then began shoveling the food into his mouth with his hands, eating with the gusto of the starving man he was. Gail, Margaret, and I looked at each other with surprise. We sensed that Alvin understood about the stay of execution, and we wept tears of joy, rage, and relief. Alvin Ford would live beyond Florida's latest attempt to electrocute an insane man. Thank God.

"Please help Alvin to feel your love, to know he won't be killed. Amen."

* * *

Gail, Margaret, and I and other members of the defense effort for Alvin had a celebratory dinner at a local eatery. We laughed and cried, reviewing the story of working over the years with a man who had been driven into insanity by the machinery of state killing. Gail had a wicked wit and a wonderful repertory. With a hand puppet gowned in a black robe, she did a spot-on mimic of Justice Lewis Powell of the US Supreme Court. Gail could keep us in stitches for hours, and this time the comic relief was a plinth anchored to Alvin's survival of the death warrant.

On June 26, 1986, the US Supreme Court ruled in *Ford v. Wainwright* that the Constitution of the United States prohibited the execution of the insane. The 5–4 decision meant Alvin Ford would live indefinitely unless the state could make him competent through treatment. Then he could be executed. Justice Powell provided the key vote. Justice Thurgood Marshall is believed to have later said, "I did not think I would live to see the Court prohibit the execution of the insane."

Unfortunately for Alvin, he never came back from his descent into madness. Removed from the deathwatch area of Q wing and taken back to the "bug" area of Q wing where guys with mental problems were kept, Alvin lingered on death row. He carried on his monologue of madness. Of course, the state made desultory attempts to make him competent so they could kill him, but Alvin was too far gone to be reached.

Alvin Ford died in February of 1991 while on Florida's death row. I was enjoying a Merrill Fellowship at Harvard University at the time, a welcome break from the Southern killing ground. But I heard about the strange circumstances of Alvin's death in a telephone call from Margaret Vandiver.

Since the medical staff at the Florida State Prison regarded Alvin as a malingerer, they were in no hurry to come to his aid when a runner serving breakfast trays discovered Alvin unconscious in his cell. It took at least ten minutes to get a medical orderly to the cell and another thirty minutes to get a stretcher to carry him to the medical clinic. Then there was a ninety-minute delay before an ambulance reached the prison.

The arriving paramedics, unencumbered by the lack of concern suffered by the prison health professionals, quickly determined that Alvin's blood sugar was extraordinarily high and transported him to Shands Hospital in Gainesville. Two days later, on February 28, Alvin Ford died. Connie Ford, Alvin's mother, who had cherished her son through the ordeal of imprisonment and madness, did not even learn that her son had been hospitalized until she was notified of his death.

A strange symmetry emerged from the process of Alvin's disintegration into insanity. The young, sane Alvin had worked in the criminal justice system as a guard at Union Correctional Institution just down the road from the Florida State Prison, where he was later incarcerated. In his early days at FSP, he talked of how he had wanted to make a contribution to society while he was on the streets, but it just never worked for him. Ironically, his madness resulted in a precedent-setting case, *Ford v. Wainwright*. Alvin's contribution to society came because he lost his mind and ultimately his life. A modicum of justice emerged from a cruel, crazy system that had no room for justice, only finality. It took a madman to move the US Supreme Court a step away from the madness of state-sanctioned killing.

CHAPTER EIGHTEEN

Dreamland

MY DREAMS BEGAN in earnest during the early morning hours of March 15, the Ides of March. We had arrived at my sister's house in Oakland, California, just the evening before, for a family reunion.

I'm not much of a dreamer normally, but just the previous week Becca had awakened me several times in the night because I was thrashing and calling out in my sleep. In the March 15 dream, I had witnessed a murder. No one saw me observe this murder, or so I thought. Then I realized that one person *had* seen me. Next, a lot of people I didn't know, male and female, were gathered in a large circle. The leader, a woman, was asking each person in the circle if he or she had seen the murder. When it was the turn of the person who had seen me witness the murder, she shook her head and said she didn't know the murderer. I too denied seeing the murder.

The dream changed. Next, I was at Camp Hanover outside of Richmond, where I had spent four consecutive summers, 1966–1970, as a counselor. It gave me a sense of safety being among friends. Except that, in my dream, I was at Camp Hanover fleeing my pursuers from the circle, who had concluded that I *had* seen the murder after all. They were attempting not just to apprehend me but to kill me. A group of children had unloaded from a school bus, and after telling their teachers how to get to the waterfront, I took a kayak and paddled to the beaver dam at the far end of the lake, thinking no one could find me there. I spent several hours watching the beaver, blue heron, and other wildlife. Then I went back up the hill to the main camp area.

When I arrived, a white school bus drove up and parked. I asked the driver if I could help. He said, "I have a delivery for Bob Pryor." Bob was the camp director.

I called out to Bob across the field: "Bob, you have a package."

He yelled back: "I'm tied up with these campers. You take it."

I told the delivery man I would sign for it, but he replied, "No. This is for Bob Pryor. He has to come with me to Richmond to sign for it."

I was just communicating this to Bob when I saw my pursuers rushing down the dirt road toward me. I fled.

That's when Becca awakened me and told me that she'd already wakened me six previous times during the night because I was calling out and thrashing about with my arms and legs.

The next night brought more of the same. I was violent, kicking and hitting as if in a fight, again with no awareness of it. Becca woke me four times. But that night, the dream was different again. It featured a silver disc about three feet in diameter. The disc seemed to be alien. It sucked me into its side, and no matter how hard I struggled, I could not prevent the disc from pulling me inward. Desperately, I looked around. Some ten feet away, an infant lay on the ground. I watched in astonishment as the infant grew into a boy, an adolescent, and then a young man. This, I suddenly realized, was my son. He strode to the disc, grabbed my arms, and began pulling me out of it. I was being pulled in two directions at once, but my son seemed to be slowly prevailing. Then Becca woke me.

As she and I discussed the dreams, she told me that I'd been speaking during my dreams, as my arms and legs flailed about, but she hadn't been able to understand what I was saying. She would awaken me, and shortly after I went back to sleep I would return to the violence until, after several repetitions, I would finally fall into normal rest.

The next night was perhaps the worst. She woke me only once, but it was after I had hit her squarely on the nose. That night, I had no recollection of what the dream had been about.

We returned home after a good visit with Kay and Sterling, wondering what was going on with me. In all the years of my work against the death penalty, I had never really dreamed much—other than the nightmares I sometimes had just before or after executions. In those, I sometimes saw myself or a loved one executed. But these recent dreams had become a continuum, not an occasional experience. I had never experienced anything like it.

Next came a couple of fairly routine nights of sleep—and then a doozy of a nightmare in the early morning hours of March 21. Chris Minton, one of Ed Zagorski's lawyers through the years, had become a good friend in the fight to save Philip Workman from his frame-up by Memphis cops and prosecutors. Recently, Chris and I had been having an occasional lunch. In this dream, Chris and I were back at Ed's trial some thirty-five years before. I was desperately trying to introduce some of the evidence we had uncovered post-trial that demonstrated that Ed was being poorly served by defense counsel and that he was not guilty of killing the two men he was charged with killing. Somehow, Chris and I had been able to interest several jurors in the evidence we had obtained, and we were transmitting it to them. Suddenly, I was standing before a bunk bed, reaching for an item on the top bunk. I thought I was back at Camp Hanover but then noticed that these bunks were wooden. The bunks at camp were metal. Then I realized I was at Auschwitz, which I had visited in January of 1994. The housing block I was in was crowded with people; to me, it felt as if I had been transported to 1944.

Next came a couple of fairly routine nights of sleep— and then a doozy of a nightmare in the early morning hours.

Once again, Becca woke me. I had been violent, hitting, yelling, and kicking. This time, she understood what I was saying: "I'm reaching for something on the top bunk."

Among the blessings of my life are the friendships I have been fortunate to make over the years. Art Gatewood and Bob Pryor were two such friends from our college days. They rolled into town to help me prepare the blueberry plants for the summer, and we spent March 21 and 22 composting and mulching, laughing and acting the fool, as only old friends can do.

After Art and Bob left, I noticed the bed of my pickup truck littered and dirty from our work, and I recalled that just a year ago I had driven my truck, similarly dirty with the detritus of compost and coffee grounds, into the prison parking lot after Art, Bob, and I did the work last spring.

So many changes had taken place in that year. Tennessee had gone on a killing spree, executing three people in the fall. As a result of my involvement in trying to prevent or ameliorate those killings, I was emotionally shattered. My dream life in March was extreme, much like the weather, which had turned from the cold of the first week of the month to erratic warmth and cold at the end of the month. It felt as if nearly everything in my life had changed dramatically, externally and internally. Working with Art and Bob, friends of fifty years, had been a welcome respite. Throughout the chaos, Becca and my friends, the dogs and Jack the cat, along with good medical care, had been my continuing support.

246

Tennessee had gone on a killing spree, executing three people in the fall. As a result of my involvement in trying to prevent or ameliorate those killings, I was emotionally shattered. My dream life in March was extreme, much like the weather, which had turned from the cold of the first week of the month to erratic warmth and cold at the end of the month. It felt as if nearly everything in my life had changed dramatically, externally and internally.

When I talked with my psychiatrist on March 25, I first vented my anger at a development trying to impact our rural neighborhood in an unwelcome manner. I was actually angry—and had the energy to be mad! Then I shared my dreams with him. He said, "You seem to be feeling better." I reflected and, to my surprise, realized that despite the traumatic dreams, he was correct.

On Tuesday and Wednesday, March 26 and 27, I felt good. Not just the Tweener state, but actually good.

Then came the night and early morning hours of March 27 and 28. Becca woke me five times because I was thrashing and talking unintelligibly. The last time she woke me, I said clearly, "There's a man over there who is hungry."

Becca responded, "Honey, it's only a dream."

"It's not a dream," I said. "That man is hungry."

"Who is he?" she asked.

My reply was instantaneous and matter-of-fact. "Me."

* * *

At the end of *The Plague*, Albert Camus describes the feelings of those who have survived. Rambert, who had worked closely with Dr. Rieux, had seen countless people die in the city. Yet he had survived, and in this scene he was on the train platform, awaiting the arrival of his wife, whom he had not seen in months because she had been away from the city when the quarantine was put in place.

> If only he could put the clock back and be once more the man who, at the outbreak of the epidemic, had only one thought and one desire: to escape and return to the woman he loved! But that, he knew, was out of the question now; he had changed too greatly. The plague had forced on him a detachment which, try as he might, he couldn't think away, and which like a formless fear haunted his mind.[1]

In the forty-plus years of working with the condemned, I had always managed to find my way back to myself after the trauma. The events of the fall of 2018, culminating in the two deathwatches with Ed Zagorski, had left me at a loss of self that I had not previously

---

1 Albert Camus, *The Plague* (Everyman's Library, 2004), 115.

experienced. I felt like Rambert in that all I desperately desired was to return to my wife, Becca, whole and intact.

In 1976, Becca and I met at a house on Seventeenth Avenue in Nashville, where I was living with a group of friends. We called it Ma's Boarding House and shared the good life of young people post-college age. On a hot August day, I was lying on the ratty old couch in the living room. The ceiling fan was on, and I was weary, seeking relief from the heat.

My tiredness stemmed from, besides the heat, a fast I had begun as a moral witness against the death penalty. The US Supreme Court had reauthorized capital punishment with three decisions on the eve of the weekend celebrating the two-hundredth anniversary of the United States. I was working with the condemned across the South and knew what that meant. An article about the fast from the *New York Times* described our protest for the nation.

Oct. 10, 1976

COLUMBIA, Tenn.—The Rev. Joe Ingle quietly refused a menu here the other morning, when a waitress proffered it in the dining room of the Holiday Inn.

"I'll have two glasses of tomato juice," he said, "and a cup of decaffeinated coffee."

"Not much breakfast," a companion said, and Joe Ingle smiled. Joe Ingle is 29 years old and has been fasting since the Supreme Court ruled last July 2 that the death penalty is not necessarily cruel and unusual punishment under the 8th Amendment to the Constitution. The ruling upheld death penalty laws in Georgia, Florida and Texas, opening the way to executions in those and other states with similar laws.

On the 94th day of his fast, Joe Ingle and the 190

men and women on Death Row in those three states got more bad news. The Supreme Court has vacated a stay on actual executions and said its July 2 ruling could be applied immediately in those states which have constitutional death penalty laws.

So, as he began the 95th day of his fast, having already lost 45 pounds—"I was carrying around maybe 15 too many anyway"—Joe Ingle was gloomy but not despondent. No doubt about it, he said, there soon would be an execution, many executions, probably the first coming in Florida. As a member of the Southern Prison Ministry, he has been regularly visiting and helping in the cases of 42 people on Death Row in Tennessee; as publisher of the Southern Coalition Report on Jails and Prisons, he is as much in touch as anyone with Death Rows [in] the South.

Actually, in Tennessee, the situation is less acute than in some other Southern states. Tennessee's death penalty law may not be constitutional under the July 2 ruling, a question on which the state supreme court is expected to rule sometime soon, and Gov. Ray Blanton says he will not permit an execution while he is in office.

But in Florida, Attorney General Robert Shevin is agitating for quick action to put to death one or more of the 50 persons on Death Row there. If Florida does become the first state to execute an offender in this country since 1967—the first in Florida itself since 1964—the deed will be done at Raiford Prison in an electric chair made by prisoners in 1924 and jovially known to some as "Old Sparky."

It's at least possible that Old Sparky's first victim—it claimed 196 from 1924 to 1964—could be George

Vasil, 17, white, convicted at age 15 of killing and mutilating a 12-year-old girl. But when the theory was advanced that it was statistically likely that the first person to be executed would be black, Joe Ingle politely, disagreed.

"They're too sophisticated," he said. "They know that would look too bad, cause too much protest."

If that's true, a 17-year-old boy probably wouldn't be first, either. In its current issue, Corrections Magazine suggests that a Florida white man, Charles Profitt, might be electrocuted first. Whoever it is, Joe Ingle—like his visitor—believes that the spectacle will be revolting to a public long unaccustomed to state executions. Meanwhile, he and others are doing what they can to mobilize public opinion for life, not death.

A day or so earlier, about 140 persons had met in Nashville, just north of Columbia, for a workshop and strategy session sponsored by 26 organizations and some individuals grouped into "Tennesseans Against the Death Penalty." They heard Millard Farmer, a lawyer with the Southern Poverty Law Center, express the hope that Tennessee might yet "present a view of the future" by abolishing the death penalty. But John Lozier, state director of the Southern Prison Ministry, told the group that at least 25 capital punishment bills would be presented on the first day of the Legislature, if Tennessee's present law is struck down.

All across the South, where execution is most imminent, such groups are working against time— Florida Citizens Against the Death Penalty for example, and the Southern Prisoners' Defense Committee. Theirs looks like a losing fight—Louisiana and Oklahoma have

Too Close to the Flame

passed new death penalty laws since July—but for Joe Ingle and others like him, there's nothing to do but go on.

"Instead of killing these people, we should be forgiving them," the young minister, a native North Carolinian, told the Nashville Tennessean last month. "If you are a Christian, forgiveness is the norm, not vengeance."

Joe Ingle doesn't know when he'll end his fast, whether before Old Sparky strikes or not. "The Lord led me into it," he said, "and He'll lead me out."[2]

As a result of being over a month into the juice fast, I had lost my desire to eat. My main challenge was to keep hydrated in the summer heat. I was just thinking of rising from the Ma's Boarding House couch to refill my water glass when I heard a knock at the front door. I shouted, "Come in. It's not locked." The door opened and my life changed.

A lovely brunette with hair down to her shoulders walked in. She wore blue jeans and a white cotton sweater with a silver dove of peace hanging from a chain around her neck.

I sat straight up and rose from the couch, asking, "May I help you?" She asked if Tish Crane, one of my housemates, was around. I called for Tish, who was upstairs, and introduced myself. The brunette said, "I'm Becca Joffrion."

From the moment Becca walked through the door of Ma's Boarding House, through our wedding in October of 1979, and then forty years of marriage, it had all led to this place of trauma and my attempts to reclaim myself. The past six months had not been easy for her. My prayer was, "God, give me myself back and by so doing bring back her Joe once again!"

---

2 Tom Wicker, "Old Sparky's Ready," *New York Times*, October 10, 1976.

Dreamland

Despite my nightmares, spring was moving forward. The daffodils gave way to the spring beauties. The peach and cherry trees bloomed. The grass turned green, and spring green began to appear in the tops of the trees. I saw a pileated woodpecker flit from tree to tree out back. He stopped to hammer a tree with a staccato sound loud enough to be a drum in the symphony orchestra. His red-plumed head, black-and-white body, and eighteen-inch length were stunning. After a few minutes, he was gone.

April rolled out its magic carpet ride of wildflowers—purple and white trillium, phlox, Virginia bluebells, bloodroot, early spurge, wild ginger, shooting stars, dwarf iris, and the glory of the redbud trees. Whether it was the long, gray winter or my internal lassitude, the colors seemed unusually vivid this spring.

On April 2 and 3, I experienced the three Ds: detachment, dislocation, and disconnection. Once again, it was the random appearance of these feelings, and my utter lack of control over them, that unbalanced me.

The first chapter began on Maundy Thursday of 2018, when Ed Zagorski and Don Johnson asked me to stand deathwatch with them. By Maundy Thursday of 2019, Ed had been killed by the state of Tennessee and Don Johnson had a May 16 execution date. After struggling through two deathwatches in eighteen days with Ed, I had told Don I couldn't do it with him. I spent the evening of Maundy Thursday of 2019 in a class on Albert Camus rather than going to the foot-washing service at church. I was looking forward to seeing my trauma therapist, who had returned from her jaunt abroad, the next day.

I started the session by recounting my emotional roller-coaster month, my nightmares, and my utter lack of energy. I pointed out that this spring was the fortieth anniversary of John Spenkelink's killing by the state of Florida, the trauma that initiated my first disassociation experience. I told her my psychiatrist thought my dreams were signs things were "percolating." He was concerned about Becca's safety, considering my striking out in the dreams.

After a full and enlightening session, we concluded with my therapist asking me to draw my dream of the hungry guy—me—beside the road. Then she asked me to explain it. I studied the drawing I'd made: I was sitting, Buddha-like, beside the road, as people walked by. Green lines extended from my mouth to the people, signifying that I was talking with them about their experiences. At the end of the road, awaiting the pilgrims, was a crucifix and an electric chair.

"And what does that mean?" she asked. The pilgrims who were parading down the road in front of me were others who were on that journey of fighting this criminal legal system. I was responding to them. I felt I had something to share, perhaps something that would ameliorate or prevent the killing at the end of the road.

The overriding question throughout the preceding six months of therapy had been, Would I someday go back to death row? When we began, I couldn't even have considered it. The prison was a trigger that so traumatized me I could rarely even allow myself to think about it. Now, through the therapy and support of Becca and friends, through the passage of time and the grace of God, I was slowly returning to myself. I had begun to accept that I was good at what I did, and the drawing illustrating my dream revealed a willingness to share my knowledge—definitely not yet, but sometime down the road.

The dream revealed that I was hungry for life. As I told my therapist, "I feel as if I have been under a thousand-pound weight. I want to laugh, to feel, to shrug this weight off me and stand up again." That would take more time—but I could feel it lifting.

I took stock after the session, comparing myself with where I'd been emotionally a year before. My thoughts ran something like this:

Even though I am hesitant and tentative, I feel as if I am getting better. The flashbacks are gone. I am taking two-mile walks. I'm watching a lot of Vanderbilt baseball at Hawkins Field and following some detective mysteries I greatly enjoy streaming on television. Interestingly, the first detective series I watched in the depths of my trauma was *Bosch*—which is about to begin a new season. Perhaps that new season will serve as a bookend to my emotional shipwreck.

In my struggle to understand what I am experiencing, I think I have reached a new stage. I don't think I'm riding the boulder up and down Sisyphus Mountain any longer. Nor am I perched on the ledge, halfway up. Rather, I am free of the mountain altogether. I am walking again, on the green grass Ed Zagorski so fondly recalled from his dream with Laurie. Only *my* green grass is quite literal—it stretches throughout our rural neighborhood. It is as if this coming of spring has freed my emotional bonds, and I am slowly getting back to myself. Not quite there, but no longer experiencing extreme mood swings.

It is all so new and tentative, I feel I have to proceed gently.

LEFT: Joe as a silversmith apprentice—Colonial Williamsburg, Virginia, Fall 1968

BELOW: Joe and his wife, Becca, with their dogs and Angus cattle, 1982

Joe speaking at the 1977 Witness Against Executions in Atlanta

Witness Against Executions in Atlanta – Floyd Craig, Ramsey Clark, and Joe (in Stetson) with 3,000 protestors

Musician Joan Baez protesting the death penalty
in Atlanta, Spring 1979

Dr. Hugo Bedeau, Joe, and Dr. Mike Radelet at the National Coalition
to Abolish the Death Penalty meeting in Philadelphia, 1990

Neighborhood Justice Center Opening

LEFT: Guest Pass to Parchman Prison

BELOW: Davidson County Jail Minister's Pass

United Church of Christ clergy before a death row visit

Art, Christ help death-row inmates find humanit[y]

Holly Meyer
Nashville Tennessean
USA TODAY NETWORK - TENNESSEE

Jesus is laying on the cross in the painting, his arms splayed wide as one of his executioners hammers a nail into his hand.

The artists who created it — selecting the caramel color of Christ's skin and the silver of the nail drawing the red pool of blood on his palm — are inmates on death row who, like Jesus, are facing their own state-sanctioned executions.

Those who visit with the prisoners in Unit 2 at Riverbend Maximum Security Institution in Nashville say the new Stations of the Cross artwork helps show the humanity of men often defined solely by their crimes.

Derrick Quintero, sentenced to death in 1991 for first degree murder, is one of the artists who collaborated on the new piece that depicts the biblical account of Jesus' trial, crucifixion and resurrection.

He explained, in a statement accompanying the artwork, why he and fellow prisoners created the piece as well as the open and honest dialogue that it inspired.

"This piece of art is a commentary on the continuing battle for our collective moral world view," Quintero said. "I asked my fellow community members to help me create this project to begin a conversation about what justice looks like."

It took more than two months to complete their piece. During the process, the religious and nonreligious artists talked about their own understandings of Jesus' death and appearance and welcomed feedback from other prisoners, correctional officers and volunteers.

Artwork travels from church to church

While they remain behind bars, the artwork, painted on two long scrolls, now is traveling to churches and other religious institutions in Middle Tennessee that want to display it.

Deacon W. James Booth, of Holy Family Catholic Church in Brentwood, is helping facilitate the exhibition of the piece. He anticipates that it will eventually be put on permanent display, potentially at Holy Family.

He visits death row nearly every Saturday morning to help with a Catholic infused, but ecumenical service and study group. The weekly meeting is attended by Quintero, who was baptized Catholic in prison, and a h[...]

A new Stations of the Cross art piece is traveling around to churches and religious institutions in Middle Tennessee. The piece was created by death row inmates at Riverbend Maximum Security Institution in Nashville.
PHOTOS BY HOLLY MEYER/THE TENNESSEAN

push policy, Booth said. The hope is that it can serve as a bridge of faith between the inmates and the outside world, he said.

State renews push to execute inmates

But the artwork is circulating at time when the state is renewing its push to execute inmates on death row. The state Supreme Court has set a handful of new execution dates for later this year, put legal debates on how inmates can be put to death are ongoing and not all efforts to delay some executions have been exhausted.

In Tennessee, 61 people, including one woman, are currently on death row. The last execution happened in 2009.

Capital punishment remains a controversial issue. Fifty-five percent of U.S. adults support it for those convicted of murder, according to an October 2017 Gallup report. While still a majority, that is the lowest support in 45 years, Gallup said.

The Catholic church opposes the death penalty, but that does not mean the people who fill the pews all agree, said Booth, who does not support capital punishment.

But h[...]

out, in a way does some of that work without some of those individuals having to leave the comfort of their neighborhoods and parishes."

The piece stirred healthy conversations about Jesus and justice behind bars, too. In his statement, Quintero said he did not know if any of his fellow prisoners changed their opinions as a result of it. But their open and honest dialogue is in keeping with the community model the prisoners have created on death row.

"We tackle all the positive and destructive social issues that were a part of our lives," said Quintero, who was convicted of the 1988 slayings of an elderly Stewart County couple that occurred during his escape from a Kentucky prison.

"How we got to today, finding healing, and making better overall decisions is critical to the security of the prison system and society at large."

They do so with the blessing and cooperation of corrections officials, Quintero said.

Neysa Taylor, a state Department [...] that idea in h[...] grams behind b[...]
The Tenne[...] on embrac[...] allow offen[...]

Meghan Gwaltney Manrique and [...] Ingle view the new Stations of the Cross artwork that was on display [...] Christ Church Cathedral on May 2[...] was created by inmates on death r[...] at Riverbend Maximum Security Institution in Nashville and is curr[...] traveling around to churches and religious institutions in Middle Tennessee.

Some of the artists who worked on new Stations of the Cross artwork signed their names on the back of [...] of the scrolls. They are all inmates death row in Nashville.

"It's a powerful piece," he said.
A handful of people, including [...] wife, were standing over them that [...] day morning, taking in the details reading Quintero's statement. It Manrique Barrenchea's first time se[...] the piece. Although, he had heard al[...] it from his friend and death row inn[...] Billy Ray Irick, who helped paint [...] landscape in the scenes.

Irick was convicted of the 1985 [...] and murder of a 7-year-old girl. In Je[...] [...] Supreme Court set his [...]

Minister's long fast over death penalty ends

By RAY WADDLE
Religion News Editor

The Rev. Joe Ingle of Nashville was so hungry to see the death penalty abolished that he stopped eating for nearly six months.

Ingle, nationally known for his fight against death row, sat down last night to his first solid meal since Feb. 24 — ending his fast after a Texas inmate's imminent execution was blocked Monday.

"I'm really drained. I'm tired," Ingle, 46, said yesterday afternoon before eating soup and bread after nearly six months on juice under a doctor's supervision.

"My 5-year-old is very excited because Daddy is going to eat again. Both she and my wife were getting concerned about my health.

Ingle put himself through the long fast, he said, not to drum up publicity but to perform an act of "penance" for the "racist" practice

of capital punishment that has killed 18,766 inmates in the United States since 1608. Only 31 of those were whites who killed a black person, he said.

Ingle started what he thought would be a six-week Lenten fast in February to protest the pending execution of Texas inmate Leonel Herrera, who insisted on his own innocence in the shooting deaths of two policemen.

But Herrera's execution date kept getting postponed.

The ordeal stretched to 174 days, more than a month longer than the 134-day fast Ingle kept in 1978 when the U.S. Supreme Court reinstated the death penalty.

Herrera lost the legal battle, and his life, after the U.S. Supreme Court ruled no new evidence could be entered after a federal trial.

But another Texas death row inmate, Gary Graham, came to Ingle's attention in April, and he decided to extend his fast until yesterday, Graham's scheduled execution. The execution was blocked Monday by the Texas Court of Criminal Appeals to allow new evidence in his case. ∎

These Tennesseans of faith forge connections with inmates living on death row

Befriending the condemned

The Rev. Joe Ingle of United Church of Christ sits at his Nashville home with "Winds of Change," a painting by Endume Olatushani. Ingle, a longtime death penalty abolitionist, helped Olatushani get off death row. Ingle also helped start the visitation on death row program in the 1970s. MARK ZALESKI/FOR THE TENNESSEAN

August 18, 1993, article in *The Tennessean*, upon the ending of my second fast against the death penalty

---

TOP: A May 28, 2018, *Tennessean* news article with photo of 22-foot Stations of the Cross painted by death row prisoners

ABOVE LEFT: December 18, 2019, article in The Tennessean, showing Joe with Ndume's painting "The Winds of Change"

Rev. Tom Feamster speaking at the state capitol with the Spenkelink family to his right and Joe to his left, May 1979

John Spenkelink, Florida's Death Row, 1979

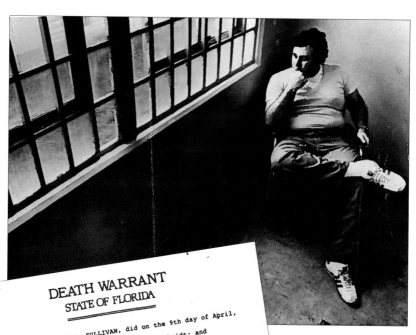

DEATH WARRANT
STATE OF FLORIDA

WHEREAS, ROBERT A. SULLIVAN, did on the 9th day of April, 1973, in Dade County, Florida, murder Donald Schmidt; and

WHEREAS, ROBERT A. SULLIVAN was found guilty of murder in the first degree and was sentenced to death on the 12th day of November, 1973; and

WHEREAS, on the 27th day of November, 1974, the Florida Supreme Court upheld the sentence of death imposed upon ROBERT A. SULLIVAN and Certiorari to the United States Supreme Court was denied on the 6th day of July, 1976; and

WHEREAS, it has been determined that Executive Clemency, as authorized by Article IV, Section 8(a), Florida Constitution, is not appropriate; and

WHEREAS, attached hereto is a copy of the record pursuant to Section 922.09, Florida Statutes;

NOW, THEREFORE, I, BOB GRAHAM, as Governor of the State of Florida and pursuant to the authority and responsibility vested by the Constitution and Laws of Florida do hereby issue this warrant directing the Superintendent of the Florida State Prison to cause the sentence of death to be executed upon ROBERT A. SULLIVAN on some day of the week beginning noon, Wednesday, the 23rd day of November, 1983, and ending noon, Wednesday, the 30th day of November, 1983, in accord with the provisions of the laws of the State of Florida.

IN TESTIMONY WHEREOF, I have hereunto set my hand and caused the Great Seal of the State of Florida to be affixed at Tallahassee, the Capitol, this 2nd day of November, 1983.

GOVERNOR

ABOVE: Bob Sullivan on Florida Death Row

LEFT: Death Warrant for Bob Sullivan, 1983

Derrick Quinterro, Joe, and Terry King, Tennessee Death Row

Jimmy Lee Gray, Mississippi
Death Row, electrocuted
September 2, 1983

Robert Wayne Williams,
Louisiana Death Row,
executed December 14, 1983

James Adams behind glass, with girlfriend, Jackie,
and brother Willie Lawrence, on death watch visit, 1984

Jimmy Lohman and Rose Williams comfort Willie Lawrence Adams
on the day of his brother James' electrocution, May 1984

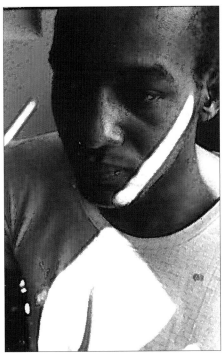

LEFT: David Washington, Florida Death Row, electrocuted July 1984

BELOW LEFT: Willie Darden, Florida Death Row, electrocuted March 1988

BOTTOM RIGHT: Morris Mason, photo he gave to Joe at 4:30 p.m. prior to his electrocution at midnight, August 1985, Richmond, Virginia

BELOW RIGHT: Alvin Ford, Florida State Prison, hours before scheduled execution, May 30, 1984

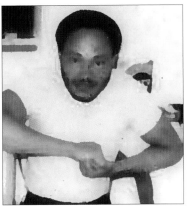

TOP: Philip Workman in the visiting gallery at Riverbend Maximum Security Institution, executed May 9, 2007

MIDDLE LEFT: Philip Workman reading his Bible
LOWER LEFT: Joe, holding the cover of Philip's book
LOWER RIGHT: Philip and Joe talking

ABOVE: Holding cell where prisoners are kept for seventy-two hours prior to execution, Riverbend Maximum Security Institution

LEFT: Electric Chair Mechanism, Riverbend Maximum Security Institution

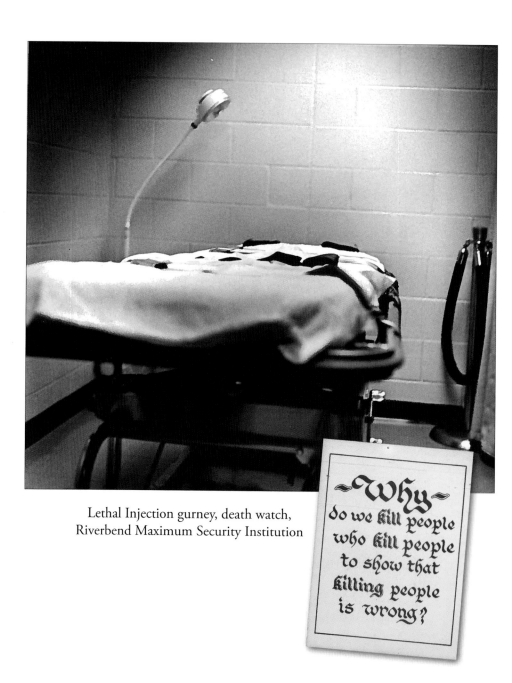

Lethal Injection gurney, death watch,
Riverbend Maximum Security Institution

~Why~
do we kill people
who kill people
to show that
killing people
is wrong?

Outside Riverbend Maximum Security Institution,
Nashville, Tennessee

Joe leaving his home for a prison visit

Joe picking blueberries on his farm in Nashville

River Rats

CHAPTER NINETEEN

Attica

In this life spent voluntarily in and out of death row, I've sometimes found myself recalling the events that led me to it—and they date back to a memorable national scandal that mesmerized the nation while I was living in New York, attending Union Theological Seminary.

Prisoners took over Attica prison in upstate New York on September 9, 1971, holding hostages and issuing demands for better treatment. I lived in a major urban ghetto—East Harlem—but I had no experience with jail or prison. I had never been in one, even though incarceration was a reality in the lives of many in the East Harlem community.

Prisoners took over Attica prison in upstate New York on September 9, 1971, holding hostages and issuing demands for better treatment.

Following the Attica story in the *New York Times* and on television news, I was impressed by the powerful and articulate statements of the prisoners. As the crisis dragged on, I had a sense of foreboding. Attica symbolized our divided country in the late sixties and early seventies. Before us all, a chasm gaped between political leaders who talked about the need for law and order and many citizens who wanted their leaders to think in terms of justice and even mercy. The crisis of mistrust and misunderstanding was coming to a head at Attica. Full of fear and dread, I watched on our small black-and-white television in the tenement apartment on East 105th Street as the Attica crisis built to a climax.

Under the orders of Governor Nelson Rockefeller, on September 13, 1971, prison guards and highway patrol officers armed with shotguns stormed the prison after blanketing it with tear gas. The casualty report read like the results of a Vietnam firefight. Thirty-nine people killed, another hundred injured. News reports implied that the "good guys" were victorious against the "bad guys." But when the prison was stormed, almost all thirty-nine people killed—ten hostages and twenty-nine prisoners—were shot by the bullets or buckshot fired by those retaking the prison. As one relative of a dead hostage put it, her loved one was killed by "a bullet that had the name Rockefeller on it."

The Attica rebellion was crushed by a slaughter that left me sick at heart, even though it accomplished the prison authorities' goals and may have boosted the political career of Governor Rockefeller. After Attica, I felt compelled to learn about these places and the people who were locked up in them, and what their life was like there. I decided to make my nine-month seminary project of the East Harlem Urban Year Program visiting prisoners in the Bronx House of Detention.

As I drove my little blue Toyota up to the Bronx for my first visit, I had no idea what to expect. My orientation from the chaplain at the jail had been thorough, but I was anxious and apprehensive nevertheless. Tension knotted inside me as I parked my car and walked inside.

I showed my ID card at the entrance and rode the elevator to the sixth floor. I showed my ID again to the guard and followed him around the outside of the huge, barred cage that was the cellblock containing the individual cells. The doors to the cellblock were closed and locked, but unbeknownst to me the doors of the individual cells were open so the prisoners could move around in the walk. My hands were sweaty. As we neared the corner of the rectangular cellblock, the guard motioned to a room on the left.

"You can visit in here, where lawyers and clergy visit."

I stood for a moment, silent, then said, "I'd prefer to get into the cellblock and talk with the men." He raised an eyebrow at me, then shrugged and opened the door leading into the cellblock. I stepped through. The door slammed shut behind me. The crash of the steel-barred door rang in my ears. I looked at the cells—their doors were open. My mind surged with fear. *Oh, God! What am I doing here? I'm locked in here with all these animals!* I stood frozen.

"Man, what are you doing here?" someone said.

I looked toward the voice. In the cell on my right, a young man sat on his bunk, looking up at me. Laughing nervously, relieved at making my first contact, I explained to him that I was there to visit with anyone who wanted to talk and that I'd be coming back regularly until June. He invited me to sit on his bunk, and we chatted for a while. Then he took me around the walk and introduced me to the men in each cell.

Two hours later, I left the House of Detention and climbed into my car for the short drive back to East Harlem. My mind was a tangle, but I tried to sort through my thoughts and feelings. Those two hours had completely changed my perception of jails. With one exception, all of the twenty-four or so men I talked with were

Black or Puerto Rican. Some of them had been convicted of crimes and were serving their sentences. But most were there because they had been arrested and charged but couldn't post bond. A man who couldn't make bail could expect to wait an average of *eighteen months* before he would go to trial.

I felt as if I had just visited a different world. I was shocked and ashamed to realize that my own socialization process had conditioned me so that my first reaction, when the cellblock door slammed behind me, was to fear these men and see them all as animals. I was beginning to see hints as to why the prisoners at Attica had rebelled. I was stunned.

I felt as if I had just visited a different world. I was shocked and ashamed to realize that my own socialization process had conditioned me so that my first reaction, when the cellblock door slammed behind me, was to fear these men and see them all as animals. I was beginning to see hints as to why the prisoners at Attica had rebelled. I was stunned.

* * *

260

As the weeks passed, I struggled with my visits to the Bronx House of Detention. I discussed my work with others in the Urban Year Program, and their support, as well as our meetings for group sharing and reflection, helped me as I struggled to find a Christian response to the jail system. As the months passed, a framework of faith slowly emerged from my experiences and my studies.

I had always taken the Bible seriously as the basic tool for understanding the Christian faith. What the Bible has to say about prisons and jails is striking. Jeremiah, John the Baptist, Joseph, Paul, Peter, and Jesus had all been in jail. These men were not criminals. Each was a man acting on his understanding of what God called him to be and do. Yet they suffered the common lot of ordinary criminals. The theologian Karl Barth said that the first Christian community did not arise following the Pentecost experience but rather with the two thieves crucified with Jesus. It was a crucified thief who confessed that Jesus was Lord when almost everyone had deserted Jesus. At a place called the Skull "was the first Christian fellowship, the first certain, indissoluble and indestructible Christian community . . . directly and unambiguously affected by Jesus' promise and his assurance . . . to live by this promise is to be a Christian community." At this crucifixion of criminals on Golgotha was the initial Christian recognition.

As I studied the scriptures, I realized that the law, whether it be the Hebrew Torah or the Pax Romana, was often a cold, rational juggernaut that could not comprehend the Spirit of God moving individuals. This was equally true of the Pax Americana, as it locked thousands of civil rights demonstrators and war protesters in the nation's jails and prisons. I came to believe that secular law, which society conceived as its absolute guide to human behavior, should be merely a tool for the furtherance of the will of God. When that tool proved useless, God would summon someone to direct the people on the path of righteousness. Many times, from the time of Moses and Jeremiah to the time of Martin Luther King Jr., this path led to conflict with the law.

But how did all of this apply to the "common criminals" I visited each week in the Bronx? Each had either been convicted of a crime or accused of a crime and arrested; this fact alone made it hard to see them in the same category as the prophets and apostles who went to jail.

The study of the scriptures and my experiences in jail led me to reevaluate the meaning of "righteousness." When that cellblock door slammed behind me, I had thought of those men as "animals" not so much because of what they had done or were accused of having done but because I believed I was better than they were—because of what I had *not* done. I was self-righteous. It was this position of moral superiority that I found conspicuously absent in the biblical studies of the prophets and Jesus.

Indeed, I found Jesus himself giving definitive instruction about judgment and punishment in the eighth chapter of the Gospel of John. Not only did Jesus forgive a woman who had been accused of and confessed to a capital crime, but he posed a dilemma for her accusers who wanted to carry out the death sentence then and there. "Let him who is without sin among you be the first to throw a stone at her," Jesus said. He not only forgave the woman charged with the crime but he also questioned the authority of those who sought to condemn her and execute her. Clearly, when I reacted as I did to that cellblock door slamming behind me for the first time, I had shown myself to be among those willing to cast the first stone. Yet I knew I certainly was not without sin.

That particular gospel story was part of a pattern of Jesus urging followers to turn the other cheek, to fulfill the law by transcending it, to render evil to no one, to constantly forgive people regardless of who they were or what they had done. This teaching led me to see that the law as I knew it, the law that locked people up in the jails and prisons of our country, was rooted in a presumption of moral judgment. This presumption helped maintain law and order in society, but it had little to do with the agape love Jesus was calling people toward in discipleship. What Jesus taught was antithetical to the values of any earthly society, be it Marxist or American Christian, because his message is a scandal to those who desire to dwell and rule in any earthly domain.

Slowly, I came to see the men at the Bronx House of Detention as my brothers in Christ. I began visiting them simply as a friend, not as someone who had all the answers, nor as someone who could help them in any material way, nor as someone who had to visit them for a school project. All I could offer were the little things: to contact their families, to give them postage stamps when I could afford them, to telephone their lawyers. I was the one with the seminary education and the minister's ID card, but I soon began to wonder who was ministering to whom. As I tried to minister to the men in jail, they were also ministering to me. Within those concrete walls and behind those steel bars, the Spirit of Christ was manifest. Jesus taught us that whenever we served "the least of these," we were serving him—and he specifically mentioned visiting them in jail.

These men locked in the cages of the Bronx House of Detention helped me to see that God was calling me to work with people locked up in jails and prisons. It was a significant first step, and one that I would never have envisioned when I moved to New York.

CHAPTER TWENTY

Homeboy

WHEN GOVERNOR BOB Graham signed John Spenkelink's death warrant in mid-May of 1979, he also signed Willie Darden's. I asked David Kendall, John's lawyer, if Willie was in imminent danger. In what would prove to be an understatement, David said, "Joe, Willie has a lot of appeals left."

I would visit Willie Darden throughout the 1980s as he survived death warrant after death warrant. Indeed, ABC's *20/20* did a segment on Willie titled "The Dean of Death Row."

Willie called me "homeboy" because we grew up in adjacent counties of North Carolina. He was born in Greene County and I in Pitt County. He came of age in the segregated Black world as I had in the white one. Water fountains were labeled *colored* and *white*, as were restrooms and restaurants. Blacks sat in the balcony of the movie theater. It was an apartheid society. The white Southern oligarchy ruled as it had since Reconstruction ended in 1876.

Willie was born in 1933 and I in 1946. His skin was ebony, mine white, and although we were seemingly completely different, we were bonded through our visits at the Florida State Prison and our status as neighbors growing up in North Carolina. Funds were meager in our family when I lived in Pitt County; the year after my father's death we lived with Mom's parents in their rented house in Greenville, but our penury certainly didn't compare to Willie's situation in Greene County. As the Reverend Leon White wrote, on behalf of Willie's clemency, "In 1860, slaves constituted half the total population of Greene County; in 1930, Blacks constituted half the population. [In the entire state] Blacks owned only 4% of taxable wealth and the average Black income was less than $1,000 annually. Four out of five Black families were tenant farmers or sharecroppers."[1]

Willie Darden's mother gave birth to Willie in a state where infant mortality was fifth highest in the United States, with nine out of every one thousand infants perishing. Willie's mother, who was fifteen when she birthed Willie, died in childbirth two years later.

Willie's maternal grandfather, with whom he was very close, was the son of a slave and ran a "two-horse" farm. The horses were used to plow the fields. As soon as Willie was old enough, he was helping his grandfather in the field as well.

In a segregated world with no money, education was hard to come by. However, Willie persevered at the Zechariah School for the Colored through the eighth grade. In those days in North Carolina, the average grade completed by Blacks was the second. But with Willie's grandfather's death, school became a luxury and Willie became the man of the family. His aunt recalled him as a child: "Because I spent so much time with Willie Jr., I was as close to him as if he were my own. He went to Sunday School every week with my children, and I know for a fact that that child was always a solid rock." She described Willie's family as a "first-class colored family in Greene County. The white families would hire our husbands and children to work in the tobacco factories during the season because [we] were known to be a hard-working and religious family."[2]

---

1 Unpublished letter submitted by the Reverend Leon White to the governor of Florida on September 1, 1980, seeking clemency for Willie Darden.
2 Unpublished letter to the Reverend Leon White.

In his aunt's words lay the reality of life in rural Greene County. The white people ruled through ownership of land and what little industry there was, dominated and controlled the political process, and determined what tax money was spent for whom. It was the classic separate and unequal caste system that existed throughout the state and the region. Although Willie and I were born only a few miles apart, the social reality was that we were separated by light years.

The white people ruled through ownership of land and what little industry there was, dominated and controlled the political process, and determined what tax money was spent for whom. It was the classic separate and unequal caste system that existed throughout the state and the region. Although Willie and I were born only a few miles apart, the social reality was that we were separated by light years.

In our visits at the Florida State Prison, we bonded through our backgrounds, and our affection for each other grew. My visiting days at FSP were long, and I saved my visits with Willie for last because we always relaxed and enjoyed ourselves, ending an exhausting day on a high note. The "homeboys" had a good time.

The US Supreme Court issued *McCleskey v. Kemp* in April of 1987. (Warren McCleskey was a friend of mine on Georgia's death row.) The court made it clear that two facts prevailed in the administration of the death penalty: First, the law was demonstrably racially discriminatory. And second, the court would not redress the issue. Justice Lewis Powell authored the majority opinion (5–4), a decision he would publicly regret in retirement. As Steve Bright aptly titled his book, it was *The Fear of Too Much Justice.*

As in Warren McCleskey's case, race was the theme of Willie Darden's life that led to death row at FSP. After his grandfather's death, Willie's stepmother deserted the family. He was placed in foster care, where he found himself in a state of virtual slavery, working in the field like a beast. Willie began to steal to obtain food and clothing. Caught stealing from a farmer's mailbox, he was sent to the National School for Boys at the age of sixteen. A segregated facility in North Carolina, it served as Willie's apprenticeship in how criminal behavior enables one to survive in an apartheid society.

Willie began to steal to obtain food and clothing.

After his release, Willie began a series of odd jobs. In 1953 he met his future wife; they married in 1955. In January of 1956, Willie was arrested for cashing a forged check for $48.00. He was sentenced to four years in prison. His wife recalls, "It broke my heart that they put him away so long because I knew that he had done it to buy us some food."[3]

When Willie and I were growing up, white people in the South divided Black people into distinct categories: "good niggers" and "bad

---

3 Unpublished letter to the Reverend Leon White.

niggers." The law decided under which of those categories a Black person might fall. Of course, the law was merely an instrument of social control by an apartheid society, as it had been since the 1600s in the colony of Virginia. In North Carolina in the mid-1950s, the judges were white, the jurors were white, the lawyers were white, the prosecutors were white (even today, 98 percent of prosecutors in death penalty cases are white), and Black people were under the boot heel of a segregated regime. The law kept them that way. You could call that system *neo-slavery*.

> ## *Black people were under the boot heel of a segregated regime. The law kept them that way. You could call that system* neo-slavery.

So, in January of 1974, it was no surprise when Willie walked into the courtroom in Inverness in rural Florida, facing a murder charge, and everyone except Willie was white. As Willie told me, "Joe, I looked around at all those white faces and I knew how it was gonna come out. I was like a raisin in a bowl of milk."

It was a classic recipe for the death penalty in the South: a Black man accused of killing a white man. It was white justice versus Black bestiality. Throughout the trial, the prosecutor described Willie as subhuman: "Willie Darden is an animal who should be placed on a leash." The prosecutor expressed the desire that Willie be seated at the counsel table "with no face, blown away by a shotgun."[4]

---

4 *Darden v. Wainwright*, 477 US 168 (1986), Justice Blackmun dissenting in a 5–4 vote.

That savage attack by the prosecutor was unchallenged by defense counsel. The court-appointed lawyer, as is true in nine out of ten death penalty cases, was worse than inept. He refused to put on the stand an eyewitness who vouched for Willie's whereabouts near the time the crime occurred.

That witness was Christine Bass, a white woman from Lakeland, Florida (where the murder Willie was being tried for had occurred). She came to the courthouse with information that provided a clear alibi for Willie. She communicated that information to Willie's lawyer.

Christine Bass had been at home in Lakeland when a Black man—Willie Darden—rang her doorbell and explained that his car had broken down and asking if he could use her phone to call a tow truck. She allowed him to make the call, then he went back outside to stay with his car. She estimated that this occurred between 4:00 and 5:30 p.m. on September 8, 1973.

The police estimated that the crime at a furniture store in Lakeland took place between 6:00 to 6:30 p.m. There was no way Willie could have been at Christine Bass's home with a broken-down vehicle and made it to the furniture store for a robbery-murder.

Willie's lawyer, as is so often the case, assumed his client was guilty. After all, all the other white people were telling him Willie Darden had committed the crime. So what should he do with Christine Bass? He didn't investigate her story, nor did he allow her to testify.

The only testimony linking Willie to the crime was eyewitness testimony. Although laymen often think eyewitness testimony is a sure thing, those familiar with such testimony know it can be highly suspect. This is especially true in a cross-racial crime. As Southern whites have a long history of saying about Black people, "They all look alike." The eyewitnesses in Willie's case were white, and their eyewitness testimony was highly suspect.

The widow, Mrs. Turman, and her husband operated a

furniture store in Lakeland. Mrs. Turman at first told police she couldn't remember what the perpetrator looked like or what he was wearing. On the day after her husband's funeral, she was led by the police into a small courtroom where only one Black person was present, sitting at the defense table. The prosecutor asked Mrs. Turman, "Is this man sitting here the man who shot your husband?" The Black man sitting at the defense table was Willie Darden. Since the assailant had been identified as a Black person, Mrs. Turman identified Willie as the murderer.

The prosecution had one other eyewitness, a neighbor who came when he heard shots and in turn was shot himself. Still in his hospital bed, he was shown six photographs. Willie Darden's picture was among them—and it was the only one labeled, "Sheriff's Department, Bartow, Florida." He chose Willie as the man who'd shot him.

There were major discrepancies in the eyewitness accounts, but the police seemed to airbrush those inconsistencies in order to identify Willie. The discrepancies included the color of the assailant's shirt, whether he had a mustache, and his height (eyewitnesses suggested heights of five feet six, five feet eight, five feet ten, and finally six feet). But in the end, all that really seemed to matter was the unanimous agreement that the assailant was "colored." If they all look alike, and this one was a bad dude according to his criminal record, what difference did it make as long as you got one of them off the streets?

When "they all look alike" eyewitness testimony combines with a legal system that discriminates in the application of the death penalty, justice is rare.

* * *

On January 23, 1974, Willie Darden, forty-four years old, was sentenced to death by electrocution. I imagine that the white people in that courtroom didn't expect to hear anything more about this uppity Black until he was electrocuted at the Florida State Prison. But they had launched a high-profile death case with their prejudicial and unjust treatment of Willie.

Christine Bass didn't forget about Willie, and she kept talking about the case until, finally, in a 1979 post-trial hearing, her testimony was given for the record. Unfortunately, her story was not corroborated, and the case continued to wind through the courts until 1986.

Governor Graham made a point of mentioning Willie's case as he campaigned across the state for reelection in 1983. He had by that time signed two death warrants on Willie, and the courts had stopped each one for further consideration. He was making Willie into a "poster boy" for the death penalty in Florida. Graham's bid for reelection was successful, and he signed Willie's third death warrant, setting the execution for September 2, 1985.

This warrant brought me to Starke for what I feared would be a final visit with Willie. The US Supreme Court was considering Willie's case—but given the politically rightward march of the justices under Chief Justice William Rehnquist, it was not a hopeful scenario.

During a deathwatch, the most difficult aspect is the pain experienced by the family and loved ones of the condemned. As the emotional vise tightens with each passing minute, the pressure on loved ones often becomes excruciating. That's why I was most concerned with Felicia, Willie's girlfriend. She was a middle-aged Hispanic woman with an incomplete grasp of English. The legalities of the killing machinery totally eluded her; she just loved Willie.

The first day of September found Margaret Vandiver, Felicia, and I in our friend Mike Radelet's house in Gainesville, Florida. We were waiting to hear from the US Supreme Court before driving to our scheduled visit with Willie at the prison in Starke, about an hour's drive. The electrocution was set for 7:00 a.m. on September 2, almost twelve hours away.

Margaret, Mike, and I were deciding who would drive whom to the prison while Felicia watched television. The local news was full of Willie's pending execution. Suddenly, a piercing wail slammed into us. Felicia jumped up, grabbed her purse, and ran out the door. We turned to catch the last of the television broadcast. Willie had been turned down by the Supreme Court. I bolted out the door to catch Felicia—I didn't want her driving while she was so distraught.

I slid into the passenger seat of her car and grabbed Felicia's hand just as she started to turn the keys in the ignition. "Felicia, don't drive. You're too upset. You won't do Willie any good if you wreck this car trying to drive to the prison."

Felicia broke down. Sobbing in my arms, she moaned, "They're going to kill Willie."

"We haven't heard from the lawyers yet," I said, trying to comfort her. "We don't know exactly what the decision says or what it means for Willie. We need to hang on until we can make a plan."

In truth, I was despairing as well. Felicia's wail had been an outward manifestation of the desperation we all felt about this decision. "Sweet Jesus, have mercy upon us," I muttered.

I drove us to the prison, where we waited for Margaret Vandiver to bring the official word from the lawyers so we would be able to explain to Willie all we knew.

The Supreme Court vote, which had come at around 6:00 p.m., had been 5–4 against Willie. He had no legal recourse left. We entered the prison to be with him one final time.

As was customary under deathwatch, this visit would last until midnight. It would be a noncontact visit, through the glass partition. Then Willie would have a one-hour contact visit with Felicia. At 1:00 a.m., I would accompany Willie back to his cell and spend the night with him outside the cell as his spiritual adviser.

We had brought a tape player with us and played Sweet Honey in the Rock. Their songs of oppression and liberation, of freedom and joy, echoed through the noncontact visitation room. Willie's life, and his impending execution, would have made a good song for them.

Willie tried to keep things upbeat. Margaret and I migrated to the end of the partition so he and Felicia could have as much time as they needed. He summoned us all back together after a long visit with Felicia. He wanted us to "be keeping up the struggle. Not letting these people defeat us."

A few minutes before midnight, our parting time, I eased out the door and sat in one of the ubiquitous plastic chairs of death-watch. I shut my eyes, prayed, and tried to make this nightmare go away.

Suddenly, I heard the sound of rapid footsteps. It was one of Willie's lawyers, running down the hallway and calling something about a stay of execution. I was incredulous. How could that be?

Margaret rushed out to join us in the hallway and we heard the incredible story. Although denied 5–4 on the request for a stay of execution, the lawyers realized they had the four votes needed for the case to be accepted as a certiorari petition, which meant the court would hear oral argument. Justice Lewis Powell, realizing four of his colleagues felt very strongly about this case, switched his vote to grant the stay of execution upon petition of the lawyers. The courtly Virginian saved Willie's life as a courtesy to his fellow justices.

Willie would, for now, survive Governor Graham's repeated efforts to kill him. Governor Bob was about to become Senator Bob, in large measure due to his relentless signing of death warrants; he had initialed 155 in eight years and electrocuted eighteen people. Some political observers saw him as a possible presidential candidate. It appeared the political reward for killing citizens, especially Black citizens, was a continued political career at a higher level.

Unfortunately, barring an unexpected change of judicial heart, the votes were not there for Willie Darden to prevail in the Supreme Court. The case was briefed and argued. Bob Martinez, a Republican former mayor of Tampa, succeeded Bob Graham as governor. There was no hope of clemency from Martinez, as he embarked on an even brisker pace of signing death warrants than his predecessor's.

With all political and legal avenues closed, none of us were hopeful about Willie's fate. When the Supreme Court ruled 5–4 against Willie, Justice Harry Blackmun penned a bitter dissent:

> Thus, at bottom, this case rests on the jury's determination of the credibility of three witnesses . . . I cannot conclude that McDaniels' [the prosecutor's] sustained attack on Darden's very humanity did not affect the jury's ability to judge the credibility question on the real evidence before it. Because I believe that he did not have a trial that was fair, I would reverse Darden's conviction; I would not allow him to go to his death until he has been convicted at a fair trial. I believe this Court must do more than wring its hands when a state uses improper legal standard to select juries in capital cases and permits prosecutors to pervert the adversary process. I therefore dissent.[5]

Justice Blackmun clearly had Willie's case on his mind in the summer of 1987. He spoke at a judicial conference of the Eighth Circuit Court of Appeals: "If ever a man received an unfair trial, it was Darden. He may be guilty, I don't know, but he got a runaround in that courtroom."[6]

The public campaign on Willie's behalf intensified. Thousands of petitions flooded Governor Martinez's office in Tallahassee. ABC's

5 *Darden v. Wainwright*, 477 US 168 (1986), Justice Blackmun dissenting in a 5–4 vote.
6 Colman McCarthy, "Reasonable Doubts and Unreasonable Punishments," *Washington Post*, January 3, 1988.

program *20/20* and CBS's *West 57th* did news magazine stories on Willie, which aired in January of 1988.

The problem was the inability to overcome the trial court record. Willie was a lone Black man in a sea of white in the courtroom. His own lawyer, Willie said, referred to him as a "nigger." The prosecutor portrayed him as inhuman. Christine Bass was not put on the stand. With an all-white jury, it was a historic Southern recipe for a modern lynching.

Christine Bass, after being haunted by this case for years, one day mentioned it to Reverend Sam Sparks, a chaplain she knew at a local hospital. Reverend Sparks was startled to hear what Christine Bass had to say, because he already had some firsthand knowledge of the day of the murder—he had rushed to the scene of the crime as the minister to the victim and his widow. He had a clear recollection of the widow's trauma and of the time of day he had arrived. Like many others, he had assumed Willie was guilty and beyond that hadn't paid any attention to the facts of the case. When Ms. Bass explained to him what time Willie was at her house that day and Sparks recalled what time he had arrived at the victims' furniture store, he realized that to commit the murder Willie would have to have been in two places at once. Sparks and Bass filed affidavits on the record verifying Willie's alibi story. Unfortunately, despite finally obtaining corroborating evidence, no court would give a hearing on the innocence claim.

Among those contacting Governor Martinez about Willie's case was Andrei Sakharov, the 1975 winner of the Nobel Peace Prize. His message came to the heart of the matter:

> I ask you to intervene in the affair of Willie Darden. I am convinced that capital punishment is an inhuman institution for which there can be no room in a civilized, democratic society.

Homeboy

Injustice, a mistake in relation to an innocent person, cannot be set right. Moreover, capital punishment may not be applied in cases where there's at least a shadow of doubt of the legality of the sentence, or the unbiased nature of the legal system for racial or other reasons. I asked that the death sentence for Willie Darden be revoked.[7]

The torrent of words, deeds, and protests crashed on Florida— but to no avail. Governor Martinez, on March 8, 1988, signed Willie Darden's seventh death warrant and set the execution for the Ides of March, just a week later rather than the customary thirty days.

At the time, Becca and I were enjoying our newborn baby, Amelia, born on March 5. After Governor Martinez signed Willie's death warrant, I received a call from one of Willie's lawyers passing along Willie's request that I not come down to Florida to be with him the night of his execution. He knew how much our newborn daughter meant to us and didn't want me leaving Becca and Amelia to come to deathwatch.

I didn't want to leave my family. But my homeboy was about to be electrocuted. I could not remain with Becca and Amelia, no matter how much I wanted to. I flew down to Starke, bringing my Communion kit and legal pad, joining Willie on deathwatch on Q wing.

The evening of March 14 found me ensconced in the all-too-familiar noncontact visiting area at the Florida State Prison. Willie had a final visit with Felicia. We had Communion one last time. After the visit, I accompanied him back to Q wing. A final round of appeals had been denied by the US Supreme Court, and we knew that this time there would be no stopping the killing machinery.

Willie's cell was full of correspondence from around the world. He sorted through it, handing me some to respond to, giving

---

7 Amnesty International US.

instructions about others. Because this death warrant had allowed only one week, it was impossible for Willie to respond to everyone he wished to write.

After 2:00 a.m., when Willie had about five hours left to live, he said, "Joe, congratulations—you're a dad. How does that sound? I'm going to call you Dad." He smiled. "I'm so happy for you and for Becca."

We shared a couple of Jamaican cigars, smoking and visiting down the hall from the death chamber. Reminiscing about North Carolina, his children, and the struggle for justice, there was neither a dearth of conversation nor any hurry to say anything. The night moved on toward morning.

Willie asked that I witness the execution. I had a cardinal rule in ministering to the condemned: I would not watch them be killed. But Willie really wanted me there. I felt my insides turn over as I agreed to honor his request. We discussed where I would be as a witness so that he could find me when he entered the death chamber.

"I'll hold up my pendant," I said. It was a gold symbol of the Committee of Southern Churchmen.

Willie said, "Good, I like that. Now you be sure to be standing, not sitting in a witness chair. I want to be able to see you."

Even though I was exhausted, my adrenaline had kicked in and I was alert throughout the early morning hours, in a hyper-vigilant state. I noticed the daylight creeping through the window at the top of the wall and realized it would soon be time for me to go. We held hands and had a final prayer.

At 5:30, the guard arrived with the gray briefcase that contained the tools of barbering for Willie's electrocution. Willie had already shaved his head, but they would do it again and also shave the hair from his right calf. This would allow the electricity to flow cleanly into the body from the attachments.

We embraced through the bars. "I love you, Willie."

"Joe, I love you too."

I turned and walked down the hall, escorted by a guard to the cafeteria.

All the witnesses to the execution were fed breakfast in the prison cafeteria, a nice Southern amenity in the process of killing a human being, compliments of the state of Florida.

I had no desire to eat. I sat alone, sipped an orange juice, and ignored the chitchat of the other witnesses. The flag of the state of Florida and the flag of the United States hung high on the walls. Was this what those flags symbolized? An institution for killing citizens, overlaid with a patina of due process? Complete with breakfast before the witnesses observed a cold-blooded state murder. And, irony of ironies, the Florida flag had inscribed on it "In God We Trust."

Oh, yeah, I thought, *let's bring God into this unholy proceeding.* State-promulgated killing was the opposite of trusting in God. It was an exercise of the power of taking life, an act of idolatry. Just as the Gospel of John put it in describing Satan as "the murderer from the beginning," that is precisely how the death penalty functioned. It was an evil process, conceived solely to murder. It usurped the sovereignty of God.

As I looked back on all those I knew or had known on death row, not one of them was a murderer from the beginning. No one on death row was born a killer. Each had a unique story of abuse and desolation. It was these Southern states that were barbaric enough to murder from the beginning.

At 6:45 we were summoned and led outside to two white vans. It was a gorgeous morning with a blue sky and bright sunshine. We clambered into the vans and were driven to Q wing. I had witnessed this scene from across the road in the cow pasture many times as a protester. Now I was in the belly of the beast.

Our vans stopped outside the death chamber, and we got out and proceeded into the witness room. There were three rows of white, high-backed chairs facing the window. Everyone found a seat. I remained standing, as I had arranged with Willie.

The clock on the wall behind the electric chair read 6:58. Promptly at 7:00, the door opened and Willie, manacled at his ankles and with his arms handcuffed to a chain around his waist, was escorted into the death chamber. His bearing was erect and proud. The light glistened off his bald ebony head. He looked like an African king.

The guards removed the shackles and waist chain. He was put into the electric chair and strapped down, his arms, chest, and legs fastened with big leather straps. Willie looked for me as they fastened him down to the chair. He met my gaze and smiled. Willie then met the eyes of each witness, surveying each one individually.

Asked if he had a final statement, he said, "Yes." His voice came clearly and firmly. "I tell you that I am not guilty of the charge for which I am about to be executed. I bear no guilt or ill will for any of you. I am at peace with myself, with the world, with each of you. I say to my friends and supporters around the world, I love each and every one of you. Your love and support have been a great comfort to me in my struggle for justice and freedom."

Willie then fixed his vision on the gold symbol I held out before me—a symbol of God in the world, present for all of us equally and uniting us in life as he would in death.

The guards roughly pushed Willie's head back, and he winced with pain. They strapped his chin. Still maintaining eye contact with me, he winked at me. Then he lifted his thumb on his left hand upward, the "it's all right" sign. As the black mask was dropped over his face, Willie waved goodbye with his left hand. I thought I would break down on the spot.

Three charges of electricity went surging though Willie's body.

A voice announced, "The sentence of the court against Willie Darden has been carried out. He was pronounced dead at 7:12 a.m."

When I emerged from the witness van into the bright morning

sunlight, Margaret Vandiver was waiting for me. It was so good to see a dear friend.

"Joe, are you all right?"

Stunned, I said, "Yes." I grasped the cross Willie had bequeathed to Felicia; my last mission for Willie was to deliver it.

Margaret and I drove back to the airport. She was heading for Boston, and I was going home. I was hammered by the events of Willie's killing—not just the final twenty-four hours of Willie's life, but the cumulative effect of all the executions from John Spenkelink in 1979 through Willie in 1988. From Florida to Alabama, to Virginia, to North Carolina, to Louisiana, to Mississippi, to Texas, to South Carolina, to Georgia, and to Tennessee, I had visited death rows. I loved the individuals condemned there, and I hated that they were being exterminated by the state killing machinery.

In 1979, John's and Willie's death warrants had been signed together. John had been the victim of electrocution that spring. Willie had gone through six more death warrants before he was killed in the spring of 1988. Those two men had served as bookends supporting me as I worked among the condemned throughout the South.

Now both my bookends were gone, and I was falling into a vortex without the support of my homeboy and my brother.

A Letter from Hell

In the autumn of 1988, in response to Willie Darden's electrocution and at the encouragement of my therapist, I wrote this letter:

November 1988

Dear John and Willie:
My therapist suggested I write a letter to Willie. I realized I couldn't do that without writing you too, John.

After all, it seems like it all started with you.

I recall your face so clearly, John. You were such a kind man. The acknowledged leader of Florida's death row, a role you never sought, always looking out for others.

David Kendall, your lawyer, always said your case wasn't a death penalty case. He was correct, but there you were on death row nonetheless. You felt so strongly someone, somewhere in power would also see your case wasn't a death case. Despite your juvenile record, you had a real faith in the American justice system. It reminded me of the Superman line: "Truth, justice and the American way." Well, we found out the American way had nothing to do with truth or justice.

It's almost Thanksgiving in 1988. Ten years ago, the goon squad at FSP attacked you in your cell for not returning your dining tray. You were protesting the arbitrary canceling of family visits around the holiday without notice. They gave you a concussion, a broken rib, and dragged you off unconscious to Q wing as punishment for your protest. But most of all, I remember our visit the next week. The vulnerability you felt when I saw you was palpable. You couldn't believe they would beat you like that over wanting to call your mother or lawyer to notify them of the cancelled visits.

John, although I evince worldly cynicism about the criminal justice system, I guess I can't believe it either. Not only did they beat you but they killed you in the damned electric chair: May 25, 1979.

God, I'll never forget that day. I was with Lois, your mother, when they killed you just after 10:00 that Friday morning. Lois was asleep, from exhaustion and worry. I woke her up after seeing the CBS news flash on

TV. She looked right into my eyes, John, and she said: "They've killed my Johnny." Not so much a question as a statement. I said: "Yes, they have, Lois." And she wept and sobbed. When her brother called, I went into the bathroom and beat my fist on the wall, crying: "Is there no justice? God, is there no justice!"

So, here I am ten years later. I promised you I wouldn't forget the other guys and I haven't. I've ministered to and loved so many. Eighteen, including you, have been killed. Now I'm wondering if this isn't killing me.

I don't have any energy, John. I'm really depressed. Becca said last night I haven't had the energy—the full day's work go get 'em energy for a long time. Since I started writing the manuscript is when she dated it. I thought that would be cathartic and I think it was somewhat. Getting all of this stuff out of myself and onto paper. But now it's another burden. It's too much pain working on it.

I went to sleep last night thinking of you two. How I love you both. Willie, you were a leader and so funny, too. A self-educated, articulate Black man from Greene County, NC. Next to Pitt County, where I was born. You called me "homeboy." Due to segregation, you grew up in your Black world and me in my white one. We finally met at the Florida State Prison in Starke.

We worked so hard to save you guys. Jesus, the stays of execution, the roller-coaster emotional ride through the courts. But we couldn't pull it off. They killed each of you. Now, on a gray autumn day in 1988 with Amelia sleeping in her room, I wonder what it all means. I'm sad, bereft, just thinking about it. You guys were something else and I miss you.

Too Close to the Flame

I think my therapist wanted me to write you as a way of letting go, saying goodbye. But how can I do that? So much of you guys is in me. It's like letting go a part of myself.

I'm going to give a speech at UNC (University of North Carolina) tomorrow night. It will be good, even though I'm down. It will be good because I knew and loved you guys, and the others, and I can share that publicly. It seems I have a rather painful gift. The gift is your friendship. The pain is your being killed.

So what should I do, guys? What does it all mean? Right now, I'm sad and lonely. And I want to be happy and enjoy life with Amelia and Becca. I think both of you would encourage me to do that. I thought a sabbatical would help but then they killed you, Willie. I had to be with you through that. Helluva sabbatical, huh?

You guys still bring a smile to my face. Remember your smiley face in your letters, John? I just enjoyed my friendship with you two so much. A smile comes forth despite the pain.

There are several things going on in my life, seemingly contradictory. I was nominated for the Nobel Peace Prize in 1988 for the work. Amazing, isn't it? St. Andrews College gave me an honorary doctorate. And the big news: Becca and I are parents of little Amelia, now 8 months old. But I have seen so much suffering and pain it is hard to feel the joy of fatherhood.

John and Willie, thank you for your friendship. I really appreciate knowing you. We connected under the most difficult of circumstance but we really connected. I loved you both.

Joe

CHAPTER TWENTY-ONE

Illness

APRIL AND OCTOBER are glorious months in Middle Tennessee. April brings wildflowers, forsythia, redbuds, daffodils, trees leafing, and the increasing warmth and light of spring. October revels in coolness, changing foliage, fall wildflowers, and clear days with a high, blue sky. These are my favorite months to be alive and dwelling in Tennessee.

I began feeding the birds again in mid-April 2019. It was good to have the energy to do so and to watch as they gobbled up the seed. The hummingbirds returned to the feeder in the front of the house. We had a bird population explosion that year. The rose-breasted grosbeaks began to migrate through, heading north, on April 16. We were pleased to see them at the feeder out back. Becca and I spent an entire morning sitting on the back porch, watching them in all their beauty.

April 19 and 20 marked the arrival of dogwood winter—a mini-winter of several days after the spring's last frost. These small cold spells take their name from whatever is blooming at the time. By mid-April the dogwood blossoms have unfurled, hence the name.

Don Johnson telephoned me. His execution date of May 16 was less than a month away, but the main reason he called was to check in on me, concerned most not about his own problematic future but about my health. I gave him an abbreviated report and assured him I was under excellent medical care.

Don filled me in on the clemency effort on his behalf. He felt optimistic and had a positive attitude, but my stomach grew uneasy. I recalled feeling the same way when Ed Zagorski's lawyers were so confident of clemency. I said nothing as Don detailed the work being done on his behalf. It certainly seemed that his lawyers were hitting the right notes, but I was still recovering from the acts of our last Christian governor to have any faith in the newly elected Christian governor.

We talked for a half hour, and then Don closed, as he always did, by saying, "I'm too blessed to be stressed."[1]

Trauma is fickle. I thought I had been doing well. Then on Monday, April 22, I experienced mild disassociation: a feeling of being out of your body, of almost being able to stand aside and gaze at yourself. It was my good fortune to have an appointment already scheduled with my psychiatrist, who reminded me that "trauma is a roller coaster," guiding his arm in the arching up-and-down movement of a roller-coaster ride. I thought, but did not say, *I know this is a roller-coaster ride. I just want to get off the damn roller coaster.*

I know this is a roller-coaster ride. I just want to get off the damn roller coaster.

Hector Black, my blueberry mentor whose daughter had been murdered, had written a letter to Governor Lee and wanted my suggestions about it. It described Hector's experience with Trisha's murder and asked that the governor grant Don a life sentence. I

---

1 When I originally typed this quotation on April 26, 2019, I mistakenly wrote "I'm too stressed to be blessed."—a typo that described my state of being, not Don's.

assured Hector that his letter, along with mine, would be hand delivered to the governor.

We had a brief locust winter on Sunday, April 28—a time when the locust leaves with their light green coloring were abundant and stood out in comparison to the darker-hued leaves of the other hardwoods. Whitish-green blossoms filled the trees as the temperature dropped to the low forties at night and the sixties during the day.

* * *

In the fall of 1988, my right cheek went numb. I didn't know what to make of it, but my best guess was that, having lost a number of friends to the executioner, the stress of being with them just before their extinction was manifesting itself physically. Becca thought I should have it evaluated to be sure it was psychological, so I made an appointment with a neurologist. I was examined and had an MRI.

The next day I was finishing up doing the chores for our small herd of Angus cattle on our twenty-five-acre farm. As I was returning to the house for a shower before going into work, the phone rang. It was Becca. She had been paged while walking the floor in the hospital where she worked as a nurse. A doctor friend had seen my MRI results and called to tell her. She was calling me now to tell me she had heard my results and she was coming home so we could discuss this face-to-face.

"Becca, what does the report tell us?"

"I'll be home in just a few minutes," she said. "Let's wait till I get there."

"Honey, you're scaring me. I need to know what you know. What is the diagnosis?"

She paused. "The MRI indicates you have multiple sclerosis."

Dumbstruck, I mumbled something in response.

I walked out to the front porch and sat in the swing. I really didn't know what multiple sclerosis was, but it didn't sound good. Then memories from the Jerry Lewis Labor Day telethon flashed through my brain: people on crutches, in wheelchairs, their limbs at odd angles. I was in shock. I just sat on the porch swing, gazed at the gorgeous October day, and waited for Becca.

It's about a twenty-five-minute drive from St. Thomas Hospital, where Becca worked, to our house. Becca made it in considerably less time that day. She drove up the driveway, hopped out of the car, and we embraced. Then we headed to the porch swing to talk.

When I told her about the images I remembered from the Jerry Lewis telethons, she shook her head. "No, that's muscular dystrophy. You have multiple sclerosis. MS is a degenerative neurological disease. It can manifest itself by numbing or tingling. Loss of function can be experienced as the myelin, which is a sheath surrounding the nerve, is destroyed. We'll need to see a neurologist. I've already made an appointment."

Fortunately, as a nurse, Becca had lots of friends in the medical community. When Becca contacted the neurologist, he agreed to see us later that day.

"I don't really want to talk about this anymore until we see the neurologist," I said. It sounded serious to me, but I didn't want to speculate without knowing the facts. Becca agreed.

The visit with the doctor was factual and reassuring. As we viewed the MRI, he pointed out the lesions on my brain. That was the multiple sclerosis. "No one really understands how it gets started, although some doctors speculate that it's spread by a virus or by bacteria," he said. "It favors females and usually appears in people younger than your age of forty-one. It's prevalent in colder climates. The best treatment is rest and avoiding stressful situations, and if those things don't control it, then we can try injections of a medication called Betaseron, the brand name for a form of interferon. Betaseron slows the disintegration of the myelin around the nerves."

He thought the numbness in my cheek would go away in a week or so. If it did not, or if I had other symptoms, I should contact him immediately.

The challenge of MS was not unlike responding to an execution crisis. I had already begun practicing centering prayer, a spiritual discipline that empties the mind and enables one to be open to the spirit of God. In a literal sense, I turned the future course of my MS over to God through the practice of centering prayer. Of course, this didn't make all concern and worry disappear. It did, however, give me a framework with which to deal with it.

Although my doctor had instructed me to resume my normal life but beware of fatigue and stress, that suggestion was impractical for someone working with death row prisoners. Those I knew were exhausting their appeals as the courts made the appellate process more difficult through procedural bars to raising issues.

Witnessing Willie Darden's electrocution had killed more than one person. In crisis situations, I am always calm and clear. But beneath the surface, emotions run deep, and it is often weeks or months before I recover from an execution. Willie's killing had knocked me to my knees, and I didn't seem able to get back up.

The fall of 1988, my beloved time of year, found me gripped by a profound melancholy. I was shaking it, but only slowly. Now I had an unsettling medical diagnosis to deal with as well.

In December of that year, I was nominated for the Nobel Peace Prize by the Swedish Parliament, and that helped me realize that somebody somewhere valued abolitionist work in the United States. Maybe things weren't as dire as they seemed, and I would be able to beat this after all.

*In December of that year,
I was nominated for the
Nobel Peace Prize by the Swedish
Parliament, and that helped me
realize that somebody somewhere
valued abolitionist work in the
United States. Maybe things weren't
as dire as they seemed, and I would
be able to beat this after all.*

* * *

Becca and I continued to try to have children. Fertility treatments, an ectopic pregnancy, laser surgeries for endometriosis—we dealt with one obstacle after another. We were delighted with our daughter Amelia, whom we adopted in March of 1988, but we wanted to give her a brother or sister. A routine exam of Becca by her OB-GYN found a mass the size of a small grapefruit on her ovary. Given her history, he was confident it was a benign cyst, but he would have to remove and examine it to be sure.

On July 18, 1989, Becca underwent surgery for the cyst. As I paced the hospital waiting room for news, time passed all too slowly. Finally, I was summoned to the telephone.

The nurse from the operating room said, "The doctor has found abnormal cells. He is finishing up and will come to see you."

I was stunned. "What does 'abnormal cells' mean? Cancer?"

The reply wasn't reassuring. "The doctor will explain the

situation to you. It will be a while because he is still stitching your wife up."

I wasn't alone; my friends David Rainey and Harmon Wray were with me. I told them the news and we took a walk together around the block. I kept repeating the nurse's words: "Abnormal cells." And speculating: "How can that be? She's thirty-seven years old. I can't believe it. Cancer? Or what?" They walked with me, kept me company, and we returned to the waiting room.

Finally, in the early afternoon, Becca's doctor, Jim Growden, entered the waiting room. Becca had been downstairs in surgery since 7:00 a.m. It was Jim who had helped us navigate the infertility process, and he was someone we really respected. His explanation was very clear:

"I removed the cyst, and it was self-contained. Everything looked fine. There was a little endometriosis, which I also cleaned out. I shaved a couple of slices off the cyst to send to the lab to check. I continued the surgery, and the path report came back almost immediately: there were abnormal cells indicating that she had ovarian cancer. I had no choice at that point except to do a full staging. I had to remove everything I could to be sure we got the cancer. She has had a full hysterectomy. I think we got the cancer. It was at an early stage."

I nodded, but the reality of this sudden change was too much for me to process. We had done the surgery as a means of increasing our chances of fertility. Now, we had eliminated any chance of conception and, most importantly, discovered that Becca had ovarian cancer. I explained what the doctor told me to her parents and my friends. We waited for Becca to be brought up to her room.

Jeanne Ballinger, a good friend and a surgeon, came by. Fortunately, she was there when Becca was brought into the room. The nurses wheeling her gurney were reporting to each other as they got her situated while I struggled to figure out how I would tell her she had ovarian cancer. As I sat next to her bed, she heard one nurse tell the other, "We drew the CA125 in the OR."

Being an oncology nurse, Becca, though groggy from anesthesia, knew what that meant. She rolled her head to me and said, "Do I have cancer?"

Still in disbelief myself, I couldn't find the words.

She repeated, "Do I have cancer?"

Jeanne Ballinger responded from the foot of the bed: "You have early-stage ovarian cancer. There is every indication they got it all, and the prognosis is good."

Becca had gone into surgery hoping to come out enabled to bear children. Now that hope was shattered, and her very life was threatened. She knew the high rate of mortality for ovarian cancer from her cancer patients. She had followed Gilda Radner's battle with ovarian cancer, which had resulted in her death. Although Becca was surrounded with friends and family, this was a terrible and unexpected blow.

Once the shock of the diagnosis settled into reality, there were decisions to make. Would she take chemotherapy? Although the surgical report about clearing the abnormal cells sounded promising, as a nurse Becca had seen too much of cancer to rely solely on the hope of surgery alone. She opted for chemo, which would attack any remaining malignant cells, increasing the chance for cure. She also wanted to return to work after a month or so. And she insisted we go to Michigan on vacation in August with Jeanne Ballinger and her husband, Irwin Venick, as we had planned.

Becca came home and began her recovery. Amelia was fourteen months old and trying to understand what had happened to her mother. After the first chemotherapy treatment, Becca was very sick: nausea, vomiting, and weakness. But she wanted to try the Michigan vacation.

As we walked through the Detroit airport to make our connecting flight to Traverse City, the airport nearest Crystal Lake,

Illness

Becca's hair came out in clumps. At our Michigan vacation destination, otherwise beautiful, the cool Michigan summer air felt cold to Becca's depleted system. We returned home realizing that Becca was very sick and would not be returning to work anytime soon.

Before leaving for Michigan, we had hired a contractor to remodel the only bathroom in our old farmhouse, a step toward bringing the house up to standards. I was very clear with him that Becca was quite ill and needed a functioning bathroom upon our return. Instead, we came home to a construction nightmare.

The contractor had torn out walls and part of the floor and removed the tub. The toilet looked questionable. There was no way Becca could handle this mess with her sickness from the chemotherapy. We called Becca's sister Tina and her husband, Don, in nearby Murfreesboro, and explained our dilemma. They kindly offered to take us in until the bathroom was completed.

* * *

The impact of the chemotherapy on Becca that autumn was devastating. After subsequent treatments, she stayed in the hospital because of her fierce reaction to the drugs. At home, she couldn't tolerate the smell of cooking food. She had no appetite. She became dehydrated. She vomited repeatedly, even when there was nothing left to throw up. The drugs were destroying her blood cells, good and bad. She was wasting away before my eyes. Her hair was gone. She resembled someone who'd stumbled out of a concentration camp.

I barely noticed the glorious fall; all my concentration was on caring for Becca and Amelia and doing my job. Martha Joffrion, Becca's mother, came up from Huntsville, Alabama, for a week after each chemo treatment. Friends at church brought meals, as did other friends in the community. We would not have made it without such wonderful support.

Too Close to the Flame

Although the doctors told me Becca's prognosis was good, I saw before me a specter of the vibrant woman who was my life companion. She was bedridden, needing assistance even to go to the bathroom. On occasion she would become so nauseated I would have to drive her to the hospital so she could be hydrated with intravenous fluids. We would spend the night there until she stabilized, then return home the next day.

I feared the impact of Becca's illness on our precious Amelia. Becca was too sick to mother her, to hold her, to have her around much at all. Becca was also sensitive to noise in her state. Amelia became dependent on me for almost everything. We were all doing what we could just to get through this ordeal.

As fall became winter, we discussed with her oncologist and our friend, Alan Cohen, the possibility of changing her treatment. A new drug had been developed in Europe, carboplatin, which did not seem to have the toxic effect on the kidneys that cisplatin did. I had begun to fear the cure worse than the disease as Becca wasted away and developed kidney damage. Would she be able to recover at all?

We did switch to the new drug, and the fifth chemo experience was much better. Although our Christmas would be a quiet one, Becca was able to be up and about a bit now. In public, she wore a wig or a scarf to cover her bare head. We were actually able to go to a movie!

In January, we took a much-needed visit to Sanibel Island, Florida. Our good friend Charles Merrill offered his house, and we went south to Florida for two weeks. Amelia stayed with Tina and her family in Murfreesboro.

In the warmth and beauty of Sanibel, I finally began to believe I was going to get my Becca back. Although emaciated, she was now eating, as well as drinking liquids. She had energy to move, albeit slowly.

One day, much to my surprise, she said, "Let's go to the public pool."

"Are you sure you have the strength for that?"

"I think so. I'll take it easy."

We had the pool to ourselves. She slowly swam a few laps. The sight of Becca moving through the water was a joy to me. I was beginning to see that the doctors were right. She would be herself once again. The fear that she would die, which had been roiling in my gut since her surgery, began to release.

After nine months, Becca returned to work. It wasn't an easy decision. Although she was trained in oncology, the experience of having ovarian cancer herself was still traumatic nine months later. She wondered whether she would be able to work with cancer patients again. After easing in slowly, though, she found her own experience to be a comfort for her patients, and she once again experienced the fulfillment of working with the seriously ill.

In September, we moved from the farm to a more modern home. A newer brick house without cows seemed more fitting for two people with major illnesses to deal with.

The fall of 1990 found me again with profound melancholia— the third successive autumn with this illness. As William Styron wrote, *depression* is an inadequate word. It sounds like a rut in the road. What I had was enervating. There were times I would sit in my office and just stare at the walls. I had no energy. Although I was seeing a counselor and taking my prescribed antidepressants, I had to face reality: I could no longer continue in the work I felt called to do. I resigned from my job, effective the end of December 1990, and accepted a Merrill Fellowship to Harvard University.

The local paper carried a story about my leaving for Harvard. As I ate breakfast one December morning in the Pancake Pantry, a stranger came over and asked, "Are you the Joe Ingle who is going to Harvard?"

"Yes, I am."

"Well, good luck. But you know going there means you lose all credibility."

I smiled and thanked the man. Credibility was the least of my worries. I had to worry first about survival. I was shaken to my foundation by twenty executions of friends, by my mom's total loss of her home through an electrical fire, by Becca's fight with cancer, and by my own continuing journey with multiple sclerosis.

Still, the stranger's remark was a good send-off to northern climes. Maybe I should pack my bib overalls. Or some cow manure from the farm.

On second thought, I figured they would have enough BS at Harvard without me bringing any along.

CHAPTER TWENTY-TWO

Don Johnson

THE LAST OF OUR mini-winters rolled in on Saturday evening, May 11, 2019. The small wild strawberry fruit was in the field, and the domestic strawberries were now ready as well. The temperature dropped into the fifties: strawberry winter.

I had been interviewed on May 10 by a film crew about Hector Black, the remarkable ninety-four-year-old organic orchard grower whose daughter had been murdered in Atlanta almost twenty years before. Hector; his wife, Susie; his daughter, Annie; and I have remained friends since our restorative justice process around Trisha's murder. We were able to overcome the district attorney's desire to impose the death penalty through the powerful witness of Hector and his family as the victim's family. The two-and-a-half hours spent on this film effort and reliving so much pain in the Black family's case depleted me. After the crew left, I went directly to Hawkins Field to watch Vanderbilt baseball, where my biggest concern would be whether they continued their twelve-game winning streak.

They did. Pitcher Drake Fellows brought his win-loss record for the season up to 10–0.

Saturday, I met Chris Minton at the main gate to Hawkins Field at 11:00 a.m. The game started early to avoid the rain and cold headed our way. Chris and I had been enjoying Tuesday lunches for several months at our favorite eatery. Chris represented Ed Zagorski and Don Johnson before he left the Federal Public Defender's Office in July of 2018. In particular, Chris and I had connected through Philip Workman's execution by the state of Tennessee in 2007. Philip was framed by Memphis police and prosecutors.[1] Chris had been Philip's lawyer and I his spiritual adviser.

On this day, the Vandy team looked like they were still asleep, and their thirteen-game winning streak ended. We left just as the rain began. I actually caught a T-shirt in the T-shirt toss. Chris said, "You gotta give it to that kid," and he gestured toward a youngster about six years old across the aisle. I motioned to the kid and when he approached, I tossed him the shirt. I was rewarded with a big smile and a thank-you.

Sunday was the day before Don Johnson was to be moved to deathwatch. To distract myself from thoughts of that place, Becca and I watched the last two episodes of *Bosch*, the detective series we streamed. I had started the series in winter, never dreaming I would still be seeking distraction in May.

* * *

Just before eight o'clock Monday morning, the telephone rang. I didn't recognize the caller ID but was sure it was Don Johnson, so I answered, "Good morning, Don."

"Good morning, brother," he said, and immediately began discussing the public outcry for his execution generated by the official forces of darkness in Memphis. Evidently, people didn't think he was remorseful enough, so he should be executed—a position so ludicrous I couldn't respond. But Don took it seriously enough that he wrote a statement reiterating his remorse and shared it with his

---

1 See Joseph B. Ingle, *The Inferno: A Southern Morality Tale* (Nashville: Westview Publishing, 2012).

attorneys. I wasn't optimistic that anything would slake the thirst for blood of those who ran the criminal legal system in Memphis, the belly of the death penalty beast in Tennessee. But it was important to Don: "I am truly repentant, and I wish to explain how I feel inside."

> *Evidently, people didn't think he was remorseful enough, so he should be executed— a position so ludicrous I couldn't respond.*

He shared a remarkable development with me. Henry Hodges is probably the most difficult man on death row in Tennessee due to serious mental issues. Don had been talking to Henry—and Henry, not a man who prays, had been praying for Don. The two of them had discussed the power and benefits of prayer, and Henry had told Don he appreciated their discussions about it.

"It's really true," Don told me, "that saying that the Lord works in mysterious ways."

"His wonders to perform," I said.

This might, I realized, be the last conversation I would have with Don. Once he had been moved to deathwatch, he wouldn't be able to call me. "Don, I want to share a passage of the Bible that means the world to me. It's by the apostle Paul, Romans 8:31–39:

> What shall we say to this? If God is for us, who is against us? He who did not spare his own Son but gave him up for us all, will he not also give us all things with him? Who shall bring any charge against God's elect? It is God

who justifies; who is to condemn? Is it Christ Jesus, who died, yes, who was raised from the dead, who is at the right hand of God, who indeed intercedes for us? Who shall separate us from the love of Christ? Shall tribulation, or distress, or persecution, or famine, or nakedness, or peril, or sword? As it is written,

> "For thy sake we are being killed all the day long
> We are regarded as sheep to be slaughtered."

No, in all these things we are more than conquerors through him who loved us. For I am sure that neither death, nor life, nor angels, nor principalities, nor powers, nor things present, nor things to come, nor height, nor depth, nor anything else in all creation, will be able to separate us from the love of God in Christ Jesus our Lord.[2]

"I love that passage, too," Don said. "You know, Joe, it's like I told Henry. I'm sleeping fine. And when they move me onto death-watch, I will sleep fine there too. It's in God's hands. I'm prepared."

* * *

The warden and death squad came to Don's cell at 11:44 p.m. on Monday, May 13. Terry King, in the neighboring cell, watched the guards placing the leg shackles around Don's ankles and putting on the waist chain with handcuffs attached to a black box. Don shuffled off to deathwatch in Unit 8. As he did, he stumbled and fell. He wasn't used to being shackled. He had been an A-level prisoner for what seemed like forever. The guards helped him up, and they soon

---

2 Michael D. Coogan, ed., *The New Oxford Annotated Bible: New Revised Standard Version with the Apocrypha* (New York: Oxford University Press, 2018), 219.

disappeared through the door leading to deathwatch.

That Monday evening the visitors' gallery (VG) for Unit 2 was filled with visitors, including Shane Claiborne from Philadelphia. I had previously brought Shane into death row to visit the men, and they all knew him. This evening he was visiting Terry King, which enabled him to interact with numerous people in the VG. They were all enjoying each other's company.

Don built beautiful lighthouses out of matchsticks burnt at the tip. Shane bought three of them. He would auction them off and send the money to Cindy, Don's daughter. Don wanted his approach to clemency to be about mercy, not justice. He wanted no civil disobedience protesting his execution, because he feared it would be misinterpreted as violence.

This was an unusual situation for me. A man I had known for thirty years, a man who honored me by asking me to stand deathwatch with him, this brother in the faith, was about to be killed and I could not be with him. My trauma was such that even our phone calls gave me deathwatch flashbacks.

A man I had known for thirty years, a man who honored me by asking me to stand deathwatch with him, this brother in the faith, was about to be killed and I could not be with him. My trauma was such that even our phone calls gave me deathwatch flashbacks.

On the night of May 15, Becca and I went with Margaret Ecker to hear Mavis Staples, celebrating her eightieth birthday with a concert at the Ryman Auditorium. She was joined by many prominent Nashville singers, from Marty Stuart to Sheryl Crow. Her combination of talking civil rights and singing the gospel and blues provided an inspiring time. By the end of the concert, the audience was on its feet singing with Mavis. We sang "The Weight" by the Band and "Will the Circle Be Unbroken?" popularized by the Nitty Gritty Dirt Band. We left feeling uplifted as we walked the streets of Nashville back to our car.

The morning of May 16, I walked out onto my deck and enjoyed the cool air and clear skies above the woods that surround our house. I let the dogs out and wandered back into the house. The telephone rang. I looked at the clock. It was a little before 7:00 a.m. The telephone ID flashed "TN State Govt." I knew it was Don calling from deathwatch. In twelve hours, he would be strapped to the gurney and given a lethal injection.

"Don, how you doing, my man?"

"I'm blessed, Joe. I slept well."

Not surprisingly, Don had many things on his mind on his final morning. He was particularly pleased that the Dysinger family, who had visited him faithfully for years, had pledged to stay involved with death row work. The Dysingers and Tommy Bugg had been visiting Don for as long as I could recall. They were good friends who shared Don's Christian faith, and Don felt blessed by their friendship.

"Joe, who will take Lee to the yard to exercise, or help him with the microwave?" Lee Hall was almost blind.

"Don, there are other guys there who will look out for Lee."

"I hope he gets his *Star Wars* glasses." He was referring to some highly specialized glasses that had been promised to Lee for several years.

The reading of George Orwell's *1984* had made an impression

302

on Don. "I feel like with all the cameras we have watching everyone, we're becoming a *1984*-type environment," he said.

After a long chat, Don said, "I'm getting hoarse from all these calls, but I have more to make. I love you and appreciate you." His voice broke up. "I want to pray. Dear Father, thank you for my brother, from the bottom of my heart. Our friendship has been a moving experience. He has been able to get things accomplished that others couldn't. I know you'll guide him. Give him his health back and lead him in the direction you want him to go. From my days at the Walls, he was a comfort and joy. He didn't see strangers when he came to death row—he saw children of God. I've run my race and help me finish well. Let me put off the old body and put on the new. I'll be looking for my friends on the other side."

I responded with a quick prayer of gratitude for our friendship, for all he meant to those on death row and outside it, and for the love we had shared over the years.

Don's final words to me: "Praise the Lord, and thank you."

"Thank you, Don."

The call was completed.

I gave a deep sigh. I looked at the clock: 8:15. Don had given me over an hour of his time when he had only twelve hours to live. Sweet Jesus, have mercy.

* * *

As I said in my discussion of Billy Irick's execution and the lethal injection lawsuit, there is no doubt that Tennessee uses an excruciating process of killing disguised by the midazolam, which provides a light unconscious state but does not render the prisoner insensate. The paralytic drug, vecuronium bromide, essentially freezes the prisoner's movements so he cannot show pain or react. The entire charade is intended to give the appearance of peaceful dying. For

Don, as it was for Billy, there was nothing peaceful about it, and Don's reactions were similar to Billy's as the drugs coursed through his veins. What was remarkable is that Don sang a hymn—"Soon and Very Soon"—while strapped to the gurney. He kept singing the hymn until the drugs flowing into his veins made it impossible to continue. Don't we all feel safer now that a hymn-singing, caregiving elder in the church has been poisoned by lethal drugs rather than spending the rest of his life behind bars?

There is no doubt that Tennessee uses an excruciating process of killing disguised by the midazolam, which provides a light unconscious state but does not render the prisoner insensate.

Don had told me that the warden had come to his cell about thirty days before the execution date to ask him whether he preferred the electric chair or lethal injection. Don refused to complete the paperwork. He did not want to cooperate in the process. His decision meant that he would receive the default: lethal injection.

There was another strong protest in the field outside the prison at the time of Don's death. Many of the death row visitors were there: the Reverend Matthew Lewis led the service, Hector Black shared his ordeal, and Shane Claiborne spoke, as did others.

Only one celebrator of the execution showed up.

At the vigil, Pastor Napoleon Harris aptly summed up Governor Lee's inaction, which led to this killing: "Governor Lee and Dylann Roof [the young man who killed the members of the

Don Johnson

Emanuel African Methodist Episcopal Church in Charleston, South Carolina] have one thing in common. They both killed a minister."

I learned several years later that Governor Lee had an evangelical pastor with him as Don's execution drew nigh. The court prophet informed the governor he was sure Don Johnson would be glad Governor Lee allowed the execution to proceed because Don would be in heaven. This fellow failed to discern the following: (1) Don wanted very much to live. I knew that fact because I talked to him for an hour shortly before his killing. (2) The teachings of Jesus are clearly opposed to killing. (3) This statement bears an eerie resemblance to radical Muslims who commit terrorism in order to attain the afterlife.

This supposedly well-meaning preacher reminded me of a trip I made to Tyler, Texas, to testify before Judge William Wayne Justice in federal district court. Judge Justice was confronted by a death row prisoner wishing to drop his appeals. He was facing imminent execution. His lawyers were challenging this decision. The prisoner was under the influence of the Texas prison chaplains, who advised him to go ahead and get executed so he could go to heaven. I met with the prisoner over lunch, heard his thoughts, and spent the afternoon testifying about Jesus and the Christian faith. I detailed how it was a perversion of the gospel for the state of Texas, through its chaplains, to manipulate death row prisoners into seeking their own extermination in the name of Jesus; the man who represented life, love, forgiveness, and reconciliation. After I returned home, the lawyers called to inform me that Judge Justice had stayed the execution.

* * *

My introduction to the latent fatality of the political process began with meeting Governor Bob Graham in Florida in March 1979 and his subsequent killing of John Spenkelink on May 25, 1979.

305

In memory of John, on the eve of the fortieth anniversary of his execution four of us who were intimately involved connected on a conference telephone call. David Kendall, John's lead lawyer; Debbie Fins, the younger lawyer on the case; Susan Cary, a lawyer who has worked with so many for so long on Florida's death row; and I were conversing.

It is a revealing fact that the four of us were talking after being annealed together in that awful spring of 1979. How many people stay in touch after forty years and recall what drew them together? The intimacy of the struggle, the fight for life over death, the success and desperation, the ultimate failure—it was all indelibly etched on our souls.

As we discussed our lives now and remembered the horror of 1979, it was as if we had picked up a conversation from last week rather than years ago. As I participated in the call, I could feel the sheer goodness of these souls. Their kindness, thoughtfulness, and willingness to walk through the fire of state killing still resonated. As painful as it had been, and still was for me, we would have all done it again.

Debbie put it best when talking about John: "He was singular. I have not seen anyone else like him. Who he was made him truly singular." She was right. As was David in his eulogy for John at the memorial service at First Presbyterian Church in Tallahassee, Florida, on May 27, 1979: "He was a decent man to whom something terribly indecent was done."

CHAPTER TWENTY-THREE

Summer of 2019

THE SPRING RAIN had been abundant and there was no late frost. The blueberry harvest was the largest in the seven years I'd been doing this work. The picking, washing, and sorting, then packing them into containers and selling them, was a rewarding respite; five human beings had been killed by the state of Tennessee in a year. Tennessee hadn't executed so many so fast since 1948. And the blueberries did not know, did not care, and flourished. In doing so, they helped bring me back from the PTSD.

I completed my second op-ed for the *Tennessean*, "The Governor and the Holy Ghost." This one focused on how Governor Lee and his evangelical ilk do whatever they please because of their relationship to the Holy Ghost or Spirit, which allows them to ignore the teachings of Jesus and still carry on as "Christians." This is simply a continuation of the subjective attitude that has allowed the church to commit murder and mayhem for centuries.

As I finished this work in August, I realized I was regaining my own spirit. I was regaining my anger at this insanity that had ensnared me. That anger was definitely a good sign. My therapy continued, and the EMDR was slowly helping remove the powerful emotions brought on by my trauma.

307

Steve West was electrocuted on August 15, 2019. You could check the boxes:

1. Mentally ill.
2. Did not do the killing.
3. Suffered horrific abuse while growing up.
4. Inadequate lawyering at trial.
5. Poor.
6. Juvenile accomplice was recorded acknowledging to another inmate that he, the accomplice, had killed both women.
7. The victim was white, as are the victims in almost all cases that are prosecuted for the death penalty.
8. A Christian governor denied clemency.

Steve's last words summed it up: "God created man . . . and Jesus wept."

Shortly after West's execution, I saw something in court that, in over forty years of working against the death penalty, I had never before witnessed. It happened in the criminal court of Davidson County and concerned the case of Abu-Ali Abdur'Rahman.

Abu-Ali's case, which had been pending before Judge Monty Watkins in criminal court in Nashville for almost two years on a racial discrimination claim, had now begun moving forward. Once again, Governor Lee provided no prospect for clemency. District Attorney Glenn Funk was deeply troubled after reviewing the claims that Brad MacLean, Abu-Ali's lawyer, had assembled from the notes of the original prosecutor in the case (back in the 1980s) detailing racial discrimination in jury selection.

On August 28, beginning at 9:45 a.m., there was a hearing before Judge Watkins. MacLean began by detailing the prosecutorial misconduct in jury selection. One example of many: Mr. Thomas, a prospective juror, was described in the prosecutor's notes as "seemed uneducated, unintelligent and uncommunicative." John Zimmerman, the prosecutor, reached this conclusion because Mr. Thomas was African American. But in fact, Mr. Thomas was the college-educated pastor of a local church and a very good communicator. It also came to light that Mr. Zimmerman had led a session at a bar conference on how to get away with such racial discrimination.

After reviewing the record, Mr. Funk declared to Judge Watkins that a prosecutor's job was to be a "minister of justice." It was not about winning at any cost. "The prosecutor's job was to pursue justice with fairness. Overt racial prejudice has no place in the justice system." He then went on to discuss how the prosecutor's office operates now, emphasizing that it does not engage in the practices Mr. Zimmerman practiced in the 1980s. At the end of his presentation, he offered an agreed order to MacLean and Abu-Ali, which stated that all parties agreed to a life sentence. Mr. Funk signed it, as did Abu-Ali and MacLean. They submitted it to Judge Watkins, who said that he would review the record and reach a decision. The next day he signed the order and Abu-Ali's sentence was reduced from death to life.

Quite the day!

* * *

On the night of September 6, I had a death row dream. I was sitting around the Table of Reconciliation in Unit 2-A, visiting with Abu-Ali, Nick Sutton, Mike Rimmer, Akil, and K. B. We were relaxing and discussing life. It was a pleasant dream, although Nick's execution date in February was nearing. It was quite vivid when I recalled it after I woke up the next morning.

Attorney General of Tennessee Herbert Slatery wrote to District Attorney Glenn Funk stating he opposed the proposed agreed order with Abu-Ali. Even though Funk had made repeated efforts over the

309

summer to obtain a response from the attorney general, Funk didn't receive the letter stating Slatery's opposition until the morning of the hearing. It was no surprise the attorney general appealed the agreed order. He also requested more execution dates from the Tennessee Supreme Court.

The session with my trauma therapist on October 4 was revelatory. At the beginning of each session, I take several laminated papers on which words are inscribed, both negative and positive, and indicate which word best describes my state of mind. I also complete the Burns Depression Checklist. The therapist tallied my numbers of the Burns checklist, wrote something in each corner and handed it back to me. In the left-hand top corner, written in all capitals and circled, were the words: *NO DEPRESSION*. In the right-hand top corner, written and circled, was: *A+*. I smiled. She had said from the beginning, "This will be hard, but we will get through it. You will get yourself back." She was a woman of her word. I felt like a kid with a good report card!

Bob Dylan sang, "I dreamed I saw Saint Augustine, alive as you or me." The dream I experienced while the rain came down reminded me of Dylan's song. In it, I was in my old office in Hillsboro Village, on Twenty-First Avenue South, some blocks from Vanderbilt University, with my colleagues in the Southern Coalition on Jails and Prisons. One of them called from across the office, "Joe, come here and look." As I crossed the room, I noticed she had pulled a cardboard box from the bottom shelf of a bookcase. Looking into the box, I was stunned. There was my colleague and friend Harmon Wray (Harmon had died a dozen years before). We lifted him from the box and unfolded him until he reached his full height. He was upright, standing before us, "alive as you or me." Only he was mute. He could not speak. I went to the telephone and called my neighbor and doctor friend, Tom John. "Harmon Wray has come back from the dead," I said, "and he seems to be fine except that he can't speak."

Tom agreed to examine him. One of my colleagues left to get coffee for Harmon, and as he left he asked, "Should I get some for Tom John?" I said "No. It will take a half hour to get there and it would be cold by then." Soon we left to take Harmon to his medical exam.

When I shared the dream with Becca, she asked how it made me feel.

"Good," I said. "It was great to see Harmon again. For him to be resurrected in our presence."

After we'd discussed the dream a bit more, she said, "Now—it's your dream and make of it what you will. But I wonder: What are the three things you think of when you think of Harmon?"

My answer was quick: "Gentle. Loving. Pessimistic. A real Eeyore."

She let that statement hover in the air between us. Then she said, "And what do you see in yourself that Harmon represents?"

I thought about it for a while, and when I didn't offer an answer, she said, "Harmon was folded up in a box. You stretched him out, unfolded him. He was resurrected. You have resurrected yourself over the last year. You are straight and tall again. Also, you are loving and gentle once more and you have regained your pessimism." Indeed, I *had* recovered my pessimism, a sure sign I was no longer in despair. "And you had a shot of coffee to give you energy to get going. You have come back to yourself."

Becca, this remarkable soul mate of forty-plus years walked into my life on a summer's day when I was fasting in 1976. Even in my reduced state, I recognized what a lovely person she was in her blue jeans and cotton sweater, with her long, brunette hair and a dove of peace around her neck. As we are aging, lo these many years later, she is still a wonderful gift in my life.

October 8–11, I journeyed to the Sisters of Loretto in Kentucky, about eight miles from the Abbey of Gethsemane. I've been making this trip annually most years since the late 1970s.

Sister Elaine Prevallet, a wise and gentle soul, has led meditations for myself and the groups I bring to meet with her. We have become fast friends. She has been my spiritual mentor. She and I were able to meet on my last morning there and had a good visit.

As I made the three-hour drive home on the eleventh, I learned the Los Angeles Dodgers lost the fifth game of their playoff against the Nationals. I was too rested to even care. It appeared one World Series Championship—Vanderbilt baseball winning the College World Series—was my allotment that year.

My return to Nashville brought me immediately back into the prison world. I learned that the prison administration had turned down the request of the Episcopal bishops to share Communion with Abu-Ali during their visit with him on Monday, October 14. The reason given was that sharing Communion had not been requested at the time the visit was approved. A few emails over the weekend had resolved the problem by 11:30 a.m. Monday. The bishops, along with Dean Timothy Kimbrough of Christ Church Cathedral, where Abu-Ali was a member, were able to visit and share the Eucharist with Abu-Ali, who sang "Amazing Grace" in his lovely baritone voice for his visitors.

At my monthly psychiatric visit, we discussed phasing out my medication. I shared with him how the Burns Depression Inventory I'd recently taken had gone, and he smiled. "Most people would be happy to have that score," he said. We agreed that I would return in three months. *Joe, you've come a long way, baby*, I thought as I walked out of his office back to my truck.

A Swedish network television show was filming Nashville, focusing on many facets of the city, and the producers were interested in including Tennessee's handling of the death penalty. I agreed to two interviews, considering it an opportunity to discuss my work and what Dietrich Bonhoeffer termed the cost of discipleship.

We have a general store in our neighborhood that is hugely

supportive of Donald Trump. The employees wear Trump shirts. The electronic sign in front of the store rotates various right-wing notions. My Swedish friends, in the neighborhood for my interview, were curious about the sign and entered the store. Somewhat surprised by the Trump T-shirts and merch, they asked about it all. Soon they found themselves expelled from the store and permanently banned from reentering the premises. The Swedes were polite and as Nordic-looking as folks could be. Evidently, they failed to sufficiently worship at the altar of Trump.

My first trip to Sweden came in 1986. I was there with others to examine Sweden's criminal justice system; on that same trip, I would investigate the systems in England, France, and Germany. Our group visited Kumla, Sweden's maximum-security prison above the arctic circle. Kumla was a decided contrast to American max prisons because they provided education and vocational programs for the men to increase the likelihood that they would be successful when they returned to society. As in all European countries, the Swedes consider America barbaric for using the death penalty.

> *As in all European countries, the Swedes consider America barbaric for using the death penalty.*

Halloween Week

Sunday, October 27, Becca and I settled into the pew at Christ Church Cathedral for the 8:30 a.m. worship service. I kept my brown leather motorcycle jacket on because it was cool in the church. In the pew in front of us were Ann Walker King and Ken King. Noticing that Ann was also wearing a brown motorcycle jacket, I leaned forward and tapped her on the shoulder. Pointing at her jacket and then mine, I said, "Here's to Ed Zagorski."

She smiled and said, "Ed would appreciate our wearing these."

Halloween week in 2019 was a year removed from the trauma and killing of the same period in 2018. It had taken a year for me to be able to refer to Ed in a loving, nontraumatized manner. Now, Ann and I were able to smile at his memory with gratitude for his friendship.

When the clouds that morning gave way to a sunny fall day, with the leaves finally turning, I drove the five miles from my house to Philip Workman's grave for a visit.

The late afternoon sun backlit the trees. Three red maples near his grave showered it with their lovely red leaves. I brushed them off his marker. It had been over twelve years since the May day we had gathered here to bury him. Standing amid the beauty of creation and viewing a marker commemorating the horror of state-sanctioned killing, I whispered a prayer of gratitude, of thanksgiving, for having known this man and for our friendship.

As the week progressed, I was acutely aware of what I had been doing with Ed Zagorski at the same time the previous year. Tuesday, October 29, I was depressed. Not out-the-bottom-of-the-barrel melancholia, but really down. That didn't surprise me. I weathered the internal storm brought about not only by the events of the past but also by my mixed emotions about returning to the prison on Halloween.

I drove to the prison early in the afternoon of Thursday, October 31. As I searched for an empty parking space in the lot, I noticed the absence of deer and turkeys in the field near the prison. I shut off my truck and followed the long-familiar routine: I removed my license from my wallet, put my volunteer badge in my shirt pocket, and left my cell phone and wallet in the truck.

I chuckled, remembering a story one of the death row visitors, David Bass, likes to tell. I had oriented him to visit Terry King on death row. His first trip to the prison—as it turned out, to *any* prison—he was full of trepidation. So much so that after parking his car, he called his wife on his cell phone and said, "I'm going in"— the words countless movies have used as their protagonists rush into combat. David laughs about it now, because "going in" has transformed his life. Besides, when you enter death row, you're entering one of the most strictly controlled and safest places in Nashville—for the visitors, at least. The love David has for Terry and the other guys has become profound over the years.

On that Halloween, I headed for Unit 2. This time last year, it was day two of the second deathwatch with Ed Zagorski. The guards buzzed me into the unit, and I made my way to the center of the pod, surrounded by the pod's four wings extending away from me. Abu-Ali approached, and we shook hands. We chatted briefly and he pointed out where the other guys I'd come to see were located.

First, I walked up the steps to the second level and knocked on the hard plastic vertical strip that served as a window for Mike Rimmer's cell. Mike, who had requested that I visit, arose from his self-made desk and extended his hand through the pie flap. We shook hands and I knelt so that we could hear each other through the open flap.

First, Mike asked about me; he was concerned. We discussed how I was feeling and then moved on to several items of business he hoped I might be able to help him resolve. When his list was finished, I told him I had to go to see the other guys. We held hands and he prayed a lovely prayer for my health and safety and for Becca and Amelia.

As I made my way to the program building, 2-A, several of the guys gave me a shout out as I passed them. Terry King came over and

315

we hugged, then sat down to discuss his continuing effort to donate his kidney, which had hit yet another snare. Recently, the doctor who was championing this effort had suggested a new strategy. I explained it to Terry, and he agreed to think about it.

I walked over to the law library, where several prisoners were gathered. They stood and we exchanged hugs in a semi-circle. Soon we were teasing one another, and it felt as if I had been gone a week rather than a year.

Next stop was the art room, next door to the library. A half-dozen guys were working here. This was where Billy Irick, Derrick Quintero, and Harold Nichols had labored to create the stations of the cross scroll. The six of us teased each other and talked about various projects. Gary Sutton was part of this group. I feared he would be among the next to be "dated up." The attorney general had requested nine more execution dates, and Gary was to be one of them. I believed that he was innocent, but he'd had no luck interesting people in his case over the years. Gary speaks with that mountain, East-Tennessee accent that I love to hear.

I was feeling tired by this time, so I said goodbye and headed out of Unit 2 and through the administration building to the parking lot.

"How'd the visit go?" Becca asked when I arrived home. I was glad I had gone but surprised at how drained I felt afterward.

The next day was November 1, the anniversary of Ed Zagorski's killing by the state of Tennessee.

Dreams

PTSD has put me in touch with my dreams in a way that I did not previously understand. As my psychiatrist said, "The dreams mean things are percolating." Halloween night, after a lovely time at Ann Walker and Ken King's, handing out candy for trick-or-treaters, I slept.

My dream that night was set in Laurinburg, North Carolina, a town that has a safe and comfortable association for me because I spent four years of college there at St. Andrews. In my dream, I was waiting to visit a prisoner. Above the waist I wore only an undershirt, and as I sat waiting, I felt exposed. No one seemed to mind, but I still felt uncomfortable. After waiting a good while, I went up to the desk to ask when I might see the prisoner. A female officer told me to go ahead and asked if I remembered which room I was going to visit. "Seventeen," I said. She nodded and waved me through the door.

I opened the door to number seventeen, entered, and looked around at the bare room. On a hook on the back of the door was my shirt from the last visit. I laughed at myself.

The prisoner visit was unremarkable, and I went back to my truck after I was done.

Still in my dream: Before my next trip to the prison, I discussed local politics with African Americans who lived in Laurinburg. We were strategizing how to elect Blacks to the city council to counter the white oligarchy. The scene segued back to the prison. Again, above the waist I wore only an undershirt, no top shirt, and felt the same sense of exposure. Once again, I went to room seventeen, and once again my long-sleeved shirt awaited me there. This time, when the visit was over, I wore the shirt out of the prison.

The dream was surfacing my mixed feelings about the trip to death row. I felt exposed, vulnerable. The prison staff were polite and helpful. The prisoner visit was fine. But the entire process left me with a feeling of endangerment—but not from the prisoners or the staff. Rather, I felt a sense of imminent danger connected with the place itself.

The next night brought another dream. I was at Camp Hanover again, where I had been a camp counselor during college. It represented a safe and secure place for me.

317

My friend Bob Pryor was in charge, and we were preparing for an attack. There had been an earlier assault that we had repelled, and now we awaited another. Bob asked someone if he had checked the western perimeter. The person said, "Yes, but that side isn't solidified for an attack."

I peered out the windows of Knoxwood Lodge, through the darkness, between the trees, toward the lake. Suddenly, I saw what resembled white blossoms floating through the night and landing in the lake. *Parachutists*, I realized. The attack would come from the lake, up the hill to the lodge. I told Bob what I had seen.

Now the scene changed. I was still in Knoxwood Lodge, but now I was confronting a Nordic dude who held a long staff with a blade at the end. I had a similar weapon, but mine had no blade. We were about to engage in hand-to-hand combat. A soldier approached him and whispered in his ear. Suddenly, he disappeared, and I was left alone. I went to the door leading out of the lodge and turned the handle—locked. I felt desperate to flee—and just then a woman appeared with a key and unlocked the door. I was able to escape.

Two dreams with messages for me. The first dream reflected the exposure I experienced in returning to the prison. The unease and threat I felt was not from people but from something about the place itself. In my forty years of working in this environment, I had given the shirt off my back. I had paid a price. But I was able to return and get my shirt back. I had not lost myself permanently by going to the prison—but I had been damaged. The African Americans represented the effort to change the system, to make it more just. They knew that the politics of the white oligarchy functioned as a tyranny of the majority.

The second dream communicated that my happiness—such as I'd experienced at Camp Hanover—was under siege. Some of the people we had counted on didn't do their jobs. We withstood the initial assault, but the parachutists over the lake prevailed with the second attack. Afterward, I was alone, a captive. The Nordic guy represented all the power brokers I had dealt with over the years, and he was about to engage me in mortal combat. But then he exited, leaving me alone but still trapped, imprisoned behind a locked door. Then a woman appeared and set me free.

I was in a space of safety and security, but I felt like I was in a war. A war we, apparently, ultimately lost. I could see all the faces of my dead friends. I was trapped and locked away. The women who saved me in real life—Becca; Elaine Prevallet; Jo Ann, my trauma therapist; and the many female friends I have and have had through the years—opened the door and freed me.

The Absurd

About twenty years ago, I was told that Lee Hall was going blind. The prison health-care people had not provided needed medical help for him. I discussed this with Lee, then I reached out to the Nashville medical community for help. Because Becca worked in this community, we were fortunate to have friends there who would help when I called on them.

A wonderful ophthalmologist agreed to examine Lee and determine what was causing him to lose his vision. The diagnosis she gave was sobering. Lee had acute glaucoma, which would lead to total blindness. However, there were some sophisticated glasses—like something out of *Star Trek*—that would enable him to see. They cost several thousand dollars. There were eye drops that would reduce the pressure that caused his glaucoma to progress. This information was turned over to the prison medical staff.

Lee's execution date was December 5. On that day, I was in Durham, North Carolina, to speak to a group of progressive prosecutors (not an oxymoron). The afternoon of the fifth, I received a telephone call from Lee's lawyer, Jonathan King, who asked if I had a final message for Lee, who would be electrocuted that evening.

"Please tell Lee it has been a long and winding road," I said. "I have been honored to accompany him on this journey. I am grateful for his friendship. I know that he has obtained the mercy of God. God will be with him and enfold him in his everlasting arms with grace and love. Tell him I love him."

The next day I went down for breakfast in the hotel before my panel presentation. Mike Farrell entered the restaurant as I finished my meal, so I walked over to greet him. Knowing about my PTSD, he asked "How are you feeling?"

"A little dinged up," I said.

We discussed what each of us would say on the upcoming panel. Then I reached into my pocket and handed him a linked bracelet. Originally, the bracelet had belonged to Morris Mason. Morris gave it to my colleague, Marie Deans, as we sat outside his cell in the basement of the Virginia State Penitentiary on June 25, 1985, just a couple of hours before his electrocution. Morris gave me a picture of him in his cell on death row. Mentally challenged, Morris was childlike in his behavior. As Marie wept, he tried to comfort her: "I'm gonna be strong. I'm going to be brave. I'm gonna make you proud." He was like a child trying to please his parents. At 10:45, the death squad assembled outside his cell. "I love you," Morris told us. "Don't be sad. Don't cry." We told Morris we loved him as they shackled him and marched him to the death chamber. Later, the bracelet passed to me.

"Mike," I said, "I think you should have this bracelet." I reminded him of its history. He was grateful. And I was glad that someone else who knew and loved Marie would carry it forward. It was time to pass it on.

Mike and I walked together into the large room to make our

panel presentations. When my turn came, I shared stories of men and women I had worked with, many of whom are included in this book, who had been killed by the state. I didn't mention Ed Zagorski, though—the trauma was still too raw. Telling those stories (and summoning up that final message for my dear friend Lee just hours before his execution) took all the strength I had. Exhausted, I was glad to return home.

I arrived home with my soul stirred and uneasy. I was glad to be seeing my trauma therapist at the end of the week and I emailed her and informed her of my unease. She replied that it was to be expected, given Lee's execution and the exposure to the prosecutors. Even though these were progressive prosecutors, I had spent my adult life battling prosecutors who were trying to kill people I loved. The event plus Lee's execution was a recipe for disassociation.

We soon received a welcome piece of good news: the Tennessee Supreme Court finally ruled on the attorney general's motion to expedite Abu-Ali's appeal. In a December 11 decision, the court denied the request to expedite the process and referred it to the Court of Criminal Appeals. The court also dissolved Abu-Ali's April execution date. This could mean that even if Abu-Ali did not prevail on appeal, the process would carry the case into 2021.

On the night of December 16, I received a call from death row. Terry King was checking in to see how I was doing. He then told me of an uncanny event. He had returned to his cell after his visit that evening to discover a card from Lee Hall in his mail. Lee was thanking him for his friendship as well as thanking him for introducing me to him. Once again, I was struck by the generosity of the condemned. Lee, in extremis, scratches out a note of thanksgiving for friendship. It is astonishing and overwhelming.

Lee was thanking him for his friendship as well as thanking him for introducing me to him. Once again, I was struck by the generosity of the condemned. Lee, in extremis, scratches out a note of thanksgiving for friendship. It is astonishing and overwhelming.

Beauty

On Monday morning, December 16, Becca told me she had a surprise. I soon discovered it: familiar loud and piercing notes came through our closed bedroom window. Peering out the window, I spied a pileated woodpecker holding forth. She was in our dogwood tree eating the red berries. I could not believe she was so close. The tree was the same height as our second-story window, so the pileated was at eye level with us. If I had opened the window and extended my arm, I could have touched her. This elusive bird, which we hear year-round but see only when the leaves fall from the trees, was near us in all her splendor. The red head with the feathers swept back (the ducktail look), the black eighteen-inch-long body, the white neck stripes that seem to extend to rim the wings—what a magnificent creature! Becca and I sat and watched her for more than ten minutes until she flew away, displaying the full moon white circles under her wings. We were overjoyed that she kept coming back for ten days, and each time Becca and I were spellbound by her beauty. One day she brought with her a juvenile who joined in the berry eating. The sheer loveliness of this creature helped still my soul.

* * *

The apostle Paul has a phrase: "seeing through a glass darkly." It's a good description of my current state, as of this writing. I see vague outlines of a way forward, but I have no clarity. The trip to death row after almost a year away and the subsequent dreams have caused a reaction in me I did not expect. If I hoped to have some definitive answer for the future of my work, what I got instead was ambiguity and uncertainty.

There are some discrete tasks I can continue:

1. Work on getting approval for Terry King to donate a kidney.

2. Continue to work on Abu-Ali's clemency.

3. Help Ron Cauthern, who discovered he was a German citizen while on death row and wishes to transfer to Germany.

4. Continue to work with the visitors on death row.

There are also tasks I can no longer do:

1. I cannot go to the prison weekly. It takes too much of an emotional toll. I have recruited Matthew Lewis, a young Episcopal priest and friend, to attend to death row prisoners on a more regular basis than I can. On November 18, 2019, I took him to the prison to introduce him to everyone in Unit 2.

2. I cannot do deathwatches. That would put me so close to the flame that I may be burned beyond recognition.

3. I cannot do any more vigils, outside the prison or anywhere else. It is too much.

4. The prison is still a trigger. The trip to Durham, only my second airline trip without Becca in thirteen months, revealed how badly I am singed.

5. I cannot visit any more governors to ask for clemency.

I do not know the way forward.

I do not know the way forward.

CHAPTER TWENTY-FOUR

2020

WARREN MCCLESKEY was executed in September of 1991 by the state of Georgia. He was a dear friend.[1] Although it was twenty-eight years since his killing, I had a vivid dream of Warren on December 30, 2019—one in which Warren and I were in a tight embrace, saying goodbye as they prepared to lead him to the electric chair.

Warren McCleskey was executed in September of 1991 by the state of Georgia. He was a dear friend.

The guards were nearby, and when Warren stepped back from our embrace, they led him into the death chamber. I was in the control room. I wore no shirt—I was looking for my shirt and couldn't find it. Even though I was in the control room, I felt exposed and out of control. It was odd that the guards weren't hustling me out of there, given that the control room is where they initiate and monitor the

---

1 For a full account of his case and our relationship, see Joseph B. Ingle, *Slouching Toward Tyranny: Mass Incarceration, Death Sentences and Racism* (New York: Algora Publishing, 2015).

execution. I looked up; a guard was wheeling Warren past me in a wheelchair. His head was slumped on his left shoulder, and his eyes were closed. They had killed him. I told the guard pushing the chair, "I'll take it from here." He allowed me to take the wheelchair and push Warren out of the death house.

But once we were outside, I realized that Warren wasn't dead. I took him away from the prison, obtained medical care, and he was restored. I found him a job, and all was going well for him. And that's how the dream ended.

When I shared this with Becca, she asked which three things about Warren had most impressed me. "Kindness, generosity, and giving," I said. "Plus, he was a real Christian. As his death row brother Billy Moore put it, 'Warren is a better Christian than I am.'"

"Those same three elements," Becca said, "are strongly present in your own character."

The effort to bring Warren back to life in my dream resembled my own efforts to restore myself from PTSD.

Later, I shared the dream with my trauma therapist.

"The dream could be about self-repair," she said. "You have been damaged, a portion of you destroyed. Yet you are engaged in restoring yourself. In the dream, Warren—representing you—is well enough to actually have a job courtesy of your resurrection. Those qualities you admired in Warren, that are in you, are on the mend. The state killed Warren, but those elements of him that exemplified his character are still with you. You carry him with you. This could be about resurrection." These words came from a woman who had repeatedly stated she did not understand "the religious framework" that had held me together doing this work through the years.

I write this in January 2020, fifteen months removed from Ed Zagorski's killing. In each session of trauma therapy, I focus on the image that haunts me the most at that time. Today, I envision several of the events that revolved around my relationship with Ed. The weeks we spent talking when he shared his life story with me. Then the two deathwatches. The vigil after the execution when I read my rewrite of Dan Berrigan's poem. Seeing his body in the crematorium Saturday morning. The redness in the face with the two blackened marks from burning. Becca driving me to pick up his ashes Saturday afternoon. Placing the ashes between my feet as Becca drove me home. A man I was talking with on Thursday evening had become a reddened corpse on Saturday morning and ashes between my feet late Saturday afternoon. It was all too much.

As I focused on the images, the trauma therapist led me through EMDR, rapid eye movement. I revisited each image, recalling the feelings and the events of those days. I had felt utterly alone, help-less, overwhelmed—but I had tried to assist Ed as best I could. After each visit, when I left the prison, I had felt I was done, in the fullest sense of the phrase. I had nothing left. I was on automatic pilot through the vigil and the trip out of state that had followed. This going through the motions while totally numb is called automatic obedience. I had disassociated; I was literally not myself as I walked through my appointed tasks.

That day the therapist recounted the chain of events that had led to the end of Ed's life. Once again, she told me I had helped Ed die well. He had felt valued, loved, and authenticated. We had given each other all we had to share under the most excruciating circumstances.

When I began to see this therapist, we engaged in the process of self-repair. It has proven to be a lengthy one, and the end is not in sight. Slowly, incrementally, I have made progress. I am no longer numb, enervated, or helpless. My friends are being killed by a godless process, in the name of God, by our Christian governors. As a result, there is much EMDR in my future.

I am slowly getting myself back. Some days I am sad, but that is to be expected, given that my friends are being murdered. We are dwelling in an unholy time, and sadness is an appropriate response. As is anger.

> *Some days I am sad, but that is to be expected, given that my friends are being murdered. We are dwelling in an unholy time, and sadness is an appropriate response. As is anger.*

On January 7, 2020, Episcopal bishop Phoebe Roaf and I sat at a table in the empty C pod, visiting Abu-Ali. I mostly listened to Abu-Ali and Phoebe share their stories. She, an African American woman who against all odds had become not just an Episcopal priest in conservative Louisiana but a bishop as well—of the Diocese of West Tennessee. Abu-Ali, an African American man who had fled an abusive father in Fort Bragg, North Carolina.

Abu-Ali shared his abusive childhood, his love of the woods where he always felt safe and secure, his living with the Lakota, his prison experiences and rape, his study of Islam and Buddhism, and finally, his return to Christianity as an Episcopalian. He described his confirmation service conducted by Bishop Bauerschmidt in Building 2-A and his reading of William Stringfellow with Timothy Kimbrough's guidance. He was preparing to study to become a deacon in the Episcopal church as his next step in the pilgrimage of faith.

I asked Abu-Ali if he had received the postcard I'd sent him during my last visit with the Sisters of Loretto.

"Yes, I did," he said. "I appreciate it. It means a lot to know you remember me while you are on your journey of revival."

"It means a lot to know you remember me while you are on your journey of revival."

Abu-Ali's statement was an epiphany for me. My "journey of revival." That is exactly what I had been embarked on since All Saints' Day, November 1, 2018. And for Abu-Ali to recognize it, to name it, was an immeasurable aid to my self-understanding.

* * *

Frances Christian is one of the visitors signed up through the Visitation on Death Row program. She visited Nick Sutton weekly for five years. Nick had a February 20, 2020, execution date.

When the execution loomed just five weeks away, Frances and I met at one of my favorite restaurants for lunch to discuss how she was doing. She felt she was well supported and doing okay. She shared where Nick was in his journey.

Nick felt that he had a good case for clemency. Jurors on his trial jury had said they would have given him a life sentence if they had known all the pertinent information at trial. He'd been convicted of killing another prisoner; of the several people involved in that murder, Nick was the only one to receive the death penalty. His trial and appellate lawyer had made serious mistakes, and Nick would pay for those errors. Nick had a good institutional record since coming to death row and graduating from the mediation program. Correctional officers signed affidavits describing how Nick had saved their lives over the years.

"He is hopeful for clemency," Frances said. "But I don't see it happening."

I agreed. I told her about Don Johnson, who'd been hopeful even on deathwatch. That hopefulness seems to be part of an interior progression each condemned man goes through as he approaches the end. Each one does it differently. "In my experience," I said, "it's important to let the prisoner sort out this process. Our feelings on the likelihood of clemency are beside the point. We are there for the prisoner. We support, listen, and love. The prisoner does the hard work.

"The theologian Paul Tillich once said, 'It is all right to be cynical about all things except the Ultimate,'"[2] I told Frances. "And that's my perspective on the death penalty in Tennessee. We can't expect clemency from Governor Lee, and the courts have delivered neither justice nor mercy in these cases. It's best to be cynical about the entire process and steel ourselves for the executions that are coming. Of course we dread them, not only for Nick but for the other nine cases the Tennessee Supreme Court is considering before setting execution dates. We are on the verge of Tennessee becoming the execution leader in the country. The three in 2018 and three in 2019 catapulted the state into second place, trailing only Texas. When the Tennessee Supreme Court schedules the next nine for state killing, we will leapfrog Texas to become first in the pace of executions. Somehow, we must navigate the dread of that upcoming reality and not let it overwhelm us. I simply try to banish it from my thoughts whenever it pops into my mind."

"Matthew Lewis has agreed to be Nick's spiritual adviser,"

2 One of the benefits of attending Union Theological Seminary was learning the stories and quotes attributed to Niebuhr, Tillich, and other teachers.

Frances said. I was pleased to hear it. In a short period of time, Matthew and Nick had bonded, and clearly Nick was comfortable asking Matthew to perform that role.

Matthew and I met to discuss the ABCs of deathwatch so he would know what to expect on February 18–20. (Since every death-watch is different, this preparation is by definition incomplete.) We covered a lot in an hour and a half, and I was satisfied that he understood that it was his presence, his being more than his doing, that would mean the most for Nick.

The Tennessee Supreme Court set two more execution dates: Oscar Smith on June 4 and Harold "Red" Nichols on August 4. Seven more prisoners were still awaiting dates from the TSC. Red had applied for a hearing from a state court judge that the attorney general's office successfully opposed. The denial of that hearing kept him in line for execution. Red, Billy Irick, and Derrick Quintero had painted the twenty-two-foot "Stations of the Cross" scroll.

AFib

At 3:00 a.m. on Friday, January 17, I awoke to let the dogs out. I was quite dizzy and returned to bed as soon as they came back into the house. I awoke at seven o'clock, expecting to have slept off the dizziness. Intending to go make coffee, I slipped out of bed and stood—and the dizziness returned. I navigated carefully down the hallway to the kitchen. I had to hold on to the counter while I made the coffee. *Maybe eating breakfast will get rid of the dizziness*, I thought. It didn't. I woke Becca, who took my pulse and blood pressure.

"We're going to the ER," she said. "Your heart is out of rhythm."

At the hospital, an EKG officially determined that I had atrial fibrillation. What made that unusual was my low resting heart rate, which was sixty. The doctors suspected that I might have had a stroke, so I was admitted to the hospital. Several images were made of my neck, brain, heart, and lungs through various tests, and once the possibility of a stroke had been eliminated, the doctors turned their attention to my heart. I was given heparin via IV. If the blood thinner was not successful, I would have a cardioversion of my heart on Monday. Fortunately, Saturday afternoon my heart converted back into rhythm. I would not need the shock of the paddles on my chest.

Becca spent Friday night sleeping in the chair beside my hospital bed. Saturday morning, as I lay there with the heparin IV dripping into my arm and my eyes closed, I had a strange experience: I felt as if I were outside my body and positioned above my bed, looking down at myself. I could see Becca in the chair to my left and the IV inserted into my right arm. All seemed perfectly normal except for the bizarre fact that I was looking down on my own body. I felt no fear—I felt nothing at all. I recalled my conversation with James Adams on the eve of his execution at the Florida State Prison in May of 1984. When I asked whether he had ever felt like he was dying, he recalled a time when, as a child, he was bedridden. His family had gathered around the bed as if he were dying. Suddenly, he too was looking down on his body from above. Not only could he see all of his family, he could also see through the cracks in the floorboards to the chickens under the floor. Then he felt a pulling on his ankles and found himself back in his body.

After my heart settled into an acceptable rhythm Saturday afternoon, Becca asked if I had been afraid. The answer was no—I hadn't even considered it. I was in no pain; I was not having a heart attack. The doctors and nurses were competent. I felt well cared for and expected to return to health.

Returning home, however, found me tired and without much energy. The layering of the AFib on my lingering PTSD set me back. Ed Porter noted how tired I seemed. Slowly, though, over the next week, my strength and vitality returned.

Becca, as a member of the Christ Church Cathedral vestry, was chosen to be a delegate to the annual convention of the Diocese of Tennessee of the Episcopal Church. The convention would be held at Christ Church Cathedral on January 24 and 25. I encouraged her to go. I felt fine, if a little lethargic.

At the convention, the body passed the following resolution regarding Abu-Ali:

> *Whereas,* the Episcopal Church holds a long-standing opposition to the use of capital punishment, most recently affirmed at the 79th General Convention of the Episcopal Church (DO77); and
>
> *Whereas,* Abu-Ali Abdur'Rahman, an inmate of the State of Tennessee's death row at Riverbend Maximum Security Institution, for the past 32 years, is a member of the Episcopal Church in the Diocese of Tennessee, (his confirmation by the Rt. Reverend John Bauerschmidt, on October 15, 2014, is recorded at Christ Church Cathedral, Nashville;) and
>
> *Whereas,* the reduction of Mr. Abu-Ali Abdur'Rahman's sentence from "death" to "life imprisonment without possibility of parole" by the Honorable Monte Watkins, Judge of the Criminal Court of Davidson County, after consultation with Glenn Funk, the District Attorney of Davidson County, for reasons including their determination of racial bias in the jury selection for the trial that convicted and sentenced Mr. Abdur'Rahman to death; *therefore, be it*
>
> *Resolved,* that members of the convention pray on behalf of and for the well-being of Abu-Ali Abdur'Rahman and all death row inmates; *and be it further*

Resolved, that the Secretary of this 188th Convention of the Episcopal Diocese of Tennessee make known to any courts considering this matter and Governor of the State of Tennessee, Bill Lee, this petition that Mr. Abdur'Rahman's reduction of sentence be upheld by the Tennessee Court of Criminal Appeals, and any other courts to which the matter is appealed; *and be it further*

Resolved, that the Secretary of this 188th Convention of the Diocese of Tennessee transmit, forward, or send this resolution to the bishops of the Diocese of West Tennessee and of East Tennessee and the delegates of their respective annual conventions for their consideration.[3]

* * *

On January 31, when I crawled out of bed at approximately 3:30 a.m. to let the dogs out, I immediately felt dizzy, much to my distress. It had been exactly two weeks since the last attack of dizziness, and I realized that I was probably in AFib once again. I went back to bed and awoke Becca at 7:00 a.m. She checked my pulse, confirmed the arrhythmia, and we dashed to the hospital.

This time, once the AFib was confirmed, I was able to remain in a room in the ER. My cardiologist determined that I should stay put, hooked up to monitors, and take an oral medication to see if it would convert my heart back to normal. If the oral drug didn't do the trick by 4:00 p.m., they would do the cardioversion. At 3:50 p.m., the nurse came in to check my heart rate—and much to my relief, I was no longer in AFib.

I was discharged, with instructions to take an oral version of

---

3 Timothy Kimbrough, email to Joseph Ingle, January 10, 2022.

the drug that had helped convert my heart rate back and to remain on blood thinner.

The next day, Groundhog Day, was glorious—blue skies and sixty degrees. I was sluggish, napping for a couple of hours. But Monday I felt like myself again.

Thursday night, February 6, at a United Church of Christ clergy meeting, Jennifer Crane asked me about the vigil planned for Nick Sutton's execution on February 20. I gave her the details. I had been in touch with Kevin Riggs and Matthew Lewis about the vigil, which would be held outside the prison. Matthew, as Nick's spiritual adviser, would be inside the prison with Nick until 5:00 p.m., with the execution scheduled at 7:00 p.m., so Kevin had agreed to lead the vigil.

I settled back to listen to my colleagues. As I listened, one tear after another coursed down from the corner of my eye. The mere sharing of the vigil details had stirred my trauma. Clearly, I wasn't doing as well as I'd thought.

An advocate for those condemned to death draws fire from all sides. On February 9, the *Tennessean* published an op-ed by a local lawyer who thoroughly trashed me. Billing himself as an expert on the death penalty in Tennessee (since he'd published a book about it), he misconstrued a number of things. Using the example of a clergyman he'd heard about who prayed with a guy on the gallows before he was hanged, the op-ed writer made it clear that I too should simply be praying with the guys before their execution, commending them to God, and leave it at that. Since I don't believe God has a hand in state-sanctioned killing, and since I very much doubt that it meets with God's approval, I can't agree that my role is simply to pray with them before their execution. But the part of the op-ed that bothered me most was the writer's statement that Philip Workman had provided no evidence of his innocence. That's an insult to Philip's memory and to those who worked so hard on his case. There's substantial evidence that Philip was framed by Shelby County prosecutors and police for a murder he did not commit. Ballistics provides proof that his bullet did not mortally would Officer Oliver.

Of course, the idiocy of one op-ed writer doesn't begin to compare with the death threats to myself and my family that have come in over the years. Hazard of the trade.

Monday, February 10, I was watching television with Becca. I rose to get a glass of water, and by the time I reached the kitchen, I was holding on to the counter to keep my balance—a sure sign that the AFib had returned. Becca took my pulse and blood pressure—which revealed that I was indeed in AFib once again. What to do?

We agreed that I should take my scheduled medication, the one that had helped convert the heart rate on my latest trip to the ER. Becca would continue to monitor me, and if it became worse, we would head back to the ER. Fortunately, it converted to normal as I slept that night.

Becca and I thought that perhaps I should have an ablation, which would zap the areas firing irregularly in the heart. At my appointment with my cardiologist on February 12, he disagreed. After reviewing all the tests, he thought I had trifascicular blockage. In other words, the electrical system in my heart had a conduction problem. I needed a pacemaker to regulate the beats of my heart.

We scheduled the procedure for Tuesday, February 18. What a relief to have a plan and a remedy for the AFib. The ablation would come in June.

Meanwhile, the judge in Nick Sutton's trial had suggested that Nick deserved clemency. Which meant that we had the judge, six correctional officers whose lives Nick had saved over the years, and the victim's family, all arguing for clemency for Nick. It appeared that Nick had hit the trifecta for clemency. The only problem was that it was Governor Lee deciding his fate—Governor Lee who had given no indication that he had either mercy or justice in his heart for death penalty cases. Perhaps Governor Lee would prove me wrong. I was afraid I knew the answer.

On February 17, 2020, a Monday, I told my psychiatrist I had to beware of falling into Nietzsche's "eternal recurrence of the same." Regarding Nick, I needed to avoid giving way to despair in the belief that Governor Lee would do the same old thing again, again, and again. As much as I loved Nick, I had done all for him that I could do. I submitted my affidavit with his clemency package. I would support Frances, who had been visiting him weekly for five years and who might have had her last visit with him that very evening before he was moved to deathwatch. The vigil was organized; word had been spread. It was up to the good Lord to kick Governor Lee in the butt.

Nick reminded me of Ed Zagorski in some ways. Each was a convict, not an inmate. They lived by a code, and their word was their bond. Nick saved the lives of those correctional officers because he had the courage of his convictions. I trusted Nick. He would never have sold someone out for personal gain. He was honest. His description of the killing he was convicted of: "Joe, I've done some things I deserve the death penalty for. But this is not one of them." And now his trial judge agreed.

That night, as I showered thoroughly with anti-bacterial soap in preparation for surgery to implant the pacemaker the next day, I pondered that fact that I was being provided life-saving treatment while the same society placed Nick in a cage and was preparing to exterminate him. The incongruity at the heart of the state of Tennessee is astonishing.

We arrived for the surgery at 7:30 a.m. on February 18, and I was taken back to a waiting area. The nurse, anesthesiologist, and doctor came by to explain what to expect and answer any questions. Then I was wheeled on the gurney into the operating room.

I was already hooked up to an IV, so they transferred me from the gurney to the operating table. The room was cold. They placed a heated blanket over me. Warm air circulated beneath me. As the operating team went about their tasks, I was impressed by their competence and kindness.

A nurse explained that they were going to slide a thin platform of wood under me. She placed my right arm on her shoulder, the team elevated me slightly, and in no time the wood was in place. Then she explained that they would tie my arms down to the table so that I wouldn't try to scratch my face during surgery.

I knew the drugs that they were giving me that day and their purpose. One of them was the same drug, midazolam, used in the lethal injection protocol. This was the drug we had argued against with Governor Haslam's legal counsel, the one that eased Billy Irick into unconsciousness but did not render him insensate. Of course, on this day I was being given other drugs besides midazolam that would indeed render me insensate. Unlike Billy, I would not feel a thing.

The tying down of my arm recalled for me the guards tying Billy's arms down. Additionally, they had taped his fingers down so that they wouldn't convulse, revealing to the execution witnesses the pain he was experiencing. My last thought as I went under was of the kind nurse who had my hand on her shoulder. Billy had died with no one to extend kindness to him.

I awoke some two hours later in the recovery area. Becca was there, and as I gradually cleared from the anesthesia, I was able to understand most of what the doctors and nurses told me. I was glad that Becca could totally grasp the information, because I was woozy.

We went home that afternoon. My left side movements would be restricted for a month. I couldn't lift anything with my left hand heavier than a milk jug. I could not raise my arm above my shoulder.

After Bible study on Wednesday, Becca and I took Frances Christian to lunch. Frances had completed her last visit with Nick Sutton. We wanted to support her and allow her to share what she wished. The execution was thirty hours away.

2020

I reminded Frances that when I was out in Unit 2 a couple of weeks after having matched Frances with Nick and set up their first visit some years before, he had stopped me: "Joe, you matched me with an alpha female! She doesn't take anything from anybody. She is tough."

I had laughed. "Nick, what did you expect? I know you. I wasn't going to send someone in here that couldn't match your toughness."

As Becca and I listened, Frances shared a couple of Nick stories. At one point, Nick had been planning to go into the death chamber and cuss everybody out. But after he'd processed his own anger, he changed his mind. During their final visit, Nick had said: "Frances, you know I run hot and cold on God."

"Tell me about the cold," Frances said.

"I don't see any results."

"God isn't Santa Claus," Frances said.

Nick leaned back, looking at her. Then he looked out at the visitation area, populated at that moment with all his friends, chatting with each other. "I had never experienced love before I came here," he said. "It was on death row that I was loved for the first time. I feel like people have loved me back to God."

Nick Sutton was electrocuted on Thursday, February 20, 2020, at 7:00 p.m. His final words were not spoken out of anger; rather, they were a testimony to his faith. In the field outside the prison, in a service organized by Kevin Riggs, stood over fifty witnesses against the execution.

As I lay down to sleep hours after the execution, I prayed: "God, we need a little help here. I've got this pacemaker now and won't be able to do much. But they are killing my friends. We need a little help."

Somewhere in the border between waking and sleeping, I received a vision. I was lying on my back, arms outstretched to the side. At first, I seemed helplessly suspended in midair, but gradually

339

I became aware that I was being held up. I looked over my shoulder and saw many hands holding me up—Black hands, brown hands, and white hands. I looked past the hands to the faces. I recognized them—the men and women I'd spent the past few decades visiting in prison. All of them were now dead, most of them by execution, yet there they were uplifting me.

I wasn't able to go to Nick Sutton's memorial service. Matthew Lewis, Nick's spiritual adviser, spoke there: "Nick said to be sure to mention Joe Ingle and Ron Shelton, who had been his mentors for many years. Ron can't be here because he passed away in November—but Nick said they showed him how a real Christian thinks, prays, listens, and acts. They, like so many people who surrounded him, were among God's finest, he said. People who heard the moans of the prisoner and responded. Nick said that even if he walked among society, he would have checked the 'convict' box on every application he ever would fill out—*that* prisoner, the despised, the unforgiven—is the one they visited and cared for and showed love to. And to them he would be forever grateful."

The Governor and Pilate

My editorial "The Governor and Pilate" that appeared in the *Tennessean* on June 5, 2019, was in response to our Christian governor Lee's failure to grant clemency to Don. It placed the governor in a long line of predecessors on the road to perdition.

> Governor Bill Lee issued a statement in denying clemency to Don Johnson, who was subsequently executed on May 16th: "After a prayerful and deliberate consideration" were the words that resonated.
>
> In working with the condemned across the South since 1975, I visited governors. I began with Governor

Blanton in Tennessee, Governor Graham in Florida in 1979, Governor Edwards in Louisiana, and met with Governor Haslam. Southern governors routinely deny clemency and execute prisoners. They usually issue a religious statement in justifying their decision.

The execution reminded me of a blues song:

"Jesus is on the mainline, tell him what you want . . .

Just call him up and tell him what you want."

I called Jesus on the mainline: "Jesus, this is Joe Ingle in Nashville."

Jesus: "I know who you are, Joe."

Joe: "Jesus, I've been working with the condemned and talking to governors for over forty years. And they keep killing people, no matter how remorseful or redeemed the prisoners may be."

Jesus: "I know, Joe. I just can't deal with this. I'm transferring your call to Pilate."

I was stunned, and a voice came on the line: "Pilate here."

Joe: "Pilate, I thought I was talking to Jesus but he sent me to you."

Pilate: "Oh yeah, I handle all these calls. After Governor Graham denied clemency for John Spenkelink in 1979, Jesus passed me this job. The governors who pray automatically get referred to me, not Jesus. Jesus keeps saying 'What you do to the least of these you have done unto me,' 'Let he who is without sin throw the first stone,' and 'By their fruits you shall know them.' I don't want to hear any of that stuff, so I just do the job."

Joe: "But why am I talking to you? I'm not a governor."

Pilate: "Do you recall what I did to Jesus? How I wrestled with the decision, prayed to my gods about it, but had him crucified? I did that because I wanted to keep my job, maybe even get a better one, it was the politically correct thing to do. That is why I am talking to you."

Joe: "Yes, you thought he might be innocent but had him executed anyway."

Pilate: "What was I going to do? The law said he was guilty. Give clemency? There is no political future in that."

Joe: "You are telling me that clemency is all about politics, not about faith or mercy?"

Pilate: "Joe, how slow can you be? You've been doing this for how long and you still talk to governors about faith and mercy."

Joe: "Yes I do."

Pilate: "Look, the governors pray and I hear them out. I don't have to tell them what to do. They believe to advance politically they have to kill prisoners. It's been going on at least since I killed Jesus. Our god is political expediency. It's got nothing to do with Jesus."

Joe: "So you are telling me there is no hope?"

Pilate: "Where do you live?"

Joe: "Tennessee."

Pilate: "In what region of the country have you worked?"

Joe: "The South."

Pilate: "You are really slow. You work against the death penalty in a region that leads the country in executions. The South pioneered slavery, lynching, segregation, the convict lease system . . . I could go on."

Joe: "And your point is?"

Pilate: "It's all political expediency and those prisoners you work with don't matter."

Joe: "What about Jesus saying: 'When I was in prison you visited me.'"

Pilate: "Jesus! What has he got to do with any of this? Why do you think I'm on the prayer line with the governors? Their actions show disregard for Jesus. This is bigger than Jesus. It's their political careers. They are like me, which is why we can relate."

Then Pilate hung up. At least, as the blues song put it, I've told Jesus what I want.

Ash Wednesday

In 2020, Ash Wednesday fell on February 28. I pulled T. S. Eliot's poem "Ash Wednesday" off my shelf. The first lines of Part I struck me:

> Because I do not hope to turn again
> Because I do not hope
> Because I do not hope to turn

Yes, I do not hope to turn again toward the years 1960–99, when there were no executions in Tennessee. I do not hope to return to the days from 2000 to 2017, when we had six executions. It is because of this that the final lines of Part I sing out:

> Pray for us sinners now and at the hour of our death
> Pray for us now and at the hour of our death.

* * *

Too Close to the Flame

The situation reminds me of a Thomas Merton prayer—and his words are a perfect way to close:

> My Lord God, I have no idea where I am going. I do not see the road ahead of me. I cannot know for certain where it will end. Nor do I really know myself, and the fact that I think that I am following your will does not mean that I am actually doing so. But I believe that the desire to please you does in fact please you. And I hope I have that desire in all that I am doing. I hope that I will never do anything apart from that desire. And I know that if I do this you will lead me by the right road though I may know nothing about it. Therefore, will I trust you always though I may seem to be lost and in the shadow of death. I will not fear, for you are ever with me, and you will never leave me to face my perils alone.[4]

---

4 Thomas Merton, *Thoughts in Solitude* (New York: Farrar, Straus & Giroux, 1999), 79.

Coda

CHAPTER TWENTY-FIVE

Not Innocent Enough

IN THE SPRING of 2023, I drove my pickup truck through the greening Middle Tennessee countryside. Turning off the road, I eased my truck around the graveyard and pulled off the grass lane into the shade. I approached the grave marker and for the first time did not feel the usual pain. Since the burial of Philip Workman at this spot in the spring of 2007, each visit had been hurtful.

A blooming white dogwood stood to my left near the grave marker. Another white dogwood to the right seemed to beckon me. Fifty feet beyond the grave, a pink dogwood blossomed. The marker gave Philip's birth and death dates. The biblical quote emblazoned on the baseball cap that constantly perched on his head during his life was now inscribed on his grave: "Though you slay me, yet will I trust in you" (Job 13:15).

I quietly spoke: "Yes, you trusted in God even though you were slain. But it was the state of Tennessee that killed you. God had nothing to do with that. It was like you always said: 'I'm not innocent enough.'"

I uttered a prayer of thanksgiving for Philip and for our friendship and prayed for consolation for his family and all who loved him. I then absorbed the natural beauty surrounding me. Beauty and madness. It was the story of Philip Workman and Tennessee's twenty-five-year quest to kill an innocent man.

"Yes, you trusted in God even though you were slain. But it was the state of Tennessee that killed you. God had nothing to do with that. It was like you always said: 'I'm not innocent enough."

Question: How can you be sent to death row without killing someone?

Answer: Find yourself ensnared in the Memphis, Tennessee, criminal legal system, the belly of the death penalty beast in Tennessee.

Philip Workman stepped into the above situation when he robbed a Wendy's restaurant in the Bluff City, as Memphis is known. He was after the money in the cash register for his drug habit. He had a loaded .45-caliber pistol, but it was for show. He had no intention of harming anyone.

It was hot in Memphis on August 5, 1981. Workman enjoyed eating in the Wendy's at closing time, cooling off in the air-conditioned restaurant. The only customer there, he finished his burger and French fries.

At 10:22 p.m. he stood up, pulled the .45 pistol from his waistband, and ordered everyone to move to the office in the back of the restaurant. The employees were frightened and offered their own money, but Workman told them he only wanted the money in the cash register. He directed a female employee to gather up the proceeds of the day. She put the money in a canvas sack and gave it to

Workman. Everyone else was on the floor. After some minutes, one of the employees complained of a cramp and he was allowed to stand up and stretch. Unbeknownst to Workman, he triggered a silent alarm.

The police who responded to the alarm had been briefed at roll call that an African American man was robbing fast food establishments. When they arrived at the Wendy's, they were looking for an African American. Philip Workman, who was white, walked right out the door and spoke to Officer Ronald Oliver. Lieutenant Oliver responded and continued to look for a Black male.

For a brief moment, it appeared Workman might escape. Then, as he walked onto the asphalt, he saw a police cruiser at the corner and realized he was between two officers. He fled toward the adjacent Holiday Auto Parts parking lot. In his haste, he tripped over the curb separating the two establishments and fell to the ground. He pushed up into a kneeling position and raised his hands in surrender. He shouted, "Don't shoot! I give up!"

When Lieutenant Oliver saw Workman's gun in his hand, he responded with a blow to the head. As Workman was struck, probably with a heavy-duty police flashlight, his gun discharged into the air. Stunned by the blow, he stood up. He was concussed and bleeding from the head. He racked his pistol, forgetting it was a semi-automatic, and ejected a round to the ground. This was the second of the four rounds in the gun.

Officer Aubrey Stoddard shot at him. Responding to the flash from Stoddard's gun, Workman returned fire and wounded the officer in the arm. Meanwhile, Officer Steve Parker had arrived. He witnessed the exchange of gunfire and emptied a shotgun at Workman, striking him in the buttocks. A witness nearby, Steve Craig, saw Parker fire the shotgun two or three times.

Fearing his attempt at surrender was only going to get him killed, Workman stood up and ran across the Holiday Auto Parts parking lot. Jeff Rickard, a witness, saw Workman fleeing and holding his bleeding head. Workman stumbled at the north end of parking lot and discharged another shot in the air. It was the last of his four bullets. He hid in a nearby field and tried to collect his thoughts.

At 11:55 Philip Workman was captured in the field. He was arrested and taken to John Gaston Hospital, where he was treated for a head wound and dog bites, and shotgun pellets were removed from his buttocks. As he was being treated at the hospital, he heard a television report that an officer had been slain at the scene of the crime. He did not recall killing anyone.

In most jurisdictions, this would have been the end of the matter. A robber was apprehended, and he would be off to prison, convicted of armed robbery and wounding a police officer. It would be a long time before the individual would be released from prison.

Such was not the case in Memphis. In the Violent Crimes Unit at 5:00 a.m. the morning after the robbery, the following police personnel gathered: Inspector Hess, Captain Jackson, Captain Lewis, Lieutenant Music, Lieutenant Keenan, Sergeant Hollie, Sergeant Wilson, and Officer Ball. The policemen reviewed the photographs of Officer Ronald Oliver's fatal wound, Workman's gun, and the three shell casings and one live round from Workman's gun found at the crime scene. They also examined Lieutenant Oliver's clothing. The police log notes "an exchange of information [took] place."

In the course of reviewing the assembled evidence it became apparent that the size of the wounds in Lieutenant Oliver's body did not match the ammunition from Workman's .45. Aluminum-coated hollow-point .45-caliber bullets, which Workman used, would expand upon entering the body and create a larger exit wound than entrance wound, if they exited at all. But Oliver's body had a larger entrance wound than exit wound. This was consistent with a bullet fired from another police officer's pistol. It appeared that Lieutenant Oliver had been the victim of "friendly fire."

It appeared that Lieutenant Oliver had been the victim of "friendly fire."

The discussion in the Violent Crimes Unit focused on a different conclusion to this morality play. Clearly, Philip Workman was a strung-out drug addict who had robbed a Wendy's and wounded Officer Stoddard. Workman had no ties to the community and no one in Memphis cared what happened to him. He was just another druggie scumbag who needed to be off the streets. So what if his bullets did not actually kill Officer Oliver? They needed to be sure he would never do this again, and if he got out of prison, he would surely return to armed robbery. And who wanted to try to explain to the public how one Memphis policeman shot and killed another?

On August 18, 1981, the grand jury issued an indictment on two counts for Philip Workman: (1) Felony murder of Lieutenant Ronald Oliver. (2) Premeditated murder. Workman, with no resources, was appointed Shelby County public defenders to represent him in his capital trial.

If one word could describe Philip Workman's trial, it would be *farce*. The defense lawyer's opening statement consisted of little more than saying that Workman "was high on drugs, really messed up on drugs . . . That is simply it." The prosecution, on the other hand, was aggressive and relentless. The defense accepted the prosecution's theory that there were only two shooters, Workman and Oliver, and did no investigation before trial. This woeful performance concurred with other death penalty cases in Memphis prior to Philip Workman.

At the time of the trial, Tennessee was four years into the administration of a new death penalty law passed by the legislature in 1977. Several of the Memphis cases prosecuted under this law resulted in the death penalty. The men sent to death row in Nashville were Richard Austin, Bill Groseclose, Ronald Rickman, and in July of 1982, Gary Cone. On appeal all of these sentences were reversed due to "ineffective assistance of counsel." Despite the woeful legal representation on his behalf, Philip Workman would not be so fortunate.

By the time of the trial, Philip Workman had sobered up and realized he was being prosecuted for a murder he could not recall committing. As he watched his lawyer's performance with increasing alarm, he realized the state's theory of the case was going basically unchallenged. One particular testimony during the trial astonished him.

Despite the prosecution describing a shootout between Oliver and Workman, no law enforcement person had actually seen Workman shoot Oliver. To put the final nail into Philip Workman's coffin, the state needed an eyewitness. Enter a man named Harold Davis.

Harold Davis, an African American, testified between the testimony of Officer Aubrey Stoddard and Officer Steve Parker. He stated he saw Philip Workman shoot Ronald Oliver from a distance of no more than three feet. Workman was incredulous when he listened to this testimony because he recalled seeing no Black people in the parking lot or inside the Wendy's. Granted, he was strung out, but he did not believe he had ever seen Harold Davis in his life.

Unbeknownst to the jury, Harold Davis had contacted the Memphis police about the slaying of Ronald Oliver at 12:25 p.m. on August 6, 1981. The police asked Davis to come down to the precinct. At 2:30 p.m. he gave a statement: "As I got out of the car and went up to the door, I saw this man coming out of the back coming toward the door with a gun in his hand." Davis retreated to his car and climbed into it. "I heard the policeman tell the man to stop, and then I saw the man turn around and start shooting at the police. I saw the police return fire and I saw one policeman go down. Then I heard some more shots, and I saw the guy who shot the policeman run across the auto parts lot and he was holding his head. Then a bunch of police showed up at the crime scene." Workman's lawyers did not cross-examine Harold Davis.

As we would come to find out, Harold Davis gave this testimony after being coached by the police and prosecution. His eyewitness testimony was totally fabricated. In point of fact, Harold Davis was not at the Wendy's when the shooting occurred. And so it goes in a Memphis death penalty trial.

The advice Philip Workman received from his lawyers was to take the stand and be remorseful for killing Officer Oliver. This is hard to do when you don't recall murdering anyone, but Workman stumbled through some statements stressing that he was sorry. He did feel remorse for creating the scene. But creating the crime scene with the robbery was not killing Lieutenant Oliver. Another policeman did that deed.

In short order, Workman was found guilty and sentenced to death. He was shipped to the Tennessee State Prison in Nashville on March 31, 1982. He was the twentieth prisoner sentenced to death under the 1977 death penalty law enacted by the legislature.

This case would have become yet another typical death row case, except for the involvement of one person in particular: Chris Minton. From 1982 to 1989, Philip Workman's case chugged routinely through the appeals courts. When Minton took over the case, he brought a fresh perspective and compassion. He also listened to his client as he talked to him about the case.

Minton utilized a new law, the Tennessee Public Records Act (TPRA), and filed a request for access to the police file, the district attorney file, and any other pertinent information the state had about Workman. The prosecution complied and provided what was requested.

As Minton reviewed the files, he was impressed by the fact

that his client's story was consistent whereas the stories of the police, district attorney, and judges in the case kept changing. There were contradictions in the police log and trial statements. And there was the glaring absence of any mention of the mysterious Harold Davis, the "eyewitness." His presence was not recorded in police notes or crime scene drawings. It led one to wonder: Where did Harold Davis come from?

For Chris Minton, the initial crucial hearing in Philip Workman's case would come on July 18, 1994, in federal district court in Memphis. Minton's research had unearthed enough contradictions and inconsistencies in the state's position to deserve a hearing in federal court. He had demonstrated a "colorable" claim of innocence and material facts that would have affected the conviction if available at trial. In his filing, he listed the following issues:

Memphis police officer Parker's testimony at trial—a graphic description of Lieutenant Oliver dying from what he believed to be a bullet from Workman's gun—contradicted his initial statement at 2:10 a.m. on the night of the crime, when he stated that he did not see Philip shoot Oliver but did see him shoot Stoddard in the arm.

1. The medical examiner for the state of Georgia, Dr. Kris Sperry, provided an expert report that Lieutenant Oliver's wounds were dramatically inconsistent with the ammunition that Philip used that night.

2. Witness statements and police reports demonstrated that Harold Davis was not present to witness Lieutenant Oliver's shooting.

3. Witness statements, police reports, and medical records demonstrated that persons other than Lieutenant Oliver and Philip Workman fired weapons.

4. Witness statements, police reports, and medical records

demonstrated that Philip ran into the Holiday Auto Parts lot, where police bludgeoned him.

5. The defense's evidence demonstrated that Davis, Stoddard, and Parker had testified falsely.

6. Substantial evidence existed that prior to the shooting of Lieutenant Oliver, Philip had surrendered and was bludgeoned by police, and in the ensuing confusion another police officer shot Lieutenant Oliver.

7. The state withheld evidence and knowingly presented perjured testimony to obtain Workman's conviction.

Given the gravity of the allegations in the filing in federal district court, one would expect a hearing to ascertain the accuracy of the claims. Any two or three of these claims seemingly would necessitate a hearing to evaluate them.

The federal habeas corpus petition—*Philip R. Workman v. Ricky Bell, warden*—would be considered by Judge Julia Gibbons, a Republican appointee to the federal bench. In order to ensure her attention was attracted to the brief, a summary made the allegations unmistakably clear:

> Workman alleges that contrary to the State's case against him, he did not wrestle with Stoddard and Oliver from the Wendy's parking lot onto the Holiday lot, produce a gun, and shoot them. Rather, Workman alleges that he ran from the Wendy's lot onto the Holiday lot, tripped and fell, offered his surrender, was bludgeoned, and in the resulting confusion a fellow police officer, not Workman, shot Oliver.
>
> Workman asserts a Fourteenth Amendment claim that the prosecution withheld evidence of events

surrounding Oliver's death while it knowingly presented
false testimony. This claim requires Workman to show
that (1) the evidence the prosecution presented was actually false; (2) the prosecution knew it was false; (3) the
false evidence was material.

The legal standard was that a "colorable claim of innocence"
or of material fact that would have affected the conviction had to
be alleged. In this case, eight claims had been introduced that challenged the propriety of the conviction. Surely this would lead to an
evidentiary hearing to evaluate the merits of the claims.

One would be inclined to think that if a judge were presented
a series of claims alleging a fundamental violation of an individual's rights—in this case, framing someone for a murder he did not
commit—a hearing to determine the validity of the claims would be
warranted. Indeed, the case law was clear that in such circumstances
the merits should be weighed in a hearing. However, and not for the
last time, it must be pointed out that the proceedings under discussion took place in Memphis, Tennessee.

Memphis police and prosecutors are notorious for their corruption of justice and unethical behavior. What may be settled case law
in the courts of the land does not necessarily cross the Shelby County
line. The distance from the marble halls of the US Supreme Court to
the grime of the Shelby County criminal legal system is more than
a matter of miles. The two are light years apart and exist in entirely
different constellations of justice.

Judge Julia Gibbons, the federal judge hearing the Workman
appeal, was a product of the Memphis establishment. She had been
a circuit court judge in Shelby County and served as legal counsel
to Republican governor Lamar Alexander before her appointment
to the federal bench by President Ronald Reagan. The youngest
judge appointed to the bench, she was married to William Gibbons.

Not Innocent Enough

Mr. Gibbons, serving as county commissioner, had recently been appointed by Republican governor Don Sundquist as district attorney general for Shelby County. On November 1, 1996, he was sworn into office by Judge Julia Gibbons, his wife, in her judicial robes. The official swearing in was preceded on October 29, 1996, with Judge Gibbons granting the state's request for a summary judgment in the *Workman* case.

This matter is so egregious we must delve below the charming picture of the two that appeared in Memphis's *Commercial Appeal* on November 2, 1996. The two love birds, one a judge swearing in her husband to be the district attorney, are a smiling Memphis success story. The reality is rather different. The wife of the man who would become district attorney, the man who would preside over the cesspool of corruption that determined Philip Workman was detritus who needed to be disposed of whether or not he killed anyone, was the very person who had just dismissed a valid appeal for an evidentiary hearing to examine the machinations of the district attorney's office. The hearing in which Philip Workman could present the newly discovered evidence that he did not shoot Officer Ronald Oliver would not take place in Julia Gibbons's courtroom. It is not difficult to imagine the pillow talk that led to this decision. The light of justice would not penetrate this dark corner of the Memphis killing machinery.

The next legal step for Philip Workman was an appeal to the Sixth Circuit Court of Appeals. Surely moving the case to a level of appeal outside Shelby County, indeed outside the state of Tennessee, would provide a fair opportunity for relief.

Examining death penalty law and its application is enough to make a lawyer dizzy. For laymen, it is often bewildering. As laypeople, we turn to a journalist, Dan Horn, to lead us through the dynamics of the Sixth Circuit Court of Appeals. Mr. Horn, a writer for the *Cincinnati Enquirer*, undertook a survey of death penalty case

357

decisions by the Sixth Circuit Court of Appeals from 2000 to 2007. The article was titled, "The Politics of Life and Death: An Inmate's Fate often Hinges on Luck of the Draw." It was published on April 15, 2007.[1]

In his analysis of the judicial composition of the panels that issued death penalty decisions, Dan Horn discovered that Republican judicial appointees voted to deny relief 85 percent of the time. Democratic appointees voted to grant at least partial relief in 75 percent of cases. As the title of the article indicated, the outcome of the cases depended more on the political persuasion of the judicial panel than the matters of fact and law.

Horn's article focused on Paul House, a Tennessee death row prisoner, to illustrate his point about the political motivations of the judges in the Sixth Circuit. Paul was someone I knew well. I had watched him physically deteriorate after contracting multiple sclerosis on death row. I worked to have his diagnosis recognized and got him seen by the neurologist who treated my own MS. I then advocated for his treatment from the Department of Correction. His mother, Joyce, was the salt of the earth and devoted to her son. The facts of Paul's case and its intersection with the Sixth Circuit Court of Appeals could only make one wonder at the dispensation of justice in capital cases in America.

Paul maintained his innocence of the rape and murder for which he was convicted. He prevailed in the Sixth Circuit in 2002. On the basis of DNA, he was ordered a new trial. However, due to procedural issues the case was referred back to state court and once again appeared before the Sixth Circuit in 2004. The same facts and legal issues were present in the case. Only this time the case was put before the entire Sixth Circuit, fourteen judges. Included in those fourteen were four new Republican appointees to the bench. Paul

---

1 Dan Horn, "The Politics of Life and Death: An Inmate's Fate often Hinges on Luck of the Draw," *Cincinnati Enquirer*, April 15, 2007.

House lost before the en banc court because of the four new appointees, not for lack of evidence of his innocence. The case was appealed to the US Supreme Court. That decision stated in part, "any reasonable juror would have found Mr. House not guilty."

It was into this judicial snake pit Philip Workman's case now landed for oral argument on June 17, 1998. The three-judge panel that heard the case consisted of David A. Nelson, James L. Ryan, and Eugene E. Siler Jr. They were all Republican appointees. On October 30, 1998, the opinion was issued. The vote was 3–0 against relief.

Chris Minton, Philip's lawyer, once said to me, "Joe, my son is four years old. He can tell you how a death case will come out in the Sixth Circuit. No matter the merit, if you have a majority of Republicans on the panel, you lose."

In my study of the Holocaust, which included visits to Auschwitz, Majdanek, and Mauthausen, two meetings with Elie Wiesel to discuss the similarities and differences between the Nazi and American killing machinery, and extensive reading, it is the details of the extermination machinery that reveals the true evil of the process. Everything the Nazis did was legal. Just as state killing in the United States is legal. But none of it is moral. It is in the little things that the horror is manifested.

The details of the *Workman* case provide a classic example. The explanation of the Sixth Circuit panel in their decision takes us beyond the ugly and sinister machinations of Memphis into a realm of concocted malfeasance. It is sobering and depressing, but it is also revelatory as to the length judges will go to ensure the killing of a person, even if innocent of the murder for which he is charged.

In order to rule against Philip Workman, some issues had to be dispensed with. Dr. Kris Sperry, the medical examiner for the state of Georgia, had examined the ballistics and submitted an affidavit that stated he had seen "30 to 40 corpses with wounds from ammunition of the sort Workman used"; that in every one of these cases "the .45 Silvertip hollow-point bullet expanded upon entering the human body involved"; that approximately 90 percent of the time the hollow-point never emerged from the victim's body at all; that "in the remaining instances the exit wound created by the .45-caliber Silvertip hollow-point bullet was significantly larger than the entrance wound the bullet created"; and that it would be inconsistent with the exit wounds seen by Dr. Sperry "for a .45 Silvertip hollow-point bullet to create an exit wound smaller than the entry wound."

Judge Siler, writing for the panel, disposed of Dr. Sperry's affidavit:

"If a .45 caliber hollow point bullet had gone all the way through Lt. Oliver's chest and emerged in one piece, we have no doubt the exit wound would have been larger than the entry wound. It hardly follows, however, that Lt. Oliver could not have been shot with the type of ammunition Workman was firing—because the record in no way compels the conclusion that the bullet which killed the officer emerged from the body in one piece."

Unfortunately for Judge Siler's rationale, the record made clear, and would compel any reasonable person to conclude, that there was no fragmentation of the bullet that killed Lieutenant Oliver. Dr. James Bell, the medical examiner, found no piece of the bullet in the body. But that did not stop Judge Siler from inventing an explanation:

"Soft point bullets sometimes shed fragments after entering a human body. See, for example, the paper on 'Ballistic Injury' presented by Col. Martin L. Fackler, of the US Army Medical Corps, at the March 1986 Symposium of the American College of Emergency Physicians. The paper, accepted for publication in the *Annals of Emergency Medicine*, describes one soft point bullet wound where the percentage of bullet fragmentation was calculated at 33.4 percent. Dr. Fackler gave the following description: 'As the bullet deforms on impact, small pieces of it separate. In this case, 33.4

percent of the bullet's total weight leaves the main mass in the form of fragments. Each fragment crushes its own path through tissue as the multiple fragments spread out laterally away from the main projectile.'"

Judge Siler went into full creative mode: "If part of the bullet that killed Lt. Oliver remained in the officer's body, that would be entirely consistent with Dr. Sperry's observation that hollow point bullets remain inside the victim's body about 90 percent of the time. Dr. Bell did not recover any bullet segment, to be sure, but no X-ray was taken, and the small piece of metal could simply have been overlooked. Dr. Bell did report a gunshot wound fracture of Lt. Oliver's left seventh rib, so the bullet may have fragmented on striking the rib. But regardless of when any fragmentation may have occurred, the most obvious explanation of the quarter inch 'slit-like tear in the skin' on Lt. Oliver's back is that the wound was caused by the exit of a hollow point bullet fragment (possibly part of the aluminum jacket) and not by the exit of an entire bullet. Therefore, there is no reason to conclude that Workman was actually innocent of causing Lt. Oliver's mortal wound, just as there is no reason to conclude that the prosecution knowingly presented false evidence in this connection."[2]

This fanciful explanation is breathtaking. At the oral argument when Colonel Fackler's study was introduced for the first time by the judges, Chris Minton was taken aback. He was equally surprised by the notion of a fragmenting bullet. In the record, which is what the appellate judges are supposed to consider, there was no mention of either Fackler or a fragmenting bullet. Judge Nelson went on to ask if there was an X-ray and Minton replied he had subpoenaed all medical records and no X-ray had been produced.

Minton returned to Nashville from Cincinnati where the oral argument took place. He contacted Colonel Fackler to ascertain exactly what his study determined.

---

2 *Workman v. Bell*, 178 F.3d 759, 160 F.3d 276 (6th Cir. 1998).

Fackler was astonished at the judges' interpretation of his study. He was focused on high-velocity NATO 7.62 mm soft-point rifle bullets, not .45 semi-automatic pistol bullets. The rifle bullets regularly shed fragments on impact. This study was not of .45 bullets nor was his study of rifle bullets applicable to them. The judges had misapplied Fackler's research to the *Workman* case. Colonel Fackler's other work confirmed what Dr. Sperry's affidavit stated. The entrance wound would be smaller than the exit wound with a hollow-point bullet.

At trial, Dr. Bell had testified that "the bullet that entered Officer Oliver and eventually killed Officer Oliver exited Officer Oliver as well." Despite what the record stated, appellate court judges invented a fragmenting bullet, and misunderstood and misapplied Colonel Fackler's study of rifle bullets, in a concerted effort to deny Philip Workman relief.

The process of manufacturing a scenario that would justify killing Philip Workman began in the early morning hours after the Wendy's robbery, continued through trial and the state appellate courts, and morphed once again at the federal level. It was accomplished by dehumanizing him into a being fit for disposal: a cop killer.

Chris Minton, still the legal warrior armed with facts, truth, and a sense of justice, filed a petition back with the panel pointing out the errors in their decision. He chiefly focused on the misinterpretation of Colonel Fackler's study and attached the study, which clearly revealed it was about rifle bullets and not handguns. There was not even a gossamer thread to maintain the idea of bullet fragmentation without Fackler's research backing the theory.

How might the panel respond to the petition for rehearing when confronted with their flawed reasoning? Journalist Dan Horn and Chris Minton's son were prescient about what Republican judges would do. They denied the rehearing petition 3–0.

If the result was predictable, the judges' written opinion was

astonishing. No effort was made to explain their error of inter-
preting the Fackler study. Rather, they marked through all the words
pertaining to the study in the prior opinion and reissued the previous
opinion. The crossed-out paragraphs gutted the rationale for the
fragmenting-bullet theory. Nor was there evidence on the record to
support such a conclusion. The rehearing decision was not anchored
in fact or reason. It had become a wishing and hoping opinion, but
it was still deadly for Philip Workman.

As Philip's appeal continued, Minton turned his focus to the
mysterious Harold Davis, the African American who was the sole
"eyewitness" to Workman shooting Oliver. He went to visit Davis's
family in Cordova, outside Memphis. Jackie, Harold's sister, told
Minton to talk to Vivian Porter because she was with Harold the
night of the robbery.

Vivian Porter ran a Christian drug counseling center in
Memphis. She was willing to tell what she and Harold had done the
night of Lieutenant Oliver's slaying. It was this information that finally
provided the explanation as to how Harold Davis entered the case.

Porter and Davis were smoking marijuana and driving around
Memphis the night of August 5, 1981. A Memphis police officer
pulled them over. Porter thought, "Oh, no, he's going to smell the
marijuana and we'll get busted." As the police officer approached
their car, he heard a police radio broadcast about an officer down. He
returned to his car, jumped in the seat, and rapidly drove off. Repeating
to themselves, "Thank you, Jesus," the duo followed the police car.
They drove by the crime scene, which was already marked off with
yellow tape. They decided to return to Vivian Porter's apartment where
they partied and watched the news on television. The news informed
them a police officer had been killed at the Wendy's restaurant.

In his conversations with Jackie, Harold's sister, Minton
learned that Davis had a cocaine habit. One way he maintained his
habit was to be an informant for the police. In exchange for money

or the dropping of pending charges, Davis would state what the police desired him to say. Davis used this MO when he contacted the police at 12:25 p.m. on March 6, 1981. By 2:30, according to police logs, he had given a statement describing Philip Workman's killing Lt. Ronald Oliver. He was able to do this without identifying Philip in a lineup.

It had become clear that given the relentless effort of the federal judiciary and the state of Tennessee, finding Harold Davis was of paramount importance. Chris Minton learned Davis's mother had her son's last telephone number, and she shared it with Chris. It was a motel in Phoenix, Arizona. Minton and his colleague, Jefferson Dorsey, decided to fly to Phoenix and see if they could find Harold Davis.

After arriving in Phoenix, renting a car, and checking into a motel, they drove to the motel at the other end of Harold Davis's number. They knocked on the door they believed to be the room in which Davis was housed. A white man answered the door. It was obvious Harold Davis was not there. They checked with motel management and were informed that Davis had been there but moved on.

The two lawyers traversed a ten-mile strip of motels bordering Van Buren Street. As they went from motel to motel inquiring whether Davis had stayed there, they began to comprehend the kind of motel Davis frequented. He did not choose the top of the line nor the bottom. He preferred a Days Inn or Motel 6. Davis would wear out his welcome at one motel and move on to the next one, cobbling together temporary living quarters as he maintained his drug-addled existence. Such was the life of an itinerant drug addict.

As the search wore on, afternoon turned to evening and then the darkness of night, and there was still no Harold Davis. Finally reaching the end of Van Buren Street with nothing but the desert stretching out ahead of them, it appeared time to give up. Chris told Jefferson they had given it a good effort, but perhaps they should call it a night. Jefferson responded, "We're moving on." They kept driving and searching, following the road into the desert night.

After a mile or two, the lights of a Motel 6 brightened the night. They decided to stop and inquire, without much hope of learning anything after a long, exhausting day.

They entered the motel and went to the desk. They showed the manager the picture of Harold Davis, which was somewhat crumpled after being thrust before motel managers for the last twelve hours. The manager eyed the photo and said, "Room 240."

The duo went to room 240 and knocked on the door. Harold Davis was inside, but he was not going to let them in. They talked to Davis for twenty minutes through the door. Each took turns explaining that Philip Workman was about to be executed for a murder he did not commit, and that Harold could save his life. They told him all they knew about the case—about Vivian Porter being with Harold that night, about Harold's contacting the police and them summoning him to the station—and finally the lawyers shared their conversations with his family. Perhaps it was the reminder of his family, or maybe the cascade of facts about the case—who knew? But Harold Davis opened the door.

Minton and Dorsey audiotaped Harold Davis's account of the events of the Wendy's robbery, and he agreed to participate in a videotaped interview the next morning at 10:00. The next day the lawyers showed up at 9:15 a.m. and obtained the videotaped interview.

Upon their return to Nashville, the lawyers worked with the local CBS affiliate for a weeklong series on the *Workman* case that aired in December 1999. They also provided the facts of the case to Sonny Rawls, who wrote several lengthy articles about the case for the *Tennessean*. The television and print stories recounted the events at the Wendy's restaurant, Harold Davis's recantation of his original statement, and the illicit shenanigans of the Memphis police and prosecutors. This included Harold Davis stating that two white men, whom he assumed to be police, had come to his motel room in Memphis at the time of the crime and told him he had better cooperate with the police or his family would be in trouble.

As the legal situation, in and out of court, continued to develop, I was visiting Philip Workman on a weekly basis. We initially met at the Walls (Tennessee State Prison) and maintained the visits after the closing of TSP and the opening of RMSI in 1989. Philip had been told repeatedly by his trial lawyer, police, district attorneys, judges, and now the attorney general of Tennessee that he was a cop killer. But Chris Minton's diligent work had proven otherwise.

In January of 2000, I met with Governor Sundquist's senior policy adviser, Justin Wilson. He was polite and gracious as we discussed the case. I reviewed the details of prosecutorial malfeasance, manufacturing testimony, and the creation of a witness who was not even present at the crime. As we neared the end of the meeting, he assured me that the governor would be made aware of this knowledge, saying, "The state of Tennessee would not execute an innocent man."

I shared the details of the visit with Justin Wilson with Philip when I next went out to see him. As I concluded the story of the visit, he shook his head in a resigned manner. "They won't execute an innocent man. I'm not innocent enough. I'm just not innocent enough. I created the scene by committing the robbery, and that's all they care about. They're not about to face the fact that they killed one of their own."

This was the first instance of what I would repeatedly witness over the next seven years. Philip had a profound insight into his situation, fully understood it in ways I and his lawyers did not, and would even tell us the next steps to be prepared for. Indeed, when the most bizarre incident happened in what was truly an *Alice in Wonderland* case, Philip was the one who immediately grasped what occurred. As he said, "I'm the captain of the ship." He appreciated everyone's roles, but he wanted to be on top of it all.

Not Innocent Enough

The Tennessee Supreme Court set an execution date of April 6, 2000, for Philip and his colleague on death row, Robert Glen Coe. In mid-February, I officially registered as Philip's spiritual adviser. This would enable me to be with him on deathwatch.

Meanwhile, the case had legally proceeded, with all the new evidence and information, to the entire Sixth Circuit Court of Appeals after the three-judge panel's latest denial. Chris Minton wished to hold off on any clemency hearing until the Sixth Circuit ruled. Jefferson Dorsey and Don Dawson wanted to proceed with the hearing. The decision was made that Jefferson and Don would handle the clemency hearing on April 3, 2000, and Chris would remain available by telephone to the judges of the Sixth Circuit Court of Appeals.

Philip's scheduled execution was less than seventy-two hours away when he arrived at the clemency hearing from deathwatch. He was manacled to a waist chain. He appeared wan but determined. He fully understood the effort that was made to frame him for Lieutenant Oliver's homicide, and he was aware of the utter lack of relief that would probably issue forth from this clemency effort. Yet Philip was resolved to make his statement and try again to show that he did not kill Lieutenant Oliver. Justin Wilson would preside over the proceedings.

Jefferson Dorsey led off at 2:21 p.m. From then until 3:51 p.m., he and Don Dawson presented Philip Workman's case for clemency. Jefferson put up a map of the crime scene and pointed out the facts of what that scene revealed and the discrepancies with the police accounts of the scene. He also brought in the witness statements at the scene, which contradicted the police accounts. He reviewed the locating of Harold Davis and his subsequent statement that he did not witness the crime. Jefferson summoned Vivian Porter as a witness and she recounted her night with Harold, which eliminated any possibility he had seen Philip Workman shoot Ronald Oliver.

367

Don Dawson called Dr. Kris Sperry as a witness. He detailed his ballistics analysis and stated, "With a reasonable degree of medical certainty" the bullet that killed Lieutenant Oliver came from another policeman's weapon, not Workman's.

In the effort of preparing for the clemency hearing, Minton once again subpoenaed all medical records. Much to his shock, the latest medical examiner of Shelby County—Dr. O. C. Smith—indicated that there were X-rays of Oliver's wound. Dorsey journeyed to Memphis and obtained the X-ray for the hearing. The absence of this X-ray had allowed the Sixth Circuit Court of Appeals panel to create the fragmenting-bullet theory after crossing through Colonel Fackler's article. The X-ray revealed a "through and through" bullet according to Dr. Sperry. There was no fragmentation.

As a witness to this clemency hearing, I felt Philip's case had been presented well. There were pertinent items left out, but the limitation of time was a factor. Any reasonable person would have concluded that Philip Workman did not shoot Lieutenant Oliver.

The star for the prosecution in the clemency hearing was O. C. Smith, the Shelby County medical examiner who had admitted to the existence of the X-rays. Dr. Smith put on a PowerPoint presentation complete with medical and scientific jargon to Justin Wilson, a lawyer with no scientific, much less medical, background. Since Dr. Smith was not subject to cross-examination, he had leeway to state anything he was inclined to say with impunity. In the clemency transcripts, which I subsequently researched, his testimony goes from page 96 to page 142. He gave well over half of the state's total testimony at the hearing.

Dr. Smith's testimony was a farce. A tragic farce, for it could assist in Philip's execution, but the testimony was from cloud cuckoo land. I listened with astonishment, incredulity, and anger to his confabulation of a tale more appropriate to science fiction than any medical analysis of Lt. Ronald Oliver's killing. Smith's testimony made it abundantly clear, if there was any remaining doubt, of the determination of the Memphis and state authorities to kill Philip Workman.

In order to provide the feeling of the clemency hearing, I will quote from O. C. Smith about Q1, what we on the defense team called "the magic bullet." The following is taken directly from the transcripts of the hearing—it is not just my traumatized brain recalling events.

From page 108 of the transcript: "Bullet Q1 is a bullet recovered at the scene in the parking lot. It was recovered the next day. It is my contention that this bullet that was covered in the parking lot is the one that went through Lieutenant Oliver's body."

For anyone familiar with the crime scene and the trial court record, this was a preposterous statement. The bullet Smith referenced was found by Terry Willis, assistant manager of the Holiday Auto Parts store adjacent to the Wendy's, in his parking lot. He picked up what he thought was a "ball bearing." He later realized it was a bullet and called the police. This despite the police having previously scoured the crime scene and found no bullet. At trial, the FBI had discounted the bullet found by Willis as the fatal one. The FBI agent testified that there was no hair, cloth, skin, or any other indication that Q1 traveled through a human being; it was a pristine bullet, not a fatal bullet. But for O. C. Smith, the bullet had somehow become the bullet that killed Officer Oliver: "I think that it is reasonable to expect that this bullet could go through Lieutenant Oliver's body without expanding very much at all, but it did produce a small exit wound as a result of not having expanded or having exited base first or sideways. That it didn't deform significantly after the initial nose deformation and that it could have [done so] either by striking the 7th rib, could have either caused the nose to fold inward or to become plugged with debris and fail to expand as expected with most hollow-points."

At the Workman trial, Dr. Bell, the medical examiner and Smith's "mentor," had already testified that this pristine bullet could not have killed Ronald Oliver. This meant that Smith's testimony contradicted Dr. Bell, the FBI agent, Dr. Kris Sperry, and Dr. Cyril Wecht. It was totally fabricated, but since no cross-examination was allowed at the clemency hearing, it went unchallenged.

Smith explained this conclusion by describing how he shot into gelatin, shot into water, discussed his paper on shooting into intermediate targets, shot into cotton boxes . . . and he displayed all of it on the PowerPoint. None of which provided insight beyond his testimony and contradicted expert testimony and the trial court record.

Not content with this charade of hocus pocus, O. C. Smith addressed the problem of the X-ray. Although I thought Smith had reached the ultimate level of absurdity, I was soon abused of this notion.

Recall that the Sixth Circuit Court of Appeals panel had already choked on one decision (regarding the Fackler study they introduced) about the X-ray. They had concluded their theory was possible because there was no X-ray to reveal this was a "through and through" bullet. Now that defense had obtained the elusive X-ray, there was proof it was a "through and through" bullet. This evidence was now under consideration by the entire Sixth Circuit Court of Appeals, consisting of fourteen judges.

O. C. Smith addressed the problem of the X-ray through more razzle dazzle with the PowerPoint slides. He intended to establish "another reason why the X-ray is not of great importance." The utter folly of this presentation underscored how significant the X-ray truly was.

In conclusion, Smith shared the following comparison experiment:

This is the bullet model that went through the shirt, the
rib cage, and the gelatin . . . I think that you can take a
look at those and see that they have enough similarity to

believe as I do that this model adequately duplicated the forces that were present on the bullet that went through Lieutenant Oliver's body producing enough similarity and because it only went 104 feet beyond the blood pool that contained Lieutenant Oliver's body, that Q1 indeed is the bullet that went through the lieutenant, and that bullet, Q1, was by the FBI testing, shown to come from Mr. Workman's cold pistol to the exclusion of all other pistols in the world.

What?!

Although I was alternating moods from being stunned, outraged, angered, and full of despair, it was clear that Justin Wilson was taken with Smith's testimony. Indeed, as we later discovered by obtaining emails leading up to the clemency hearing, the entire proceeding was no more than a show trial in which the decision had already been made to dispose of Philip Workman.

Philip desired to tell his side of the story. He was allowed to do so. Shackled, he left his seat in the rear of the room and came forward to the table with Wilson. He was drawn; he fully understood that the lies he had heard from the state's witnesses did not amount to a genuine attempt to discover the truth. He spoke clearly and compellingly. After recounting his version of the crime, he turned to the process in which he was ensnared:

"Nobody wants to die, but if I have to die, I know where I'm going for the first time in my life. But I'm telling you, this is wrong. You, sir, you've got to know, nobody can go to their death, and nobody can spend a life sentence in prison on perjured testimony. This is wrong."

After a few more concluding statements, Philip closed with, "Thank you."

Philip Workman returned to deathwatch to await his fate. It

371

was clear from the tone and type of questions from Justin Wilson that he was impressed with the O. C. Smith charade. There would be no clemency from Governor Sundquist. It was up to the Sixth Circuit Court of Appeals to decide whether Philip would live or die.

On the morning of April 4, 2000, the entire court of the Sixth Circuit Court of Appeals granted a stay of execution to Philip Workman in order to review the newly discovered X-ray. The fourteen judges would determine Philip's fate by evaluating the existence of the X-ray, the panel decision with the redaction of the Fackler study from its earlier version, and Philip's claims of being framed by police and prosecutors.

After a summer of study and discussion, somewhat heated at times, the court issued an opinion on September 5, 2000. The vote was a 7–7 tie. This became the infamous "tie you die" decision. According to the rules of procedure, if the en banc court delivered a tie vote the case reverted back to the panel decision. In this instance, the earlier panel decision with the marked-out remarks about the Fackler study and now with an X-ray revealing a "through and through" bullet with no fragmentation, literally made no sense because the entire premise was built on a fragmenting bullet. The three-judge panel decision was not anchored in fact, reason, or law. However, it was full of enmity; the three Republican judges on the panel were three of the seven who voted against Philip. Seven Republican judges voted to deny relief. Seven Democratic appointees voted for it.

* * *

After Philip returned to death row from deathwatch in the spring of 2000, we resumed our weekly visits. The summer was a time of wondering what the Sixth Circuit would do. Philip had taken to the phrase, "I'm not innocent enough" to describe his situation. It seemed an apt description of the treatment his case received. But surely, I thought, the X-ray that demolishes the fragmenting-bullet theory would be the final straw and he would receive a new trial. The September 7–7 "tie you die" opinion by the Sixth Circuit made me, a veteran of twenty-five years working against the death penalty, feel naive. Attorney General Paul Summers promptly petitioned the Tennessee Supreme Court for a new execution date. He expressed the state's position: "Workman has provided this court with no good reason to defer the federal courts at this late stage. A date for execution of his lawful sentence should be promptly set."[3]

A second clemency hearing was held on January 25, 2001, at 8:30 a.m. This time the parole board would act as a clemency board and make a recommendation to the governor. I noticed that the female clemency board member had writing on a pad that she placed on the table before her as she sat down.

Dr. Cyril Wecht was a key witness for Philip. He testified as to how the Q1 bullet O. C. Smith determined to be the fatal bullet could not have been the one that killed Lieutenant Oliver. Chairman Charles Traughber asked, "State has said they found round (Q1). Would mutilation be on it?" Wecht replied, "Yes. Trace evidence, not visible to the human eye, would be there."

In the midst of Dr. Wecht's testimony, apropos of nothing that had proceeded it, clemency board member Dills commented, "I'm impressed with the Who's Who in Israel, Who's Who in the United States, you've testified in death cases many times."

"Yes, but never in a clemency," Wecht replied.

"What percentage of the time do you testify for the defense?" asked Dills.

Wecht answered, "85 percent of the time I testify for the prosecution."

At this point, Dr. Cyril Wecht, Dr. Kris Sperry, Dr. James Bell,

3 *Black v. Workman*, Case No. CIV-02-225-C (W.D. Okla., February 10, 2010).

and FBI agent Wilkes had all concluded that because of its pristine condition, Q1 could not have been the fatal bullet. There was no fabric, blood, tissue, or biological material on what O. C. Smith claimed was the fatal bullet. It was truly the magic bullet.

Philip's lawyers brought in Vivian Porter to testify about Harold Davis partying with her the night of the Wendy's robbery. She was harassed by members of the board, as was witness Wardie Parks, a juror at the trial. He testified that if he and other jurors had known Harold Davis was not there, a different verdict would have been rendered. After a series of demeaning questions, he finally blurted out, "I'm charging you all, I'm washing my hands of this situation . . . You do what's right according to the law."

Then came the police, who did as they did in the first clemency presentation—misrepresented what happened at the crime scene. This continued after the lunch break, when William Gibbons, the Shelby County district attorney, gave an opening statement. He reiterated the state's theory of the case, which was belied by the evidence, that Philip Workman and Ronald Oliver were the only shooters at the scene of the crime. He concluded, "The facts have not changed in nineteen years. He is not deserving of clemency." Officers Stoddard, Parker, and Keenan then gave versions of what happened at the crime scene that did not match the original notes recorded there but which made it look bad for Philip Workman.

Once again, O. C. Smith would be the key witness. He was the state's final witness. His prior clemency testimony had been discredited, so he presented a new theory of how Q1 was the fatal bullet. A section of the transcript is worth quoting in detail: "I took a 1980s-era MPD [Memphis Police Department] polyester uniform shirt, used the rib cage of a canine, and put 10 percent ordnance gelatin—which is a recognized human tissue stimulant—behind it, and I fired one round and one round only through this model, striking the rib and recovering the bullet back behind the gelatin . . . This is what the hollow-point bullet did. It went through the cloth, through the rib, hit here and then began to tumble and exit the gelatin."

This was displayed through PowerPoint.

"Basically, only two guns were fired, from the circumstances I was able to uncover. Lieutenant Oliver did not shoot himself."

O. C. Smith repeated all the tests he had conducted the previous year. "[In the current year,] what I did was obtain a pig's foot and shot a Silvertip ammunition through it and then excised the wound and had it analyzed by a state-of-the-art instrument called a scanning electron microscope with energy dispersant analysis of X-rays. And we see here that there are aluminum residues in the wound of the experimental firing . . .

"So, in 2001, a year later, why do we know that it was a Silvertip bullet that killed Lieutenant Oliver? First, because of the same original reasons. The model certainly explains why the bullet did not expand, and now we know that the gunshot contains aluminum." (There was no trace of aluminum found in Lieutenant Oliver's wound).

Mr. Dills of the clemency board stated, "What I'm hearing you say is that you're testifying without a doubt in your mind that the caliber .45 weapon took Lieutenant Oliver's life."

Smith responded, "There's not a doubt in my military mind."

Once again, Philip concluded the proceedings. After stating that he was "sorry for creating the scene" through his robbery, he detailed what happened and how he did not shoot Lieutenant Oliver. Then came the turkey shoot. The hostile clemency board members pounced on him. Philip finally closed with, "I'm feeling in five days I will be executed."

As I sat and listened to this show trial, I was horrified. It was clear the Memphis establishment would do anything to protect their policemen, including create a cover-up and execute an innocent man. DA William Gibbons had led off the afternoon proceedings. His wife was Judge Julia Gibbons, who initially denied Philip his day in court. The chairman of the Parole/Clemency Board was Charles Traughber, the husband of Lois DeBerry, who was speaker pro tem of the Tennessee House of Representatives. All of these folks were from Memphis. The white and Black political establishment were united in the effort to destroy Philip Workman.

The clemency board voted 6–0 to deny clemency. The female member read from the prepared remarks she brought into the room at the beginning of the meeting. We later learned that in meetings held before the clemency hearing, the members planned to recreate the crime scene post-execution. This demonstration would educate the citizenry as to "what really happened." They believed that there was a need for such a piece of theater to educate the people of Tennessee who had been gulled by the "liberal media." The fix was in before the hearing. Philip could have saved himself the humiliation and remained in his cell. The result would have been the same.

After the second clemency hearing, Dr. Werner Spitz, the leading expert in the field, gave an affidavit that a bullet does not leave traces in soft tissue, despite O. C. Smith's elaborate experiment detailed in PowerPoint. Nor was there any trace of aluminum in Lieutenant Oliver's body. This elaborate confabulation was possible because no cross-examination of witnesses was permitted. As in the first clemency, Smith was demonstrated to be a liar and a fraud in his presentation to the clemency board.

On January 28, 2001, Philip was in his cell preparing to watch the Super Bowl (prisoners may have televisions if they buy them). Although the US Supreme Court had not accepted his case and the Tennessee Supreme Court had set an execution date of January 30, 2001, he had a stay of execution. The Department of Correction had a policy of not moving a prisoner to deathwatch if he had a stay.

Suddenly, the death squad appeared outside his cell and told him to pack his things. He was going to deathwatch. Obviously he had no choice, but he told them he had a stay of execution.

Nonetheless, he was taken to the death house in Unit 8. The stay of execution remained intact, and he returned to death row seventy-two hours later. The Tennessee Supreme Court set a new execution date of March 30, 2001.

No one in Tennessee had been moved to deathwatch three times and lived to tell the tale, but Philip would now make this third trip to the killing ground. The second clemency hearing, like the previous one, proved to be a mockery of justice. We learned that the chairman of the clemency board, the state's attorney general, the governor's legal counsel, the commissioner of corrections, and the governor's senior policy adviser had planned the state's post-execution press reenactment of the crime to demonstrate their version of events before the clemency hearing even took place.

And so it goes.

∗   ∗   ∗

As the time ticked down to the new execution date, I could feel the tension in my body. It was specifically in my chest. Philip and I continued the weekly visits. We began to prepare for the next trip to deathwatch.

I had registered to be Philip's spiritual adviser as a minister in the United Church of Christ and the person Philip wished to be with him the last hours of his life. I was surprised when Warden Ricky Bell stated that I would be denied the opportunity to be with Philip for the last three hours. The state's reason was "security."

A lawyer friend agreed to handle a suit in chancery court about my access to Philip. At 10:00 a.m. on Thursday, March 30, 2001, we were before Chancellor Ellen Hobbs Lyle to determine if I could be Philip's spiritual adviser for the last three hours of his life. The state wished to have the state-paid institutional chaplain perform this role.

The state statute said the minister "preparing the condemned prisoner for death" should be present. I fit that definition through our long relationship; the prison chaplain had only a casual relationship with Philip.

Chancellor Lyle listened carefully to each side's arguments and asked the assistant attorney general, "In the course of Rev. Ingle's twenty-five years of ministering to death row in Tennessee, has he been a security threat to any institution?"

"No, your honor," came the state's reply.

At 2:35 p.m. Chancellor Lyle faxed her decision to the parties involved in the litigation. I would be allowed to spend the last hours of Philip's life with him as his pastor.

During the afternoon of March 29, 2001, Philip had his final visits with his brother Terry (the only member of his family who could bear the ordeal) and with friends. At the conclusion of the visits, he was offered the opportunity to choose a final meal. He opted for a vegetarian pizza and requested it be given to the homeless in Nashville. When his request was denied, he decided to go without a final meal.

At 7:30 p.m. I arrived at deathwatch within Riverbend prison. The area is located in Building 8 behind the large visiting room for the general population. The physical components of deathwatch are four holding cells, a darkened control booth, a noncontact visiting booth, the witness room, and the death chamber that houses the electric chair and the lethal injection paraphernalia, complete with gurney.

After signing the logbook, the third book I had signed after clearing the first checkpoint, I walked toward Philip. He was saying farewell to his lawyers through the glass of the noncontact visiting booth. As I awaited their departure, a guard informed me that Philip and I would visit in the noncontact booth. I pointed out I had obtained a court order that enabled me to visit just outside Philip's cell. The guard replied, "I have my orders from the warden."

I stopped Philip's legal team as they emerged from the visiting booth. As I explained the situation, they nodded and told me Philip had informed them about the warden restricting my visit despite the court order. I gave them Chancellor Lyle's home telephone number, and they agreed to check into the matter.

The guards brought Philip into the foyer. He was shackled at the waist. We awkwardly embraced and sat down in the molded plastic chairs. After talking about how his family was doing, I sighed and said, "Philip, I know all this is real. But it seems surreal. I can't believe it's happening."

"Me either, Joe," he replied. "I just can't believe it's come to this. After all the evidence we've found. But it's real all right."

As Philip and I sat in the deathwatch foyer, we recalled his long-held belief that he was "not innocent enough." *Surreal* was a mild description of where we found ourselves, in the bowels of Riverbend, less than five hours from Philip's being strapped to a gurney and poisoned to death by lethal injection.

Our initial hour of visitation was soon completed. Philip needed to make final phone calls to his family, and I needed to find the defense lawyer stationed at the prison to see if Chancellor Lyle's court order would be enforced. We hugged goodbye, and I left deathwatch as Philip returned to his cell.

At 9:30 p.m. I signed back in to the deathwatch log. The lawyers had clarified matters with the warden, as had the judge, and I could go back to Philip's cell and remain there until they came to take him at 12:55 a.m. As I signed back in, I wrote "minister" under the category "role." In the space above my signature, I noted someone had written "observe the minister" for his role. The name next to this was that of the Catholic deacon who ministered to death row prisoners. I was certain that there were two reasons for this note: (1) I was not the in-house chaplain, and (2) I was a longtime opponent of the death penalty. As I headed to Philip's cell, Jerry Welborn, the institutional chaplain, stopped me to talk. At that point I had been fighting to be with Philip since 10:00 a.m., and I did not want to tarry and visit with Jerry—or anyone else. After speaking a few words of condolence and concern, Jerry asked to see my Communion kit, which had already been inspected. I opened the portable kit and showed him the wine and wafers. He gave the okay sign to the guards behind the darkened glass, and I walked to Philip's cell.

Philip was in the holding cell at the end of the tier farthest from the death chamber. After passing through the larger cage door, I pulled up a plastic chair outside his cell. As I settled into the chair, I noticed how bare the cell was. His leather-bound Bible was his primary companion. I brought Philip up to date on Chancellor Lyle's enforcement of her order on pastoral visits. Philip mentioned that the Catholic chaplain wanted to come and say goodbye. I told him that was fine and observed that it shouldn't be difficult for him since the chaplain was in a chair about twelve feet behind me. We discussed Philip's children and grandchildren, who had visited Becca and me in our home. He was concerned about his brother Terry, who was determined to be strong and to shoulder this burden alone for the family. Then we discussed the funeral service, where Philip wished to be buried, and the final details of a healthy man preparing for his imminent destruction.

At 10:30 p.m., we heard that the US Supreme Court had declined to accept Philip's appeal on the clemency hearing. Once again, Philip had fallen one vote short. This time Justice John Paul Stevens wrote a dissent. Philip and I decided to share Communion. I opened my Communion kit, spread the linen cloth over a small table, and set up the wine and wafers. We prayed together, and then after blessing the elements we partook of the bread and wine. When the service concluded, we prayed for God's blessing to strengthen us through this ordeal.

The Catholic chaplain came over to visit Philip. I scooted my chair away and waited for them to finish. When they said goodbye, the chaplain returned to his chair of observation directly behind me. Philip and I discussed his odyssey through the courts and, as Jerry Garcia of the Grateful Dead sang, "What a long, strange trip it's been."

At midnight Philip said he wanted to pray by himself. I nodded and concurred. He retreated to the rear of his cell, dropped to his knees with folded hands, and looked through the narrow vertical window as he offered his prayers to God. The sight of Philip with his head uplifted in prayer focused on the night sky almost unhinged me. A man prostrate before his God, sweating the proverbial blood of Jesus in Gethsemane, resembled a specter in his hospital-white attire. I prayed for strength for us to endure this madness.

I read the 139th psalm as Philip prayed. Time slipped by and it was soon after midnight, execution day, March 30, my sister's and father-in-law's birthday. Philip remained on his knees, lost in prayer. At 12:10 a.m. I glanced up at the television, mounted on a shelf outside the cell. A local reporter narrated the scene outside the prison, and a bulletin flashed across the bottom of the screen: "THE TENNESSEE SUPREME COURT HAS GRANTED A STAY OF EXECUTION TO PHILIP WORKMAN." Transfixed, I heard the reporter reiterate the bulletin, and it scrolled across the screen again. Then I shuddered from prior experience.

Oh my God, I thought. *They're going to delay this temporarily, maybe for an hour or so, and then do it.*

I strained to listen to the reporter and read the bulletin a third time. I glanced at Philip. He was still praying, oblivious of the news, whatever it meant. I waited for the phone call from the lawyers who would explain. Time passed. No phone call. No clarifying reports.

At 12:20 a.m. Philip stood and brushed off his white pants. He turned and walked toward me. As he approached the cell door, I informed him, "Philip, you have a stay of execution from the Tennessee Supreme Court. I don't know what the grounds are or how long it will last. But you have a stay."

Philip staggered in midstride and took a step back. My words had the effect of a punch delivered to his solar plexus. Bewilderment, consternation, and confusion flashed across his face. He had prepared himself, steeled his will to deal with his slaughter, and this sudden turn of events was unnerving. He steadied himself and walked toward me.

"What does it mean?" he said. "Do I have my evidentiary hearing?" He grasped my shoulders through the bars, and I grabbed his shoulders in return.

"I don't know. All we know is the Tennessee Supreme Court granted a stay. I don't know why and for how long." Neither of us knew there was any more litigation ongoing. I nodded in the direction of the television. Philip asked the guard to turn it up. The news was the same from the reporter outside the prison, and the bulletin at the bottom of the screen remained unchanged.

"Philip, let me get ahold of the lawyers," I said. The guard dialed the number of defense lawyer Jefferson Dorsey, with whom I had earlier discussed the pastoral visit. "Jefferson, what's going on? Philip is on an emotional roller coaster here. Do we have a stay? How long?" The words rushed from me. "Do we have an evidentiary hearing?"

Jefferson responded, "We have a stay. The Tennessee Supreme Court clerk is on the other line. They're faxing the order. Let me check on the evidentiary hearing." A pause, then Jefferson returned. "We have an evidentiary hearing."

Incredulous, I shouted, "We have an evidentiary hearing!"

Philip stood on his tip toes, elation flushing his face. He addressed the deathwatch guard: "That's all I've wanted for ten years! A chance to put on the evidence to show I didn't kill Officer Oliver."

I hung up the telephone and Philip and I embraced through the bars. Then he began talking about who we could put under oath and what we could now prove that had been unknown at the time of the 1982 trial. His words cascaded over me with enthusiasm. It felt like a verbal waterfall. Through the joy, the television blurted, "The evidentiary hearing will be held in Memphis later today." Philip and I were stunned into silence. As we looked up at the television, the reporter was saying that the evidentiary hearing would go forward almost immediately.

Philip and I looked at each other in horror. He grabbed my shoulders in a strong grip. Looking directly into my eyes, he delivered a plea. "Joe, you've got to tell them to go ahead and kill me. I can't take anymore. A hearing later today will be a joke, and they'll move me back here again. I can't go through this anymore."

I looked into those pained brown eyes and said, "Philip, hang on, man. This is just a news report. Let me check with the lawyers. It can't be right."

Philip was deflated, wounded. The immense pressure of the state machinery of killing had driven him to his wit's end. I motioned the guard to dial Jefferson Dorsey again. "Jefferson, you have to read me the court order. The news is reporting the hearing will be in Memphis in a few hours. What's going on?"

"Joe, look that can't be right. Let me check." In a few minutes he came back. "The news media are wrong. The order will be transmitted to Memphis today, but the hearing is not set."

I thanked Jefferson and told Philip the news. We embraced and decided to pray. Holding hands through the bars, we offered a prayer of thanksgiving. We praised God, gratefully mentioning those who had helped, and then began to realize the imminent danger had passed.

We finished the prayer and the guards wanted to hustle me out of deathwatch. Philip would be going back to his cell on Unit 2. I teased him, "Man, you're going back to a clean cell." (Philip meticulously cleaned his cell before going to deathwatch. He wanted the next man to have a freshly scrubbed "home.")

Philip laughed and said, "Yeah, it will be good to get back

there." We hugged each other goodbye, and I exited.

Before leaving the prison, I sought to confirm the accuracy of our latest information. I was in a state of astonishment, almost disbelief. As I passed several glum prison administrators, I received all the confirmation I needed. After walking out of the stale, recycled air of Building 8 into the fresh air of spring, an African American guard smiled and extended his hand in fellowship. As we shook hands, he said, "Tell Philip I'm so glad. God is good." As I shook his hand, I replied, "I'll let Philip know. God is good."

After signing out of the prison, I noticed the paramilitary display for the execution was not to be seen. All that remained of the state troopers, who had searched all cars and frisked everyone entering the parking lot, was a lone car pulled off to the side of the road. The helicopter that had buzzed overhead for "security purposes" had flown back to base. The crowd of three hundred protestors and four celebrants of the execution had returned home.

As I eased my truck into a parking space at the motel where Philip's friends and family awaited my return, I gripped the steering wheel as hard as I could and breathed deeply. The tension in my body was palpable. I recalled the somber scene I'd left earlier in the evening inside this motel. Philip's loved ones were preparing for the worst. We had read scripture and prayed, and we created a scenario we would enact at 12:55 a.m. before they walked him into the death chamber. The plan was that Philip and I would read the apostle Paul's letter to the Romans 8:31–39. Then he and I would join hands in prayer, each of us extending a hand toward those in the motel room so that they could join us spiritually, if not physically. It would be a circle of prayer. The loved ones in the motel room would be holding hands and extending a hand to unite with us.

I knocked on the door and heard the reply from within: "It's Joe! Open it up!" There were hugs, shouts, laughter, and unmitigated joy. I exclaimed, "Jesus kicked butt tonight! He may have been wearing lawyer's shoes, but he kicked butt!" As the energy release of the pandemonium eased down, we exchanged stories of what had transpired during the evening. I munched on some leftover Chinese food, finally feeling hungry. My adrenaline and exhaustion were intermingled, and I could not relax. At 3:00 a.m. we had a final prayer.

I drove home through the early morning spring darkness with my window down. When I reached our long, winding gravel driveway, I turned off the headlights and drove in the moonlight. The spring peepers were quite loud. A barred owl hooted from across the way. The stars shone brilliantly. The eighth psalm came to mind: "O Lord, when I consider the beauty of your creation, what are we humans that you are mindful of us?"

Entering the house from the basement, trying to be quiet so as not to awake Becca and Amelia, I came up the stairs to the main floor. Becca was waiting for me. She seemed sad and worried.

"Are you okay?" she asked.

I realized she had not heard about Philip's stay of execution. I grinned. "Philip got a stay from the Tennessee Supreme Court. He's alive."

Becca's face transformed into disbelieving joy. "What? How?" she asked, eager for information.

We hugged each other, and I sat down beside her and retold the evening's events. She then shared what she and Amelia (thirteen years old at the time) had experienced while I was at the prison with Philip.

Early in the evening they attended a service for Philip at Christ Church Cathedral, the Episcopal church we attend. Terry, Philip's brother, spoke at the service. Amelia had grown close to Philip through phone calls to our house from the prison and she served as an acolyte during the service. After the service they drove out to the prison to take part in the protest.

As the mother and daughter joined the protestors, they saw

a woman weeping and wailing in the field. It was Susan, Philip's former girlfriend, who had been our houseguest a year before when Philip came within thirty-four hours of execution.

After recognizing Susan, Amelia began to sob and exclaim, "I want my daddy. I want my daddy."

Becca held her. "Daddy needs to be with Philip right now. Philip needs him. He'll be out as soon as he can."

"I want my daddy," Amelia continued to cry. Becca caressed her, loved her, and comforted her. Then two guards approached.

"Are you all right?" one of the correctional officers inquired.

"Yes, we are fine, thank you," Becca replied.

"Just wanted to be sure you were okay," said the officer.

As the guards walked off, Amelia burst out, "Boo ya!" Although the officers did not hear the remark, Becca and Amelia laughed at her teenage audacity and determination.

After they came home, Amelia went to sleep crying, worried about Philip. Shortly after 1:00 a.m., the telephone rang. Becca answered. It was a hate call. Then at 2:20 a.m. an elderly African American woman telephoned and asked that I pray for her vision. Amelia slept as Becca fielded the phone calls.

When Becca and I completed our sharing of the night's events, I moved Amelia over on our bed so Becca would have room to sleep. I was too hyper-alert to sleep myself. As I moved her, Amelia awoke. She whispered, with her bottom lip trembling, "Did they kill him, Daddy?" I pulled her to me and whispered in her ear, "Philip is alive and well, honey. He got a stay of execution." Before my second sentence was completed, she showered my face with kisses. And together the three of us tumbled on the bed, laughing.

It was 4:00 a.m., and for the third time in a year, Philip had survived the state of Tennessee's effort to kill him. Now, three hours past the appointed killing time, we laughed and celebrated life. As the guard at the prison put it, "God is good."

Not Innocent Enough

*   *   *

What had happened to change impending doom into a lifeline? Robert Hutton, a Memphis defense lawyer, had filed an error coram nobis petition on Philip's behalf several weeks before the execution reciting the newly discovered evidence in the case. Filed in the trial court, it was treated as all legal matters were in Memphis pertaining to Philip Workman: denied. Amid all the frenetic activity of the weeks leading up to the execution, it was forgotten. The petition reached the Tennessee Supreme Court on the eve of the execution and in a 3–2 vote, Philip was granted an evidentiary hearing at the last minute. The key vote and the opinion were by Justice Frank Drowota from Nashville. "At the hearing, Workman will have the opportunity to establish that newly discovered evidence may have resulted in a different judgment if the evidence had been admitted at the previous trial."[4]

Given the chaos of events and changes of course in the *Workman* case, it is worth reviewing the facts pertaining to the crime scene, discovered through Chris Minton's filing of a Tennessee Public Records Act request and the notes of the policemen at the scene. It was a decidedly different picture than the one painted by the state at trial, on appeal, and in the two clemency hearings.

There were three citizen witnesses to the events at the crime scene: Garvin Null, Jeff Rickard, and Steve Craig. Null and Rickard drank beer inside Null's truck, which was parked at the Gulf gas station across from the Wendy's restaurant. Null saw a bunch of police cars pull into the Wendy's. Several cars departed the restaurant, leaving two officers outside talking. Steve Craig followed two police cars pulling into the Wendy's and drove into the Holiday Auto Parts lot adjacent to observe. He exited his vehicle to go talk to his

---

4 *Workman v. State*, 41 S.W.3d 100 (Tenn. 2001).

friend, Officer Stoddard. When Officer Parker arrived, Craig saw Workman fleeing the scene. Null saw Lieutenant Oliver hit Philip on the head with a flashlight. Stoddard shot at Philip, and Philip fired a return shot that hit Stoddard in the arm. (It could be that in this exchange of gunfire from Stoddard and Workman, Stoddard accidentally shot Officer Oliver.) A police report from that evening states: "M/W [Male/White] runs north thru the parking area and was caught by the officer and during the struggle . . . Stoddard was shot in the arm . . . Oliver was shot in the chest." Craig was back in his car lying down when he heard six more shots. He raised up and saw Oliver on the ground.

Despite the prosecution's two-shooter theory advanced at trial, quite a few bullets were fired that night by several people. Philip fired three shots and ejected one: one went up in the air when he was struck on his head by Officer Oliver's flashlight while in the act of surrender; the second was fired at a "flash," which was Philip's return fire that struck Stoddard in the arm; the third one was ejected when Philip forgot he had a semi-automatic; and the fourth shot was fired in the air as Philip climbed over a fence while fleeing.

Memphis policeman Stewart heard three gunshots, a volley of six rounds, then a couple more shots. Memphis policeman Geil heard two shots, which he mistook for a car backfiring, then another shot, then seven to eight shots. Memphis policeman T. L. Cobb heard eight to twelve shots. Null heard about nine shots in five seconds. Jeff Rickard heard nine to twelve shots. This was more shots than Philip (three) and Oliver (six) fired. The Memphis police maintained Oliver emptied his gun at a fleeing Workman while on the ground after being shot. This is highly dubious, and since the police secured Oliver's gun at the scene, no one really knows how many bullets were in it.

Steve Craig saw Officer Parker shoot his shotgun two or three times at Philip as he fled. When treated at the hospital after being apprehended, Philip had shotgun pellets removed from his buttocks. Officer Stewart arrived at 10:35 p.m. and saw Parker "going around the Northeast corner of Holiday building with a shotgun." Officer Stoddard fired several times at Philip after he was struck on the head. Null, Rickard, and Craig all saw Philip holding his head as he fled the scene.

Also, there was the matter of Harold Davis. The man who wasn't actually at the crime scene but who testified at trial as the sole eyewitness who observed Philip shoot Oliver.

There was the X-ray that somehow the state misplaced for twenty years until it became available in preparation of the first clemency hearing. This X-ray established it was a through and through bullet, demolishing the fragmenting-bullet theory advanced by the Sixth Circuit Court of Appeals panel and O. C. Smith.

And there was also the fact that when Robert Hutton checked with the two people who worked with O. C. Smith on firing the bullet into the pig's foot, neither recalled the results Smith testified occurred. Mr. Koontz and a female associate analyzed the samples, observed the result of the test, and gave statements that there was no aluminum found in the first test sample. The second test sample was conducted on an aluminum slide, so any aluminum would have been conveyed by the slide. The sample examination utilized what O. C. Smith described as "the state-of-the-art instrument called a scanning electron microscope with energy dispersant analysis of X-rays."

Given this picture of factual distortion and creative fantasy by the state of Tennessee in its persistent effort to kill Philip Workman, one would not only welcome an evidentiary hearing to set the record straight but would hope these matters could be addressed in a fair manner. For instance, why not hold it in a jurisdiction outside of Memphis? Any major city would do—Nashville, Knoxville, or Chattanooga. Given the record of Memphis authorities in the handling of this case, why would one expect fairness at a hearing in Memphis?

A foreshadowing of what was to come with the evidentiary hearing had already occurred in 1990. Chris Minton was new to the *Workman* case and filed a Tennessee Public Records Act (TPRA) request. Based on the information discovered through the TPRA effort (police notes from the crime scene and the prosecutor's files), he realized that his client was consistent in his description of events, but that the stories by the police and the district attorney kept changing. There was contradiction in the police log of the crime scene and the statements given at trial. Given this newly discovered information, Minton filed an amended motion for state post-conviction relief.

A status conference was scheduled on Minton's motion. Judge John P. Colton Jr. would preside. Minton drove the three hours to Memphis from Nashville for the status conference. Upon arrival, rather than a status hearing, he was given a decision denying his amended motion petition. Judge Colton would not even hold a status conference, much less a hearing to consider the issues. Years later, Judge Colton would preside over the evidentiary hearing for Philip Workman.

Robert Hutton would be Philip's lawyer in the evidentiary hearing. On Friday, March 30, 2001, Hutton appeared on a local radio show hosted by Mike Fleming. As a devout Catholic, Hutton thought his role was to discuss scripture and the Catholic teaching on the death penalty. However, Fleming had other ideas and pressed him with questions about the *Workman* case. O. C. Smith had appeared on Fleming's show the prior week in an effort to counteract the "liberal media," which had been so persuasive in presenting Workman's side of the story. Fleming asked Hutton to evaluate Smith's two clemency performances. Hutton minced no words and stated that Smith was "a liar."

Three days after Hutton's radio appearance, he received a letter threatening O. C. Smith. It stated, in part, "A greater task you have given me to destroy the LIAR who would bear false witness." Hutton turned the letter over to state and local authorities. The assumption was that some nut case who was a Workman supporter sent the letter.

The Workman defense team had waged an effective public education campaign. The first thing Judge Colton did, sua sponte, meaning on the court's own initiative, was enter a gag order on April 6, 2001. The attorneys would not address the media, and that included all of Workman's lawyers.

On April 9, 2001, a scheduling conference took place before Judge Colton. Robert Hutton arrived, and the state presented him a motion requesting production of Harold Davis's statements forty-eight hours before his testimony. The defense did not know where Davis was at the time.

Hutton responded to the haste with which Judge Colton was acting. He pointed out that Colton did not even have jurisdiction of the case because the mandate had not issued from the Tennessee Supreme Court. He also indicated he would be filing a rehearing petition, which would further delay issuance of the mandate.

Judge Colton insisted it was his case despite the procedural rules stating he did not have jurisdiction yet. "Now, the court's going to find that it has jurisdiction to rule on matters before it at this time. Also, the court is going to grant the motion of the state directing the defendant to produce any audio or written tapes of statements of Harold Davis and an order of protection. I'll need an order from the state." Colton set an April 23, 2001, date for the evidentiary hearing.

Once these matters reached the Court of Criminal Appeals, Judge Colton was reversed on May 2, 2001. The hearing had not taken place on April 23 because the Court of Appeals had stayed the proceedings pending the outcome of their ruling. In motions filed with Judge Colton, the prosecution was never denied.

They found Harold Davis in the Jacksonville, Florida, jail. He was charged with shoplifting. They brought him to Memphis for the

August 13 evidentiary hearing. The prosecution did not inform the defense they had Harold Davis in custody.

In an effort to keep their secret of bringing Harold Davis to Memphis, the prosecution put him in the Germantown jail at 9:25 a.m. on Sunday, August 12. The defense would have discovered if he was in the Shelby County Jail, so he was placed in a suburban jail in hopes of maintaining the secrecy of his presence.

Unbeknownst to prosecutors, when Harold Davis was escorted through the Memphis airport after his flight from Jacksonville, a minister who had known him since childhood spotted him. After speaking with Harold and learning he was in town to testify at the Workman hearing and was being held in the Germantown jail, the minister called Davis's sister to let her know his whereabouts. She contacted Workman's defense team.

Later that Sunday afternoon, prosecutors Kitchens and Campbell met with Davis. Kitchens called Hutton from Campbell's home phone after the visit. He informed him they had Harold Davis. Davis's family had already contacted Hutton to let him know where Harold Davis was sequestered.

After the prosecutors spoke with Davis, the investigator Ron Lax and clemency lawyer Pierotti spoke with him. Harold Davis's sister also spoke with him, and she read him the riot act. He was told in no uncertain terms that he needed to tell the truth, no matter what deal he had cut with prosecutors. The family name was at stake. They were the children of a minister, and everyone needed to know the truth that he did not see Philip Workman kill the police officer.

CHAPTER TWENTY-SIX

The Evidentiary Hearing

THE *WORKMAN* CASE had been characterized by mendacity, deceit, and deception prior to the evidentiary hearing. It featured police officers suborning perjury; prosecutors misrepresenting facts at trial, on appeals, during two clemency hearings, and in the press; judges denying relief that was called for; federal judges literally creating theories by distorting a study to justify the conviction; and two clemency hearings decided in advance. Really, one could not make this stuff up. And since the evidentiary hearing was to be conducted in Memphis, by the same authorities whose hostility toward Philip Workman had been unrelenting, why would one expect things to change?

Prior to the hearing, Robert Hutton asked Judge Colton to recuse himself. That motion, like every other pretrial motion Hutton filed on Workman's behalf, was denied. Undaunted, at the beginning of the August 13, 2001, evidentiary hearing, he moved for the recusal of the prosecutors. He made this unusual request because the prosecutors had deceived him about having Harold Davis in custody and were not forthcoming of Davis's whereabouts before getting him to Memphis. Judge Colton saw no problem with this failure of disclosure, despite the issuance of a subpoena. He denied the recusal motion.

The **Workman** *case had been characterized by mendacity, deceit, and deception prior to the evidentiary hearing. It featured police officers suborning perjury; prosecutors misrepresenting facts at trial, on appeals, during two clemency hearings, and in the press; judges denying relief that was called for; federal judges literally creating theories by distorting a study to justify the conviction; and two clemency hearings decided in advance. Really, one could not make this stuff up.*

Harold Davis took the stand as the prosecution's witness. He had a long history of being apprehended for crimes and cutting deals with prosecutors to tell them what they wanted him to say in exchange for a reduced or dismissed charge. This was certainly what the prosecution expected from Davis as he began his testimony. It soon became clear that Harold Davis was no longer certain about what happened that night. Despite repeated questions, he would not confirm he was at the Wendy's the night of the crime. The prosecution became increasingly frustrated. Defense lawyer Robert Hutton asked him a direct question about whether he saw Philip Workman shoot Officer Ronald Oliver. The answer stunned the prosecution because Davis, their witness, replied, "I did not see Workman shoot Officer Oliver."

Prosecutor Jerry Kitchens went after Davis in a hostile, vindictive manner. For several hours he harassed, pressed, and harangued Davis. Despite defense objections, Judge Colton allowed the aggressive questioning to continue. Davis grew weary and weak from the verbal assault. He weaved and wavered in his testimony over time. He indicated that drugs, the loss of his father, and living on the streets for the last twenty years made it difficult to remember.

"I remember being behind a police car and a police car turned into Wendy's. But after that I'm not sure," he said.

Davis was emotional, sometimes crying under the pressure from the prosecutor.

"A man's life is at stake and it's not right for me to say what's true or not because my mind is not fully there. I've lived on the street twenty years where it's easy to lie. It's self-preservation." Davis also stated that after Workman's trial, two white men came to the motel and insinuated that if he changed his testimony, people he knew might be harmed. He indicated he thought those men were policemen.

Harold Davis was the only witness for the state. Clearly, his testimony had not gone well for the prosecution. He was not a reliable witness.

Given the life Harold Davis had lived for the last twenty years, he was lucky to be alive. Strung out on drugs, wandering from one cheap motel to another, one step ahead of the law or in jail, his health was not good. He was in a weakened state before the fierce questioning of the prosecution. Yet they brought him back on Tuesday morning for more examination.

Kitchens coaxed Davis to say that the defense lawyers had scared him two years ago when they showed up at his motel in Phoenix. "I told them what they wanted to hear. I was coming down off of drugs, and I would have said anything to keep my freedom. I took it otherwise they were going to drag me back to Tennessee and put me in jail."

The statement by Davis was ludicrous for at least two reasons: (1) Chris Minton and Jefferson Dorsey had no power, no authority to coerce him back to Tennessee. (2) They were officers of the court and any effort to transport Davis against his will could have cost them their law licenses.

Robert Hutton led Harold Davis through his testimony in the 1982 trial of Philip Workman. The defense lawyer read a series of answers Davis had given at trial, including the reenactment when he came down off the witness stand and demonstrated how Workman allegedly shot Oliver. After reading the testimony, along with other parts of Davis's "eyewitness testimony," Hutton asked: "True or not true, Mr. Davis." Davis responded without hesitation to each question, including the reenactment of the murder: "Not true." He concluded, "I'm coming forward with the truth today."

After returning to the Germantown jail, Davis suffered severe headaches. He was taken to a hospital and his brain was scanned. The stress of the prosecution's relentless attack had a profound physical and emotional impact on him.

On Wednesday morning, Davis took the stand at 8:30 a.m. After telling defense lawyers he did not see Philip shoot Lieutenant Oliver, he told prosecutors he remembered turning into the Wendy's behind the police car and remembered leaving, but beyond that he could not "distinguish fact from fiction. I just don't know."

At 8:45 a.m., the testimony was interrupted and the court was informed by medical personnel (who had examined Davis the previous night in the Germantown Methodist Hospital) that a brain scan revealed swelling of the brain. Davis had to be returned to the hospital. Davis was removed from the courtroom on a gurney and hospitalized. He received treatment for high blood pressure and swelling of the brain.

Davis returned on Thursday, August 16, for a final day of testimony. There was little added to the record and the prosecution and defense battled to ask the last question in hopes of obtaining a definitive answer. Davis stated his poor memory was the result of drug use, personal problems, and possibly a series of small strokes. Even the prosecutor admitted Davis had a history of strokes.

No one with an objective perspective would believe this man had the credibility to send someone to the death chamber.

Vivian Porter was the next witness. She testified that Harold Davis had been with her the night of the Wendy's robbery and Lieutenant Oliver's slaying. She said they had driven past the crime scene but did not drive into the parking lot. She also told of how she and Davis learned of the police killing on television at her dwelling.

The hearing concluded with the scheduling of the date of August 24, 2001, for the testimony of further witnesses who could not make the dates of this evidentiary hearing.

As one who had sat through two clemency hearings that starred Dr. O. C. Smith and his misleading PowerPoint presentations, it was interesting to note that he was not called as a witness. The reason was obvious: If he testified, he would be subject to cross-examination. His experiments and explanations would disintegrate like wet tissue paper. This meant that Harold Davis, who contradicted his own trial testimony, was the only state witness.

After witnessing the evidentiary hearing, I headed back to Nashville. The hearing would conclude with testimony from Dr. Cyril Wecht in October. As I drove the two hundred miles back home over I-40 east, the hearing percolated in my mind.

Harold Davis, who contradicted his own trial testimony, was the only state witness.

I had witnessed a Memphis judge who consistently favored the prosecution throughout the proceedings—a prosecution that placed so much pressure on a witness that he had to be treated in a hospital for stroke-like symptoms after his testimony. On Wednesday, after a mere fifteen minutes of testimony, he was removed from the stand and placed on a gurney to return to the hospital with swelling of the brain. There was simply no limit to what Memphis police, prosecutors, and judges would do to maintain the twenty-year cover-up of Lieutenant Oliver's death by friendly fire.

On October 13, 2001, the evidentiary hearing continued with the testimony of Dr. Cyril Wecht. As he had pointed out in the second clemency hearing, a hollow-point bullet expands once it enters the body. If it exits, the exit wound is larger than the entry wound. Philip Workman had hollow-point bullets. Yet Lieutenant Oliver's entrance wound was larger than the exit wound. It could not have been Workman's bullet. He was able to make that conclusion "to a reasonable degree of medical certainty."

On cross-examination the prosecutors tried to portray Dr. Wecht as someone whose opinion was shaped by defense counsel. Wecht responded forcefully: "I have no bias in this case. I have no cudgel to bear, no axe to grind and no flag to wave."

The prosecutors were intensely hostile to Dr. Wecht because his testimony undid the trial court record and established that Philip did not shoot Oliver. They kept him on the stand the entire afternoon, pounding him with questions. Wecht clearly stated he did not agree with police and prosecutors who asserted that the bullet found the day after the shooting, in a parking lot 104 feet from where Lieutenant Oliver was shot, was the bullet that killed Oliver. Dr. Wecht was adamant that what we termed "the magic bullet" showed very little of the damage that would have occurred if it had hit Lieutenant Oliver, striking his rib and passing through his body. "A soft-jacketed hollow-point bullet would be expected to deform or fragment when it hit a bone and it's not designed to exit the body," he said.

The final witness in the evidentiary hearing was juror Wardie Parks. Parks testified strongly that if the jury had known the scientific evidence that demonstrated it was not Philip's bullet that killed Lieutenant Oliver, and that the "sole eyewitness," Harold Davis, was not actually at the crime scene, the jury would not have voted to convict Workman of murder, much less sentence him to death. Judge Colton ruled Parks's testimony was "not relevant," although he preserved it on the record for appeal. I suppose the five other jurors who had been contacted post-trial with the same evidence, and who stated they would not have voted for death, were not relevant either.

The Tennessee Supreme Court ruling ordering the evidentiary hearing set the standard for the hearing: "At the hearing, Workman will have the opportunity to establish that newly discovered evidence may have resulted in a different judgment if the evidence had been admitted at the previous trial." Clearly, that standard had been met through the testimony of Harold Davis, Vivian Porter, Dr. Cyril Wecht, and Wardie Parks.

Judge Colton indicated he would rule within thirty days, and so he did. He denied Philip Workman relief. Welcome to Memphis.

CHAPTER TWENTY-SEVEN

You Can't Make This Stuff Up

ON MARCH 13, 2002, a janitor found a bomb and two smaller explosive devices in the stairwell outside of the Shelby County Regional Forensic Center. Dr. O. C. Smith was summoned and examined the devices. He confirmed that they were explosives, and the police were called. The suspicion was that the bomb was the work of a writer of a series of threatening letters who seemed to be a Philip Workman supporter. He signed the letters "STEEL in the hand of the KING OF KINGS."

From a letter to Lawrence Buser, a writer for Memphis's *Commercial Appeal*:

> GOD BLESS YOU for your articles about the fearful conspiracy of deceit and LIARS trying to CRUCIFY an INNOCENT man, a LAMB OF GOD beloved of our LORD and SAVIOUR.
>
> I received HOLY ORDERS from a MESSANGER OF GOD on Friday in the FORM of Robert Hutton, son of the ONE TRUE CHURCH speaking to me through the Mike Fleming show. He told me the LIAR,

O. C. SMITH, a DOCTOR-KILLER committing two MORAL SINS. He is bearing FALSE WITNESS with his lies deceit and untruths in an effort to MURDER PHILIP R. WORKMAN.

Long have I waited for my HOLY ORDER to fight against the DOCTOR-KILLER abortionists but now I Know OUR LORD was saving me for something bigger.

Through your help I understand better the "Little General" commands of DEMONS doing the work of SATAN on CESAR'S WORLD.

GOD BLESS YOU A THOUSAND TIMES.

JOHN 15:13

Steel in the hand of the KING OF KINGS

This is only one example of letters sent to numerous people, including District Attorney William Gibbons. We had no clue where these letters came from.

Philip Workman's birthday was June 1. On that day in 2002, a bizarre incident occurred involving O. C. Smith. After leaving work earlier in the day, Smith returned to the Regional Forensic Center at 9:00 p.m. He informed the only employee on duty that he was there. A little after 10:00 p.m., as Smith once again left the building, he was walking to the parking lot when someone threw an "acid-like" substance in his face to subdue him and then wrapped him in barbed wire, head to toe, with a bomb strapped to his chest. Smith was found by a security guard at 12:30 a.m. on June 2. He had been locked to the security bars of a window. It was reported his arms were outstretched in the form of a crucifixion.

In a June 3, 2002, press conference, Jim Cavanaugh, an agent of the federal ATF (Bureau of Alcohol, Tobacco, and Firearms) stated:

"There is a good chance that the man who wrote the letters is the bomber . . . This person is someone in this area who has strong religious beliefs, and we are asking for the public's help to find him because he is dangerous. The explosives make him a danger to a personal level toward Dr. Smith.

"The attacker is described as a white man, 20–30 years old, 5'8" to 6,' and pale complexioned . . . Authorities say he attacked the medical examiner because Smith was a prosecution witness in the long-running case of convicted cop killer Philip Workman."[1]

Memphis police investigators and bomb-squad officers were interviewed for an episode of the nationally syndicated television show *America's Most Wanted*. Agents later said the program produced some "very interesting" tips.

ATF agent Gene Marquez stated, "We're confident we can solve the case." He also said it was "our priority investigation right now." The ATF said it had evidence linking the attack to previous bombings and threatening letters.

In a November 8, 2002, interview with the *Memphis Flyer*, Agent Cavanaugh said that the bomber may have gone underground like the Unabomber. The attacker had worn gloves, punched Smith in the stomach, and jumped on him, did not carry a gun or knife, and chained Smith to a window grate in a "semi-crucified" position. Asked if he thought the attack might have been staged, Cavanaugh responded, "I've been a cop too long to not think that there might be something else. I'm open to any angles."

As Philip's case meandered its way through the appellate courts, our weekly visits continued. The events of the spring and his third death warrant had taken their toll. He was more somber but still had

---

1 *Commercial Appeal*, June 4, 2002.

his sense of humor. It was in one such discussion of the bizarre events in Memphis that Philip opined, "Joe, I think O. C. Smith wrapped himself in barbed wire and placed the explosive device on his chest." This observation caught me by surprise. I knew Memphis was the belly of the death penalty beast in Tennessee, but the thought that the medical examiner could be utterly mad did not cross my mind. But given we were talking Memphis, all possibilities were on the table.

Philip's forty-ninth birthday was June 1, 2003. He did not think he would live to see it, but he was in Unit 2, back with his friends. Life had resumed a regularity if not normality. Then on June 2, 2003, the Tennessee Supreme Court set his fourth execution date for September 24, 2003.

* * *

It was hard to imagine how Philip would survive a fourth death warrant.

It was hard to imagine how Philip would survive a fourth death warrant. The tension that gradually builds as the days move toward deathwatch is palpable. In an effort to ascertain how Philip was doing mentally, Dr. George Woods was brought in to evaluate him. Dr. Woods is a renowned neuropsychiatrist with an expertise in trauma. Excerpts from his report follow:

> Mr. Workman described his first exposure to the Deathwatch protocol on April 3, 2000. "My heart started to explode." He talked about the level of self-denial he

had experienced, which included not packing his belongings until the last possible moment.

As he was discussing the counter rituals that condemned inmates develop to deal with the protocols put in place by the prison, the steps described are very similar [to] those of someone who is dying from a terminal disease or attempting to commit suicide. He gives his possessions away to those he has come to believe would appreciate them, his pencils, extra clothing, his caps.

Mr. Workman couldn't sleep the night before he assumed he would be taken. Understanding that there was someone waiting to take his cell as soon as he was executed, he cleaned the cell, out of courtesy. About 3:00 a.m. Philip took a shower and got dressed. It seemed but a few minutes, and "There they were . . . come in numbers." The team that comes for Deathwatch inmates are dressed completely in black, and are volunteers that, because of their size, responsibility, and willingness, are even more intimidating.

After being strip searched, Mr. Workman was shackled, and walked to the Deathwatch cell. None of the other Death Row inmates said anything to him as he walked by their cells. It was his sense that every inmate was glad this time wasn't their time, and couldn't find much to say. He could see their faces in the openings of their cells.

Mr. Workman described an " . . . almost dreamlike state . . . You're there, but you're not there . . . It's not you."

Mr. Workman received a stay on April 4, 2000, a day and a half before he was to be executed. He remembers feeling a "rush of energy . . . " and feeling elated. However, returning to his cell on Death Row, he knew that his life had changed.

"I didn't know whether to unpack," Mr. Workman recalled. Since that first exposure, he has never unpacked immediately.

In September of 2000, a fellow inmate woke him up to tell him that his stay had been lifted. When the extraction team, the similar assemblage of large men dressed all in black, came the second time, on January 28, 2001: "My breath was taken away."

In spite of clearly recognizing the circumstances he was facing, again, experiencing the execution ritual, Mr. Workman had developed a pathological denial, an inability to face the execution ritual as straightforwardly as he had the first time. He had not packed, although he had been, again, giving things away since Christmas. . . .

Mr. Workman started experiencing dreams of being executed. He also had nightmares of being in the Death Chamber, 20 to 30 feet from the electric chair, and it is malfunctioning. He dreamed of watching others being executed and being in an electric chair that is being driven through a mall.

Mr. Workman noted that one of the experiences that imprinted the execution procedures most on him was the number of strip searches. He would take off all his clothes, sometimes his upper garments first, at other times his pants and underwear. He would be told to squat in the event something had been secreted in his anus. He was strip searched upon each visit, even though they were all noncontact. On certain days, this would mean being strip searched 16 times.

On the second Deathwatch to which he has been exposed, Mr. Workman received a stay, and was returned to Death Row from Deathwatch 11 hours before he was to be executed . . . Mr. Workman recognized this experience was not over. "You're on pins and needles."

Mr. Workman hardly unpacked anything after his second exposure to the execution procedures. He found himself continually anxious. His concentration was becoming impaired. He found himself unable to focus on those things that had occupied [him] the last 22 years, his Seventh Day Adventist ministry, his daughter and grandchildren, his belief that he was factually innocent.

The third time the extraction team came to take Mr. Workman to Deathwatch was, according to Mr. Workman, round 11:00 a.m. on a Tuesday, within a few months of his previous exposure . . . The five guys, dressed in all black, made him, again, " . . . anxiety ridden."

Mr. Workman remembered those few administrative persons responsible for carrying out the execution procedures that were also willing to talk to him, including the Warden, saying the same thing, "Workman, it's that time again."

He received the denial of clemency. The night before he was facing execution, for the third time, his attorneys came to visit him (and) he could tell by their faces that the news was not good for him.

Mr. Workman called his daughter. She had not been able to bring herself to come to the third Deathwatch. The time was about 12 o'clock. Mr. Workman remembers specifically not asking the Lord if this was his final one.

He described himself as, " . . . not really there."

With 40 minutes remaining before being executed, Mr. Workman received a stay.

RELEVANT FAMILY HISTORY

Philip Workman was born into a family of abuse and neglect. Mr. Workman was running away from home early in life, attempting to escape physical beatings. The trauma derived coping skills continued throughout his adolescent years.

He was abandoned by his mother at an early age, and subjected to an alcoholic, abusive father. After 22 years on Death Row, he understands the impact of his nuclear family on his own emotional growth, and has done well for 22 years, until now.

MENTAL STATUS EXAMINATION

. . . His mood was anxious, and he started tearing, then crying immediately. Mr. Workman said, "This is going to be very hard for me . . . it's one of those things you don't want to show."

He denied perceptual disorders, hallucinations, delusions, etc. He was certainly oriented to person, place, time, and circumstances. He acknowledged nightmares during the periods he has been on Deathwatch, and in the interims between . . . Thought processes were ruminative. This ruminative thought process was impairing his concentration, in his estimation.

Mr. Workman found himself hyper-vigilant, even taking into consideration the proscribed circumstances he found himself. He had found his responses increasingly impaired from his first execution procedure to this, his fourth.

Thought contents were mildly paranoid, anxiety-ridden. He denies suicidal ideation.

DIAGNOSES
Axis 1: Post Traumatic Stress Disorder, acute

ANALYSIS
Mr. Workman fits the criteria outlined in the Diagnostic and Statistical Manual-IVTR for Post Traumatic Stress Disorder. . . . There is no question that Mr. Workman has experienced repeated stressors that would quality for Criteria A.

Mr. Workman dreamed—and says he continues to dream—distressing nightmares of the execution procedure he has described in detail. Intrusive thoughts, particularly of the multiple strip searches, are discussed by Mr. Workman. Starting this interview was difficult for him, and he specifically noted that discussing these previous exposures would be difficult for him. He began to cry. These Symptoms meet Criterion C.

Mr. Workman describes an inability to organize himself, giving his things away later and later, closer to the time he would possibly go to Deathwatch; an increasing difficulty unpacking his possessions each time he came back from Deathwatch. He believes this impairment in organization is secondary to problems with concentration, not memory. "I can't get this stuff out of my mind." Mr. Workman feels there has been an escalating degree of anxiety related to each Deathwatch, with its attendant execution procedures.

The rituals that have worked for Mr. Workman for the 22 years he has been on Death Row have started to deteriorate, not in the face of his execution, but, he believes, due to the repeated, acute, exposures to dying. He describes a decrease of activity, which he attributes to his paralyzing anxiety and concomitant hyper-arousal, an oxymoron if there ever was one. The first and second time Mr. Workman was escorted from Deathwatch to Death Row, he told the members of the Extraction Team that he hoped he didn't have to see them again. He didn't say anything to them on the third Deathwatch. . . .

Although problems sleeping may have occurred prior to Mr. Workman's first exposure to the execution procedures, these problems were certainly magnified during his multiple exposures to the execution procedures.

Mr. Workman experiences significant problems with his concentration, due primarily to his ruminative thoughts. Repeated exposures to highly regimented execution procedures have heightened his vigilance. A constant expectation rooted in reality, but augmented by repetition of such a costly, definitive protocol.

Mr. Workman has been under Deathwatch three times in a 12-month period. He was symptomatic, with distressing dreams, ruminative thinking, hyper-vigilance, intrusive thoughts, and impaired concentration; since his first exposure to the execution procedures. The course of his symptoms, therefore, meets Criterion E. . . .

The repeated exposures of Mr. Workman to the execution procedures are consistent with Complex Post Traumatic Stress Disorder, which occurs more commonly with repeated exposure to stressors. The stressor of sure death is the ultimate stressor, and there have been medical protocols developed to ensure interrater reliability when evaluating multiple exposures to execution. The Physicians for Human Rights, in collaboration with the United Nations, have developed both medical and psychological protocols that may be relevant.

At the time I saw Mr. Workman, he was less than ten days from being placed on Deathwatch a fourth time. There is no reason to assume that a fourth trip to Deathwatch would not, to a reasonable degree of medical certainty, retrigger the symptoms of Mr. Workman's post-traumatic disorder.

Thank you for allowing me to examine Mr. Workman.

George Woods, MD

* * *

In Distrust of Merits
The world's an orphan's home. Shall
We ever have peace without sorrow?
Without pleas of the dying for
Help that won't come? O
Quiet form upon the dust, I cannot
Look and yet I must. If these great patient
Dyings—all these agonies
And wonderings and bloodshed—
Can teach us how to live, these
Dyings were not wasted.
— Marianne Moore[2]

2 Marianne Moore, "In Distrust of Merits," in *Nevertheless* (New York: Macmillan, 1944), 843-845.

Marianne Moore's poem characterized my feelings as time wound down in the summer of 2003. In my work against the death penalty through the South since 1975, I had seen too many "dyings." And I cannot imagine "peace without sorrow." "All these agonies and wonderings and bloodshed" from Texas to Florida, Georgia to Virginia, Alabama and Mississippi, North and South Carolina, Louisiana and now Tennessee. Sweet Jesus. What a slaughter I have witnessed. Perhaps Marianne Moore is correct that this experience "Can teach us how to live" and if so, "these Dyings were not wasted." That was yet to be determined.

In my work against the death penalty through the South since 1975, I had seen too many "dyings." And I cannot imagine "peace without sorrow."

Of course, the work had taken its emotional toll. John Laurence, who wrote *The Cat from Hué: A Vietnam War Story*, was a journalist in the field and in Hué for the Tet Offensive by the North Vietnamese and the Viet Cong in 1968. His description of entering into a battle zone rang true: "My physical perceptions were ultra alert. Colors were brighter, sounds sharper, my reflexes quicker. Everything appeared with precise clarity. And yet the speeding, fast-moving fight unfolded in slow motion, like a macabre ballet . . . the sight and sounds . . . [were] holding me in the grip of overwhelming powerlessness, a feeling of being on the border of madness myself, not knowing nor being able to change or caring what might happen next."[3]

3 John Laurence, *The Cat from Hué: A Vietnam War Story* (New York: PublicAffairs, 2002), 15.

You Can't Make This Stuff Up

Laurence's description of his feeling was on the mark for my own work under death warrants. Of course, I wasn't being shot at, but I was, as my therapist put it, "dying little deaths" when my friends were killed. The hyper-vigilant status, everything totally concentrated and focused, the "overwhelming powerlessness, a feeling of being on the border of madness myself, not knowing nor being able to change or caring what might happen next" could have been a description of me. I could not flee or fight, so I was frozen. Just trying to function and survive while being pressured in an emotional vise, with the state cranking it shut.

* * *

As Chris Minton discovered, his client's story was consistent and true. The version the police, prosecutors, and medical examiner told was an inconsistent, misstated, one-dimensional attack to kill Philip Workman.

On the other hand, Philip continually expressed regret for "having created the scene" that resulted in Lieutenant Oliver's death. As he always put it, "I'm not innocent enough." He was an adult with a fully developed moral consciousness who accepted responsibility and felt sorrow for his deeds.

In reality, though, Philip could never be innocent enough for the Memphis and state authorities. They had foreclosed that possibility when they decided to frame him in 1982. Since that point, they had not moved an inch. Despite all the evidence brought forth that Philip Workman did not shoot Ronald Oliver, there was a single view of Philip by the power structure: robber, drug addict, shot a policeman, would do it again, not really a human being, so let's erase him from the face of the earth. From the articles in the *Commercial Appeal* to clemency hearings and judges' decisions, Philip was not viewed as a human being but a cop killer. The response was to advocate this position rather than admit a mistake had been made: that one policeman accidentally killed another policeman, and everyone was sorry for such a terrible mistake.

It was Philip Workman who was the adult who developed moral character. The opposition were like children who could not get their way. They whined, pouted, and tried over and over to do the wrong thing. They would not acknowledge culpability in their behavior. It was all about power and authority that had nothing to do with truth or fairness. Unfortunately, there was no adult to discipline them and assist them in their moral growth, so they remained stuck in their relentless, shallow, cold-blooded, killing attitude toward Philip.

In this morality play, I am too generous referring to the Memphis cabal as *children*. They, the supposed good guys, did the killing, covered it up, invented fairy tale explanations for their behavior, and were hell-bent on killing a guy who had not killed anyone. Even the case law, *Severs v. Tennessee*, on consideration of the facts, would not allow Philip to be tried for murder. But who was concerned with the actual law? Certainly not the upholders of it.

All of this while Philip took responsibility for "creating the scene." He felt sorrow for Lieutenant Oliver's killing and publicly acknowledged it in the trial and two clemency hearings. The guy on death row did not actually kill anyone and felt bad for the officer who died. The ones who did the killing covered it up, took no responsibility for it, and pinned it on someone they deemed worthless. It was too much to bear.

Yes, in the summer of 2003 I knew that as Philip awaited his fourth deathwatch, the people who sought his death were determined to finish the job. Although the entire tapestry woven at trial was unspooled by Philip's lawyers on appeal, Memphis authorities were unyielding in protecting one another. They needed Philip Workman to die in order to maintain their charade of denial.

Joe Cocker sang, "I'm not feeling too good myself." That rang

414

true with me as the summer of 2003 inevitably moved toward the September 24 execution date. The tightness in my chest grew but I had no heart problems. Rather, it was the prospect of Philip going back to deathwatch a fourth time and my accompanying him that generated the increasing discomfort. Good God, how would we survive this ordeal?

I had nightmares. On August 13 at 2:15 a.m., I awoke in a cold sweat. In my dream I was in the death house with Philip awaiting his execution. I was outside his cell as we waited for the death squad to come and take him to the killing chamber. But in the dream, nobody came, and the time for the execution passed. There had been no word from the courts or the governor. The deathwatch guard did not know what was going on either. I decided to find someone with information. I was full of anxiety.

I awoke with pressure building in my chest. The house was still. My heart was racing. After glancing at the clock, I arose from the bed and went to the study. I wrote the nightmare down. After writing all I could recall, I turned out the light and sat in the darkness. The dread of going back to deathwatch with Philip coursed through me. I prayed for God to deliver Philip from this ordeal. Then I sat quietly in the dark. There would be no more sleep for me.

I crawled back into bed at 5:30 a.m. to be near Becca. She put her arms around me. I told her I had a bad dream about Philip, and she pulled me to her. I rested my head on her chest, listening to her heartbeat. There was strength in that beating heart. As I lay quietly and listened to her heart, I thought how blessed I was to have this woman as my wife. Through her ovarian cancer, my multiple sclerosis, all the state killings I had endured, the vicissitudes of daily life, Becca had been there with me. Her beating heart seemed to tell me everything would be all right. Somehow, some way, it would be all right.

My weekly visits with Philip continued. We discussed the case, his family, passages in the Bible, and what was going on with my family. We closed with a prayer, which Philip concluded by praying for me: "Place a hedge of protection around my brother and his family."

On September 4 I received a postal notice of an attempt to deliver a certified letter. Becca wondered what it could be. Looking at the date and calculating we were three weeks from Philip's execution, I knew what the notice meant. It was the official invitation from the warden and the state of Tennessee, sent by certified letter, informing me I was authorized to witness Philip's execution as his spiritual adviser. I told Becca I would pick it up at the post office the next day.

Judge Bernice Donald, a federal district judge in Memphis, scheduled a hearing on Philip's case for September 15. She would consider whether or not to grant a stay of execution. There would be no discussion of the merits of the case. Given the lateness in the scheduling of the hearing, it could once again mean a battle in the Sixth Circuit Court of Appeals with a decision rendered while Philip was on deathwatch for the fourth time.

The night of September 10 Philip called me at home. His voice was somber. He told me he was packing his possessions and preparing to wash down his cell for its next occupant. The process of dividing his property and preparing to leave his "house" was a sad one.

In a telephone conversation I had with Philip's brother, Terry Workman, we discussed the cruelty of the death warrant process. Terry aptly described its impact: "It's like forcing Philip to play Russian roulette. We can't appreciate or understand what that does to his mind. This is the fourth time." I agreed and told Terry that was why Dr. George Woods had diagnosed him with acute PTSD.

My next visit with Philip began with a hug. I was exhausted, working long days and devoting time to raise money for his defense, clemency team meetings, public speaking, utilizing all the energy

I had to fight an execution. I was totally drained of strength. He looked at me and asked, "Will you bury me?" For a man expecting to move to deathwatch in a mere nine days, it was a natural question. But it caught me by surprise. All of my actions had been devoted to keeping Philip alive. I had neglected the obvious: the state of Tennessee planned to kill him in twelve days.

> *"Will you bury me?" For a man expecting to move to deathwatch in a mere nine days, it was a natural question. But it caught me by surprise.*

"Yes, Philip," I said. "I will bury you."

We moved into a painful discussion of what it was like for him to experience his fourth death warrant. As the visit progressed, I realized Philip was attenuated emotionally. He was in a place very similar to his last hours on deathwatch in 2001. His somber, painful tone reflected the cruelty of the last three deathwatches and the toll exacted upon him yet again. *My God*, I thought, *this whole process is obscene!* Even if they failed to kill him, the torture inflicted upon him in carrying out this premeditated, cold-blooded murder is cruel and unusual punishment.

After the visit, Psalm 116 welled within me. It was God "who rescues from death, my eyes from tears, and my feet from stumbling." Both Philip and I were swirling in the powerful tide of death that sucked us into the vortex of state killing. "The cords of death entangled me; the grip of the grave took hold of me; I came to grief and sorrow." The challenge was to maintain our faith and sanity, as the psalter put it, "Then I called upon the Name of the Lord: 'O Lord, I pray you, save my life.'"

Tennessee had elected a new governor, Phil Bredesen, a Democrat. It was hard to know what this would mean for the death penalty and for Philip Workman. My experience with John Spenkelink in 1979 on through the events surrounding Philip Workman revealed that political party, Democrat or Republican, did not always matter regarding the death penalty. They were all equal-opportunity killers.

The weekend prior to September 15, 2003, I invited Terry Workman and Michelle, Philip's daughter, to come to Nashville for media interviews. They did an excellent job as we sought to keep the case in the spotlight.

I was in my office on September 15, nine days before Philip's execution. I had my invitation to the state killing and it appeared the state was good to go. It was a somber time.

At 10:15 a.m., I received a telephone call. The voice on the phone was instantly recognizable: "Joe, this is Dave Cooley." Dave was the deputy governor. I knew Dave prior to his joining the new administration. He was dedicated to Governor Bredesen. On election day he stood on Broadway at the intersection of the interstates with a sign urging folks to vote for Phil Bredesen for governor.

"Hello, Dave, how are you?" I said.

"The governor wanted me to let you know that at 10:30 he is holding a press conference to announce a 120-day reprieve for Philip Workman pending the outcome of a federal criminal investigation." He urged me to tell no one and watch the press conference.

I immediately called Terry in Kentucky and Michelle, who was still in town. We were all shocked by the news. I told them all I knew. I then called the lawyers.

The press conference was televised live. Governor Phil Bredesen and Attorney General Paul Summers spoke. Summers, who had done all in his power to have Philip executed under the prior administration, read a statement:

"Based upon information that I recently received regarding the pendency of an investigation that indirectly relates to the Philip Workman case, I recommended to the governor that he issue a temporary reprieve of the execution of Mr. Workman's death sentence. At the risk of compromising the investigation, I cannot at this time be specific with regard to the nature and subject of it. In the interest of fairness and justice, the execution of Mr. Workman's death sentence did not need to proceed as scheduled."

Attorney General Summers had been deeply involved in the two clemency hearings that had tried to kill Philip. In the spring of 2001, he had vetted himself to news media as a possible prime candidate for governor largely on the basis of getting Philip Workman executed. Now he was announcing a reprieve. I knew that Summers must be choking on every word of his statement, and the expression on his face revealed taking this action was the last thing in the world he wished to be doing.

Governor Phil Bredesen then spoke:

"The attorney general recently informed me of a federal criminal investigation under way that may be related to this case. As a result, today I am issuing a postponement of Philip Workman's execution until this investigation is completed and we can assess its relevance to the case.

"So long as there are outstanding issues that may be related to this case, the only proper thing to do is wait until those questions have been answered. I am a supporter of the death penalty, but committed that it be carried out in a judicious manner."

Philip's clemency team met that Tuesday night. It was a relaxed group with lemonade and champagne in full supply. We discussed what the events may mean and toasted Philip, the lawyers, the governor, and one another. Although we could only speculate, the key piece of the puzzle seemed to be the attorney general's reference to an ongoing "criminal investigation." The only federal criminal investigation we knew of that had been ongoing in conjunction with the *Workman* case was that of O. C. Smith, the Shelby County medical examiner.

This investigation began because of O. C. Smith's attack on June 1, 2002 (Philip's birthday), when he was wrapped in barbed wire in a semi-cruciform position with a crude bomb strapped to his chest. The bomb endangered the first responders who rescued him. This placed it under federal authority of the Patriot Act and resulted in the ATF agents investigating. This meant the *Workman* case, for the first time, would have an investigation with an agency outside of Memphis and with no agenda, unlike the Memphis cabal who were hell-bent to frame and kill Philip.

It appeared that O. C. Smith, feeling discredited after his two clemency performances and receiving public criticism (such as Robert Hutton calling him "a liar" on the Memphis radio), had created a scenario to elicit sympathy. As Philip Workman told me, Smith had wrapped himself in barbed wire and planted a bomb on his own chest. After countless interviews, the ATF realized that Smith had done this to himself.

It was tempting to believe that the house of cards the Memphis authorities had constructed for the *Workman* case was about to fall. But we'd had that feeling previously. Chris Minton stated, "When Harold Davis recanted, I thought it was the end of the death penalty case. The only eyewitness changes his testimony, so that should be it." Of course, that wasn't it, nor the X-ray, perjured testimony, Fackler's study, contradictory ballistics, and on and on. The ATF appearance had created a logjam in the proceedings, but it was a long way from deliverance.

When I went out to Riverbend to see Philip the evening of the governor's morning press conference, I was profoundly relieved. I was cautious and just wanted to see Philip to talk with him and get his take on things.

Philip was strung out. Not on drugs but from the tension of anticipating a fourth deathwatch and its sudden dissolution. He was decompressing from the sword no longer hanging over his head. The countdown to execution had led him to pack all of his things in boxes and wash down his cell again. As I observed him, it was not so much relief but a feeling of being stunned that he expressed. He was frayed, his nerves attenuated, the ordeal of it all had taken its toll. Four death warrants in three years was nothing less than torture.

Philip opened his big, leather-bound Bible. It looked like he or another prisoner had designed the cover. It was a red-letter Bible, with the words of Jesus written in red. We had a lively discussion about the emperor Constantine and his impact on the Christian church. Neither of us had a high opinion of Constantine. He had called together the Council of Nicaea and made it clear the bishops would not leave without a means of maintaining order in the church. The emperor did not care for the disputes and disagreements among the bishops as to who Jesus was. He wanted to enforce law and order in his empire. He was rewarded with the Nicene Creed.

I shared with Philip the narrative of *Constantine's Sword* by James Carroll. It documents the anti-Semitism in Christianity through the history of the church. The former priest delivered a compelling and horrible read.

After a two-hour visit, we held hands and closed with a prayer. I prayed for a "hedge of protection around my brother and his family." Then I left the prison and went into the darkening autumn evening.

On September 24, the day Philip was scheduled for execution, I returned to the prison to visit him. We greeted each other with a hug, and I exclaimed, "Happy September twenty-fourth!" He chuckled and responded: "Yeah, let's see. They would have me dead by now and about to be buried." We smiled at each other. There was

421

much to talk about, but we were both exhausted and drained from the events leading to this day. Philip began relaying the emotional toll this fourth warrant had extracted from him. He detailed the scrubbing of his cell, the packing of his personal possessions in boxes, giving items away to his fellow prisoners, the feeling of heartbreak and lassitude.

Then we transitioned from the experience of trauma to the realm of the absurd. O. C. Smith had appeared before a grand jury in Memphis. A special prosecutor from Arkansas was appointed to the case. Smith had been trained, while in the military, in the manufacture of explosive devices. When the ATF raided his farm, they found barbed wire and the material necessary to make an explosive device like the one attached to his chest. Given the questions about his behavior regarding the *Workman* case, the mayor asked him to take a leave of absence from his job as medical examiner. Smith refused to do so and the district attorney vouched for him. This was expected since they had collaborated in the two clemency schemes. The mayor held firm.

Philip and I shared a sermon I had preached and read Psalm 116. We discussed the biblical stories of God championing the poor, the widow, the orphan, and the prisoner. He returned to the pain he had experienced, the trauma of the last death warrant and the previous deathwatches. Clearly, there was a cumulative effect of this torturous process. Philip was a deeply wounded man. We closed with a prayer.

The latest act in the theater of the absurd of the *Workman* case, O. C. Smith wrapping himself in barbed wire and rigging an explosive device to his chest, brought a fantastic dimension to the case. A frame-up for a murder he did not commit, transformed into an exercise in judicial folly, had now morphed into the bizarre. However, for the Memphis criminal legal system, it probably seemed logical to solicit sympathy for their star clemency diva by portraying him as a victim. It was extreme but normal for them to think that Smith wrapping himself in barbed wire and attaching a bomb to his chest was the next step in the process. It never crossed anyone's mind that the world beyond Memphis might raise questions about this behavior. Or that this action would move the case beyond their clutches to the federal level with the ATF. In *Alice and Wonderland*, it was the Red Queen who declared, "Sentence first. Verdict afterward." The Red Queen was the embodiment of the Memphis way.

As autumn became vibrant with the coloring of the leaves in October of 2003, Philip called me at home one night. "I'm just waiting for the who, what, when, where, and if, to come out of Memphis," he said. It was a succinct description of the feelings of all involved with his case. We were awaiting the conclusion of the investigation of O. C. Smith. Grand juries moved deliberately in determining when to issue an indictment, but surely after a fifteen-month investigation, a decision would come soon.

On Thursday, November 6, I went out to the prison to see Philip. We had a good visit. He caught up on my daughter's soccer team going to the state tournament in Chattanooga, and we discussed his case. There was a worship service next door, and they were singing "Were You There When They Crucified My Lord." Philip read Hebrews 11:6 and Isaiah 43:11 and verse 25. I opened my Bible to Isaiah 61 and shared it. I then read Jesus reading from that scripture in his inaugural "sermon" in his hometown of Nazareth (Luke 4:18). Philip revisited the deathwatch psalms, 27 and 31:1–4. These were songs of succor provided to those under attack. I shared Psalm 146:4–9, a song proclaiming God as one "who executes justice for the oppressed, who gives food to the hungry. The Lord sets the prisoners free; the Lord opens the eyes of the blind. The Lord lifts up those who are bowed down; the Lord loves the righteous. The Lord watches over the sojourners, he upholds the widow and the fatherless; but the way of the wicked he brings to ruin."[4]

I found it very helpful to discuss the scriptures with Philip. I didn't consider it unusual at all that the most moving Bible study I experienced was on death row. It seemed appropriate for someone on the path of discipleship whose savior suffered execution to share the Bible with the condemned.

When we concluded the visit, I prayed. We held hands and bowed our heads, and I reminded God that Isaiah and Jesus had proclaimed "release to the captives." I prayed for Philip's freedom from this insanity.

Visiting Philip in the winter meant arriving and departing in the darkness. A killdeer often accompanied me as I made my way through the sliding gates and down the sidewalk to Unit 2, death row. The bird's keening cry in the night seemed to make her my companion. Sometimes I glimpsed her as she flitted over the razor wire that sparkled from the glare of the prison security lights.

My next visit with Philip found him in a buoyant mood. He asked that I read the legal brief his lawyers had filed before Judge Donald in Memphis. He thought the brief presented the best recounting of the contradictions in the state's position of what had happened at the crime scene. As we talked, the hymn singing by the worship group next door seeped through the wall. Once again it was "Were You There When They Crucified My Lord." When the hymn concluded, the preacher took off with his sermon. Philip smiled and said, "Preach it, brother."

In all our visits outside deathwatch (no caps were allowed on deathwatch) Philip wore his black baseball cap. The cap was emblazoned in white letters with Job 13:15: "Though you slay me, yet will I trust in you." The purple band underneath the white cross said What Would Jesus Do? The cap summed up Philip's theological perspective.

4 NRSV.

On December 4, I arrived at Riverbend again to visit Philip. The windy, rainy evening was accompanied by temperatures in the forties and dropping. The killdeer again cried in the night as I walked from checkpoint to Unit 2; I saw her winging beneath the arc lights that kept the compound lit. When I arrived outside Unit 2, all the canna lilies and impatiens next to the entrance were gone. The bare, cold earth was all that remained from their presence last week. Winter had come to Middle Tennessee.

During our visit the strains of "O Come All Ye Faithful" and "Silent Night" penetrated the wall to the larger visiting room. The heartfelt Christmas singing underscored the power of God to move people, even in the heart of the killing machinery.

I shared with Philip that I recently viewed Dixie Gamble's movie about Robert Glen Coe: *Beyond Right and Wrong*. It was the story of Robert growing up in utter poverty in West Tennessee. Dixie could relate to Robert because her own son was mentally ill. She knew that if he had his medications removed, as was true with Robert, he too could confess to a crime that he did not commit. There was serious doubt about Robert's guilt of the rape and murder of the young girl. There was no doubt about the rural community's fear and dislike of Robert Glen Coe.

Philip knew Robert. They had been taken to deathwatch together at 4:00 a.m. on April 3, 2000. The death squad "looked like linemen on a professional football team." On the way over to Building 8, Philip and Robert did not talk. Robert was placed in deathwatch cell one, with his possessions in cell two. Philip was put in cell four with his stuff in cell three. They obtained stays of execution and were moved back to Unit 2 at 11:00 a.m. that Tuesday. For Philip, there was no doubt that Robert was profoundly mentally ill.

Robert's stay was dissolved, and he was to be moved back to deathwatch for a final time. He came by Philip's cell with the guard escorts. Robert clasped his hands in a gesture of prayer toward

425

Philip and nodded as he passed by the cell. Robert Glen Coe, on the verge of his own extermination, indicated he was praying for Philip Workman.

As Philip described the story of his interaction with Robert around deathwatch, I could only focus on how cruel this process was for Philip. Four serious execution dates had been set for him. They had taken him to deathwatch three times—coming within forty-five minutes of execution on his third trip—and he prepared to take a fourth trip to Building 8. His neighbor on deathwatch had been exterminated by the state of Tennessee. The two clemencies were from cloud cuckoo land. Sweet Jesus, how much can one man take? Dr. George Woods diagnosed him with "acute PTSD" and that was prior to the resolution of the fourth death warrant. My silent and urgent prayer as I sat listening to Philip was simple: "Lord, keep him from returning to deathwatch." I did not know if it was mentally possible to survive a fifth deathwatch, even if he was physically saved.

My silent and urgent prayer as I sat listening to Philip was simple: "Lord, keep him from returning to deathwatch." I did not know if it was mentally possible to survive a fifth deathwatch, even if he was physically saved.

* * *

On January 9, 2004, Governor Phil Bredesen issued the following statement:

"After conferring with the attorney general, I have decided to extend Mr. Workman's reprieve until the federal investigation is completed and its relevance to the case is determined. As a result, I am extending the temporary reprieve until April 15.

"I believe the death penalty should be carried out judiciously. As long as there continue to be outstanding questions related to this case, the proper thing to do is wait until those questions have been answered."

As Philip and I visited on a bitterly cold night in mid-January of 2004, he talked about his feeling of being on a ledge.

"Since my first deathwatch in 2000, I feel like I'm just hanging on a ledge. We keep finding more facts, but I'm still here. To sit here and know they're doing all in their power to cover up for O. C. Smith . . . I mean, think about it. Sergeant Parker, who shot my butt full of shotgun pellets and then denied it, is now in the US attorney's office in Memphis. And that other Memphis guy, Kitchens, he is in the US attorney's office too. I'd sure like to know what is going on with that grand jury."

When I arrived at the prison on February 3 to see Philip, the checkpoint officer called back to Unit 2 to inform them I was coming. Sergeant Rushton, whom I have known since the Walls, broadcast back on the radio, "Send him on down, because we are getting a cell ready for Ingle, too."

O. C. Smith was indicted by the grand jury on February 10, 2004. There were two counts in the indictment: (1) illegal possession of a destructive device and (2) lying to federal investigators. In response, Smith submitted a resignation letter of sorts. The Shelby County district attorney, Bill Gibbons, who had earlier written Governor Bredesen urging him not to extend Philip's reprieve, issued a statement indicating they would continue to use Smith in their cases.

Too Close to the Flame

The district attorney and his Memphis cohorts in the criminal legal system had had things their way for so long in the *Workman* case that their arrogance enabled them to continue in a manner inimical to their self-interest. The Shelby County authorities had pushed for Philip's killing since 1981 and subsequently worked with the attorney general of Tennessee, the governor's office, and the clemency board to ensure his extinction. The fact that O. C. Smith could perjure himself under oath in two clemency hearings, wrap himself in barbed wire with a "destructive device" on his chest, lie to federal investigators, and be indicted on two counts did not stop the Memphis criminal legal system using him as medical examiner in other cases.

In response to O. C. Smith's indictment, Governor Bredesen appointed Dr. Bruce Levy to investigate Smith's clemency testimony. Levy, the state medical examiner hired by Bredesen, came from New York City. Since he owed his job to Bredesen, we expected he would do what the governor indicated he wished to be done. He was to report back by April 24, 2004.[5]

Dr. Cyril Wecht was informed of the developments in the *Smith* case. He succinctly appraised the situation for the *New York Times*: "If he could fabricate a story like this that a Hollywood screenwriter on LSD would have difficulty coming up with, who could believe him in a courtroom?" However, the Memphis DA was unconcerned. The day after the indictment was issued, he had O. C. Smith testifying in a case.

When I visited Philip in mid-February, I was concerned with his demeanor and tone of conversation. He was saying that no matter the justice or truth of the situation, he was going to be killed. This was different than his usual attitude, and it really

5 I had seen Levy provide inaccurate testimony in a lethal injection hearing. It was only years later that I realized the true mendacity of the man. He was forced to resign as medical examiner because he stole marijuana out of the evidence room and was indicted for it. This guy fit right in with the Memphis crew.

428

concerned me. An almost fatalistic feeling came through in the weariness of his soul.

As the visit progressed, I realized I just needed to be there for him. It was not a rational discussion; he was emotionally strung out and in physical discomfort (pain in his chest). I reflected on the four death warrants, three deathwatches, and twenty-three years in prison for a murder he did not commit. No wonder he was weary and despairing.

We closed with a prayer, and I asked for guidance for all of us—lawyers, family, friends, and Philip—to lead us on a path of justice and righteousness. Finally, I prayed for a day when Philip would experience freedom as an exonerated man.

The next visit with Philip brought a different conversation. He was deeply concerned his lawyers would accept any clemency offer the governor might provide. He felt strongly he should not do time for killing Lieutenant Oliver since he did not shoot him. He looked directly at me: "The lawyers don't understand. They don't know what it's like in here. They think life without parole is a victory. I'd rather die than do that. I've done twenty-three years. I'm tired. I can't go on like this indefinitely. My body is letting me know it's breaking down. I can feel some things aren't right. I did some dumb things to myself when I was young that are costing me. I won't take a life sentence. I have to see some light. They've had me on a ledge for too long. I have to see some light."

After listening for quite a while, I said, "You are in a totally different frame of mind than last week. When we last talked, you were worried about being killed. Now you're talking about clemency. What accounts for the change?"

Philip said his lawyers had visited him and they were hopeful about clemency. They seemed to have some inside information. I was relieved to hear the change in his tone and hope in his voice. But frankly, I would believe clemency when it was actually given. I have been down this road too many times to think otherwise.

When Governor Bredesen assigned Dr. Bruce Levy to evaluate O. C. Smith's clemency testimony, I felt conflicted. I hoped for the best, but I feared the worst. My fear was rooted in political reality, which always seemed to triumph over justice in Philip's case. In this instance, Mayor (of Nashville) Phil Bredesen had appointed Bruce Levy the medical examiner for the city. Then upon becoming governor, Bredesen appointed Levy the state medical examiner. If the governor wished the report on Smith to angle in a certain direction, I felt Levy would accommodate him. The report would reveal as much about Governor Bredesen as it did about Dr. Levy.

Levy's report was released in April, once again affirming the truth of T. S. Eliot's line: "April is the cruelest month." The conclusion was that it was Philip Workman's bullet that struck and killed Lieutenant Oliver.

Philip and I reviewed the report during our next visit. It relied totally on the prosecution's record at trial. It stated that the prosecution's theory was true: only two shooters, Workman and Oliver. In a television interview, he debunked all the post-trial evidence as the "grassy knoll theory" of the crime. This sounded more like a prosecutor than an objective scientist. And the prosecution's two-shooter theory, endorsed by Levy, had at least the following problems:

1. The treating physician's report at the hospital documented Philip's injuries from the Wendy's escape. They included dog bites and shotgun pellets in the buttocks.

2. The police records indicated that police weapons at the crime scene were not properly checked for firing, despite sworn testimony to the contrary.

3. The FBI testimony at trial that the infamous "magic bullet," Q1—the bullet O. C. Smith swore with 100 percent of his "military mind" was the fatal bullet—could not have

been the mortal bullet. There was no trace of blood, bone, tissue, or fabric on it.

Dr. Levy had the gall to write the following about O. C. Smith: "I believe the high regard and respect that he has for Dr. Bell [Smith's predecessor] motivated him the breath [*sic*] and depth of his investigation."

Really? Dr. Bell said at trial that Q1 was not the bullet that killed Officer Oliver. I think a better of explanation of the "breadth and depth" of Smith's testimony was that he was in cahoots with Memphis prosecutors and state actors framing Philip Workman. There was no scientific proof in the report; it was all speculation and belief. It was a rehash of the prosecution's trial efforts.

I was chilled to the bone reading this report. I knew it indicated what Governor Bredesen was going to do on clemency. The spring was lovely, but this document was another nail in Philip Workman's coffin.

May of 2004 found Philip and I continuing our Thursday evening routine. We read some psalms and focused on 146, "put not your trust in princes." He reminded me of how much that psalm meant to him on deathwatch. We also examined the First Letter of John. It was one of my favorite epistles, and we discussed the meaning of love the writer shared.

The Tennessee Supreme Court set an execution date for Philip Workman of September 22, 2004. It was his fifth execution date and likely meant another trip to deathwatch.

When I visited Philip after the setting of the date, he was fired up. He was incensed about the treatment of Iraqi prisoners by American military personnel in Abu Ghraib prison. "When they put a bag over your head, they don't have to look at you. It makes it easier for them to do whatever they want. That picture of the woman soldier dragging that Iraqi like a dog on a chain just makes me sick."

After a thorough discussion of the Iraq situation, Philip looked and me and said, "I called it." Indeed, he had predicted the month the Tennessee Supreme Court would set his fifth execution date.

Philip was frustrated. And I felt I had fallen down the rabbit hole in *Alice in Wonderland*. Everything was upside down. The officials whose duty was to obtain justice—police, prosecutors, attorney generals, judges, governors—had subverted justice for twenty-three years in this case. Instead of justice, there were lies, deceit, perjury, falsified reports, evidence withheld, and a manufactured witness. The attitude was, "We're the good guys and you must believe what we say." In this case, the police and the thin blue line must be supported at all costs. Facts are inconvenient and we will proceed on our murderous way.

In one of our summer visits, Philip brought up the difficulty he was experiencing in trying to cope with the latest execution date. Although he had anticipated it, he described his feelings as "being in a storm. The sea is overwhelming you. You are sinking and there is nothing you can do." As he talked, I recalled Dr. George Woods's diagnosing him with acute PTSD before his fourth execution date. Philip felt Dr. Woods misestimated when difficulties begin emotionally. "It's not when you get to deathwatch. It starts right after you get the execution date. The guys don't know how to relate to you. You don't want to be glum, you want to carry on and try to be normal, but the emotions are stirred inside you. You try to maintain a normal way of doing things, but it's hard. Of course, it's worse with each execution date you get."

I asked, "How do you deal with it?"

"Prayer. Yeah, prayer and watching too much television. Working out, trying to keep my mind blank about it."

"Does it affect your dreams?"

"No, not yet. I just don't sleep much. The most I can get is six hours. My mind is always racing."

We continued to converse about the mental anguish the killing machinery exerted on those trapped in its maw. I sat and listened to a man who was trying to maintain his sanity in the midst of his fifth death warrant.

"It's hard for my visitors. Sometimes they don't know what to say. The execution date just brings pressure into everything. I can't write letters . . . It's just too much.

"Clemency. I don't think I can go through that again with the parole board. Then I think maybe I just need to represent myself before them. I know the case better than anyone. Of course, they say it is a fool of a lawyer that represents himself. But I could lay it all out to them. I don't know what to do."

Philip looked at me and asked, "What do you think is going to happen?"

"I don't know, Philip. But I think there is a good chance the US Supreme Court will take the 60(b) issue, which is also in Abu-Ali's case. So, everything should halt if the Supremes decide to review it. The Eleventh Circuit Court of Appeals ruled one way, and the Second Circuit went the other way. Whatever the Sixth Circuit does will be a closely divided decision. When there is a split in the circuit courts of appeal, it can lead to the Supremes taking the case. And there is the fact that they took it once before, so there are members of the court interested in the issue."

We hugged goodbye after our prayer. I forgot to pray for a hedge of protection around my brother. He certainly needed it.

The hottest part of the summer hit us and my multiple sclerosis flared up and I took to bed. Philip called me Sunday afternoon after hearing about the flare-up. He brought me up to date on his visitors, wished me well, and told me to take care of myself. He sounded good.

I made it out to the prison in late July. Philip was frustrated with his lawyers; he wanted to present issues that were procedurally barred, but he was quite determined to file a petition about the political dynamics of his case. He had his fighting spirit back.

My next weekly visit, which was in August, was shocking; it was the polar opposite of our previous encounter. The weariness in Philip's voice, the lines around his eyes, his fatigue with the fight— it was clear that the fifth death warrant was exacting an enormous emotional toll. I was filled with deep sadness. We talked for about an hour and a half. He was in despair. Basically, Philip wished to be alone. He just wanted to lie in his bunk to pray and think. He would call me over the weekend if he wanted me to come back. He didn't want me to tell his lawyer. He would talk with him personally. We closed with prayer, hugged, and I walked out of the unit into the summer twilight.

Our next visit was in mid-August and Philip's good spirits had returned. Perhaps it was the interview he did with the *48 Hours* news program that was fascinated with the behavior of O. C. Smith. Philip downplayed the interview. He had done so many, this was just another one.

Philip laughed as he discussed what he would do once he obtained a trial before his peers. "Here I am about a month from being executed and I'm worried about a new trial." I think he had become hopeful about the 60(b) issue in the federal courts. We closed with a prayer, each of us asking for a "hedge of protection" around the other.

Chris Minton and his legal crew were going to file a stay of execution request with Judge Donald in federal court in Memphis. They would do so by September 19 if the federal appellate courts had not decided the 60(b) issue. And there was the O. C. Smith case, which should have come to trial by the end of the year in Judge Donald's court.

I told Philip there were a lot of issues to discuss. Out of the blue he responded, "I know. Where am I going to be buried? It really doesn't matter—just put me in a ditch." He smiled.

We chuckled together at that prospect. I had been reading the psalms and Philip asked me to read him one. "Philip, this psalm has your name written all over it." It was Psalm 64 and I read it:

"Hear my voice, O God, in my complaint; preserve my life from the dread enemy. Hide me from the secret plots of the wicked, from the scheming of evildoers, who whet their tongues like swords, who aim bitter words like arrows, shooting from ambush at the blameless; they shoot suddenly and without fear. They hold fast to their evil purpose; they talk of laying snares secretly, thinking, 'Who can see us? Who can search out our crimes? We have thought out a cunningly conceived plot.' For the human heart and mind are deep."[6]

Philip and I closed with prayer. "May the God of David, credited with writing the sixty-fourth psalm, deliver Philip Workman from his enemies. Or as the psalmist put it, 'Hear my voice, O God, in my complaint; preserve my life from the dread enemy. Hide me from the secret plots of the wicked.'"

In mid-September Federal District Judge Bernice Donald granted Philip a stay of execution so she could consider the 60(b) petition. This effectively stopped the gears of the killing machinery that were grinding with Philip's fifth death warrant. But I remained worried. Although Judge Donald was a federal judge, she was still a Memphis judge. All levels of the judiciary and law enforcement in Memphis had proved unrelenting in their hostility toward Philip since 1981.

One lovely fall evening in October, when the leaves were changing colors and I was outside in the cool air enjoying the autumnal splendor, Becca called me to come in because Philip had telephoned from the prison.

I walked briskly back to the house and picked up the phone. As Philip spoke, the tone of his voice indicated something was

---

6 NRSV.

terribly wrong. In a subdued monotone, Philip informed me that Judge Donald had denied his petition. Then he said, "Joe, I'm tired of all this. These people are never going to give me a new trial." The cumulative effect of five death warrants and over two decades on death row echoed through his voice on the phone. We both knew this decision could bring a sixth death warrant in the spring. And he was concerned about his good friend Don Johnson, who had an execution scheduled in four days. I reassured him about Don and told him I would be out to see him the next day.

Reading Judge Donald's opinion illustrated the judicial problems with the death penalty. She would not go into the merits of the petition—how could she? It was an indictment of the Memphis criminal legal establishment. Hence, she dismissed it on procedural grounds.

When I visited Philip, driving in the autumn darkness to the prison, he was in a good mood. Don Johnson had received a stay of execution, and Philip was happy for his friend. He described Don thusly: "He's more refined than I am. I did a lot of dumb stuff, although I didn't kill anybody. I think the Lord has put me through what I've gone through as a way of purging me for my foolishness. My soul needed a lot more work than Don's. Don is more refined." Philip was acknowledging the misdeeds of his youth, and in comparing himself to his good friend, he believed Don was purer in a spiritual sense.

In the many years I visited Philip, he was always an honest evaluator of himself. He inventoried his spiritual state and was all too aware of his shortcomings. This is a rare quality inside prison—and outside as well. It was an honor to be his spiritual adviser.

We closed with the "hedge of protection" prayer, then gave each other a parting hug. I was out the door of Unit 2 into the chilly autumn night.

Later that fall, Chris Minton informed me of the affidavit they had obtained from Matthew Ian John. Mr. John had been in the Memphis training academy learning to be a policeman from June 1995 until November 1995. In the course of his instruction, the question of officer safety was addressed. One aspect was the risk of injury by "friendly fire" when trying to make an arrest. The training officers used the shooting of Lt. Ronald Oliver as an example of "friendly fire" killing a fellow police officer. "Those officers explained the Oliver shooting as a situation where friendly fire could have resulted in the death of Lieutenant Oliver."

The question became a simple one: Does anybody care?

The 60(b) litigation continued to bounce around the appellate courts through 2006. It was ultimately resolved by the Supreme Court, and it would provide no relief. Meanwhile, lethal injection litigation percolated in California, North Carolina, and Ohio; Florida halted executions pending review of lethal injection problems.

The lawyers working for Philip were dedicated and brilliant. They had milked the cow of litigation for many years. Yet the legal remedies were almost all gone. I could see nothing between Philip and yet another deathwatch.

The attorney general's office petitioned the Tennessee Supreme Court for a sixth death warrant in the *Workman* case. On January 16, 2007, the Tennessee Supreme Court set May 9, 2007, as Philip's execution date.

Philip's case not only proved Oscar Wilde's saying, "The Truth is rarely pure and never simple," it established that truth could be found despite long odds. The only question was if justice would flow forth from the truth.

The lethal injection litigation provided another avenue of appeal. The legal landscape had changed dramatically since the prior ruling of the Tennessee Supreme Court that the unconstitutionality of lethal injection was "less than remote."

This scenario provided an interesting context for the status conference that Judge Aleta Trauger held in Nashville federal court. The petition, filed on behalf of E. J. Harbison on death row, allowed the parties to discuss the way to proceed in a status conference with the judge. Given the seriousness of this issue (the drugs caused unnecessary pain and suffering) she suggested the parties undertake a method of addressing the problem before a trial took place. In particular, she suggested the attorney general contact Governor Bredesen and have him halt executions until the matter could be fully studied by competent professionals. The attorney general, Bob Cooper, replied that he would not contact the governor because the Tennessee lethal injection protocol had no problems. This reasoning defied belief; Tennessee had the same protocol that existed in Florida, California, and North Carolina . . . states that had stopped executions to examine the drugs.

At three o'clock on February 1, 2007, Governor Phil Bredesen held a press conference to announce the halting of all executions until the execution protocol had been examined and remedied. He designated the commissioner of the Department of Correction, George Little, to appoint a committee and deliver a report to him by May 2, 2007. This halted four pending executions.

When I visited Philip the evening of February 1, he was happy for the men whose executions had been delayed. But he was leery of his situation. "I don't think it's an accident this report comes out May 2. They can still try and get me on May 9. I have a bad feeling about the governor. I feel like a target is on my chest."

As I listened to Philip's analysis, the euphoria of the stopped executions melted away. Of course, he was correct. And the only real legal options he had left involved challenging the lethal injection protocol. As Bob Dylan put it, "You don't need a weatherman to know which way the wind blows."

Liz Garrigan, the editor of the *Nashville Scene*, filed a public records request for all information the state had pertaining to the development of the new lethal injection protocol. The state replied with a mountain of paper. Buried in it was a document that indicated they had consulted with the Federal Bureau of Prisons on designing a lethal injection concoction. Yet they withheld the notes from the two-day-long meetings in February, citing client privilege. The *Scene* prepared to go to court to get the documents.

As I visited Philip through this period, he described feeling he had a "cruise missile pointed at [his] chest." Given Governor Bredesen had postponed all executions prior to Philip's date, it was an understandable feeling.

The lethal injection mandate Governor Bredesen issued directing the Department of Correction to "fix" the lethal injection protocol by May 2 had consumed the DOC. A public hearing was held on April 5, 2007, for citizens to comment.

April 5 was Maundy Thursday on the Christian calendar. The South, which perceived itself as the most religious section of the country, had the state of Tennessee holding a hearing on how to kill people on one of the most important days for Christians—the day that commemorates the Last Supper, when Jesus says farewell to his disciples and prepares for his betrayal unto death on Good Friday.

This date made the mundane, bureaucratic function of the state of Tennessee, as it prepared to rev up the killing machinery, quite ironic. This date would be the public readying of killing for Philip Workman. Several of us testified, including my friend Harmon Wray who had worked with me against the death penalty for thirty-two years. The hearing seemed a mere formality. A series of secret meetings had already determined how the lethal injection protocol would go forward. The big controversy was whether it be a one-drug or three-drug protocol. By the conclusion of the hearing, it was clear the deadline of May 2 for issuance of the report would be met. A mere week before Philip's execution date.

On April 12 I took the Reverend Jim Lawson to visit Philip

and Abu-Ali on death row. Jim was teaching at Vanderbilt University after retiring from his Methodist church in Los Angeles. Vanderbilt had expelled Jim when he was a student in the divinity school in 1960 for training and leading the nonviolent protests that resulted in Nashville desegregating. Upon his return as a faculty member, Jim had lunch with Harvey Branscomb, the former chancellor who had presided over his dismissal. Reverend Lawson and Mr. Branscomb reconciled their differences of some forty some years ago.

> ## *The hearing seemed a mere formality. A series of secret meetings had already determined how the lethal injection protocol would go forward.*

As for me, it was hard to imagine a living soul on the face of this planet that I admired as much as Jim Lawson. I did not think he had received his due for the force he had been in the civil rights struggle. But that was my issue, not Jim's. I was glad he was going out to death row with me.

Abu-Ali was in good spirits, and we had a delightful visit. He shared the history of his case and his spiritual pilgrimage. Looking directly at Jim, he said, "The only time I see Black ministers out here is when Joe brings them out. That's one of the reasons I moved away from the Christian church." Jim, a Methodist minister wearing his clerical collar, nodded. We closed our visit with prayer led by Reverend Lawson. Then we waited for Philip to come out.

As we waited for Philip to arrive, I summarized his case. The six death warrants, the post-trial evidence revealing his innocence of the murder of Lieutenant Oliver, and the status of the lethal injection process. Jim was struck by the fact that this was Philip's sixth death warrant.

Philip came into the small visiting room and we hugged. I introduced him to Jim, and Philip explained his case. We talked a lot about clemency. Philip was clear he did not want to go through another kangaroo court with the clemency board. This time he decided to send Governor Bredesen some religious tapes he found important and "let the Holy Spirit work with him."

Throughout the history of his case, Philip had proven to be the most eloquent spokesman. Now he was limiting the media to one interview with CNN. Not doing clemency would also limit his public exposure. Although there was a residual base of Tennesseans who supported him from two prior near-executions over five years before, the public needed to be re-educated on the case. But as I listened to him speak, I realized the reality was that Philip was emotionally exhausted and simply could not do any more.

Jim reminded Philip of the book of Exodus chapter 3. It was the story of Moses being summoned by God to be a spokesman for the Lord and lead the people out of bondage. He pointed out two salient facts: (1) Moses felt inadequate and did not wish to do it, and (2) after seeing the Hebrew people suffer, God was moved to act, and God did so through Moses. Jim went on to talk about his experience with God through the civil rights movement. He said God worked through people in that struggle to accomplish justice. Jim thought that God might be using Philip and his case to advance the cause of justice regarding the death penalty.

As I listened to Philip and Jim converse, I realized that Philip was weary in an existential sense. The pressure of the sixth death warrant was exacting its inevitable, torturous toll. The machinery of killing was designed to take people to extinction. What was less understood was the emotional cost of this process. Dr. George

441

Woods's report on Philip resonated in my mind, and I realized that "acute PTSD" came closest to describing what was happening with Philip. Since that report during the fourth death warrant, Philip had endured more caging, strip searches, the repeated threat of imminent doom, and the ennui of death row. It seemed that Philip, although he wanted to live, also wanted it to be all over one way or another. He had been tortured into emotional depletion and the edge of insanity.

I tried to speak to his exhaustion, but mostly I just listened. Listening seemed to be the most important thing I could do in this visit. As the visit wound down, I asked Jim Lawson to close with a prayer. He articulated a powerful prayer of comfort and compassion. We then embraced Philip and left the prison. The execution date of May 9 was three weeks away.

The American Bar Association released a report examining the administration of the death penalty in Tennessee. The report, "The Tennessee Death Penalty Assessment Report,"[7] was issued on April 23. In a press conference in Legislative Plaza, Karen Mathis, the ABA president, discussed woefully inadequate defense counsel, too many Blacks being condemned, and a system that was fundamentally broken. The report broke the system into twelve categories:

1. Collection, preservation, and testing of DNA and other types of evidence
2. Law enforcement identifications and interrogations
3. Crime laboratories and medical examiner offices
4. Prosecutorial professionalism
5. Defense services
6. The direct appeal process
7. State post-conviction proceedings
8. Clemency

7 *Evaluating Fairness and Accuracy in State Death Penalty Systems: The Tennessee Death Penalty Assessment Report, An Analysis of Tennessee's Death Penalty Laws, Procedures, and Practices*, American Bar Association, March 2007.

9. Capital jury instructions
10. Judicial independence
11. Racial and ethnic minorities
12. Mental retardation and mental illness

In none of these categories was Tennessee's administration of the death penalty adequate. The report recommended numerous reforms. The silence from the governor's office in response to the report was ominous and deafening. It looked like it didn't matter what kind of process sent people to the death chamber just so they were killed. The question was no longer whether anyone cared. It was apparent those in authority did not.

The *Nashville Scene* filed a petition in chancery court seeking all the documents the Department of Correction maintained regarding designing the lethal injection protocol. Since the DOC was operating on tax dollars, the material should have been available through the Tennessee Open Records Act (TPRA). Chancellor Claudia Bonnyman heard the arguments from both sides on April 25. After the arguments were presented, she summarized from the bench the position of the parties. She also announced that she had previously read all the briefs and, given the timeliness of the matter, she would have a decision in an hour.

As promised, Chancellor Bonnyman returned to the bench within an hour and read her opinion. She found for the plaintiff, the *Nashville Scene*, and ordered the DOC to yield all documents and emails that had been written in preparation of the revised lethal injection protocol. The state indicated they needed to consult with the commissioner of corrections, the attorney general, and the governor before deciding on appeal. The parties agreed to file their respective briefs on how to proceed by the close of court on April 26, 2007.

Two Weeks

I picked up Jim Lawson in my pickup truck and we drove to the prison for his second visit to see Philip. When we arrived in Unit 2, Philip was concluding a visit with his lawyer. The lawyer left and Philip waved us into the small visiting room. We exchanged hugs and sat down for our visit.

Philip gestured at the legal papers next to him. "That's the papers to keep them from doing an autopsy. I don't want my body desecrated. They know how to kill me, so they don't need to do that. We'll file it in federal court."

Philip informed us that his brother Terry was driving down from Kentucky for a visit. He was planning to tell Terry he did not want him to witness the execution. "In that situation, you have to be strong. Seeing my family there, that would make it hard. I know Terry wants to be there, but I really don't want him to be there. I have to be strong, and seeing him just wouldn't help me." Philip smiled and looked at me: "But you know Terry. He takes a notion to be stubborn. But he's just going to have to go with me on this one. If I have to, I'll talk to the warden."

Jim and I had entered death row with its recycled air, leaving behind a cool, lovely spring afternoon with pansies blooming brightly outside the door leading to Unit 2. We were now plunged into conversation with a man who was anticipating the state's killing him in less than two weeks. Philip was gearing himself up, trying to muster the strength to endure yet another trip to deathwatch. Meanwhile, the case remained in routine appellate posture before the Sixth Circuit Court of Appeals without an expedited briefing schedule. If this were a normal death penalty case on appeal, Philip would have months if not a year or two remaining. But his was not a normal case. The Republican judges on the Sixth Circuit had demonstrated they would do anything to see him executed. It was a surreal situation. From outward appearances, the case was chugging along. But there was a repeated effort to exterminate Philip by those wearing judicial robes. And here he was with attenuated emotions trying to cope with the dissonance of it all. It seemed as if we were all disassociating.

"It looks like I'm headed for deathwatch," Philip said. "With Judge Donald waiting to issue the certificate of appealability, the Sixth Circuit won't have time to process the case. Plus, with the lethal injection protocol coming out May 2, that's only one week before my execution. That is going to be litigated, so it looks like I'll be over there when it's decided. I'm not going to pack my stuff. There are six of them that come to get you. They can pack it themselves. The one good thing is I get to use the phone lying on my bed while I'm on deathwatch. That's the way I like to talk. Here you have to stand and talk through the bars. At least I'll be comfortable talking on the phone." Philip smiled. "Of course, I'd just as soon not have the opportunity." We all chuckled.

Philip was wrestling with some scriptures, and we discussed them. He loved the King James Version of the Bible, and he had several editions along with an annotated one by Ellen White, the Seventh-day Adventist teacher of one hundred years before. Philip liked to be sure his understanding of the words in the Bible was as clear as possible.

Unexpectedly, Philip looked me directly in the eye and asked, "Where am I going to be buried?" We had discussed this several years before. I reminded him of the discussion.

"I can't remember what we decided," he stated. "There was just so much going on."

I shared the decisions we had reached during his last trip to deathwatch. I asked him if that was okay. He nodded that he approved. Then I inquired, to be sure, "You want to be buried, not cremated, right?"

"No cremation," he replied vigorously. "That's just desecration of the body."

Philip returned to the scriptures and did a biblical riff on Isaiah. He was fascinated by Isaiah's death. Someone had told him, probably a televangelist, that the prophet was buried in a tree and the tree was later cut down. Jim Lawson and I assured Philip that such a description was nowhere in the Bible. Jim explained it was probably a legendary account the preacher had taken at face value. I had an earthier description in mind, but I held my tongue.

Philip seemed comforted by Jim's pastoral presence. Jim listened well, and when it came time to pray our prayer of departure, we held hands and Jim articulated the spirit of the prisoner, what he was experiencing now as well as in the Bible, and offered it to God. We hugged Philip goodbye, then had a visit with Abu-Ali. Again, Jim closed with a powerful prayer.

One Week

On April 29, Philip called to discuss his family visits. He had decided to relent and have the visits as long as they could be done before he went to deathwatch. Prior final visits had been emotionally damaging for his family. I agreed to set this up with Warden Ricky Bell.

The legal battle had evolved to the Sixth Circuit Court of Appeals. Judge Donald had issued a certificate of appealability, noting the case had merit. It would go before two Republicans and one Democrat. The Republicans were sure no votes based on their records and Dan Horn's study showing that the Rs voted against relief 90 percent of the time. In the twenty-five-year history of this case, there was not a single Republican judge who voted for relief for Philip Workman.

In preparing for the final family visits, I telephoned Terry Workman. He mentioned he would be staying in the motel where

446

he usually resided for his visits. I opined that maybe his stay there would bring us good luck. He responded, "What we need is justice. All we've ever wanted in this case is a little justice."

The Tennessee Department of Correction issued the revised lethal injection protocol on April 30, 2007. In hopes of avoiding protracted litigation if they changed the recipe, TDOC kept the same three-drug protocol: (1) sodium thiopental, which is highly unstable and should not be used as an anesthetic, but is so utilized here; (2) pancuronium bromide, a paralytic agent that freezes all muscles, thus creating a chemical veil over the killing that would make it easier for witnesses even though by freezing the prisoner one cannot know how painful the process may be; and (3) potassium chloride, which delivers a maximum amount of pain to the cardiovascular system as it stops the heart.

This poisonous cocktail would be administered by untrained, unprofessional, noncredentialed correctional personnel using a long tube (some twenty-one feet in length) and a complicated delivery system.

The greatest irony of all is that the Tennessee legislature and the Tennessee Veterinary Association had joined to enact legislation to ban the use of pancuronium bromide in euthanizing animals. Now it was possible to use it to kill a human being.

Governor Phil Bredesen issued the following statement upon publication of the revised execution protocol: "As this completes the work that I asked the commissioner to undertake, the moratorium on executions will expire on schedule on May 2, 2007." So much for making a constitutional lethal injection protocol. So much for designing a system that works fairly, under the ABA recommended guidelines, and finally, so much for Philip Workman. He was right to feel he had "a cruise missile pointed at [his] chest."

Warden Bell and I met to confirm the final visiting schedule for Philip's family. On Saturday, May 5, the family would visit. This

447

would take place prior to Philip moving to deathwatch in the early morning hours of Sunday, May 6. Terry would visit with Philip on Sunday.

The lawyers filed an appeal of the 60(b) petition into the Sixth Circuit Court of Appeals on May 1. Another petition that contained the appeal of the error coram nobis hearing generated from Judge Colton's court was filed. It stressed Dr. Cyril Wecht's unchallenged testimony that the bullet O. C. Smith and the state testified was the fatal bullet could not be the bullet that killed Lieutenant Oliver. Additionally, a challenge to the lethal injection protocol was to be made in federal district court before Judge Campbell. All of this litigation was a race to the wire because there was no stay of execution in effect and there was a May 9 execution date.

Philip was jaunty when I visited him the afternoon of May 5. He was in remarkably good spirits for a guy with an execution date four days away. He reviewed the administrative hurdles the lethal injection petition had to clear before it was filed in federal court. It would probably be May 7 before it was filed. Philip reiterated his belief that he would be on deathwatch when this was decided.

We talked about the schedule of family visits. I thought the visits would be good for Philip, although I anticipated some of their normal tension. He would be moved to deathwatch in the wee hours of Sunday, May 6, and Terry would visit that afternoon.

More than ever, I felt like I was in *Alice in Wonderland*. At every turn in this case, we had found evidence that should have obtained a new trial: (1) The only eyewitness recants. (2) The Sixth Circuit panel of Republican judges misconstrued a study and refused to recant when it was pointed out they had done so. (3) The discovery of the X-ray, concealed by the prosecution for over twenty years, that revealed it was a through and through bullet. This fact exploded the fragmenting-bullet theory of the Sixth Circuit panel of Republicans. (4) Lieutenant Keenan testifying in clemency that he had found the fatal bullet, but at trial Terry Willis testifying that he was the person who found it. (5) O. C. Smith's nefarious role with his clemency charade, and wrapping himself in barbed wire with an explosive device on his chest, which resulted in his indictment and prosecution.(6) Matthew Ian John swearing that while attending the Memphis police academy, his instructors referenced the slaying of Lieutenant Oliver as probably friendly fire. These were just some of the reasons Philip Workman should have gotten relief.

However, I had been doing this work a long time. It was twenty-seven years since John Spenkelink's state killing in Florida on May 25, 1979. I had the scars on my soul to inform me that this process was not about justice or fairness. Rather, it was all about politics. The politics of state killing is what drove the death machinery. In this case, there was not a single Republican vote in the judiciary for Philip. He had been demonized as a "cop killer," and that allowed for egregious transgressions to be sure he was exterminated. In fact, he was not a cop killer, but not enough people in authority seemed to believe the evidence and facts. I thought he should get a stay of execution from somewhere, but I did not see where it would come from. I steeled myself for Philip's killing.

On May 4, with a 2–1 vote against Philip, two Republicans against one Democrat, the Sixth Circuit panel denied his 60(b) appeal. However, in the federal district court of Middle Tennessee, Judge Todd Campbell issued a stay of execution to consider the new lethal injection protocol. Judge Campbell set a hearing on the merits for May 14.

* * *

It is 1955 in Asheville, North Carolina. The early October cool of the mountains has descended on this autumn day. The leaves are beginning to change, edging their way to a fulsome explosion of color the

449

third weekend of the month.

The radio crackles in my mother's car as I strain to hear the announcers in New York. They are broadcasting the seventh and final game of the World Series on October 4, 1955. The Brooklyn Dodgers are playing the New York Yankees. The Dodgers are trying once again to slay the mighty Yankees, who thwart them repeatedly in the World Series.

As a nine-year-old, I can easily imagine Yankee Stadium and the position of each Dodger player. I want the Dodgers to win because they just can't ever quite pull it off against the Yankees. Maybe this is the year.

The Dodgers have eked out a 2–0 lead by the sixth inning. Johnny Podres, who pitched the third game and is not the best pitcher on their staff, is holding the threatening Yankees at bay. The Dodger manager, Walter Alston, substitutes Sandy Amoros in left field and moves Jim Gilliam to second base to begin the bottom of the sixth inning.

Billy Martin walks and Gil McDougald singles for the Yankees. It appears Podres is tiring. Yogi Berra, the Yankee catcher and a fearsome hitter, comes to the plate. Berra rips one fair down the left field line. It looks like extra bases and the runners are off and running. It appears the game will be tied. My heart begins to sink for the Dodgers. Then Sandy Amoros is described running at full speed with glove arm (his right arm) extended. Stunningly, he catches Berra's screaming line drive and throws to Pee Wee Reese, who is playing short stop. Reese fires it on to first baseman Gil Hodges. McDougald was running and could not get back to first base in time after the catch. It is a double play. The Dodgers are out of danger, and they go on to win their first World Series.

This moment and this World Series made me a Dodger fan. They moved to Los Angeles, and I remained a fan. One of my fondest experiences was seeing Jackie Robinson on 125th Street in New York as I awaited a bus in 1971. He climbed out of the backseat of a black car, stood, and then walked into a bank. I could not believe my good fortune. The man who integrated baseball and stood for civil rights was right across a busy 125th Street.

I try to make some Dodger games each year. I have seen them in Atlanta, Cincinnati, and St. Louis. I am a modern version of Paladin, the star of a television western of my youth. His motto was: Have gun, will travel. Mine was: Have car, will travel—to a Dodger game in a nearby state.

Becca and I planned our foray to Atlanta to watch the Dodgers versus the Braves in the spring of 2007. We did so rather innocently since we anticipated no death row drama to interrupt our trip. But as fate would have it, we were to be in Atlanta as the legalities went to the wire with Philip Workman. When Judge Campbell issued his stay of execution, it seemed all right to drive to Atlanta. We caught a game Friday night and one on Saturday. I had discussed the trip with Philip, and he pushed me to go and not worry about developments in his case.

We returned on Sunday, May 6, and Philip telephoned me at home that night. Although I had stayed in touch with the lawyers by phone, he described the legal developments and prospects. Philip reiterated that the Republicans were "Pharisees." He was convinced they had ulterior, political motives and were not merely interested in upholding the law. "The right wing talks about activist judges, but it's the Republican judges that are the activist judges. They don't enforce the law; they just want to get people executed."

Philip really enjoyed the family visits over the weekend. The visitation room was a bit crowded, especially with the Workman grandchildren. "I sure did enjoy having those Workman kids climb all over me." His stay of execution was intact, so he had not been moved to deathwatch. The lawyers expected to know by noon Monday if the stay of execution would remain in place.

CHAPTER TWENTY-EIGHT

The Wheels Come Off

AS WE AWAITED the decision from the Sixth Circuit Court of Appeals's three-judge panel, which was reviewing Judge Campbell's stay of execution and setting a May 14 hearing date on the lethal injection claim, I was reminded of Chris Minton's young son being able to determine results of a decision by noting the number of Republican appointees on the court. As Dan Horn's account in the *Cincinnati Enquirer* had revealed, the odds were overwhelmingly against any death row prisoner who faced a majority of Republican appointees. Philip's panel was composed of two Republicans and a Democrat. This did not bode well, despite Judge Campbell issuing a temporary restraining order, which are usually not appealable.

The two Republicans were the former attorney general of Ohio, Jeffrey Sutton, and Eugene Siler Jr. Judge Siler had distorted Colonel Fackler's study in a previous opinion in order to create the fragmenting-bullet theory. He crossed out that rationale after the rehearing petition pointed out it was erroneous. The order no longer made sense, but it was still lethal. Clearly Siler's personal animosity toward Philip would play a role in this decision as well.

On Monday, May 7, the three-judge panel ruled against Philip

Workman. The 2–1 vote, two Republicans and one Democrat, revealed how the majority would contort the law to kill Philip. Judge Cole's dissent eloquently stated the hypocrisy and extraordinary measures taken by the majority.

The 2–1 vote, two Republicans and one Democrat, revealed how the majority would contort the law to kill Philip. Judge Cole's dissent eloquently stated the hypocrisy and extraordinary measures taken by the majority.

The majority's opinion rests on a profound jurisdictional defect. There is no appealable order before the Court. The district court issued a temporary restraining order (TRO), not a preliminary injunction. It is well established that "[a]n order granting, denying or dissolving a temporary restraining order is generally not appealable. TROs have the modest purpose of preserving the status quo to give the court time to determine whether a preliminary injunction should issue . . . The short duration of a TRO—no more than 10 days under Rule 65(b)—is one of its chief distinctions from a preliminary injunction. Indeed, as the Court recently acknowledged, [t]he rationale for this rule (i.e., the nonappealability of

TROs) is that TROs are of short duration and usually terminate with a prompt ruling on a preliminary injunction, from which the losing party has an immediate right of appeal.

The district court's TRO cannot be magically transformed into a preliminary injunction, which is an appealable order, even though the State and the majority of this Court may wish it. This makes the majority's heavy reliance on the unpublished decision in *Alley v. Little* . . . which involved a preliminary injunction—entirely inapposite. True, in certain situations not applicable here, courts will treat TRO's as appealable preliminary injunctions. For instance, if a TRO is extended beyond the 10-day limit provided for in Rule 65(b), then it may be treated as a preliminary injunction . . . This is not an issue here because the district court's order sets a preliminary injunction hearing date on May 14, 2007, and specifies that the TRO will dissolve at that date. . . .

The TRO does not interfere with the State's conviction of Workman; it does not interfere with the State's ultimate imposition of the death sentence; and it does not indefinitely preclude the State from executing Workman. The TRO does no more than prohibit Workman's execution on May 9, so that the district court may determine—a mere five days later— whether a preliminary injunction should issue. I cannot conclude that the State's interest—whether described as avoiding delay or achieving finality—is so compelling as to necessitate what is manifestly a TRO as a preliminary injunction . . .

Because I believe that there is no doubt that

the district court issued a TRO and not a preliminary injunction, I would deny the State's appeal for lack of jurisdiction.

If the judiciary was willing to alter established law, and the governor accept a bogus lethal injection report, there was little light at the end of this tunnel. The Sixth Circuit had a clear majority of Republicans on the court, so the panel decision would stand. There was nowhere to go for relief.

I arrived at RMSI on the afternoon of May 7 and it was gearing up for an execution. The state highway patrol was on hand, creating a paramilitary presence and a preliminary checkpoint before turning to drive up the road to the prison. After passing muster with my ID and being on the memo of visitors for Philip, I was directed to the parking lot.

After parking the truck, I proceeded to the warden's office. I had a brief visit with Warden Ricky Bell and he provided me a soft drink for my visit with Philip. I left his office, and a guard escorted me to the deathwatch area of Building 8. I signed into the logbook and entered the foyer that contained Philip on the other side of the glass in a noncontact visiting booth. His daughter Michelle and brother Terry were visiting him. He waved me into the visiting booth.

Philip was garbed in medical whites, which is what one wears on deathwatch. It creates the illusion that the killing is a medical procedure, which concludes with the gentle putting down of a person, much like a dog. The fiction of that perspective was belied by the fact that the lethal injection protocol included a drug that was banned in the euthanasia of animals. And there were the tears streaming down Michelle's face.

As I gazed at Philip, I knew he was struggling. The rapidity of the changing of events, even though he had girded himself for this possibility, had shaken him. Michelle wiped away her tears and Terry maintained his stoic demeanor that masked a breaking heart. Philip was trying to be strong. He noticed my soft drink can. "Don't let them see you with that." I told him the warden had provided it. He shook his head.

We went over Philip's wishes for the last twenty-four hours. I confirmed I would be on deathwatch with him outside his cell. The warden stated I had to leave at eleven. He wondered why, since I had been with him to the end of deathwatch three. I reminded him we had to go to court to win that right. Now we were spread too thin to fight this legally. He nodded.

Philip spoke firmly about not wanting anyone he loved in the execution chamber as a witness. He told us he needed to be strong at that time and he did not want to see Terry or me there. "I can't be weak. If I saw you, I would break." Terry and I agreed to honor his request. Neither of us wished to be in the witness room, but if Philip had desired it, we would have been there.

He reviewed the rapid action of the Sixth Circuit Court of Appeals. I agreed that it appeared they were trying to clear the decks. His reply was telling: "They're not clearing the decks. They're clearing me." As usual, he had come to the heart of the matter.

"They're not clearing the decks. They're clearing me."

Michelle, Terry, and I concluded our visit with Philip at 4:00 p.m. We closed the visit with a prayer, placing our hands against the glass to meet his hands on the other side. He invoked "the hedge of protection" prayer that he always prayed for his loved ones. I echoed it: "O Lord, place a hedge of protection around Philip. Support him with your strong right arm. May he feel your grace and strength. Deliver him from those who seek to kill him, and bring him safely through this ordeal." Then we left.

Tuesday, May 8, dawned fair. The lively coolness of April had extended into May. This was welcome after a bizarre March of eighty-degree-plus temperatures ushering in a premature blooming of plants and trees. Now the early glory of spring had been hammered with three consecutive nights of twenty degrees or lower. Spring shriveled before the eyes, and an ugly brown blighted many of the recently glorious natural wonders.

Philip's situation seemed to change like the weather. After a promising beginning on appeal, the killer judges were on hand to terminate the proceedings. Tuesday brought a swirl of activity in response to those judges. I spent time with the family and the funeral home people, designed the kind of funeral service Philip wished, and finally arrived at the prison to be with Philip from nine until eleven. The frenetic continuum of events created a feeling of suspended animation amid the activity. I was encased in a process that was a cold-blooded, state-sponsored murder. All for a man who killed no one. Despite the efforts of the Memphis cabal and the judges and governors who supported them, even Lieutenant Oliver's own daughter did not believe Philip Workman killed her father. Her view reflected what the majority of Tennesseans felt as well.

As I made my way back to deathwatch, I was stunned. The dissonance between truth and reality echoed through me. I was functioning and taking care of the tasks at hand, but I had a profound feeling of dislocation. It was like being in a cocoon. Signing various logbooks, being hand-stamped, searched, and escorted to deathwatch, the entire chain of events I knew so well seemed unreal. I could not comprehend that seventeen years of visits, the last decade on a weekly basis, would conclude with this final visit tonight.

The guards led me back to the cell. Philip was on the telephone finishing a conversation with Michelle. These were the goodbye calls, the calls made to a loved one for a final expression of love and appreciation. He motioned for me to sit down.

Philip appeared wan. In his deathwatch whites, without his ever-present baseball cap with Job 13:15 imprinted across the front with a cross superimposed in the middle, his balding head shone beneath the fluorescent light. Although we had not heard from the US Supreme Court, he knew he would be killed in four hours.

Wiping the tears from his eyes, he said, "That was hard. That was Michelle. I just hope she can make it through. I also talked to Bubba" (his nephew who had brought his children to visit Saturday). "I sure did enjoy those Workman children climbing all over the place." He managed a smile through the tears.

Philip wiped his nose on a brown paper towel, brushed the tears from his face with his sleeve, and looked at me through the bars. "Can you help me with these telephone calls?" he asked. "I just don't know if I can do any more, and there are people to talk to. I just haven't had enough time since they brought me over here yesterday. You usually have seventy-two hours, but this has all been so compressed because of the lifting of the stay of execution yesterday."

I replied, "Philip, you know I will help you. How do you want me to do it?"

Philip smiled, snuffled, and said, "Let's just take some time here. See if I can get myself back together. Let's just talk for a while."

So, two friends visited with each other. The conversation unrolled, easily but painfully, until Philip looked up and said, "Okay, I've got to call Lori," a friend of fifteen years. "You have to do this one with me. I want you to start it." I knew Lori well, so I nodded I would begin the conversation. He dialed the number and thrust the phone to me between the bars. I heard it ring.

Lori was on the line immediately since she was expecting the call. "Lori, it's Joe. Philip and I are sitting here drinking some great grapefruit juice and wish you were here."

She caught my inflection. "Oh, it sounds like a party."

I nodded to Philip. "Yes, Lori, a party it is. The grapefruit juice seems to be all gone, but I understand they will give us as much as we want. Why don't you come over?"

Lori chuckled at my humor, knowing that a prisoner can receive almost anything he wishes just prior to execution. The last thing the authorities wanted to see was a dustup over some minor issue. Above all, the killing machinery had to operate smoothly.

As I chatted with Lori, Philip was composing himself. He washed his face in the lavatory and wiped it dry. He sat back down and took some deep breaths. As he moved around, Lori asked how he was doing. I answered as positively as I could. I explained he was hoarse from all the phone calls of the last few hours and said, "So don't be alarmed if he doesn't sound like himself." I told her he was literally talked out. Philip nodded, indicating he was ready to talk. I passed the telephone back to him through the bars, and he began his conversation with Lori. I flipped open my Bible and began reading passages for guidance and consolation.

When Philip concluded his talk with Lori, he rose from the bed. He went back to the lavatory and grabbed some paper towels. As he passed the stainless-steel toilet, tears or mucus fell onto the rim of the toilet. He noticed and took a paper towel, wiped the toilet rim all the way around. Philip, the original neat freak, the guy who washed his cell down for the next guy before each trip to deathwatch, was meticulous to the end. He could not bear a stained toilet rim. "Philip, you are so neat! I can't believe you just wiped that toilet rim." We smiled.

Philip had one last telephone call to make, the one to Terry, who was in a nearby hotel. Terry and I had agreed to rendezvous after I left Philip at 11:00 p.m. We would remain in a room in the administration building of the prison until either the US Supreme

Court intervened or the execution occurred.

As Philip and his brother talked, I recalled my conversations with Terry through the years. Philip had lived with Terry and his wife when Philip was sixteen. Then their dad, whose abuse Philip had fled, came to bring Philip home to Texas. Terry allowed Philip to go back with his father but regretted that decision. He thought things might have turned out differently if Philip had remained with him rather than returning. It was the path not taken, and I encouraged Terry to let it go, because he believed at the time he was doing the right thing. He did not know how brutal their father was to Philip, and who knew what was to come?

Philip completed the phone call. He came over and we held hands through the bars. We prayed. As we prayed, each taking turns as the Spirit moved him, the tears dripped from our faces onto our hands. Each teardrop was a visible symbol of the love of Christ that united us in Philip's hour of suffering. It was also a manifestation of the utter heartbreak we shared.

After being strapped down on the gurney, Philip thought he would quote the words of the apostle Stephen as he was stoned by the crowd. These words pierced me like daggers, but I felt no pain. Indeed, my tears ceased. I was there but did not feel there. My subconscious insulated me because the pain was too great, the trauma too profound. The cocoon-like state totally encapsulated me. I was fully functioning but traumatized beyond emotional overload in such a manner that I was inured to feeling all that occurred around me.

Philip was concerned about being brave through the killing procedure. He reiterated that was why he wished neither Terry nor I to be there in the witness room. Then he randomly inquired, "You know I have false teeth?" He hesitated and plunged ahead: "I take pride in my appearance and I'm wondering" and the sentence trailed off. He picked it up again: "How am I going to make a final statement

461

if the drugs hit me and my head flops over and my teeth come out?"

In preparing for my testimony before the Lethal Injection Protocol Committee, I had familiarized myself with all the sickening details of this poisoning process. I knew the painful, cruel, and torturous effect of these drugs. I had a ready answer: "Philip, it's a three-drug protocol. They are given sequentially. You will be paralyzed before it kills you. Your head won't flop over because you will be immobilized. Don't worry about your teeth. They will be fine."

The statement about final cosmetics randomly reminded me of the dying words of the Confederate cavalry general J. E. B. Stuart: "Do I still look pretty in the face?" Everyone wants to die with dignity.

In seminary, I had taken an excellent course on death and dying. Although it had proved valuable, there was nothing in that course, or in my subsequent reading of the literature, that prepared me for working with someone who was being officially murdered, which is a significantly different dynamic. There is nothing natural about taking a fifty-three-year-old man and cold bloodedly killing him in an officially sanctioned manner. Death is a natural process, be it a winding down of the body or a sudden death. There was nothing natural about state killing. It was a coerced and unnatural act. A healthy person is informed of how he will be killed and when, and several dry runs occur (in Philip's case, five of them). The process can be stopped by the courts or governor, but one usually does not know if that will happen until the very end. In a phrase, this is torture in a legal, "civilized" manner.

When Philip came to death row in 1982, Kenny Campbell had befriended him at the Tennessee State Prison. Kenny and Philip became close through the years. When Kenny received a new sentencing hearing and was given a life sentence some fifteen years after they met, he and Philip remained in touch after Kenny's transfer to another prison. Philip told me he had a message to share with Kenny, which he imparted to me. I assured him I would deliver it.

Don Johnson was also a close friend and a fellow Seventh-day Adventist. Don had come within four days of execution in 2006. Don and Philip were very close, and Philip conveyed a message for him that I also promised to carry to Don.

Philip and I held hands through the bars and prayed. He uttered a poignant and beautiful prayer for my daughter, who was undergoing teenage difficulties. His compassion in reaching out to her and our family in his direst hour enabled pain to penetrate my shocked, insulated state of mind. He invoked, as he did in our weekly visits, "Lord, place a hedge of protection around Amelia, Becca, and my brother," meaning me. "Keep this family safe and guard them. Keep the hedge of protection around them."

He then prayed for those who sought his death. Although clearly suffering, with tears rolling down his face onto our hands as we held them together, he bore no ill will to those who were in the process of killing him. Finally, he offered a prayer for his own family—and, for the first time, for himself.

Philip rose and fetched another paper towel. He blew his nose and wiped the tears away. He splashed cold water on his face bending over the lavatory. He came back over, and we spoke again. He asked, "What should I put on my gravestone? It seems like something should come to me, but I just can't think. What do you think?"

The image of him during our weekly visits welled up within me. "The Job quote on your baseball cap. What is it? Job 13:15?"

He smiled. "The Lord must have put that on your heart. That's it."

We prayed some more and talked. The time was slipping away. Soon it was 11:00 p.m. There was no doubt in my mind I had witnessed a Gethsemane experience. As the Gospel of Mark described Jesus in the garden, prior to his arrest and subsequent execution, he

463

agonized in prayer with God. Jesus prayed, "Father, if you are willing, remove this cup from me; yet not my will but your will be done." Six years before this night, Philip had been on his knees beseeching God at the rear of his cell as the execution grew nigh. He obtained an unexpected stay of execution forty-five minutes before his killing. This time, however, we knew there would be no last-minute reprieve. He shared his agony with me as we held hands and wept. The Lucan gospel writer wrote about Jesus wrestling with God as follows: "In his anguish he prayed more earnestly, and his sweat became like great drops of blood falling down on the ground." So it was with Philip. Just like Jesus, an innocent man facing extermination, Philip knew his murder was at hand. That knowledge caused profound anguish. It was not his will to die, but if it was God's will, he would go faithfully. As the book of Job inscription on his hat put it, "Though he slay me, yet will I trust in him."

The guards made some not-so-subtle noises of rattling handcuffs and keys outside the barred door behind me. Philip and I continued to pray and talk. Our foreheads touched through the bars, and I felt the four-inch scar the Memphis police had caused when they hit Philip on the head as he tried to surrender. Our leaning of heads together made the experience beyond intimate and unbearable. I knew we had to part.

At 11:10 p.m. we stood facing each other. I embraced his shoulders through the bars. He grabbed me under my arms. It was a cruel replication of our posture after his unexpected stay of execution six years earlier. He spoke first: "You are my brother."

I affirmed: "You are my brother too."

"I love you."

"I love you too."

Earnestly, Philip spoke his last words to me: "I'll see you."

"I'll see you," I firmly replied.

We squeezed each other and I turned to leave. There was a

rattling of keys and the door swung open. I looked back over my shoulder at my weeping brother. I gave him the thumbs-up as my heart finished breaking.

At this point, I was completely encased in the moment, and the pain had driven me beyond the experience of it into a state of shock. I automatically went through the motions of signing out and being escorted back to the administration building. Many of the guards were dressed in the color for killing: black.

After approximately ten minutes, Terry Workman joined me in a small room in the administration building. We talked and awaited word from the warden about the course of events. We discussed the Supreme Court. Philip came one vote shy on his last appeal to that body. It was the continued pattern of his case falling one vote short in the courts. We discussed how the various family were dealing with the ordeal. Although he maintained his stoicism, pain radiated from the expression on Terry's face.

The logistics of our situation soon proved uncomfortable. The witnesses to the execution were in an adjacent room behind us, waiting to be escorted to the death chamber. Although we could not hear the specifics of their conversations, we could hear laughter. Whether it was nervous or vindictive, we could not tell, but the sound of it emanating through the wall was disconcerting. Finally, Terry looked up at me and said, "I can understand someone being for the death penalty. What I can't understand is someone not having some respect at a time like this."

I responded: "Terry, none of this is about respect. It's all about power and control." My hands gestured at our environment as I continued: "There is no respect here. It's all about killing Philip."

A short time later, the warden opened the door and informed us the US Supreme Court had denied Philip's appeal. He was once again one vote short. The warden asked me if I wanted to witness the execution with the other witnesses. Recalling my promise to Philip, I told him I would stay with Terry. I asked the warden to let us know when it was over, and he said he would.

Terry and I prayed. We both had words to share with the Lord. We both wept. I found myself once again asking for a hedge of protection around Philip.

The associate warden opened the door to the room where Terry and I awaited the news. He informed us that the execution had been completed. He asked if we wished to leave now and offered an escort for us. Terry and I conferred. We requested to remain in the room until the witnesses to the execution left the building. He agreed to notify us when that was the case. Soon we heard the witnesses in the foyer of the administration building a few feet from our room. After some ten minutes, the babble died down and the only sound was the guards exiting the prison. The associate warden came by and told us we could leave with no problem. He provided a guard escort to our pickup trucks.

I drove to the motel where Terry and his wife, Shelley, were staying. Terry's daughter and her husband were also there. On the drive from the prison, I was disconsolate and exhausted. Upon joining everyone in the room, I heard the television broadcasting from outside the prison. I had no stomach to listen to that, so we just talked. We discussed Philip and what he meant to us. We all vented quite a bit of anger about all that had taken place. After about thirty minutes, I said goodbye. We would meet the next day to discuss the funeral. I went home and crashed into Becca's arms. There was not much to say, and I finally fell asleep.

The remainder of May 9 unspooled with phone calls to Terry, the funeral home, and the lawyers. It became clear as the day progressed that the state wished to do an autopsy of Philip's body. Philip had filed an affidavit stating it was his religious belief that an autopsy would be "desecrating" his body. Federal district court judge Todd Campbell set a hearing for May 14 on the matter. In the meantime, he gave specific orders to the medical examiner, Dr. Bruce Levy, that he not undertake any penetration or probing of Philip's body.

Prior to his execution, Philip ordered a vegetarian pizza for his last meal. He directed it be given to the homeless of Nashville. The Department of Correction refused to do so. They would not "donate to a charity." CNN picked up the story and ran it nationally. The story prompted thousands of people throughout the country to order vegetarian pizza for their homeless populations, and more than 170 pizzas came to the Nashville Rescue Mission in honor of Philip.

The thoughtfulness of Philip donating his final meal to the homeless and his final words forgiving those who killed him and commending his spirit to Jesus resonated throughout the country. The naked display of power by the state and the courts in pushing through this killing despite evidence of innocence stood in direct contrast to Philip's final witness.

The state was determined to show that the lethal injection protocol was efficient and caused no suffering. For that, they needed an autopsy. We were battling that autopsy in court, so the funeral would have to wait. As we awaited the hearing on May 14, I completed final arrangements. I received word that one of Philip's dear friends, Lori, was in a psychiatric wing of a local hospital, and I went to see her. As I made my way through the psych unit, I felt like I would welcome a stay here as well. At every juncture in the *Workman* case, we had been thwarted. Justice was turned upside down time and time again. I was suffering from profound trauma.

I entered Lori's room and she was lying in the bed. I immediately went to her and we hugged each other long and hard. There were no words. Just hugging and she sobbed. My eyes misted, but I could not cry.

I pulled a chair next to the bed and we talked. After her final phone call with Philip, she had started losing control. She thought she could handle it, but she could not. She had been in the psychiatric unit for several days and was beginning to feel calmer. We had a relaxed visit. She wanted to know how it was with Philip at the end, and I put the best possible spin on it that I could. I wanted her to recover, and she did not need to dwell on the final specifics of Philip's life. We reminisced over the years we shared with Philip. We laughed about the idiosyncratic things Philip would do on occasion. His attitude toward women was a work in progress. He had a traditional Southern male view, and we joked about it. Soon it was time to go. I did not want to exhaust my fragile friend. We had a prayer and a goodbye hug.

Judge Campbell ruled against Philip after the hearing on May 14. We still had an appeal to the Sixth Circuit Court of Appeals, but that did not offer much hope; they had repeatedly ruled against Philip for years. But the five-day delay for filing an appeal did give us a bargaining chip. Each passing day meant the half-life of the chemicals used to poison Philip dissipated. The state was anxious to get the body as soon as possible. And we were desirous of having the funeral quickly. We compromised and allowed the state to draw chemicals from the body in a minimally invasive procedure. The state gave us the body on May 12, Saturday morning.

We held a graveside service, which I assisted with, on the afternoon of May 14. I was still on task, totally numb, hyper-vigilant and functioning, more like a block of wood than a human being. I recruited help for the service. Philip had requested a Seventh-day Adventist talk about the afterlife, and John Dysinger was kind enough to fulfill that role. His family sang, providing lovely gathering music prior to the service. Terry Workman spoke for the family. The Reverend Victor Singletary, a friend, led the service. We sang "The Old Rugged Cross." I did the commendation and committal, observing that we all go "from earth to earth, ashes to ashes, dust to dust." I invited those who wished to join me to come forward and place a spade full of earth on Philip's coffin. I shoveled the first dirt. Others came forward and did the same. When the final ritual was complete, the burial crew filled in the hole around the coffin.

I arranged for the funeral to be videotaped for the guys on death row to view. It was important that they know Philip was treated with dignity, respect, and honor by those who loved him. It was contrasted to the humiliation and abuse of power the state inflicted on him.

Philip's grave marker reads:

Philip R. Workman
June 1, 1953 – May 9, 2007

THOUGH HE SLAY ME,
YET WILL I TRUST IN HIM

He was prophetic from our first meeting until the end. He was not innocent enough.

NOT INNOCENT ENOUGH
By Nanci Griffith

What the hell was I doing there
In that fast-food parking lot
They say I robbed the restaurant
and a Memphis cop got shot
I was trying to feed my habit
I was scared and I was high
It was never my intention
That anyone should die

Just how many of us are innocent enough
Just how many of us are innocent enough
Just how many of us are innocent enough
My name is Philip Workman
And I'm not innocent enough

It's not a long walk from a trailer park
to a Tennessee cell block
But I got saved behind these bars
Soon I'll give my soul to God
Reverend Joe is praying for me
And the family left behind
They say my bullet took his life
but that bullet was not mine

Just how many of us are innocent enough
Just how many of us are innocent enough
Just how many of us are innocent enough
My name is Philip Workman
And I'm not innocent enough

I had no money for a lawyer
To fight the system from within
There's no justice for the poor
From the witness they brought in
Circumstance and random chance
I never meant to do no harm
Now that cop and I, we've both died
from that needle in my arm

And there where those who called for mercy
In those final days
Even the officer's daughter
cried to grant me stay
but I'm not innocent enough
I'm not innocent enough
I'm not innocent enough
I'm not innocent enough

Just how many of us are innocent enough
Just how many of us are innocent enough
Just how many of us are innocent enough
My name is Philip Workman
And I'm not innocent enough

2am ⟨Harold Davis⟩ was not there Joe 242 5179

Inspired by a true story

What the hell was I doing there
in a fast food parking lot
They say I robbed the restaurant
& a Memphis cop got shot
I was trying to feed my habit
I was scared & I was high
It was never my intention
That anyone should die

Just How many of us
Aren't innocent enough
Just How many of us
Aren't innocent enough
Just how many of us
Aren't innocent enough
My name is Philip Workman
I'm not innocent enough

It's not a long walk from a trailer park
To a Tennessee cell block
But I got saved behind these bars
& Soon I'll give my soul to God
Rev. Joe is praying for me
& the family left behind
They said my bullet took his life
But that bullet was not mine

Chorus

Oliver — officer's name
daughter

I had no money for a lawyer
To fight the system from within
There is no justice for the poor
From the witness they brought in
Circumstance & random chance
I never meant to cause him harm
Now that cop & I, we've both died
From a needle in my arm

bridge | There were those who called for mercy
In those final days
Even the officers daughter
Cried to grant me stay
But I'm not innocent enough
Not innocent enough
Not innocent enough

Chorus

To free,
of all purpose

Acknowledgments

THERE HAS BEEN so much assistance in this living/writing process, it is difficult to know where to start thanking people. I choose to begin with Bill Webber, the man who brought me to New York City and the East Harlem Urban Year Program. Bill's vision was that our theology emerge not only from classrooms but community involvement. He and my colleagues there, especially Doug Magee, Raymond Nance, Michael and Anni Powell, and my tenement roommate, San Williams, helped me discern what became my calling through a year of visits at the Bronx House of Detention. It was then I began the process of understanding Jesus of Nazareth, the Bible, and the relationship with prisoners.

When I came to Nashville, Will Campbell and Tony Dunbar lassoed me into Southern Prison Ministry. We, along with others, created the Southern Coalition on Jails and Prisons. My colleagues over that seventeen-year period are too numerous to mention, but we sustained each other in the uphill fight against the death penalty and mass incarceration in our eight project states in the South.

Charles Merrill, who became a dear friend, helped to sustain our efforts in the struggle. His daughter Amy is a good friend without whom this book would not be before you. Bill Styron and Mike Farrell became supporters and friends as well. Gigi Cohen, photographer extraordinaire, spent countless hours on the *Workman* case. Without all of these good folks, I would not have

Acknowledgments

been able to survive and write this book.

It was my good fortune to learn of David Lambert. David is a superb editor who brought this narrative into focus. Wes Yoder, my agent, is really a friend who guided me through what was a bewildering process of publishing. His efforts led to Forefront Books and publication. Victor Judge, a source of a wealth of learning, was kind enough to translate the Albert Camus quote in the epigraph.

I have been blessed with good friends throughout my life. Three of them have sustained me and maintained my joie de vivre for fifty years. We met in college, became camp counselors together, and have been River Rats ever since (we love to kayak the rivers of the South). For Bob Brewbaker, Art Gatewood, and Bob Pryor, their love and friendship, I am eternally grateful.

Finally, there are many I have loved and lost to the killing machinery. There are many I still love behind bars and in cages facing extermination or obliteration through lengthy sentences. Our society has settled on a way of destroying and killing people through the criminal legal system that is as horrific as it is obscene. For those caught in its maw, I only hope we find a way to liberate them. As Jesus put it in his inaugural words to the hometown folks in Nazareth, it is time "to free the captives."